THE SHORT PROSE READER

THE SHORT PROSE READER

TENTH EDITION

Gilbert H. Muller
The City University of New York
LaGuardia

Harvey S. Wiener
Marymount Manhattan College

Boston Burr Ridge, IL Dubuque, IA Madison, WI New York
San Francisco St. Louis Bangkok Bogotá Caracas Kuala Lumpur
Lisbon London Madrid Mexico City Milan Montreal New Delhi
Santiago Seoul Singapore Sydney Taipei Toronto

THE SHORT PROSE READER
Published by McGraw-Hill, a business unit of The McGraw-Hill Companies, Inc., 1221 Avenue of the Americas, New York, NY, 10020.

This book is printed on acid-free paper.

2 3 4 5 6 7 8 9 0 DOC/DOC 0 9 8 7 6 5 4 3 2

ISBN 0-07-249554-5

President of McGraw-Hill Humanities/Social Sciences: *Steve Debow*
Executive editor: *Lisa Moore*
Senior developmental editor: *Carla Kay Samodulski*
Senior marketing manager: *David S. Patterson*
Senior media producer: *Todd Vaccaro*
Project manager: *Jill Moline*
Production supervisor: *Susanne Riedell*
Cover designer: *Gino Cieslik*
Supplement producer: *Nathan Perry*
Photo research coordinator: *Ira Roberts*
Photo researcher: *Alice Lundoff*
Typeface: *10.5/12 Times Roman*
Compositor: GAC *Indianapolis*
Printer: *R.R. Donnelley Company*

Library of Congress Cataloging-in-Publication Data
The short prose reader / [compiled by] Gilbert H. Muller, Harvey S. Wiener. -- 10th ed.
p. cm.
Includes index.
ISBN 0-07-249554-5 (softcover : acid-free paper) -- ISBN 07-119861-X (ISE : acid-free paper)
1. College readers. 2. English language--Rhetoric--Problems, exercises, etc. 3. Report writing--Problems, exercises, etc. I. Muller, Gilbert H., 1941- II. Wiener, Harvey S.
PE1417.S446 2003
808'.0427--dc21

2002069587

INTERNATIONAL EDITION ISBN 0-07-119861-X

www.mhhe.com

ABOUT THE AUTHORS

Gilbert H. Muller, who received a Ph.D. in English and American literature from Stanford University, is currently professor of English at the LaGuardia Campus of the City University of New York. He has also taught at Stanford, Vassar, and several universities overseas. Dr. Muller is the author of the award-winning study *Nightmares and Visions: Flannery O'Connor and the Catholic Grotesque, Chester Himes, New Strangers in Paradise: The Immigrant Experience and Contemporary American Fiction,* and other critical texts. His essays and reviews have appeared in *The New York Times, The New Republic, The Nation, The Sewanee Review, The Georgia Review,* and elsewhere. He is also a noted author and editor of textbooks in English and composition, including *The McGraw-Hill Reader* and, with John Williams, *The McGraw-Hill Introduction to Literature.* Among Dr. Muller's awards are National Endowment for the Humanities Fellowships, a Fulbright Fellowship, and a Mellon Fellowship.

Harvey S. Wiener is Vice President of Adult Programs and Community Outreach at Marymount Manhattan College. Previously University Dean for Academic Affairs at the City University of New York, he was founding president of the Council of Writing Program Administrators. Dr. Wiener is the author of many books on reading and writing for college students and their teachers, including *The Writing Room* (Oxford, 1981). He is coauthor of *The McGraw-Hill College Handbook,* a reference grammar and rhetoric text. Dr. Wiener has chaired the Teaching of Writing Division of the Modern Language Association (1987). He has taught writing at every level of education from elementary school to graduate school. A Phi Beta Kappa graduate of Brooklyn College, he holds a Ph.D. in Renaissance literature. Dr. Wiener has won grants from the National Endowment for the Humanities, the Fund for the Improvement of Postsecondary Education, and the Exxon Education Foundation. His book *Any Child Can Write* was an alternate selection of the Book of the Month Club and was featured on the *Today* show. His writing has appeared in *Anglia College English, College Composition and Communication,* and *WPA Journal,* as well as in the London *Times,* the New York *Daily News,* and *Gentleman's Quarterly.*

To the memory of George Groman

CONTENTS

CHAPTER 2

CHAPTER 3

CHAPTER 6

CHAPTER 7

CHAPTER 8

CHAPTER 9

CHAPTER 10

CHAPTER 11

THEMATIC CONTENTS

Childhood and Family

Education

Social Problems and Issues

Men and Women Today

The Minority Experience

City and Country

Psychology and Behavior

Science, Technology, and Medicine

Language and Thought

Humor and Satire

PREFACE

The tenth edition of *The Short Prose Reader* maintains the best features of the earlier editions: lively reading selections supported by helpful apparatus to integrate reading and writing in college composition and reading courses. In working through the text, the student progresses from key aspects of the writing and reading processes to chapters on the essential patterns of writing and then to more rigorous forms of analysis and argument. Each chapter provides diverse and lively prose models suited for discussion, analysis, and imitation.

New features for the tenth edition include the following:

- **Sixteen new reading selections,** including essays by Russell Baker, Judith Ortiz Cofer, Annie Dillard, Katha Pollitt, David Brooks, Shelby Steele, and Ronald Takaki. We balance these readings with favorites from the earlier editions of *The Short Prose Reader:* Langston Hughes's "Salvation," Malcolm X's "Prison Studies," Jonathan Kozol's "Are the Homeless Crazy?" and Judy Brady's "I Want a Wife" continue to offer timely and controversial subjects for reading and writing.
- A **new appendix on research and documentation,** including a step-by-step guide to the research process, a section on using MLA style to document sources, and a sample student research paper on body image and advertising.
- An expanded treatment of the **reading process** in Chapter 2, with a more detailed discussion of the steps involved in critical reading and more on evaluating arguments.
- Expanded **biographical introductions** for every author in the text, giving students more tools for reading the essays critically.

- New **"mixing patterns" boxed questions** for selected essays in each chapter that encourage students to look closely at how writers use more than one pattern to support their ideas.
- Expanded **"Summing Up" sections,** with more questions that encourage students to make connections among the essays.
- **From Seeing to Writing** activities at the end of each chapter, with an engaging visual accompanied by a question that prompts students to write a response.
- A new **"Writing about the Text"** subsection for all essays that encourages students to respond to themes and strategies in the selection.
- A **major revision of the "Argumentation and Persuasion" chapter,** which now contains two pro/con pairs of essays on the issues of reparations for slavery and the death penalty as well as thematic groupings of essays around the themes of *Identity* and *Political Rights.*

These new features enhance the key elements of *The Short Prose Reader* that have made the previous nine editions such an enduringly popular text.

ORGANIZATION

The organization of *The Short Prose Reader* is one of its major strengths. Chapter 1, "On Writing," and Chapter 2, "On Reading," offer students brief overviews of these two interdependent skills; each chapter offers four unique views on the crafts of writing or reading by well-known writers. Each of the following eight chapters contains four short essays that illustrate clearly a specific pattern or technique—description, narration, illustration, comparison and contrast, definition, classification, process analysis, or causal analysis. The final chapter is on argumentation. Students learn to build upon earlier techniques and patterns as they progress through the book.

READABILITY

From the beginning, we have chosen selections for *The Short Prose Reader* that are readable yet substantial and representative of many different types of writers. The essays, which range typically between 300 and 1200 words, achieve their goals succinctly and clearly and are easy to understand. They exemplify both the types of college writing expected of students and the length of essay they are frequently assigned to write. The detailed questions that follow each essay can be used in reading as well as writing classes since they ask the student to analyze both the content and the form of the prose selections.

APPARATUS

The questions and activities we have included for each piece are comprehensive and integrated—designed to develop and reinforce the key critical-thinking skills required in college writing.

- **Extensive biographical notes:** The headnotes preceding the selections provide valuable information about each writer.
- **Prereading questions:** Before each essay, students encounter an activity called "Prereading: Thinking about the Essay in Advance," which encourages them to think and talk about the topic before reading what the writer says about it. Studies show that such prior discussion arouses interest and holds the reader's attention.
- **Vocabulary exercises:** Each selection includes two vocabulary exercises. "Words to Watch" alerts students to words they will read in context, and "Building Vocabulary" uses other effective methods of teaching vocabulary, including attention to prefixes and suffixes, context clues, synonyms and antonyms, and abstract vs. concrete words.
- **Questions that emphasize critical thinking:** To emphasize critical thinking as the main reason for questioning and discussion, we have grouped our conversational prods and probes under the heading "Thinking Critically About the Essay." The questions titled "Understanding the Writer's Ideas" reinforce reading comprehension. The questions titled "Understanding the Writer's Techniques" and "Exploring the Writer's Ideas" provide excellent bases for class discussion and independent reading and analysis.
- **Prewriting prompts:** These sections help students record informal thoughts for writing in advance of producing an essay.
- **Guided Writing Activities:** A key exercise for each essay and a novel feature of *The Short Prose Reader,* the Guided Writing Activities offer a dynamic approach to writing projects. These activities tie the writing project to the reading selection, but instead of simply being told to write an essay on a certain

topic, students can use the "Guided Writing" to move from step to step in the composing process.

- **Collaborative activities:** "Thinking and Writing Collaboratively" activities encourage students to work together in groups on essays and ideas for writing.
- **Reader response activities:** "Writing About the Text," a new activity, asks students to examine closely the language and ideas in each selection and to write thoughtfully about them.
- **Additional writing projects:** "More Writing Projects" provide students with additional ideas for writing on the topic of the selection.

At the end of each chapter is a "Summing Up" section, a means for students to focus their attention on issues raised by several of the chapter's selections and on more writing topics, and a "From Seeing to Writing" activity, an engaging visual assignment that gives students another means of coming up with ideas for writing.

FLEXIBILITY

Students and teachers alike can use *The Short Prose Reader* flexibly and effectively. An alternate table of contents suggests thematic groupings of readings. The text is simple yet sophisticated, inviting students to engage in a multiplicity of cultural and traditional topics through essays and exercises that are easy to follow but never condescending. Weighing the needs and expectations of today's first-year students, we have designed a rhetoric/reader that can serve as the primary text for almost any composition course.

ANCILLARIES

- **The Instructor's Manual** by Igor Webb of Adelphi University provides teaching approaches for each chapter and essay, along with answers to the vocabulary and critical-thinking questions that follow each essay.
- **The companion website at www.mhhe.com/muller/shortprose** offers three types of links—cultural, bibliographical, and biographical—to further information on selected authors within *The Short Prose Reader.*
- **Teaching Composition Faculty Listserv (www.mhhe.com/tcomp),** moderated by Chris Anson at North Carolina State University,

this listserv brings together senior members of the college composition community with newer members—junior faculty, adjuncts, and teaching assistants—in an online newsletter and accompanying discussion group to address issues of pedagogy, in theory and in practice.

ACKNOWLEDGMENTS

For this edition of *The Short Prose Reader,* we enjoyed the support of Lisa Moore, Executive Editor for Composition, who has brought a fresh perspective and calm persistence to the project. We are also deeply grateful for the patient and extraordinary efforts of Carla Samodulski, our Senior Development Editor, as well as the careful attention to the manuscript and excellent advice offered by editor Randee Falk. We also owe a debt of gratitude to Igor Webb, who assisted us throughout the revision process and produced the instructor's manual. Finally, we want to thank Meg Botteon, whose invaluable efforts helped bring the research appendix from an idea to an accomplishment.

We wish to thank our colleagues across the country for their support and are especially grateful to those who reviewed the manuscript for this edition:

Leslie Kennedy Adams, *Houston Baptist University*
Marla Ahlgren, *Fond du Lac Tribal Community College*
Nancy Allen, *Angelo State University*
Doyle Burke, *Mesa Community College*
Suzanne Campbell, *Southeastern Louisiana University*
Olivia Castellano, *California State Univ., Sacramento*
Joanna Chrzanowski, *Jefferson Community College*
Michael Dinielli, *Chaffey College*
Marty Ennes-Marvin, *West Hills College*
Roy Flannagan, *Francis Marion University*
Tammy Frankland, *Casper College*
Clifford Garner, *SUNY Rockland Comm. College*
Winboune Gautreaux, *Southeastern Louisiana University*
Mary Gervin, *Albany State University*
Kurt Gravenhorst, *Foothill College*
Harry Hamel, *Central Community College—Hastings*
W. Dale Hearell, *Stephen F. Austin State University*
Robert Heckathorn, *Peru State College*

Robert Irwin, *City College of San Francisco*
Dennis Jerz, *University of Wisconsin—Eau Claire*
Amy Jurrens, *Northwest Iowa Community College*
Rita Kahn, *California State University—Pomona*
William Ketchum, *Delta College*
Joan Koplow, *Los Angeles Valley College*
James Kosmicki, *Central Community College—Grand Island*
Karen Lewis, *Louisiana Tech University*
Ronald Link, *Miami-Dade Community College*
Joe Lostracco, *Austin Community College*
Frances Lozano, *Gavilan College*
Debbie Luoma, *Gavilan College*
Marjorie Lynn, *Eastern Michigan University/Washtenaw Community College*
Lisa McClure, *Southern Illinois University*
Nancy McNeely, *University of Southern Indiana*
Homer Mitchell, *SUNY College at Cortland*
Rhonda Morris, *Lake City Community College*
Heather Neff, *Eastern Michigan University*
Troy Nordman, *Butler County Community College*
Thomas Patchell, *Mount Saint Mary's College*
Joel Perez, *San Diego Mesa College*
Virginia Pruitt, *Washburn University*
Dawn Reno, *Lake City Community College*
Arlene Rodriguez, *Springfield Technical Community College*
Terry Schifferns, *Central Community College*
Robert Scott, *De Anza College*
William Sheldon, *Hutchinson Community College*
Terry Spaise, *University of California—Riverside*
Virginia Streamer, *Community College of Baltimore County*
Geralyn Strecker, *Ball State University*
Eric Sullivan, *University of Florida*
Mary Waguespack, *Loyola University*
Diane Wahto, *Butler County Community College*
Carroll Wilson, *Raritan Valley Community College*
Julie Wishart, *Butler County Community College*
and Diana Zilberman, *Baltimore City Community College*

Gilbert H. Muller
Harvey S. Wiener

THE SHORT PROSE READER

CHAPTER 1

On Writing

WHAT IS WRITING?

Writing helps us to record and communicate ideas. It is a definitive and essential part of daily human experience. Whether we write a shopping list or a great novel, we use a tool without which we would find ourselves isolated. Without writing we cut ourselves off from vital processes like the expression of political opinions, the description of medical emergencies, and the examination of our feelings in diaries and letters.

Writing crosses many cultures. Whether we consider historic cave drawings or the transmission of fax messages after the World Trade Center disaster, we find evidence of the human instinct to communicate ideas to other people.

In the past, writing brought about change. African-American slaves were frequently forbidden to learn to read or write, but some managed to find ways to gain literacy anyway. Their narratives of slave life helped fire the abolition movement. Women in the nineteenth century used writing to advance the cause of suffrage, winning votes with passionate speeches and articles in newspapers. Immigrants struggled to learn English in order to find a better life in the New World.

Writing celebrates human achievement. In religion, in love, in wartime and in peace, in astronomy and medicine and archaeology, in the arts and humanities, writing reminds us of our shared human identity. From the Song of Solomon in the Bible to the words of Martin Luther King, Jr.'s "I Have a Dream," from the Declaration of Independence to song lyrics by Bruce Springsteen or Gloria Estefan, writing helps us to come to terms with who we are and what we want.

What is writing, exactly? For most of us, writing is so familiar that the question seems silly. We all know what writing is. Yet when we try to write ourselves, we may find that asking and answering the question are vital.

Writing is both a product and a process. Writing is, of course, *what* we write: a letter, a law brief, a term paper, an inaugural address. Since it is a product, we must think of writing as having a public as well as a private purpose. While some writing, like shopping lists or a diary, may be meant only for our own eyes, most writing is intended for an audience. In learning what writing is, we need to think about who the audience is, and what the purpose of the writing is.

Writing is also a process; it is *how* we write. In learning to write well, we examine the process of transferring ideas from head to hand. We realize that the actual, mechanical practice of writing out ideas helps us to think more carefully, to plan and arrange ideas, to analyze our vague thoughts into solid words on a page.

HOW DO WE WRITE?

The process of writing is not absolute; there is no one sure way to learn to write well. However, there are some common elements in this process that will help anyone getting started as a writer.

Warming Up: Prewriting

Like an athlete, the writer benefits from warm-up exercises. Usually called prewriting, these steps help a writer prepare gradually and thoughtfully for the event of writing a long essay. Writers stretch their intellectual muscles by thinking about a topic before they write about it. They talk to friends and colleagues. They visit a library and flip through reference books, newspapers, magazines, and books. Sometimes, they make notes and lists as a way of putting pen to paper for the first time. Some writers brainstorm: they use free association to jot down ideas as thoroughly as possible in an unedited form. Others use "timed writing": they write nonstop whatever comes to mind in a set time period—fifteen or twenty minutes, say. Freewriting like this loosens up ideas without the worry of correctness in language too early in the writing process. After these preliminary warm-ups, many writers try to group or classify ideas by making a rough outline or drawing boxes or making lists to try to bring some plan or order to their rough ideas.

Once the writer has a rough topic area outlined, he or she may return to the audience and purpose for the essay. Who will read the essay? What material would best suit this audience? What language would be most appropriate for this audience? What is the purpose of the essay? A thesis sentence is important here. The thesis is your main point, the essential idea you want to assert about your subject. It's always a good idea to write out your thesis whether or not you ultimately use it in your essay.

Often the purpose or intent becomes clearer as the writer continues to think and write. Choosing the audience and purpose carefully—and stating the thesis succinctly—make the writer's as well as the reader's task easier.

Look at the following prewriting by a student who wanted to write about her impressions of a hospital. She made a list of free associations with the intent of using her notes to prepare the draft of an essay.

Roller skating accident
Go to the hospital for tests
My mother drops me off and has to go to work in the supermarket
I'm alone, I never stayed in a hospital before
I did visit my aunt in Atlanta when she was in the hospital and I was
 there for the summer
Doctors and nurses whispering
Tray drops suddenly and scares me out of my wits
A nurse helps a girl but she pulls the curtain & I can't see
My third grade class wrote letters to one of the children who was in
 the hospital but we never saw the hospital room
I can't sleep, there's too much noise
The nurse takes my temperature, I have 102 she gives me pills
Nobody tells me anything about what's happening or what to expect
 they just do things to me
The nurses heels squeak on the floor and give me the shivers
A red lite goes on and off in the opposite room

As she reviewed her prewriting list, the student realized that her purpose was to write about her own short stay in the hospital after an accident. Most of the items recorded relate directly to that incident. She saw that she had included on the list a number of impressions that, although hospital related, did not suit her purpose for this essay. She wanted to write about her own particular experiences, and so she ultimately rejected the items about her aunt in Atlanta, her mother going to work, and the third-grade classmate. With a clearer sense of how to proceed, she thought about a thesis sentence. The essay needed focus: exactly what point did she want to make in her essay? Simply presenting descriptive details might give readers a picture of the hospital but would not make an assertion about the experience. In fact she intended to write about how uncomfortable she felt and how the sights and sounds of the hospital contributed to that discomfort. She developed this thesis sentence:

I was uncomfortable in the hospital after my accident.

This thesis states an opinion, and so it helps the writer narrow her topic. Yet it is very broad, and some of the details on the list suggest a thesis that could more accurately express the writer's main point. After several more tries, she developed the thesis which includes, as you can see, an error in spelling and verb use, that appears in the draft:

> There I layed stiff and silent in the night listening to the noises outside my room in the long corridors and watching everything that went on around me.

First Draft

Prewriting leads to the first draft. Drafts are usually meant for the writer's eyes only; they are messy with rethinking, rewriting, and revision. Drafts help the writer figure out what to write by giving him or her a place to think on paper before having to make a public presentation of the writing. Everyone develops a personal style of draft writing, but many writers find that double-spacing, leaving wide margins, and writing on only one side of the paper are steps that make rewriting easier. If you write on a word processor, you'll find you can easily revise and produce several drafts without discarding earlier versions of the essay.

In a first draft, a writer begins to shape paragraphs, to plan where to put each piece of the essay for maximum effect. Sometimes, a first draft doesn't have an introduction. The introduction can be written after the writer has finished the draft and has a better sense of what the essay is about. The audience will see only the final draft, after all, and will never know when the writer wrote the introduction.

Having finished the first draft, the writer tries to become the audience. How will the essay sound to someone else? Does it make sense? Are the ideas and expression clear? Is there a main point? Do all the ideas in the essay relate to this main point? Is there a coherent plan to the essay? Do ideas follow logically one from the next? Would someone unfamiliar with the topic be able to follow the ideas? Should more information be added? What should be left out?

In attempting to answer these questions, writers often try to find a friendly reader to look over the draft and give advice. Whatever else they may look for at this stage, they do not pay too much attention to spelling or grammar. A helpful reader will enable the writer to see the essay as the audience will see it, and suggest ways to reorganize and clarify ideas.

Here is an early draft of the essay written from the prewriting sample you observed on page 3.

DRAFT

All Alone

There I sat all alone in my hard bed at the hospital. This was the place I most definitely did not want to be in. But because of my rollerskating accident I had no choice. I had to listen to the doctors and go for the necessary tests. There I layed stiff and silent in the night listening to the noises outside my room in the long corridors and watching everything that went on around me.

As I layed there bundled up in my white sheets and the cold, hard steel bars of the bed surrounding me. I could hear everything that was happening on my ward. Nurses would pass up and down the corridor with their white rubber heal shoes squeeking on the white freshly polished floors. The squeaking would send shrieking chills up my spin. Soft whispers were heard as doctors and nurses exchanged conversations. If they only knew how disturbing it was for me to hear these slight mutters. The most startling noise, though, was when a tray must have accidentally slipped out of a nurses hand. The clatter of the tray echoed down the long, endless white corridors setting my nerves on end, I must have sat there shaking for at least five minutes.

Watching what was going on outside and inside my room was no picnic either. In the hall a bright light shown enabling me to view the room next door. As I was peering out my door, I noticed the little red light above the opposite door light flash along with a distantly faint ringing of a bell down the hall. The nurse, in a clean white uniform, was there in an instant to help the young curly haired girl. With a sturdy thrust of her hand the nurse pulled the white cloth divider across the room concealing the two of them in the corner.

Two other nurses were making their rounds when they noticed I was awake. One was in her mid forties, had brown hair, brown eyes and was slim. The other nurse looked slightly older, taller than the first one, had white streaks throughout her dark hair and was of medium build. The first nurse said to me, "What are you doing up at this hour." I told her I could not sleep. They noticed that I was perspiring and decided to take my temperature. The first nurse left and returned with the thermometer. She placed the cold, thin piece of glass into my warm mouth and put her cool fingers around my wrist to take my pulse. They discovered I had a fever of a hundred and two. The second nurse disappeared this time and returned holding a little silver packet with two tylonal aspirins in it. I took out the two white tablets and swallowed them with water. Every so often until the following morning either one of the nurses would saunter into my room to check on me. All this happened in one night.

Hospital visits can be very frightening. Nobody realizes the trauma patients go threw.

After discussing her draft with students in the class and with her teacher, the writer of the hospital essay knew to make revisions. As she weighed her options, she knew that an even more clearly stated thesis would help her readers understand what she was trying to accomplish, and so she revised it further. The thesis from the revised draft appears below:

I was supposed to be in the hospital to recuperate; instead of sleeping, though, I lay there all night stiff and silent, uncomfortably listening to the noises outside my room off the long hallway and watching everything that happened around me.

Friendly readers suggested further that the writer needed to fill in more information about the reason for her hospital stay and also to provide more snapshots of the scene around her. If in fact her objective was to portray the hospital as producing further discomfort, she needed to offer more sensory details than she had presented to her readers. (See pages 3–5.) Some readers felt that the writer should better organize these details, perhaps considering the sights and the sounds separately or pointing out first the activity in the room and then the activity in the hallway, both places apparently contributing to the writer's unhappiness. And to improve the coherence of the essay, the writer knew that in revising she should look carefully at sentence transitions, particularly from paragraph to paragraph.

Several readers felt that the conclusion was flat and that somehow the writer had to figure out a way to raise the issue of the hospital's indifference to her discomfort. It was not enough to record the unpleasantness; she also wanted to recommend some ways hospitals could avoid distressing their patients, and she decided that the conclusion might be a good place to raise those issues.

Errors distracted readers even at the draft stage. These included the sentence fragment on lines 7 and 8 and the comma splice on line 17. Some spelling, usage, and grammar errors needed attention—*layed* in line 7 (the correct verb form needed here is *lay*) and *squeeking* for *squeaking* in line 10, for example. The use of the passive voice in line 12 does not help the descriptive and narrative flow, and the writer knew to change the passive to active as she revised. Simply by revising sentences some errors vanish and others appear, and attentive writers know that a careful editing prior to producing the final draft is critical.

Additional Drafts

After getting responses from a reader, the writer begins the second draft. And the third. And maybe the fourth. No one can predict how many drafts are necessary for a final essay, but very few writers get by with fewer than two or three drafts. Revision usually involves working first on the clear expression of ideas and later on revision for spelling, grammatical correctness, and good sentence structure.

Here is a revised draft of the essay "All Alone." Note the comments in the margin.

REVISED DRAFT

All Alone

Introductory paragraph: fills in accidental details; leads comfortably to the thesis.

Thesis: last sentence of the first paragraph.

I spent a long, unpleasant weekend in a bed at University Hospital, the result of a bad roller skating accident I had one Saturday afternoon last October. There might be a concussion; there might he broken bones—and so I had no choice but to listen to the doctors and go for necessary tests. I was supposed to be in the hospital to recuperate; instead of sleeping, though, I lay there all night, stiff and silent, uncomfortably listening to the noises outside my room off the long hallway and watching everything that happened around me.

Concrete sensory details ("white sheets," "cold steel bars," "rubber heels squeaking," etc.): heighten readers' awareness of hospital room scene.

Frustration at disturbing room noises now clear; readers perceive essay's unity with repeated references to sounds.

"Perhaps the most startling noise"—effective link to thesis.

Bundled up in my white sheets and surrounded by the cold steel bars of my bed I heard every little sound in my ward all night long. Nurses, their rubber heels squeaking on the freshly polished floors, passed up and down the corridor. I heard soft whispers as one doctor in a green shirt spoke to two orderlies leaning against the wall with their arms folded. Occasionally one of them would laugh and the other two would giggle and say, "Sh! Sh!" If they only knew how disturbing it was for me to hear their muttering! At one point I almost shouted "Would you all get out of here!" but I didn't have the courage, and I pulled the blanket over my head instead. Perhaps the most startling noise, though, was the sound of a tray that must have accidentally slipped out of a nurse's hand far beyond my view. I jumped up as the clatter echoed down the long, endless white corridors, setting my nerves on end. Perspiration streaming down my face, I must have sat there in my bed shaking for at least five minutes.

Transition from paragraph 2 to paragraph 3: "All the noises aside" links the topic of paragraph 3 to the topic of paragraph 2 and to the thesis.

All the noises aside, watching the activity outside and inside my room disturbed me, too. Across the hall a little red light above the door of the opposite room suddenly flashed on and off. A nurse in a clean white uniform was there in an instant to help a young, curly haired girl twisting and crying on her bed. A bright light in the hall enabled me to see the actions clearly. With a sturdy thrust of her hand the nurse pulled the white cloth divider across the room, concealing the two of them in the corner. However, I saw the nurse's shadow moving up and down, back and forth, until the child quieted down.

Soon after I noted all this, two other nurses making their rounds saw that I was still awake. One, a slim woman in her mid forties with brown eyes, said in a loud voice, "What are you doing up at this hour, dear? It's after two AM." When I said I couldn't sleep, they saw how clammy I was, and the one who spoke to me rushed off for a thermometer. Placing the rigid glass rod in my mouth, she took my pulse with cool fingers at my wrist. "A hundred and two," she said. "Wanda, bring this girl something for her fever." The second nurse disappeared this time and returned holding a silver packet of Tylenol, and I swallowed the pills with water from the drinking glass on my bedstand. Every so often until morning one of the nurses would saunter in, touch my brow, and make cheerful but noisy conversation. I knew they were trying to help, but all this activity did not make me feel any better. It made me feel worse.

Because hospital stays can be very frightening, hospital employees must realize the trauma patients go through just lying in their beds wondering what will happen to them next. The slightest sound, the barest visible action magnifies a million times in a tense person's mind. Couldn't the admitting clerk, a floor nurse, or an intern explain to patients about what to expect at the hospital? I would have liked knowing all about the tests I'd have to go through, but also would have liked knowing not to expect much sleep. If I knew in advance of all the noise and activity I might have relaxed.

The words "watching the activity outside and inside my room disturbed me, too" set the topic of the next part of the essay.

Concrete sensory detail holds readers' interest and brings scene to life: "red light above the door"; "clean white uniform"; "curly haired girl twisting and crying on her bed"; "nurse's shadow moving up and down, back and forth."

Clear connection to previous paragraph; "Soon after I noted all this" provides transition, helping to build essay's coherence.

Nurses' spoken words add life to the essay.

Short, succinct final sentence very effective in this paragraph.

Conclusion adds depth to the essay; it places narrative and descriptive details in a larger, more profound framework.

We call attention particularly to the greatly improved last paragraph in the revised draft, the writer's conclusion. This is no mere restatement of the topic. The writer has used the experience that she revealed in the rest of the essay to establish a new context for the topic. What did her unpleasant stay in University Hospital tell her? Hospitals don't realize the trauma even a short stay can produce in a patient, and if only hospital staff would explain what to expect in advance, patients might not have such a rough time. We can see how the body paragraphs lead her to reach this conclusion and feel satisfied that the writer has led us to new insights based on her experiences.

Throughout the revised essay, the writer has tightened her sentences by combining a number of them and by eliminating unnecessary words and phrases. In addition, we note a reduction of distracting errors in sentence structure and spelling. Efforts to eliminate errors and improve language and sentences will continue as the writer moves toward producing a final draft and formally edits her paper.

Final Draft

The final draft is intended for public, rather than private, reading. It must be the writer's best effort. Most editors and teachers require final drafts to be double-spaced, neatly written or typed with wide margins, and clearly identified with the writer's name, the date, and information to locate the writer (such as class code or home address). The four writers in this chapter represent a variety of approaches to both the inspiration and the craft of writing. Russell Baker recalls his decision in high school to become a writer. Kurt Vonnegut, Jr., sees style as the defining essence of good writing. Amy Tan finds her writer's voice when she realizes that her mother is the ideal audience. Like William Zinsser pleading for the preciseness that comes only with simplicity, Tan advises us to aim for direct and simple language instead of academic jargon or pretentious style.

The four writers represented here also introduce expository techniques discussed in subsequent chapters. Careful examination of their sources of inspiration *and* their revelations about the nuts and bolts of how to get the writing done prepares the way for later chapters and writing assignments.

Finally, though the Internet and CD-ROMs increasingly replace the printed page, the basic medium of communication is still words. Whether we scratch them onto stone tablets, draw them on parchment with turkey feathers, or type them into a computer, we still use words. Without writing, we risk the loss of our political freedom and our personal history. With words, we pass ideas and values on from one generation to the next. The words of Henry Miller will always ring true: "Writing, like life itself, is a voyage of discovery."

This brief overview sketches in some of the important steps in the writing process. But you don't want to lose the idea that writing is a process both of inspiration and of craft. Many writers have tried to explain how the two connect in their own particular efforts to create. The novelist and short story writer Katherine Anne Porter, for example, tells how inspiration becomes communication in her writing: "Now and again thousands of memories converge, harmonize, and arrange themselves around a central idea in a coherent form, and I write. . . ." Jean Cocteau, the playwright, asserts the need to shape inspiration into language for a page of writing: "To write, to conquer ink and paper, accumulate letters and paragraphs, divide them with periods and commas, is a different matter from carrying around the dream of a play or a book." The point made by Porter and Cocteau is that writing emerges from both creativity and skill, instruction and technique, talent and effort. As we said, writing is a process *and* craft.

On Becoming a Writer

Russell Baker

Russell Baker recounts in his Pulitzer Prize–winning memoir, *Growing Up* (1982), from which this selection is taken, that his mother decided that he should become a writer. Baker was eleven. When he was eight, his mother, a schoolteacher, had started him out selling magazines on street corners around town, with the idea that he needed to begin training for a job. But when, at the age of 11, he came home with "A+" on an essay, she abruptly changed her mind and concluded that he would be a writer. "I clasped the idea to my heart," Baker says. "I loved stories and thought that making up stories must surely be almost as much fun as reading them." He adds, with characteristic humor: "What writers did couldn't even be classified as work." Baker, born in Virginia in 1925 and reared in Belleville, New Jersey, began his career with the *Baltimore Sun* in 1947, working his way up from police reporter to White House correspondent. In 1954 he joined the *New York Times* and in 1962 began writing his "Observer" column for the *Times;* the column was nationally syndicated, and Baker continued to write it for 36 years. In his farewell column, printed Christmas Day 1998, Baker noted that he had written three million words. A member of the American Academy of Letters, Baker has published more than a dozen books, including *An American in Washington* (1961) and *Poor Russell's Almanac* (1971).

PREREADING: THINKING ABOUT THE ESSAY IN ADVANCE

How does someone "become" a writer? Does this idea suggest something grand and elevated, or something matter-of-fact, no different from "becoming a dentist"? Why? Do you identify with the idea of becoming a writer? Or do you think becoming a writer is reserved for a particular breed, and hence is not for you? Why? Is an essay with the title "On Becoming a Writer" naturally interesting, or distant and intimidating? Explain your answers.

Words to Watch

lackluster (par. 2) lacking sheen or vitality

chloroform (par. 2) a toxic liquid with a strong odor, at one time used as a general anesthetic

notorious (par. 3) widely and unfavorably known
prim (par. 3) stiff, exaggeratedly precise, prudish
listless (par. 4) sluggish
irrepressible (par. 4) impossible to keep down
antecedent (par. 6) something that comes before; in grammar, the word a pronoun refers to
exotic (par. 8) foreign; fascinating because unfamiliar
reminiscence (par. 10) an account of remembered events
repress (par. 12) squelch

1 The only thing that truly interested me was writing, and I knew that sixteen-year-olds did not come out of high school and become writers. I thought of writing as something to be done only by the rich. It was so obviously not real work, not a job at which you could earn a living. Still, I had begun to think of myself as a writer. It was the only thing for which I seemed to have the smallest talent, and, silly though it sounded when I told people I'd like to be a writer, it gave me a way of thinking about myself which satisfied my need to have an identity.

2 The notion of becoming a writer had flickered off and on in my head since the Belleville days, but it wasn't until my third year in high school that the possibility took hold. Until then I'd been bored by everything associated with English courses. I found English grammar dull and baffling. I hated the assignments to turn out "compositions," and went at them like heavy labor, turning out leaden, lackluster paragraphs that were agonies for teachers to read and for me to write. The classics thrust on me to read seemed as deadening as chloroform.

3 When our class was assigned to Mr. Fleagle for third-year English I anticipated another grim year in that dreariest of subjects. Mr. Fleagle was notorious among City students for dullness and inability to inspire. He was said to be stuffy, dull, and hopelessly out of date. To me he looked to be sixty or seventy and prim to a fault. He wore primly severe eyeglasses, his wavy hair was primly cut and primly combed. He wore prim vested suits with neckties blocked primly against the collar buttons of his primly starched white shirts. He had a primly pointed jaw, a primly straight nose, and a prim manner of speaking that was so correct, so gentlemanly, that he seemed a comic antique.

4 I anticipated a listless, unfruitful year with Mr. Fleagle and for a long time was not disappointed. We read *Macbeth.* Mr. Fleagle

loved *Macbeth* and wanted us to love it too, but he lacked the gift of infecting others with his own passion. He tried to convey the murderous ferocity of Lady Macbeth one day by reading aloud the passage that concludes.

> . . . I have given suck, and know
> How tender 'tis to love the babe that milks me.
> I would, while it was smiling in my face,
> Have plucked my nipple from his boneless gums. . . .

The idea of prim Mr. Fleagle plucking his nipple from boneless gums was too much for the class. We burst into gasps of irrepressible snickering. Mr. Fleagle stopped. 5

"There is nothing funny, boys, about giving suck to a babe. It is the—the very essence of motherhood, don't you see." 6

He constantly sprinkled his sentences with "don't you see." It wasn't a question but an exclamation of mild surprise at our ignorance. "Your pronoun needs an antecedent, don't you see," he would say, very primly. "The purpose of the Porter's scene, boys, is to provide comic relief from the horror, don't you see." 7

Late in the year we tackled the informal essay. "The essay, don't you see, is the . . ." My mind went numb. Of all forms of writing, none seemed so boring as the essay. Naturally we would have to write informal essays. Mr. Fleagle distributed a homework sheet offering us a choice of topics. None was quite so simple-minded as "What I Did on My Summer Vacation," but most seemed to be almost as dull. I took the list home and dawdled until the night before the essay was due. Sprawled on the sofa, I finally faced up to the grim task, took the list out of my notebook, and scanned it. The topic on which my eye stopped was "The Art of Eating Spaghetti." 8

This title produced an extraordinary sequence of mental images. Surging up out of the depths of memory came a vivid recollection of a night in Belleville when all of us were seated around the supper table—Uncle Allen, my mother, Uncle Charlie, Doris, Uncle Hal—and Aunt Pat served spaghetti for supper. Spaghetti was an exotic treat in those days. Neither Doris nor I had ever eaten spaghetti, and none of the adults had enough experience to be good at it. All the good humor of Uncle Allen's house reawoke in my mind as I recalled the laughing arguments we had that night 9 about the socially respectable method for moving spaghetti from plate to mouth.

10 Suddenly I wanted to write about that, about the warmth and good feeling of it, but I wanted to put it down simply for my own joy, not for Mr. Fleagle. It was a moment I wanted to recapture and hold for myself. I wanted to relive the pleasure of an evening at New Street. To write it as I wanted, however, would violate all the rules of formal composition I'd learned in school, and Mr. Fleagle would surely give it a failing grade. Never mind. I would write something else for Mr. Fleagle after I had written this thing for myself.

11 When I finished it the night was half gone and there was no time left to compose a proper, respectable essay for Mr. Fleagle. There was no choice next morning but to turn in my private reminiscence of Belleville. Two days passed before Mr. Fleagle returned the graded papers, and he returned everyone's but mine. I was bracing myself for a command to report to Mr. Fleagle immediately after school for discipline when I saw him lift my paper from his desk and rap for the class's attention.

12 "Now, boys," he said, "I want to read you an essay. This is titled 'The Art of Eating Spaghetti.' "

13 And he started to read. My words! He was reading *my words* out loud to the entire class. What's more, the entire class was listening. Listening attentively. Then somebody laughed, then the entire class was laughing, and not in contempt and ridicule, but with openhearted enjoyment. Even Mr. Fleagle stopped two or three times to repress a small prim smile.

14 I did my best to avoid showing pleasure, but what I was feeling was pure ecstasy at this startling demonstration that my words had the power to make people laugh. In the eleventh grade, at the eleventh hour as it were, I had discovered a calling. It was the happiest moment of my entire school career. When Mr. Fleagle finished he put the final seal on my happiness by saying, "Now that, boys, is an essay, don't you see. It's—don't you see—it's of the very essence of the essay, don't you see. Congratulations, Mr. Baker."

15 For the first time, light shone on a possibility. It wasn't a very heartening possibility, to be sure. Writing couldn't lead to a job after high school, and it was hardly honest work, but Mr. Fleagle had opened a door for me. After that I ranked Mr. Fleagle among the finest teachers in the school.

BUILDING VOCABULARY

1. Repetition can be a very effective stylistic device. Baker, for example, describes his teacher, Mr. Fleagle, by repeatedly using the word "prim" (par. 3). Rewrite par. 3, substituting another word for "prim." What is the effect of maintaining the repetition but substituting this other word?
2. As a humorist, Baker is especially attuned to the importance of vivid writing. One way he achieves his effects is by the use of emphatic modifiers, mainly adjectives and adverbs. Retaining Baker's meaning, substitute your own word for the adjectives in the pairings below:
   - **a.** comic antique (par. 3)
   - **b.** unfruitful year (par. 4)
   - **c.** murderous ferocity (par. 4)
   - **d.** irrepressible snickering (par. 4)
   - **e.** grim task (par. 7)
   - **f.** vivid recollection (par. 8)
   - **g.** exotic treat (par. 8)
   - **h.** pure ecstasy (par. 13)
   - **i.** heartening possibility (par. 14)

THINKING CRITICALLY ABOUT THE ESSAY

Understanding the Writer's Ideas

1. As a sixteen-year-old, Baker pictures the writing life as full of significant drawbacks. What are they? Given these drawbacks, why does Baker want to become a writer anyway?
2. Why did Baker see being assigned to Mr. Fleagle's class as a signal of "another grim year in that dreariest of subjects" (par. 3)?
3. In what ways was Baker's anticipation proved correct?
4. Why did Baker decide to write about how to eat spaghetti?
5. Why did Baker think that to write about eating spaghetti in the way he wanted to "would violate all the rules of formal composition" (par. 9)?
6. What do you think Baker wants us to conclude from the fact that Mr. Fleagle, far from hating Baker's essay, loved it?
7. What was it about hearing his essay read aloud that produced in Baker a feeling of "pure ecstasy" (par. 13)?

8. Having his essay read out loud was, Baker says, "the happiest moment" of his school career. What made it the happiest moment?

Understanding the Writer's Techniques

1. Baker's piece begins without any gesture of introduction: he just starts right in. Do you find this opening effective? If you do, why? If you do not, why not? What would you have preferred?
2. Humor depends a great deal on *tone* (see Glossary). *Tone,* the quality of writer's voice (angry, objective, sarcastic), reflects the writer's attitude towards his subject. How would you characterize Baker's tone in this essay? Cite three or four especially telling examples to support your answer.
3. One of the rhetorical ploys that Baker uses to entertain us is *reversal,* that is, raising expectations that will turn out more or less the opposite of what we may expect. You might say that, in a grand way, this is just what happened to Baker in his life as a writer: he expected that if he became a writer he couldn't possibly earn a living, but in fact he has as a writer earned not only a living but a place of respect at the height of American society. What *reversals* can you find in the essay? How do they add to your reading pleasure?
4. Among the elements of vivid writing is vivid *diction,* the use of lively, appropriate words. How effective are the italicized words in the following sentences taken from par. 7: "I took the list home and *dawdled* until the night before the essay was due. *Sprawled* on the sofa, I finally faced up to the *grim* task, took the list out of my notebook, and *scanned* it." What other examples of vivid diction caught your eye?
5. Baker devotes four paragraphs, a third of the selection, to the drama of Mr. Fleagle's singling out of Baker's essay for special attention. How does Baker sustain the momentum of his narration while actually pausing at length over a single event? (You might note his use of transitions, for example.)
6. Why is the final sentence an especially satisfying conclusion?

Exploring the Writer's Ideas

1. Writing requires something to write about—you can't just "write." So can we believe Baker when he says, "The only thing that truly interested me was writing" (par. 1)? Are we expected

to take this as literally true, or do you think he is exaggerating for comic effect? Answer these questions in a paragraph.

2. Was Mr. Fleagle as bad as Baker makes him sound? What makes you think so? What makes you think otherwise?
3. Is powerful writing inevitably produced, like Baker's spaghetti essay, simply for the writer's own joy (par. 9), or can powerful writing be produced "on assignment"? What assumptions would underlie one answer or another?
4. Baker's essay is not uproariously funny, but it is gently amusing, even endearing. What qualities in the essay justify characterizing it as "endearing"?

IDEAS FOR WRITING

Prewriting

What would *you* like to become? Is there a particular event or time that you associate with the realization that *this* is what you want to be or do (doctor, surfer, teacher)? What about your intended occupation or role stands out for you as especially appealing? What's the downside of your ambition?

Guided Writing

Write an essay entitled "Becoming a(n) __________."

1. Begin briskly, as Baker does, recounting when the idea of becoming X first struck you as a possibility, and why. Use a slightly ironic, bemused tone, suggesting, as Baker does, that your understanding of what it means to become X was a little wobbly, but something powerful drew you to the idea anyway.
2. Tell the story of the idea actually becoming more of a reality by means of an exceptional event. Perhaps, like Baker's experience, it was an event that you anticipated would be "grim" and would have anything but a happy conclusion.
3. Characterize this event in a vivid paragraph.
4. In the next paragraph, discuss your preparation for the event. If applicable, discuss your effort to avoid the event and then your collapse into preparing for it.

5. Begin now to lay the ground for your reaction to the event and, if applicable, the *reversal* of your/our expectations when you suddenly see a glimmer of light within your preparation for the event.
6. End your essay by showing how the event changed your ideas about becoming X. If you expect the worst and it turns out to be the best, clinch the point by ending on a reversal that overturns the things you were most dreading about the event.

Thinking and Writing Collaboratively

In groups of three or four discuss the relation between the experience of school and the dream of becoming X. Does school stimulate or squelch the dream of being all that you can be? Be as specific as possible in your discussion. Then write a series of recommendations to a high school principal about how school could best encourage and inform the desires of students to "become . . ."

Writing About the Text

What motivates achievement? Wanting to become a writer, a painter, a dancer, a lawyer, or a president inevitably involves ego. In some ways ambition is selfish. Discuss the relation of selfishness to achievement, based on this selection. Is "the power to make people laugh" a joy to a writer because he can do good? Or because . . .?

More Writing Projects

1. Baker's decision to become a writer seems to have been at least significantly affected by the assertiveness of his mother. In your journal, write a version of Baker's story from the point of view of his mother.
2. In an extended paragraph, explain the role of parents in the ambitions and achievements of their children.
3. Famously, it's fruitless to try to explain a joke to someone who doesn't find the joke funny. Humorists must have a pretty good handle on what makes others laugh—or they wouldn't be humorists. Write a short personal essay that aims to be funny—and then read it to several people or give it to them to read. Ask them to tell you what they did or did not find funny, and why.

How to Write with Style

Kurt Vonnegut, Jr.

Kurt Vonnegut, born in 1922 in Indianapolis, Indiana, is one of America's most imaginative writers. Called by some a modern-day Mark Twain, he frequently draws on science fiction to cast a fresh light on earthly life. In so doing, he highlights the powerful presence of randomness and coincidence in human society, but he also discovers reasons for wonder and, not least, humor. Some of his best-known books, such as *Slaughterhouse-Five* (1969) and *Breakfast of Champions* (1973), are biting satires on American politics. Vonnegut says that he owes his outlook, at least in part, to the sometimes dismaying facts of his biography, such as that his mother committed suicide on Mother's Day 1942, or that, during World War II, he had to live through the firebombing of Dresden by the United States and Britain because he was being held there by the Germans as a prisoner of war. In this iconoclastic selection, Vonnegut, who has not been shy about creating an interesting persona for himself as a hook for his readers, recommends the same to young writers and gives other secrets of his trade.

PREREADING: THINKING ABOUT THE ESSAY IN ADVANCE

What are your thoughts about "writing with style"? What does the phrase mean? What qualities of writing do you admire? What qualities of writing do you not admire?

Words to Watch

piquant (par. 10) pleasantly disturbing
galvanized (par. 10) coated
locutions (par. 11) speaking style
higgledy-piggledy (par. 15) in disorder or confusion
egalitarian (par. 20) equal rights for all citizens
aristocrats (par. 20) members of the nobility

Newspaper reporters and technical writers are trained to reveal almost nothing about themselves in their writings. This makes them freaks in the world of writers, since almost all of the other ink-stained wretches in that world reveal a lot about themselves to 1 readers. We call these revelations, accidental and intentional, elements of literary style.

2 These revelations are fascinating to us as readers. They tell us what sort of person it is with whom we are spending time. Does the writer sound ignorant or informed, crazy or sane, stupid or bright, crooked or honest, humorless or playful—? And on and on.

3 When you yourself put words on paper, remember that the most damning revelation you can make about yourself is that you do not know what is interesting and what is not. Don't you yourself like or dislike writers mainly for what they choose to show you or make you think about? Did you ever admire an empty-headed writer for his or her mastery of the language? No.

4 So your own winning literary style must begin with interesting ideas in your head. Find a subject you care about and which you in your heart feel others should care about. It is this genuine caring, and not your games with language, which will be the most compelling and seductive element in your style.

5 I am not urging you to write a novel, by the way—although I would not be sorry if you wrote one, provided you genuinely cared about something. A petition to the mayor about a pothole in front of your house or a love letter to the girl next door will do.

6 Do not ramble, though.

7 As for your use of language: Remember that two great masters of our language, William Shakespeare and James Joyce, wrote sentences which were almost childlike when their subjects were most profound. "To be or not to be?" asks Shakespeare's Hamlet. The longest word is three letters long. Joyce, when he was frisky, could put together a sentence as intricate and glittering as a necklace for Cleopatra, but my favorite sentence in his short story "Eveline" is this one: "She was tired." At that point in the story, no other words could break the heart of a reader as those words do.

8 Simplicity of language is not only reputable, but perhaps even sacred. The Bible opens with a sentence well within the writing skills of a lively fourteen-year-old: "In the beginning God created the heavens and the earth."

9 It may be that you, too, are capable of making necklaces for Cleopatra, so to speak. But your eloquence should be the servant of the ideas in your head. Your rule might be this: If a sentence no matter how excellent does not illuminate my subject in some new and useful way, scratch it out. Here is the same rule paraphrased to

apply to storytelling, to fiction: Never include a sentence which does not either remark on character or advance the action.

The writing style which is most natural for you is bound to 10
echo speech you heard when a child. English was the novelist Joseph Conrad's third language, and much that seems piquant in his use of English was no doubt colored by his first language, which was Polish. And lucky indeed is the writer who has grown up in Ireland, for the English spoken there is so amusing and musical. I myself grew up in Indianapolis, Indiana, where common speech sounds like a band saw cutting galvanized tin, and employs a vocabulary as unornamental as a monkey wrench.

In some of the more remote hollows of Appalachia, children 11
still grow up hearing songs and locutions of Elizabethan times. Yes, and many Americans grow up hearing a language other than English, or an English dialect a majority of Americans cannot understand.

All these varieties of speech are beautiful, just as the varieties 12
of butterflies are beautiful. No matter what your first language, you should treasure it all your life. If it happens not to be standard English, and if it shows itself when you write standard English, the result is usually delightful, like a very pretty girl with one eye that is green and one that is blue.

I myself find that I trust my own writing most, and others 13
seem to trust it most, too, when I sound most like a person from Indianapolis, which is what I am. What alternatives do I have? The one most vehemently recommended by teachers has no doubt been pressed on you, as well: that I write like cultivated Englishmen of a century or more ago.

I used to be exasperated by such teachers, but am no more. I 14
understand now that all those antique essays and stories with which I was to compare my own work were not magnificent for their datedness or foreignness, but for saying precisely what their authors meant them to say. My teachers wished me to write accurately, always selecting the most effective words, and relating the words to one another unambiguously, rigidly, like parts of a machine. The teachers did not want to turn me into an Englishman after all. They hoped that I would become understandable—and therefore understood.

And there went my dream of doing with words what Pablo 15
Picasso did with paint or what any number of jazz idols did with

music. If I broke all the rules of punctuation, had words mean whatever I wanted them to mean, and strung them together higgledy-piggledy, I would simply not be understood. So you, too, had better avoid Picasso-style or jazz-style writing, if you have something worth saying and wish to be understood.

16 If it were only teachers who insisted that modern writers stay close to literary styles of the past, we might reasonably ignore them. But readers insist on the very same thing. They want our pages to look very much like pages they have seen before.

17 Why? It is because they themselves have a tough job to do, and they need all the help they can get from us. They have to identify thousands of little marks on paper, and make sense of them immediately. They have to *read,* an art so difficult that most people do not really master it even after having studied it all through grade school and high school—for twelve long years.

18 So this discussion, like all discussions of literary styles, must finally acknowledge that our stylistic options as writers are neither numerous nor glamorous, since our readers are bound to be such imperfect artists. Our audience requires us to be sympathetic and patient teachers, ever willing to simplify and clarify—whereas we would rather soar high above the crowd, singing like nightingales.

19 That is the bad news. The good news is that we Americans are governed under a unique Constitution, which allows us to write whatever we please without fear of punishment. So the most meaningful aspect of our styles, which is what we choose to write about, is unlimited.

20 Also: We are members of an egalitarian society, so there is no reason for us to write, in case we are not classically educated aristocrats, as though we were classically educated aristocrats.

21 For a discussion of literary style in a narrower sense, in a more technical sense, I commend to your attention *The Elements of Style* by William Strunk, Jr., and E. B. White (Macmillan, 1979). It contains such rules as this: "A participial phrase at the beginning of a sentence must refer to the grammatical subject," and so on. E. B. White is, of course, one of the most admirable literary stylists this country has so far produced.

22 You should realize, too, that no one would care how well or badly Mr. White expressed himself, if he did not have perfectly enchanting things to say.

BUILDING VOCABULARY

Use *context clues* (see Glossary) to determine the meanings of the words below. Use a dictionary to check your definitions.

a. intentional (par. 1)
b. compelling (par. 4)
c. intricate (par. 7)
d. reputable (par. 8)
e. eloquence (par. 9)
f. illuminate (par. 9)
g. exasperated (par. 14)

THINKING CRITICALLY ABOUT THE ESSAY

Understanding the Writer's Ideas

1. What is the difference between newspaper reporters and technical writers and the "ink-stained wretches," as Vonnegut puts it?
2. According to the writer, what is the best way to begin a "winning literary style" (par. 4)?
3. Why does Vonnegut believe that simple writing is best, and how does he try to prove his point?
4. What is the writer's attitude toward standard language versus the language "you heard when a child" (par. 10)?
5. For Vonnegut, writers should avoid "jazz-style" writing. Why?
6. How does the writer come to the conclusion that reading is "an art so difficult that most people do not really master it" (par. 17)?
7. Why does Vonnegut say it is good news that writers in America are "governed under a unique Constitution" (par. 19)?
8. What is the benefit of being a writer in an "egalitarian society" as opposed to an "aristocratic" one, according to Vonnegut (par. 20)?

Understanding the Writer's Techniques

1. What is the thesis of this essay? Who is Vonnegut's audience here? How can you tell?

2. Why does Vonnegut begin his essay with references to newspaper reporters and technical writers if he does not mention them in the rest of text?
3. Why is the *transition* (see Glossary) at the beginning of paragraph 3 effective, given the title of this essay?
4. Vonnegut suggests that writers use sentences that are almost "childlike." How can you tell that he follows his own advice?
5. What purpose does using direct quotes from William Shakespeare and James Joyce serve?
6. What is the effect of Vonnegut's switching to the first person in paragraph 13, pointing to the Indianapolis speech in his own writing?
7. How does the question "Why?" (par. 17) serve as a clear shift in the idea development of the essay?
8. The word "Also" in paragraph 20 is followed by a colon to signal a transition. Check a grammar handbook. Is this the way transitions should be punctuated?
9. Why does Vonnegut recommend the book *The Elements of Style?* Hasn't he already instructed us in these matters himself?
10. Explain how and why Vonnegut's last paragraph returns the reader to the essay's main idea in paragraph 3.

Exploring the Writer's Ideas

1. Vonnegut believes that since newspaper reporters and technical writers reveal almost nothing about themselves, they are less fascinating to us. Based on your experiences as a reader, do you agree? Why or why not?
2. If you care deeply about a subject, Vonnegut claims this will make your writing more interesting to others. Has this been true in your experiences as a writer? Explain.
3. Vonnegut makes the case (par. 12) that using nonstandard English can make a writer's work "beautiful." Do you agree with him? Why or why not?
4. Vonnegut says you should use the speech you heard as a child (par. 10) to achieve a successful writing style. Then he says that if he broke all the rules of language, he "would simply not be understood" (par. 15). Is Vonnegut contradicting himself? What if a person's childhood language is not understandable outside his or her community?

5. Vonnegut reminds us that we live in an "egalitarian" society. What implications does this have for the development of your writing style?
6. Given a choice, which writers would you rather read—those that reveal "nothing about themselves" or those whose "revelations are fascinating"? Explain your preferences.

IDEAS FOR WRITING

Prewriting

Make a list of the steps you take in the process of doing something that you have excelled in (for example, gardening, cooking, playing sports, making friends, and so on).

Guided Writing

Write an essay called "How to __________ with Style." Fill in the blank with something you do well, such as skiing, painting a room, and so on. Instruct the reader on how and why he or she should also do this activity and what you mean by doing it with style.

1. Begin by defining the most important quality you think someone needs to be successful at this activity.
2. In the next two or three paragraphs, elaborate on how and why this quality will help ensure a person's success in this activity.
3. Describe another quality needed to be a success at this activity. Give two or three paragraphs of supporting detail to show how others have been successful at this activity because they too have had the quality you just described. Here you should make clear what doing the activity "with style" means.
4. Tell if there is any reason why this activity can or cannot be done by most people. Is a special quality needed? Is this something a child can do? Why or why not?
5. Give personal testimony of how and why being a success at this activity is simple or complicated for you. What personal traits have you relied on to be a success at this activity?
6. Warn readers about the most common mistakes made by those who do not succeed at this activity, and suggest how to avoid such mistakes.

7. End with why you think this activity might (or might not) be well suited for people living in a society where they have the constitutional right to live freely. (Consider recommending a book that might assist the reader with this activity.)

Thinking and Writing Collaboratively

Write a short letter using the words of love you would share with someone close to you. Then write out a dictionary definition of "love." Form groups of three students each and share your letters and definitions with the members of the group, asking them: Which words would most appeal to you? Why? Note the responses and write an essay on how to write a love letter.

Writing About the Text

Here is an essay on style that argues "genuine caring" about the subject is the secret of style. Do you think this is true of Vonnegut himself in this essay? What evidence would you cite, for and against? Write an essay about this selection in which you examine whether Vonnegut himself actually applies the ideas he prescribes for young writers.

More Writing Projects

1. In your journal, write a short entry in language that you heard as a child. Try to capture the sounds and traits that will amuse and delight readers.
2. Write two paragraphs that contrast your language use. In paragraph one, describe with examples the kind of language you use with your friends and family. In paragraph two, describe with examples the kind of language you use with your professors or strangers.
3. Write an essay on something you care strongly about, using the language you feel best reveals something personal about yourself, as Vonnegut suggests.

Mother Tongue

Amy Tan

Amy Tan is a novelist and essayist who was born in California only two and a half years after her parents emigrated from China to the United States. Her first novel, *The Joy Luck Club* (1989), was extremely popular, and was followed by *The Kitchen God's Wife* (1991), *The Hundred Secret Senses* (1995), and, most recently, *The Bonesetter's Daughter* (2001). In 1987 Tan traveled to China for the first time, to meet her older sisters from her mother's first marriage. Her complex relationship with her mother, Daisy, who died of Alzheimer's disease in 1999, at the age of 83, is at the heart of much of her work. Among the experiences that shaped their relationship was the death of Tan's older brother and her father when Tan was 14. The two died of brain tumors within six months of each other.

Although she is a writer whose work has enjoyed impressive commercial success, Tan chose to publish this selection in 1990 in a small West Coast literary magazine, *The Threepenny Review,* edited by the writer Wendy Lesser. You might want to ask why she made this choice. The essay's title is a pun, referring at once to the language that nurtures us and, literally, to the language spoken by Tan's mother. Tan presents herself here as a writer and not a student of language, although she holds an M.A. in linguistics from San Jose State University. Speaking and writing in standard English is essential, Tan argues, but the diversity of cultures in America requires that we acknowledge the different "Englishes" spoken by immigrants. As you read her essay, think about your own experience in learning English and about how you respond to the other Englishes you may have heard spoken by your family or neighbors. Consider why Tan chooses to write in standard English.

PREREADING: THINKING ABOUT THE ESSAY IN ADVANCE

What varieties of English do you speak? In other words, do you speak different kinds of English in different situations and to different individuals or groups of people? Why or why not?

Words to Watch

intersection (par. 3) crossroad

wrought (par. 3) made; worked

belies (par. 7) misrepresents; disguises
wince (par. 8) cringe; shrink
empirical (par. 9) relying on observation
guise (par. 10) outward appearance
benign (par. 14) not harmful
insular (par. 15) like an island; isolated

1 I am not a scholar of English or literature. I cannot give you much more than personal opinions on the English language and its variations in this country or others.

2 I am a writer. And by that definition, I am someone who has always loved language. I am fascinated by language in daily life. I spend a great deal of my time thinking about the power of language—the way it can evoke an emotion, a visual image, a complex idea, or a simple truth. Language is the tool of my trade. And I use them all—all the Englishes I grew up with.

3 Recently, I was made keenly aware of the different Englishes I do use. I was giving a talk to a large group of people, the same talk I had already given to half a dozen other groups. The nature of the talk was about my writing, my life, and my book, *The Joy Luck Club.* The talk was going along well enough, until I remembered one major difference that made the whole talk sound wrong. My mother was in the room. And it was perhaps the first time she had heard me give a lengthy speech, using the kind of English I have never used with her. I was saying things like, "The intersection of memory upon imagination" and "There is an aspect of my fiction that relates to thus-and-thus"—a speech filled with carefully wrought grammatical phrases, burdened, it suddenly seemed to me, with nominalized forms, past perfect tenses, conditional phrases, all the forms of standard English that I had learned in school and through books, the forms of English I did not use at home with my mother.

4 Just last week, I was walking down the street with my mother, and I again found myself conscious of the English I was using, the English I do use with her. We were talking about the price of new and used furniture and I heard myself saying this: "Not waste money that way." My husband was with us as well, and he didn't notice any switch in my English. And then I realized why. It's because over the twenty years we've been together I've often used that same kind of English with him, and sometimes he even uses it with me. It has become our language of intimacy, a different sort of English that relates to family talk, the language I grew up with.

So you'll have some idea of what this family talk I heard sounds like, I'll quote what my mother said during a recent conversation which I videotaped and then transcribed. During this conversation, my mother was talking about a political gangster in Shanghai who had the same last name as her family's, Du, and how the gangster in his early years wanted to be adopted by her family, which was rich by comparison. Later, the gangster became more powerful, far richer than my mother's family, and one day showed up at my mother's wedding to pay his respects. Here's what she said in part: 5

"Du Yusong having business like fruit stand. Like off the street kind. He is Du like Du Zong—but not Tsung-ming Island people. The local people call putong, the river east side, he belong to that side local people. That man want to ask Du Zong father take him in like become own family. Du Zong father wasn't look down on him, but didn't take seriously, until that man big like become a mafia. Now important person, very hard to inviting him. Chinese way, came only to show respect, don't stay for dinner. Respect for making big celebration, he shows up. Mean gives lots of respect. Chinese custom. Chinese social life that way. If too important won't have to stay too long. He come to my wedding. I didn't see. I heard it. I gone to boy's side, they have YMCA dinner. Chinese age I was nineteen." 6

You should know that my mother's expressive command of English belies how much she actually understands. She reads the *Forbes* report, listens to *Wall Street Week,* converses daily with her stockbroker, reads all of Shirley MacLaine's books with ease—all kinds of things I can't begin to understand. Yet some of my friends tell me they understand 50 percent of what my mother says. Some say they understand 80 to 90 percent. Some say they understand none of it, as if she were speaking pure Chinese. But to me, my mother's English is perfectly clear, perfectly natural. It's my mother tongue. Her language, as I hear it, is vivid, direct, full of observation and imagery. That was the language that helped shape the way I saw things, expressed things, made sense of the world. 7

Lately, I've been giving more thought to the kind of English my mother speaks. Like others, I have described it to people as "broken" or "fractured" English. But I wince when I say that. It has always bothered me that I can think of no way to describe it other than "broken," as if it were damaged and needed to be fixed, as if it lacked a certain wholeness and soundness. I've heard other 8 terms used, "limited English," for example. But they seem just as bad, as if everything is limited, including people's perceptions of the limited English speaker.

9 I know this for a fact, because when I was growing up, my mother's "limited" English limited *my* perception of her. I was ashamed of her English. I believed that her English reflected the quality of what she had to say. That is, because she expressed them imperfectly her thoughts were imperfect. And I had plenty of empirical evidence to support me: the fact that people in department stores, at banks, and at restaurants did not take her seriously, did not give her good service, pretended not to understand her, or even acted as if they did not hear her.

10 My mother has long realized the limitations of her English as well. When I was fifteen, she used to have me call people on the phone to pretend I was she. In this guise, I was forced to ask for information or even to complain and yell at people who had been rude to her. One time it was a call to her stockbroker in New York. She had cashed out her small portfolio and it just so happened we were going to go to New York the next week, our very first trip outside California. I had to get on the phone and say in an adolescent voice that was not very convincing, "This is Mrs. Tan."

11 And my mother was standing in the back whispering loudly, "Why he don't send me check, already two weeks late. So mad he lie to me, losing me money."

12 And then I said in perfect English, "Yes, I'm getting rather concerned. You had agreed to send the check two weeks ago, but it hasn't arrived."

13 Then she began to talk more loudly. "What he want, I come to New York tell him front of his boss, you cheating me?" And I was trying to calm her down, make her be quiet, while telling the stockbroker, "I can't tolerate any more excuses. If I don't receive the check immediately, I am going to have to speak to your manager when I'm in New York next week." And sure enough, the following week there we were in front of this astonished stockbroker, and I was sitting there red-faced and quiet, and my mother, the real Mrs. Tan, was shouting at his boss in her impeccable broken English.

14 We used a similar routine just five days ago, for a situation that was far less humorous. My mother had gone to the hospital for an appointment, to find out about a benign brain tumor a CAT scan had revealed a month ago. She said she had spoken very good English, her best English, no mistakes. Still, she said, the hospital did not apologize when they said they had lost the CAT scan and

she had come for nothing. She said they did not seem to have any sympathy when she told them she was anxious to know the exact diagnosis, since her husband and son had both died of brain tumors. She said they would not give her any more information until the next time and she would have to make another appointment for that. So she said she would not leave until the doctor called her daughter. She wouldn't budge. And when the doctor finally called her daughter, me, who spoke in perfect English—lo and behold—we had assurances the CAT scan would be found, promises that a conference call on Monday would be held, and apologies for any suffering my mother had gone through for a most regrettable mistake.

I think my mother's English almost had an effect on limiting 15
my possibilities in life as well. Sociologists and linguists probably will tell you that a person's developing language skills are more influenced by peers. But I do think that the language spoken in the family, especially in immigrant families which are more insular, plays a large role in shaping the language of the child. And I believe that it affected my results on achievement tests, IQ tests, and the SAT. While my English skills were never judged as poor, compared to math, English could not be considered my strong suit. In grade school I did moderately well, getting perhaps B's, sometimes B-pluses, in English and scoring perhaps in the sixtieth or seventieth percentile on achievement tests. But those scores were not good enough to override the opinion that my true abilities lay in math and science, because in those areas I achieved A's and scored in the ninetieth percentile or higher.

This was understandable. Math is precise; there is only one 16
correct answer. Whereas, for me at least, the answers on English tests were always a judgment call, a matter of opinion and personal experience. Those tests were constructed around items like fill-in-the-blank sentence completion, such as, "Even though Tom was __________, Mary thought he was __________." And the correct answer always seemed to be the most bland combinations of thoughts, for example, "Even though Tom was shy, Mary thought he was charming," with the grammatical structure "even though" limiting the correct answer to some sort of semantic opposites, so you wouldn't get answers like, "Even though Tom was foolish, Mary thought he was ridiculous." Well, according to my mother, there were very few limitations as to what Tom could have been and what Mary might have thought of him. So I never did well on tests like that.

17 The same was true with word analogies, pairs of words in which you were supposed to find some sort of logical, semantic relationship—for example, "*Sunset* is to *nightfall* as __________ is to __________." And here you would be presented with a list of four possible pairs, one of which showed the same kind of relationship: *red* is to *stoplight, bus* is to *arrival, chills* is to *fever, yawn* is to *boring*. Well, I could never think that way. I knew what the tests were asking, but I could not block out of my mind the images already created by the first pair, "*sunset* is to *nightfall*"—and I would see a burst of colors against a darkening sky, the moon rising, the lowering of a curtain of stars. And all the other pairs of words—red, bus, stoplight, boring—just threw up a mass of confusing images, making it impossible for me to sort out something as logical as saying: "A sunset precedes nightfall" is the same as "a chill precedes a fever." The only way I would have gotten that answer right would have been to imagine an associative situation, for example, my being disobedient and staying out past sunset, catching a chill at night, which turns into feverish pneumonia as punishment, which indeed did happen to me.

18 I have been thinking about all this lately, about my mother's English, about achievement tests. Because lately I've been asked, as a writer, why there are not more Asian Americans represented in American literature. Why are there few Asian Americans enrolled in creative writing programs? Why do so many Chinese students go into engineering? Well, these are broad sociological questions I can't begin to answer. But I have noticed in surveys—in fact, just last week—that Asian students, as a whole, always do significantly better on math achievement tests than in English. And this makes me think that there are other Asian-American students whose English spoken in the home might also be described as "broken" or "limited." And perhaps they also have teachers who are steering them away from writing and into math and science, which is what happened to me.

19 Fortunately, I happen to be rebellious in nature and enjoy the challenge of disproving assumptions made about me. I became an English major my first year in college, after being enrolled as pre-med. I started writing nonfiction as a freelancer the week after I was told by my former boss that writing was my worst skill and I should hone my talents toward account management.

20 But it wasn't until 1985 that I finally began to write fiction. And at first I wrote using what I thought to be wittily crafted

sentences, sentences that would finally prove I had mastery over the English language. Here's an example from the first draft of a story that later made its way into *The Joy Luck Club,* but without this line: "That was my mental quandary in its nascent state." A terrible line, which I can barely pronounce.

Fortunately, for reasons I won't get into today, I later decided 21
I should envision a reader for the stories I would write. And the reader I decided upon was my mother, because these were stories about mothers. So with this reader in mind—and in fact she did read my early drafts—I began to write stories using all the Englishes I grew up with: the English I spoke to my mother, which for lack of a better term might be described as "simple"; the English she used with me, which for lack of a better term might be described as "broken"; my translation of her Chinese, which could certainly be described as "watered down"; and what I imagined to be her translation of her Chinese if she could speak in perfect English, her internal language, and for that I sought to preserve the essence, but neither an English nor a Chinese structure. I wanted to capture what language ability tests can never reveal: her intent, her passion, her imagery, the rhythms of her speech and the nature of her thoughts.

Apart from what any critic had to say about my writing, I 22
knew I had succeeded where it counted when my mother finished reading my book and gave me her verdict: "So easy to read."

BUILDING VOCABULARY

Tan uses technical words to distinguish standard English from the English her mother speaks. Investigate the meanings of the following terms, and find examples to illustrate them for your classmates.

a. scholar (par. 1)
b. nominalized forms (par. 3)
c. transcribed (par. 5)
d. imagery (par. 7)
e. linguists (par. 15)
f. semantic opposites (par. 16)
g. word analogies (par. 17)
h. freelancer (par. 19)
i. quandary (par. 20)
j. nascent (par. 20)

THINKING CRITICALLY ABOUT THE ESSAY

Understanding the Writer's Ideas

1. Why does Tan start her essay by identifying who she is *not?* What does she see as the difference between a scholar and a writer?
2. What does Tan mean when she says, "Language is the tool of my trade"? What are the four ways she says language can work?
3. Tan speaks of "all the Englishes I grew up with" in paragraph 2, and later of the "different Englishes" she uses. Why does her mother's presence in the lecture room help her recall these Englishes? Why does she give us examples of what was "wrong" with her talk in paragraph 3?
4. In paragraph 4, Tan recognizes that she herself shifts from one English to another. Which English is "our language of intimacy"? Why?
5. Tan describes how she recorded her mother's words. Why does she give us her technique in paragraph 5 before presenting her mother's exact words in paragraph 6?
6. What do we know about Tan's mother when we learn she reads the *Forbes* report and various books? Why is it important for Tan to understand the way her mother sees the world? What connection does Tan make between the way we use language and the way we see the world?
7. In paragraph 8, Tan tries to find a suitable label for her mother's language. Why is she unwilling to use a description like "broken" or "limited" English? What does her mother's English sound like to you?
8. In what ways did outsiders (like bankers and waiters) make judgments of Tan's mother because of her language? Were the judgments deliberate or unconscious on their part?
9. How does Tan use humor as she contrasts the two Englishes in the telephone conversations she records? How does the tone change when Tan shifts to the hospital scene? Why do the authorities provide different service and different information when the daughter speaks than they do when the mother speaks?
10. How does Tan connect her math test scores with her mother's language? Why does she think she never did well on language tests? Why does she think the tests do not measure a student's language use very well? Why does Tan ultimately become an English major (par. 19)?

11. In paragraph 20, why does Tan show us the sentence: "That was my mental quandary in its nascent state"? How does it compare with the other sentences in her essay? What is wrong with this "terrible" sentence? What does it mean?
12. In her two final paragraphs, Tan returns to her mother. Why does selecting her mother as her reader help Tan learn to become a better writer? What are the elements of good writing her mother recognizes, even if she herself cannot write standard English?

Understanding the Writer's Techniques

1. What is the thesis statement in Tan's essay? Where does it appear?
2. Throughout her essay, Tan uses *dialogue,* the written reproduction of speech or conversation. Why does she do this? What is the effect of dialogue? Which sentences of dialogue do you find especially effective, and why?
3. In paragraph 3, Tan writes fairly long sentences until she writes, "My mother was in the room." Why is this sentence shorter? What is the effect of the short sentence on the reader?
4. How does identifying her mother as her intended audience help Tan make her own language more effective? Does Tan suggest that all writing should be "simple"? Is her writing always "simple"? Why does her mother find it "easy" to read?
5. Why does Tan put quotation marks around "broken" and "limited"? What other words can describe this different English?

MIXING PATTERNS

Narration (see Chapter 4) is the telling of a story or series of events. *Anecdotes* are very short narrations, usually of an amusing or autobiographical nature. Point out uses of narration and anecdote in Tan's essay. Why does she use narration in this essay? How does the technique of narration interact with description here?

Exploring the Writer's Ideas

1. Why is an awareness of different kinds of English necessary for a writer? Why are writers so interested in "different Englishes"? Should all Americans speak and write the same English?

2. What is the role of parents in setting language standards for their children? How did your parents or other relatives influence your language use?
3. Reread Tan's essay, and look more carefully at her *point of view* (see Glossary) about other Englishes. How do we know what her point of view is? Does she state it directly or indirectly? Where?
4. Listen to someone who speaks a "different" English. Try to record a full paragraph of the speech, as Tan does in paragraph 6. Use a tape recorder and (or) a video camera so that you can replay the speech several times. Explain what the difficulties were in capturing the sound of the speech exactly. Write a "translation" of the paragraph into standard English.
5. Tan explores the special relation between mothers and daughters. How would you describe the author's relation with her mother?

IDEAS FOR WRITING

Prewriting

Free-associate on a sheet of paper about the language you use in daily communication, its delights, difficulties, problems, confusions, humor—in short, anything that comes to mind about the language you use in your daily life.

Guided Writing

Write a narrative essay using first-person point of view in which you contrast your language with the language of someone who speaks differently from you.

1. Begin by making some notes on your own language and by deciding whom you will choose as your other subject. It should be someone you can spend time with so that you can record his or her speech.
2. Following Tan's model, create a narrative to frame your subject's language. Tell who you are and why you speak the way you do. Introduce the other speaker, and tell why his or her speech is different.

3. Use dialogue to provide examples of both Englishes.
4. Analyze how listeners other than yourself respond to both types of speech. What are the social implications of speech differences?
5. Show how listening to the other speaker and to yourself has helped you shape your own language and write your essay. What can you learn about good writing from this project?
6. Be sure the essay has a clear thesis in the introduction. Add a strong conclusion that returns to the idea of the thesis.

Thinking and Writing Collaboratively

Exchange a draft version of your Guided Writing essay with another writer in the class. As you read each other's work, make suggestions to help the writer produce the next draft. Is the thesis clear? Is the introduction focused? Is the conclusion linked to the thesis idea? Is the dialogue realistic?

Writing About the Text

Write a critique of the language and style of this selection as though you were Tan's mother. Before writing, look carefully at what the selection tells us about Tan's mother—about what sort of person she is, about her likes and dislikes, about her reading. Write the essay in standard English.

More Writing Projects

1. In your journal, record examples of new words you have heard recently. Divide the list into columns according to whether the words are standard English or a different English. How many different Englishes can you find in your community and in college?
2. Reread question 1 in Exploring the Writer's Ideas, and write a one-paragraph response to it.
3. Tan's experience as a daughter of recent immigrants has clearly shaped her life in fundamental ways. She writes about the "shame" she once felt for her mother's speech. Write about a personal experience in which you were once embarrassed by someone close to you who was "different." Tell how you would feel about the same encounter if it happened today.

Simplicity

William Zinsser

This selection is a chapter from one of the most successful books about writing of the last quarter century, titled *On Writing Well. The New York Times* has compared William Zinsser's book, first published in 1976, with the classics in the field, saying it "belongs on any shelf of serious reference works for writers." From 1959 to 1987 Zinsser, the author of 15 books, was general editor of the Book-of-the-Month Club. He now teaches in New York City at the New School. In this selection, Zinsser begins with a fairly pessimistic analysis of the clutter that pervades and degrades American writing, and he offers many examples to prove his point. Zinsser deals with almost all major aspects of the writing process—thinking, composing, awareness of the reader, self-discipline, rewriting, and editing—and concludes that simplicity is the key to them all.

PREREADING: THINKING ABOUT THE ESSAY IN ADVANCE

Do you find writing difficult or easy? Why? What is there about the act of writing that annoys, frustrates, or satisfies you?

Words to Watch

decipher (par. 2) to make out the meaning of something obscure

adulterants (par. 3) added substances which make something impure or inferior

mollify (par. 4) to appease; to soothe

spell (par. 4) a short period of time

assailed (par. 8) attacked with words or physical violence

tenacious (par. 10) stubborn; persistent

rune (par. 10) character in an ancient alphabet

bearded (par. 12) approached or confronted boldly

1 Clutter is the disease of American writing. We are a society strangling in unnecessary words, circular constructions, pompous frills and meaningless jargon.

2 Who can understand the clotted language of everyday American commerce: the memo, the corporation report, the business letter, the notice from the bank explaining its latest "simplified"

statement? What member of an insurance or medical plan can decipher the brochure explaining his costs and benefits? What father or mother can put together a child's toy from the instructions on the box? Our national tendency is to inflate and thereby sound important. The airline pilot who announces that he is presently anticipating experiencing considerable precipitation wouldn't think of saying it may rain. The sentence is too simple—there must be something wrong with it.

But the secret of good writing is to strip every sentence to its 3
cleanest components. Every word that serves no function, every long word that could be a short word, every adverb that carries the same meaning that's already in the verb, every passive construction that leaves the reader unsure of who is doing what—these are the thousand and one adulterants that weaken the strength of a sentence. And they usually occur in proportion to education and rank.

During the 1960s the president of my university wrote a letter 4
to mollify the alumni after a spell of campus unrest. "You are probably aware," he began, "that we have been experiencing very considerable potentially explosive expressions of dissatisfaction on issues only partially related." He meant the students had been hassling them about different things. I was far more upset by the president's English than by the students' potentially explosive expressions of dissatisfaction. I would have preferred the presidential approach taken by Franklin D. Roosevelt when he tried to convert into English his own government's memos, such as this blackout order of 1942:

> Such preparations shall be made as will completely obscure all Federal buildings and non-Federal buildings occupied by the Federal government during an air raid for any period of time from visibility by reason of internal or external illumination.

"Tell them," Roosevelt said, "that in buildings where they have 5
to keep the work going to put something across the windows."

Simplify, simplify. Thoreau said it, as we are so often re- 6
minded, and no American writer more consistently practiced what he preached. Open *Walden* to any page and you will find a man saying in a plain and orderly way what is on his mind:

> I went to the woods because I wished to live deliberately, to front only the essential facts of life, and see if I could not learn what it had to teach, and not, when I came to die, discover that I had not lived.

7 How can the rest of us achieve such enviable freedom from clutter? The answer is to clear our heads of clutter. Clear thinking becomes clear writing; one can't exist without the other. It's impossible for a muddy thinker to write good English. He may get away with it for a paragraph or two, but soon the reader will be lost, and there's no sin so grave, for the reader will not easily be lured back.

8 Who is this elusive creature, the reader? The reader is someone with an attention span of about 30 seconds—a person assailed by many forces competing for attention. At one time those forces were relatively few: newspapers, magazines, radio, spouse, children, pets. Today they also include a "home entertainment center" (television, VCR, tapes, CDs), e-mail, the Internet, the cellular phone, the fax machine, a fitness program, a pool, a lawn, and that most potent of competitors, sleep. The man or woman snoozing in a chair with a magazine or a book is a person who was being given too much unnecessary trouble by the writer.

9 It won't do to say that the reader is too dumb or too lazy to keep pace with the train of thought. If the reader is lost, it's usually because the writer hasn't been careful enough. The carelessness can take any number of forms. Perhaps a sentence is so excessively cluttered that the reader, hacking through the verbiage, simply doesn't know what it means. Perhaps a sentence has been so shoddily constructed that the reader could read it in several ways. Perhaps the writer has switched pronouns in midsentence, or has switched tenses, so the reader loses track of who is talking or when the action took place. Perhaps Sentence B is not a logical sequel to Sentence A; the writer, in whose head the connection is clear, hasn't bothered to provide the missing link. Perhaps the writer has used a word incorrectly by not taking the trouble to look it up. He or she may think "sanguine" and "sanguinary" mean the same thing, but the difference is a bloody big one. The reader can only infer (speaking of big differences) what the writer is trying to imply.

10 Faced with such obstacles, readers are at first tenacious. They blame themselves—they obviously missed something, and they go back over the mystifying sentence, or over the whole paragraph, piecing it out like an ancient rune, making guesses and moving on. But they won't do this for long. The writer is making them work too hard, and they will look for one who is better at the craft.

11 Writers must therefore constantly ask: What am I trying to say? Surprisingly often they don't know. Then they must look at

what they have written and ask: have I said it? Is it clear to someone encountering the subject for the first time? If it's not, some fuzz has worked its way into the machinery. The clear writer is someone clearheaded enough to see this stuff for what it is: fuzz.

I don't mean that some people are born clearheaded and are 12
therefore natural writers, whereas others are naturally fuzzy and will never write well. Thinking clearly is a conscious act that writers must force upon themselves, as if they were working on any other project that requires logic: making a shopping list or doing an algebra problem. Good writing doesn't come naturally, though most people seem to think it does. Professional writers are constantly bearded by strangers who say they'd like to "try a little writing sometime"—meaning when they retire from their real profession, like insurance or real estate, which is hard. Or they say, "I could write a book about that." I doubt it.

Writing is hard work. A clear sentence is no accident. Very 13
few sentences come out right the first time, or even the third time. Remember this in moments of despair. If you find that writing is hard, it's because it *is* hard.

Two pages of the final manuscript of this chapter from the First Edition of *On Writing Well.* Although they look like a first draft, they had already been rewritten and retyped—like almost every other page—four or five times. With each rewrite I try to make what I have written tighter, stronger and more precise, eliminating every element that is not doing useful work. Then I go over it once more, reading it aloud, and am always amazed at how much clutter can still be cut. (In later editions I eliminated the sexist pronoun "he" denoting "the writer" and "the reader.")

---

is too dumb or too lazy to keep pace with the ~~writer's~~ train of thought. My sympathies are ~~entirely~~ with him.) ~~He's not so dumb~~. (If the reader is lost, it is generally because the writer ~~of the article~~ has not been careful enough to keep him on the ~~proper~~ path.

(This carelessness can take any number of ~~different~~ forms. Perhaps a sentence is so excessively ~~long and~~ cluttered that the reader, hacking his way through ~~all~~ the verbiage, simply doesn't know what it ~~the writer~~ means. Perhaps a sentence has been so shoddily constructed that the reader could read it in any of several ~~two or three different~~ ways. ~~He thinks he knows what the writer is trying to say, but he's not sure.~~ Perhaps the writer has switched pronouns in mid-sentence, or ~~perhaps he~~ has switched tenses, so the reader loses track of who is talking ~~to whom,~~ or ~~exactly~~ when the action took place. Perhaps Sentence B is not a logical sequel to Sentence A — the writer, in whose head the connection is ~~perfectly~~ clear, has not bothered to provide ~~given enough thought to providing~~ the missing link. Perhaps the writer has used an important word incorrectly by not taking the trouble to look it up. ~~and make sure.~~ He may think that "sanguine" and "sanguinary" mean the same thing, but ~~I can assure you that~~ the difference is a bloody big one. ~~to the reader.~~ The reader ~~He~~ can only ~~try to~~ infer ~~what~~ (speaking of big differences) what the writer is trying to imply.

Faced with these ~~such a variety of~~ obstacles, the reader is at first a remarkably tenacious bird. He ~~tends to~~ blames himself. He obviously missed something, ~~he thinks,~~ and he goes back over the mystifying sentence, or over the whole paragraph, piecing it out like an ancient rune, making guesses and moving on. But he won't do this for long. ~~He will soon run out of patience.~~ The writer is making him work too hard, ~~— harder than he should have to work —~~ and the reader will look for one ~~a writer~~ who is better at his craft.

The writer must therefore constantly ask himself: What am I trying to say? ~~in this sentence?~~

Surprisingly often, he doesn't know.

~~And~~ Then he must look at what he has ~~just~~ written and ask: Have I said it? Is it clear to someone encountering ~~who is coming upon~~ the subject for the first time? If it's not, ~~clear,~~ it is because some fuzz has worked its way into the machinery. The clear writer is a person ~~who is~~ clear-headed enough to see this stuff for what it is: fuzz.

I don't mean ~~to suggest~~ that some people are born clear-headed and are therefore natural writers, whereas others ~~other people~~ are naturally fuzzy and will ~~therefore~~ never write well. Thinking clearly is a ~~an entirely~~ conscious act that the writer must force ~~keep forcing~~ upon himself, just as if he were embarking ~~starting out~~ on any other ~~kind of~~ project that requires ~~calls for~~ logic: adding up a laundry list or doing an algebra problem. ~~or playing chess.~~ Good writing doeesn't ~~just~~ come naturally, though most people obviously think it does. ~~it's as easy as walking.~~ The professional

BUILDING VOCABULARY

1. Zinsser uses a number of words and expressions drawn from areas other than writing; he uses them to make interesting combinations or comparisons in such expressions as *elusive creature* (par. 8) and *hacking through the verbiage* (par. 9). Find other such expressions in this essay. Write simple explanations for the two above and the others that you find.
2. List words or phrases in this essay that pertain to writing—the process, the results, the faults, the successes. Explain any with which you were unfamiliar.

THINKING CRITICALLY ABOUT THE ESSAY

Understanding the Writer's Ideas

1. State simply Zinsser's meaning in the opening paragraph. What faults of "bad writing" does he mention in this paragraph?
2. To what is Zinsser objecting in paragraph 2?
3. What, according to the author, is the "secret of good writing" (par. 3)? Explain this "secret" in a few simple words of your own. What does Zinsser say detracts from good writing? Why does Zinsser write that these writing faults "usually occur, in proportion to education and rank"?
4. What was the "message" in the letter from the university president to the alumni (par. 4)? Why does the writer object to it? Was it more objectionable in form or in content?

5. Who was Thoreau? What is *Walden?* Why are references to the two especially appropriate to Zinsser's essay?
6. What, according to Zinsser, is the relation between clear thinking and good writing? Can you have one without the other? What is meant by a "muddy thinker" (par. 7)? Why is it "impossible for a muddy thinker to write good English"?
7. Why does the author think most people fall asleep while reading? What is his attitude toward such people?
8. Look up and explain the "big differences" between the words *sanguine* and *sanguinary; infer* and *imply.* What is the writer's point in calling attention to these differences?
9. In paragraph 11, Zinsser calls attention to a writer's necessary awareness of the composing process. What elements of the *process* of writing does the author include in that paragraph? In that discussion, Zinsser speaks of *fuzz* in writing. What does he mean by the word as it relates to the writing process? To what does Zinsser compare the writer's thinking process? Why does he use such simple comparisons?
10. Explain the meaning of the last sentence. What does it indicate about the writer's attitude toward his work?

Understanding the Writer's Techniques

1. What is the writer's thesis? Is it stated or implied?
2. Explain the use of the words *disease* and *strangling* in paragraph 1. Why does Zinsser use these words in an essay about writing?
3. For what purpose does Zinsser use a series of questions in paragraph 2?
4. Throughout this essay, the writer makes extensive use of examples to support general opinions and attitudes. What attitude or opinion is he supporting in paragraphs 2, 4, 5, 6, and 9? How does he use examples in each of those paragraphs?
5. Analyze the specific structure and organization of paragraph 3:
   a. What general ideas about writing does he propose?
   b. Where does he place that idea in the paragraph?
   c. What examples does he offer to support his general idea?
   d. With what new idea does he conclude the paragraph? How is it related to the beginning idea?
6. Why does Zinsser reproduce exactly portions of the writings of a past president of a major university, President Franklin D.

Roosevelt, and Henry David Thoreau? How do these sections make Zinsser's writing clearer, more understandable, or more important?

7. What is the effect on the reader of the words "Simplify, simplify," which begin paragraph 6? Why does the writer use them at that particular point in the essay? What do they indicate about his attitude toward his subject? Explain.
8. Why does the author begin so many sentences in paragraph 9 with the word "Perhaps"? How does that technique help to *unify* (see Glossary) the paragraph?
9. For what reasons does the writer include the two pages of "rough" manuscript as a part of the finished essay? What is he trying to show the reader in this way? How does seeing these pages help you to understand better what he is writing about in the completed essay?
10. Overall, how would you describe the writer's attitude toward the process and craft of writing? What would you say is his overall attitude toward the future of American writing? Is he generally optimistic or pessimistic? On what does his attitude depend? Refer to specifics in the essay to support your answer.
11. Do you think Zinsser expected other writers, or budding writers, to be the main readers of this essay? Why or why not? If so, with what main ideas do you think he would like them to come away from the essay? Do you think readers who were not somehow involved in the writing process would benefit equally from this essay? Why?

Exploring the Writer's Ideas

1. Do you think that Zinsser is ever guilty in this essay of the very "sins" against writing about which he is upset? Could he have simplified any of his points? Select one of Zinsser's paragraphs in the finished essay and explain how you might rewrite it more simply.
2. In the reading that you do most often, have you noticed overly cluttered writing? Or, do you feel that the writing is at its clearest level of presentation and understanding for its audience? Bring to class some examples of this writing, and be prepared to discuss it. In general, what do you consider the relation between the simplicity or complexity of a piece of writing and its intended readership?

3. In the note to the two rough manuscript pages included with this essay, the writer implies that the process of rewriting and simplifying may be endless. How do you know when to stop trying to rewrite an essay, story, or poem? Do you ever really feel satisfied that you've reached the end of the rewriting process?
4. Choose one of the rough manuscript paragraphs, and compare it with the finished essay. Which do you feel is better? Why? Is there anything Zinsser deleted from the rough copy that you feel he should have retained? Why?
5. Comment on the writer's assertion that "Thinking clearly is a conscious act that writers must force upon themselves" (par. 12). How does this opinion compare with the opinions of the three other writers in this chapter?
6. Reread Kurt Vonnegut, Jr.'s essay "How to Write with Style" (pages 20–23). What similarities and differences do you note in Zinsser's and Vonnegut's approaches to writing and language?

IDEAS FOR WRITING

Prewriting

For the most part, teachers have called upon you to put your thoughts in writing from your elementary school days onward. Make a list of your writing "problems"—the elements of writing or the elements of your personality that create problems for you whenever you try to produce something on paper.

Guided Writing

In a 500- to 750-word essay, write about what you feel are some of the problems that you face as a writer.

1. In the first paragraph, identify the problems that you plan to discuss.
2. In the course of your essay, relate your problems more generally to society at large.
3. Identify what, in your opinion, is the "secret" of good writing. Give specific examples of what measures to take to achieve that secret process and thereby to eliminate some of your problems.

4. Try to include one or two accurate reproductions of your writing to illustrate your composing techniques.
5. Point out what you believe were the major causes of your difficulties as a writer.
6. Toward the end of your essay, explain the type of writer that you would like to be in order to succeed in college.

Thinking and Writing Collaboratively

Form groups of two and exchange drafts of your Guided Writing essay. Do for your partner's draft what Zinsser did for his own: edit it in an effort to make it "stronger and more precise, eliminating every element that is not doing useful work." Return the papers and discuss whether or not your partner made useful recommendations for cutting clutter.

Writing About the Text

Teachers of writing tend to stress two, apparently contradictory, philosophies about writing. The first is that clear thinking makes for clear writing. This point of view assumes that thinking precedes writing, that you need to get your thoughts in order before you can write. The second is that you don't really know what you think until you write it down. This point of view assumes that writing is a process of discovery and that thinking and writing occur more or less simultaneously. Write an essay to explain which position you think Zinsser would take. What evidence does he present to support this position? Then explain your position on the matter. Draw on your own experience as a writer.

More Writing Projects

1. Over the next few days, listen to the same news reporter or talk-show host on television or radio. Record in your journal at least ten examples that indicate the use of "unnecessary words, circular constructions, pompous frills, and meaningless jargon." Or compile such a list from an article in a newspaper or magazine you read regularly. Then write an essay presenting and commenting on these examples.
2. Respond in a paragraph to Zinsser's observation, "Good writing doesn't come naturally."

3. In preparation for a writing assignment, collect with other class members various samples of junk mail and business correspondence that confirm Zinsser's statement that these tend to be poorly written. Write an essay describing your findings. Be certain to provide specific examples from the documents you have assembled.

SUMMING UP: CHAPTER 1

1. It sounds simple enough. Many writers, famous and unknown, have tried it at one time or another. Now, it's your turn. Write an essay simply titled "On Writing." Develop the essay in any way you please: you may deal with abstract or concrete ideas, philosophical or practical issues, emotional or intellectual processes, and so forth. Just use this essay to focus your own thoughts and to give your reader a clear idea of what writing means to you.
2. William Zinsser ("Simplicity") tells writers to simplify their writing. Select any writer from this section, and write an essay about whether you think the writer achieved (or did not achieve) simplicity. How did the writer achieve it? Where in the selection would you have preferred even more simplicity? Make specific references to the text.
3. Think about the message implicit in Amy Tan's essay on using her mother as an ideal audience. Find your own ideal listener. Then write a letter to that person in which you discuss your reactions to becoming a writer. Include observations you think your listener or reader will enjoy, such as your everyday life as a student, daydreams, descriptions of teachers, or cafeteria food, or of interesting people you have met.
4. Write a letter from Kurt Vonnegut, Jr., to Amy Tan on how style affects good writing. Draw on what you understand of Vonnegut's philosophy of writing from his essay "How to Write with Style," and what Amy Tan says in "Mother Tongue."
5. The writers in this chapter all give some sense of *why* they write. For the most part, their reasons are very personal. For example, Kurt Vonnegut, Jr., writes about trusting his writing when he sounds "most like a person from Indianapolis." However, many writers (including many represented in this book) feel that writing entails a certain social responsibility. For example, when Albert Camus received the 1957 Nobel Prize for Literature, he was cited for "illuminating the problems of the human conscience of our time." And, in his acceptance speech, he stated, "[T]he writer's function is not without arduous duties. By definition, he cannot serve today those who make history; he must serve those who are subject to it."

What do you feel are writers' responsibilities to themselves and to others? Do you agree with Camus? Do you prefer writing that deals primarily with an individual's experience or with more general social issues?

Write an essay concerning the social responsibilities of writers. As you consider the issue, refer to points made by writers in this section.

6. Kurt Vonnegut says that good writing comes from the heart; William Zinsser says that good writing comes from the head. Write an essay based on your experience that explores the *usefulness* of these apparently contradictory pieces of advice for the college writer.
7. In a variety of ways, the writers in this chapter stress the importance of finding your own voice as central to writing, including as a motive for writing. Explore the idea of writing as a way to be yourself (think of the meaning of writing to Russell Baker, or to Amy Tan, for example). How can you write in your own voice and yet meet the expectations of different audiences—teachers, employers, peers? What do you learn about writing in your own voice from the selections in this chapter?
8. The writers in this chapter urge clarity and simplicity of style. Simplicity can be deceiving, however: usually an artist (whether a writer or, for example, a dancer) achieves simplicity through enormous labor and through the exercise of great skill. Is simplicity, then, too ambitious a goal for the college writer? In a related vein, are clarity and simplicity necessarily interdependent? Can what you write be simple and muddy, or clear but complex? Explain.

FROM SEEING TO WRITING

Examine the cartoon and consider what it says about writing. What does Calvin say about creativity? What role does creativity play in writing? Why does Calvin say that he has to wait for his mood to be "last-minute panic" before he can write? What role does last-minute panic play in your writing? What are the advantages of last-minute panic? The disadvantages? What advice would you offer Calvin to help prevent this mood? Write an essay in which you analyze the cartoon by addressing some of these questions.

CHAPTER 2

On Reading

WHAT IS READING?

"Reading had changed forever the course of my life," writes Malcolm X in one of the essays in this chapter. For many of us, the acquisition of reading skills may not have been quite as dramatic as it was for the author of "Prison Studies," but if we are to understand the value of literacy in today's society, Malcolm X's analysis of the power of the written word is vital. Reading allows us actively to engage the minds of many writers who have much to tell us and to hear a variety of viewpoints not always available on the cable, video, and other forms of media that vie for our attention. Even the ever-present computer and its brainchild, the World Wide Web, demand active reading for maximum benefit. Learning to read well opens new universes, challenges your opinions, enhances your understanding of yourself and others and of your past, present, and future. Knowledge of books is the mark of a literate person.

But how do we learn this complex skill? Ellen Tashie Frisina's essay on teaching her grandmother to read may remind you of your own early experiences with printed words. Or, if you are a parent, you may be reading stories to your own children to help them learn to read. As we become mature readers, we read not just as we once did, for the story and its magical pleasures, but also for information and for pleasure in the *style* of writing. We learn not to be passive readers but active ones.

That early love of stories, and the self-esteem that came with mastery of a once impossible task, is, however, only the first step in understanding the power of reading. Malcolm X's "Prison Studies" extends our understanding of what reading is beyond the personal into the cultural sphere. He explores not only the power of reading to excite and inspire, but also the ways in which language connects to social identity. Malcolm X uses reading, and later writing, to challenge existing assumptions and find a place as an alert and engaged member of society. He argues that his reading outside of school made him better educated than most formally educated citizens in America.

Reading gives us access to many printed stories and documents, old and new. It lets us see beyond the highly edited sound bites and trendy video images that tempt us. With print, we can read what we want when we want to read it. We can reread difficult passages to be sure we understand them. We have time to question the author's point—and we have time to absorb and analyze ideas not only from contemporary life but also from ancient cultures and distant places. The diverse materials in libraries allow us to select what we read rather than be channeled into one point of view. On the Web we can access stories, poems, essays, even books, and can create a home library for use on a computer monitor.

Reading lets us share ideas. Reading can teach us practical skills that we need for survival in our complex world, such as how to repair a computer or how to become a biology teacher or a certified public accountant. Good reading can inspire us, educate us, or entertain us. It can enrich our fantasy lives. Reading critically also helps us analyze how society operates, how power is distributed, how we can improve our local community or the global environment. As Eudora Welty writes, reading can lead to a lifelong love affair with books and stories. The beauty of the written word and the stirrings of imagination and vision that the printed page can produce are all part of what reading is.

HOW DO WE READ?

To become a good reader, we need to think about what we read just as we think about what and how we write. In other words, we need to read *self-consciously* and *critically.* Reading, like writing, is a *process.* If we break this process down, we can say that reading involves three large steps or stages. To begin with, we want to grasp the writer's main point and the general outline of what she says. Then second, we reflect on what's being said: we probe, analyze, look more deeply, think things through. Finally, we make a judgment—"Wow!" or "Yes, I agree," or "What a lot of rubbish!"

We can focus these three stages of the reading process and enhance our understanding by pursuing certain strategies as we read. It's useful, for example, after reading a chapter to go back through it and then to *summarize* the main idea. A summary is a drastically condensed version of a piece of writing that aims to state the writer's main points by retaining only essential arguments, facts, and statements. A summary is usually brief, a sentence or two. Composing a summary, then, is one good way to help us get a clearer picture of the writer's main idea.

No essay contains just one idea, of course. In addition to the main idea, the writer usually includes a variety of supporting points in her essay. And most writers will support big ideas with facts, arguments, observations, quotations—the writer, in other words, tries to *substantiate* her major points in order to persuade you to see things her way.

Throughout the reading process, we can make sure that we are reading critically by asking ourselves a series of questions about the material in order to arrive at a fair assessment of its significance. The word *critically* here does not mean negatively, in the sense of criticizing what we read for what it's doing wrong. Rather, *critically* is intended to suggest a curious but questioning attitude, an alertness to what is being said and how it is being said, and a certain self-awareness about our responses to what is being said and how it is being said. Here are some questions we might ask ourselves as we start to read:

- What is it that we're reading? (In other words, what *genre,* or type of writing, does it belong to?)

We should first examine what we are about to read to determine what it is: Is it a romance? a history book? a religious tract? Why was it written? How do the answers to these questions shape our attitude toward the material? As readers of novels, for instance, we soon learn that a book with a cover featuring a heroine snatched from a fiery castle belongs to a particular genre of literature: the gothic romance. As potential readers, we might prepare ourselves to be skeptical about the happy ending we know awaits us, but at the same time we are prepared for a romantic tale. In contrast, if we face a hard-covered glossy textbook entitled *Economics,* we prepare ourselves to read with far more concentration. We might enjoy the gothic romance, but if we skip whole chapters it may not matter much. If, however, we skip chapters of the textbook, we may find ourselves confused. The first book *entertains* us, while the second *informs* us. In other words, our initial clue to what we might find as we read further is provided by the *kind* of book, essay, or article that we are reading. Our expectations of a romance novel are different from our expectations of a textbook.

- Who is the writer? For whom is he or she writing? When did he or she write it?

Clues to a writer's identity can often help us establish whether the material we are reading is reliable. Would we read a slave owner's account of life in slave quarters the same way we would read a slave's diary, for instance? If a Sioux writes about the effects of a treaty on Native-American family life, we might read the essay one way; if the writer were General Custer we surely would read it another way. The *audience* is also important. If we are reading a handbook on immigration policies in the United States, we might read it differently if we knew it was written for officials at Ellis Island in 1890 from the way we would read it if it were written for Chinese men arriving to work on the railroads in the nineteenth century.

Sometimes we may not know more about a writer than when he wrote. This knowledge can itself be crucial. An essay written in the sixteenth century will be different in important ways from an essay written yesterday. Not only will the sixteenth-century author use a vocabulary that is likely to diverge from ours, but he also will make allusions to people, places, and books that may be unfamiliar to us. Moreover, he will certainly have ideas and beliefs that reflect this unfamiliar world. Today, for example, we wonder only how much interest a bank will charge us on our loan; in the sixteenth century people looked on charging interest as a doubtful if not an outright wicked practice. One of the challenges in reading work from the past, then, is to read it on its own terms, remembering that what we think and what we know are different from—rather than necessarily better than—what people thought and knew in the past. The date of writing also matters with writing published closer to our own day. A writer assessing Bill Clinton before he was impeached, for example, may well have written something significantly different had she put pen to paper after Clinton was impeached. In these ways the date of writing provides important information about what to expect.

- What is the precise issue or problem that the writer treats?

During the first and second stages of the reading process, we seek to identify the writer's *exact* topic. A writer's general topic might be the Battle of Gettysburg, for instance, but if she is writing about the women at Gettysburg, then her precise topic is narrower. What is she saying, we next ask, about these women?

- What information, conclusions, and recommendations does the writer present?

The reader may find that note taking is helpful in improving understanding of a text. Creating an outline of materials after reading can help identify the writer's aims. Both note-taking and outlining will help us when we want to make a summary or when we want to pinpoint the subtopics and supporting evidence of an essay.

- How does the writer substantiate, or "prove," his or her case?

The reader must learn the difference between a writer who merely *asserts* an idea and one who effectively *substantiates* an idea. The writer who only asserts that the Holocaust never happened will be read differently from the writer who substantiates his or her claims that the Holocaust did exist with photographs of Germany in the 1940s, interviews with concentration camp survivors, military records of medical experiments, and eyewitness accounts of gas chambers.

As in the example of the Holocaust, most essays aim to persuade you to see things in a certain way. Most essays, in other words, make what is formally known as an *argument.* An *argument* is not a quarrel but rather a more-or-less formal way of making a point. Often a writer begins an essay by introducing the topic or problem in the opening paragraph or paragraphs—*the introduction*—and then offers a *thesis statement.* The *thesis statement* presents the writer's position; that is, it tells what the writer has to say about the topic or problem. It usually comes early in an essay, at the close of the introduction, frequently at the close of the first paragraph.

After stating his *thesis,* the writer will try to *prove* or *substantiate* it through use of supporting *details* and *facts,* or *reasons.* In the case of the Holocaust, a writer may use a photograph or an eye-witness account to support the position that the Holocaust did in fact occur. It is not enough, though, to see that support has been provided. We also need to assess whether this support is accurate, credible, and relevant.

Usually a writer combines generalities and specifics, facts and reasons. The writer uses reasoning. You'll find a more detailed look at reasoning in Chapter 11, Argumentation and Persuasion. Here it will be enough to say that we want to be sure that the reasoning the writer uses is sound. If the writer says that event A caused event B, we want to be sure that A and B really are related as cause and effect—that they're not two separate events. In a more general way, we want to be comfortable that a writer's conclusions are valid. Does the essay really add up to the conclusions claimed?

- Is the total message successful, objective, valid, or persuasive?

Once you have answered all of the above questions, you are ready to *assess* the work you have read. As you make your evaluation, find specific evidence in the text to back up your position.

Assessment or *evaluation* is not an exact science—assessments and evaluations are ultimately opinions. But this does not mean that we can make them recklessly—"Don't bother me with the facts!" An opinion should not be prejudice in another form. Rather, an opinion should itself be a kind of *argument,* based on fact or reason. Sometimes our deeply held beliefs are refuted by new evidence or by reasons we have not before encountered. In such cases we as educated thinkers cannot say, "Well, that may be so, but I still stick to my opinion." If the facts or reasons contradict our opinions, we have no choice but to reexamine our beliefs. That's what education is all about.

By reading critically—by reading to understand, analyze, and evaluate—you respond to an author's ideas, opinions, and arguments in an informed way. In a sense you enter into a conversation with the author. You agree or disagree with the author, "talk back," and try to understand the author's perspective on the subject. To become a critical reader, you may wish to employ a strategy, called annotation, in which you literally mark up the essay.

Here are the basic elements of this method:

- Underline important ideas in an essay. You can also, for example, use an asterisk, star, or vertical lines in the margins next to the most important information or statements.
- Pose questions in the margins. Place question marks next to the points that you find confusing.
- Take notes in the margins.
- Use numbers in the margins to highlight the sequence of major ideas that the author presents.
- Circle key words and phrases.

Examine the annotations made by one student as she read an essay by Leonid Fridman titled "America Needs Its Nerds."

America Needs Its Nerds

Leonid Fridman

Nice title! Is he serious or being funny?

1 * There is something very wrong with the system of values in a society that has only derogatory terms like nerd and geek for the intellectually curious and academically serious.

Intro / Thesis?

2 A geek, according to "Webster's New World Dictionary," is a street performer who shocks the public by biting off heads of live chickens. It is a telling fact about our language and our culture that someone dedicated to pursuit of knowledge is compared to a freak biting the head off a live chicken.

Key definition

3 Even at a prestigious academic institution like Harvard, anti-intellectualism is rampant: Many ?? students are ashamed to admit, even to their friends, how much they study. Although most students try to keep up their grades, there is but a minority of undergraduates for whom pursuing knowledge is the top priority during their years at Harvard. Nerds are ostracized while athletes are idolized.

Is this true? Where is the evidence?

Meaning?

He mentions athletes several times. Must they be separated from intellectuals?

4 The same thing happens in U.S. elementary and high schools. Children who prefer to read books rather than play football, prefer to build model airplanes rather than get wasted at parties with their classmates, become social outcasts. Ostracized for their intelligence and refusal to conform to society's

Note comparison and contrast throughout essay

anti-intellectual values, many are deprived of a chance to learn adequate social skills and acquire good communication tools.

**Call to action? Why this fragment?*

5 * Enough is enough.

6 Nerds and geeks must stop being ashamed of who they are. It is high time to face the persecutors who haunt the bright kid with thick glasses from kindergarten to the grave. For America's sake, the anti-intellectual values that pervade our society must be fought.

Geeks must rebel!

U.S. vs. rest of world

7 There are very few countries in the world where anti-intellectualism runs as high in popular culture as it does in the U.S. In most industrialized nations, not least of all our economic rivals in East Asia, a kid who studies hard is lauded and held up as an example to other students.

8 In many parts of the world, university professorships are the most prestigious and materially rewarding positions. But not in America, where average professional ballplayers are much more respected and better paid than faculty members of the best universities.

9 How can a country where typical parents are ashamed of their daughter studying mathematics instead of going dancing, or of their son reading Weber while his friends play baseball, be expected to compete in the technology race with Japan or remain a leading political and cultural force in Europe? How long can America remain a world-class power if we constantly emphasize social skills and physical prowess over academic achievement and intellectual ability?

Look up

Anti-intellectualism has negative impact on America's political and economic future. Does he prove his point?

Note series of questions. Are answers self-evident?

10 Do we really expect to stay afloat largely by importing our scientists and intellectuals from abroad, as we have done for a major portion of this century, without making an effort to also cultivate a pro-intellectual culture at home? Even if we have the political will to spend substantially more money on education than we do now, do we think we can improve our schools if we deride our studious pupils and debase their impoverished teachers?

11 Our fault lies not so much with our economy or with our politics as within ourselves, our values and our image of a good life. America's culture has not adapted to the demands of our times, to the economic realities that demand a highly educated workforce and innovative intelligent leadership.

12 If we are to succeed as a society in the 21st century, we had better shed our anti-intellectualism and imbue in our children the vision that a good life is impossible without stretching one's mind and pursuing knowledge to the full extent of one's abilities.

Essay comes full circle—reread intro

13 And until the words "nerd" and "geek" become terms of approbation and not derision, we do not stand a chance.

*Idea for essay: "My Favorite Nerd"

The process that this student follows reflects the sort of active, critical reading expected of you in college courses. Through annotation, you actually bring the acts of reading and writing together in a mutually advantageous way. Reading critically and responding to texts through annotation prepares you for more sustained writing assignments presented in this anthology.

These steps will help you engage in an active conversation, or dialogue, with the writer, sharing ideas and debating issues. At the same time, becoming a better reader will help you become a better writer. Eudora Welty and Malcolm X became readers as part of their apprenticeship to becoming world-renowned writers. For Ellen Tashie Frisina, reading remains, as it does for most of us, a personal achievement. For Welty, words came to her "as though fed . . . out of a silver spoon." Malcolm X tells us how reading was so powerful for him that it allowed him to break down prison walls. Judith Ortiz Cofer, a well-known writer, tells how reading comic books as a child liberated her imagination. Frisina reminds us that literacy is not a birthright, but a skill that can be painstakingly learned, and taught, at any age.

One Writer's Beginnings

Eudora Welty

Eudora Welty, one of America's most revered twentieth-century writers, was born in 1909 on North Congress Street in Jackson, Mississippi, in the house that she would live in almost all her long life. Although she attended the University of Wisconsin at Madison, studied business for a year at Columbia University, and traveled widely, Welty always returned to the family home in Jackson. She never married. Her brief autobiography, *One Writer's Beginnings* (1980), from which this selection is drawn, ends with these words: "I am a writer who came of a sheltered life. A sheltered life can be a daring life as well. For all serious daring starts from within." The sheltered life to which Welty alludes is the life of a white woman in the Deep South in the first decades of the twentieth century. The ways of life in rural Mississippi are the subject of most of her acclaimed writing. Her novel *The Optimist's Daughter* won the 1972 Pulitzer Prize, and her total work has been collected in two volumes for the authoritative Library of America series. But as this selection shows, her sheltered life was not limited or narrow. Rather, it was rich in sensations and emotions, and through reading she reached out to the ends of the earth and the depths of the heart. Eudora Welty died in 2001.

PREREADING: THINKING ABOUT THE ESSAY IN ADVANCE

What attitudes did your family have toward reading when you were a child? Did books surround you? Which books did your parents or other relatives read to you or suggest that you read? How did you feel about books as a child growing up?

Words to Watch

disposed (par. 4) inclined; receptive
vignettes (par. 5) charming literary sketches
roué (par. 7) lecherous, wasted man
interlocutor (par. 9) partner in a dialogue
quoth (par. 9) archaic form of word *quoted*
wizardry (par. 15) magic
sensory (par. 18) pertaining to the senses

reel (par. 19) fast dance

constellations (par. 20) positions of star groups in sky, considered to look like (and named for) mythological characters

1 I learned from the age of two or three that any room in our house, at any time of day, was there to read in, or to be read to. My mother read to me. She'd read to me in the big bedroom in the mornings, when we were in her rocker together, which ticked in rhythm as we rocked, as though we had a cricket accompanying the story. She'd read to me in the diningroom on winter afternoons in front of the coal fire, with our cuckoo clock ending the story with "Cuckoo," and at night when I'd got in my own bed. I must have given her no peace. Sometimes she read to me in the kitchen while she sat churning, and the churning sobbed along with *any* story. It was my ambition to have her read to me while *I* churned; once she granted my wish, but she read off my story before I brought her butter. She was an expressive reader. When she was reading "Puss in Boots," for instance, it was impossible not to know that she distrusted *all* cats.

2 It had been startling and disappointing to me to find out that story books had been written by *people,* that books were not natural wonders, coming up of themselves like grass. Yet regardless of where they came from, I cannot remember a time when I was not in love with them—with the books themselves, cover and binding and the paper they were printed on, with their smell and their weight and with their possession in my arms, captured and carried off to myself. Still illiterate, I was ready for them, committed to all the reading I could give them.

3 Neither of my parents had come from homes that could afford to buy many books, but though it must have been something of a strain on his salary, as the youngest officer in a young insurance company, my father was all the while carefully selecting and ordering away for what he and Mother thought we children should grow up with. They bought first for the future.

4 Besides the bookcase in the livingroom, which was always called "the library," there were the encyclopedia tables and dictionary stand under windows in our diningroom. Here to help us grow up arguing around the diningroom table were the Unabridged Webster, the Columbia Encyclopedia, Compton's Pictured Encyclopedia, the Lincoln Library of Information, and later the Book of Knowledge. And the year we moved into our new

house, there was room to celebrate it with the new 1925 edition of the Britannica, which my father, his face always deliberately turned toward the future, was of course disposed to think better than any previous edition.

In "the library," inside the mission-style bookcase with its three diamond-latticed glass doors, with my father's Morris chair and the glass-shaded lamp on its table beside it, were books I could soon begin on—and I did, reading them all alike and as they came, straight down their rows, top shelf to bottom. There was the set of Stoddard's Lectures, in all its late nineteenth-century vocabulary and vignettes of peasant life and quaint beliefs and customs, with matching halftone illustrations: Vesuvius erupting, Venice by moonlight, gypsies glimpsed by their campfires. I didn't know then the clue they were to my father's longing to see the rest of the world. I read straight through his other love-from-afar: the Victrola Book of the Opera, with opera after opera in synopsis, with portraits in costume of Melba, Caruso, Galli-Curci, and Geraldine Farrar, some of whose voices we could listen to on our Red Seal records. 5

My mother read secondarily for information; she sank as a hedonist into novels. She read Dickens in the spirit in which she would have eloped with him. The novels of her girlhood that had stayed on in her imagination, besides those of Dickens and Scott and Robert Louis Stevenson, were *Jane Eyre, Trilby, The Woman in White, Green Mansions, King Solomon's Mines.* Marie Corelli's name would crop up but I understood she had gone out of favor with my mother, who had only kept *Ardath* out of loyalty. In time she absorbed herself in Galsworthy, Edith Wharton, above all in Thomas Mann of the *Joseph* volumes. 6

St. Elmo was not in our house; I saw it often in other houses. This wildly popular Southern novel is where all the Edna Earles in our population started coming from. They're all named for the heroine, who succeeded in bringing a dissolute, sinning roué and atheist of a lover (St. Elmo) to his knees. My mother was able to forgo it. But she remembered the classic advice given to rose growers on how to water their bushes long enough: "Take a chair and *St. Elmo.*" 7

To both my parents I owe my early acquaintance with a beloved Mark Twain. There was a full set of Mark Twain and a short set of Ring Lardner in our bookcase, and those were the volumes that in time united us all, parents and children. 8

9 Reading everything that stood before me was how I came upon a worn old book without a back that had belonged to my father as a child. It was called *Sanford and Merton.* Is there anyone left who recognizes it, I wonder? It is the famous moral tale written by Thomas Day in the 1780s, but of him no mention is made on the title page of *this* book; here it is *Sanford and Merton in Words of One Syllable* by Mary Godolphin. Here are the rich boy and the poor boy and Mr. Barlow, their teacher and interlocutor, in long discourses alternating with dramatic scenes—anger and rescue allotted to the rich and the poor respectively. It may have only words of one syllable, but one of them is "quoth." It ends with not one but two morals, both engraved on rings: "Do what you ought, come what may," and "If we would be great, we must first learn to be good."

10 This book was lacking its front cover, the back held on by strips of pasted paper, now turned golden, in several layers, and the pages stained, flecked, and tattered around the edges; its garish illustrations had come unattached but were preserved, laid in. I had the feeling even in my heedless childhood that this was the only book my father as a little boy had had of his own. He had held onto it, and might have gone to sleep on its coverless face: he had lost his mother when he was seven. My father had never made any mention to his own children of the book, but he had brought it along with him from Ohio to our house and shelved it in our bookcase.

11 My mother had brought from West Virginia that set of Dickens; those books looked sad, too—they had been through fire and water before I was born, she told me, and there they were, lined up—as I later realized, waiting for *me.*

12 I was presented, from as early as I can remember, with books of my own, which appeared on my birthday and Christmas morning. Indeed, my parents could not give me books enough. They must have sacrificed to give me on my sixth or seventh birthday—it was after I became a reader for myself—the ten-volume set of Our Wonder World. These were beautifully made, heavy books I would lie down with on the floor in front of the diningroom hearth, and more often than the rest volume 5, *Every Child's Story Book,* was under my eyes. There were the fairy tales—Grimm, Andersen, the English, the French, "Ali Baba and the Forty Thieves"; and there was Aesop and Reynard the Fox; there were the myths and legends, Robin Hood, King Arthur, and St. George and the Dragon, even the history of Joan of Arc; a whack of *Pilgrim's*

Progress and a long piece of *Gulliver.* They all carried their classic illustrations. I located myself in these pages and could go straight to the stories and pictures I loved; very often "The Yellow Dwarf" was first choice, with Walter Crane's Yellow Dwarf in full color making his terrifying appearance flanked by turkeys. Now that volume is as worn and backless and hanging apart as my father's poor *Sanford and Merton.* The precious page with Edward Lear's "Jumblies" on it has been in danger of slipping out for all these years. One measure of my love for Our Wonder World was that for a long time I wondered if I would go through fire and water for it as my mother had done for Charles Dickens; and the only comfort was to think I could ask my mother to do it for me.

I believe I'm the only child I know of who grew up with this treasure in the house. I used to ask others, "Did you have Our Wonder World?" I'd have to tell them The Book of Knowledge could not hold a candle to it. 13

I live in gratitude to my parents for initiating me—as early as I begged for it, without keeping me waiting—into knowledge of the word, into reading and spelling, by way of the alphabet. They taught it to me at home in time for me to begin to read before starting to school. I believe the alphabet is no longer considered an essential piece of equipment for traveling through life. In my day it was the keystone to knowledge. You learned the alphabet as you learned to count to ten, as you learned "Now I lay me" and the Lord's Prayer and your father's and mother's name and address and telephone number, all in case you were lost. 14

My love for the alphabet, which endures, grew out of reciting it but, before that, out of seeing the letters on the page. In my own story books, before I could read them for myself, I fell in love with various winding, enchanted-looking initials drawn by Walter Crane at the heads of fairy tales. In "Once upon a time," an "O" had a rabbit running it as a treadmill, his feet upon flowers. When the day came, years later, for me to see the Book of Kells, all the wizardry of letter, initial, and word swept over me a thousand times over, and the illumination, the gold, seemed a part of the word's beauty and holiness that had been there from the start. 15

Learning stamps you with its moments. Childhood's learning is made up of moments. It isn't steady. It's a pulse. 16

In a children's art class, we sat in a ring on kindergarten chairs and drew three daffodils that had just been picked out of the yard; and while I was drawing, my sharpened yellow pencil and the cup 17 of the yellow daffodil gave off whiffs just alike. That the pencil doing the drawing should give off the same smell as the flower it drew seemed part of the art lesson—as shouldn't it be? Children, like animals, use all their senses to discover the world. Then artists come along and discover it the same way, all over again. Here and there, it's the same world. Or now and then we'll hear from an artist who's never lost it.

18 In my sensory education I include my physical awareness of the *word.* Of a certain word, that is; the connection it has with what it stands for. At around age six, perhaps, I was standing by myself in our front yard waiting for supper, just at that hour in a late summer day when the sun is already below the horizon and the risen full moon in the visible sky stops being chalky and begins to take on light. There comes the moment, and I saw it then, when the moon goes from flat to round. For the first time it met my eyes as a globe. The word "moon" came into my mouth as though fed to me out of a silver spoon. Held in my mouth the moon became a word. It had the roundness of a Concord grape Grandpa took off his vine and gave me to suck out of its skin and swallow whole, in Ohio.

19 This love did not prevent me from living for years in foolish error about the moon. The new moon just appearing in the west was the rising moon to me. The new should be rising. And in early childhood the sun and moon, those opposite reigning powers, I just as easily assumed rose in east and west respectively in their opposite sides of the sky, and like partners in a reel they advanced, sun from the east, moon from the west, crossed over (when I wasn't looking) and went down on the other side. My father couldn't have known I believed that when, bending behind me and guiding my shoulder, he positioned me at our telescope in the front yard and, with careful adjustment of the focus, brought the moon close to me.

20 The night sky over my childhood Jackson was velvety black. I could see the full constellations in it and call their names; when I could read, I knew their myths. Though I was always waked for eclipses, and indeed carried to the window as an infant in arms and shown Halley's Comet in my sleep, and though I'd been taught at our diningroom table about the solar system and knew the earth revolved around the sun, and our moon around us, I never found out the moon didn't come up in the west until I was a writer and Herschel Brickell, the literary critic, told me after I misplaced it in a story. He said valuable words to me about my new profession: "Always be sure you get your moon in the right part of the sky."

BUILDING VOCABULARY

1. Identify the following references to authors, books, and stories from Welty's essay:
   - **a.** Charles Dickens
   - **b.** Robert Louis Stevenson
   - **c.** *Jane Eyre*
   - **d.** *The Woman in White*
   - **e.** Edith Wharton
   - **f.** Thomas Mann
   - **g.** Mark Twain
   - **h.** Ring Lardner
   - **i.** *Pilgrim's Progress*
   - **j.** *Gulliver*
2. Write definitions and your own sentences for the following words:
   - **a.** quaint (par. 5)
   - **b.** hedonist (par. 6)
   - **c.** dissolute (par. 7)
   - **d.** allotted (par. 9)
   - **e.** garish (par. 10)
   - **f.** heedless (par. 10)
   - **g.** gratitude (par. 14)
   - **h.** essential (par. 14)
   - **i.** keystone (par. 14)
   - **j.** reigning (par. 19)

THINKING CRITICALLY ABOUT THE ESSAY

Understanding the Writer's Ideas

1. Why does the writer say of her mother, "I must have given her no peace" (par. 1)?
2. Why was it "startling and disappointing" for Welty to find out that storybooks were written by *people?* Where did she think they came from? Aside from the stories themselves, what is it that the author loves so much about books?
3. How did the way Welty's mother felt toward books affect her child's attitude toward reading? In what ways did the conditions in Welty's home contribute to her attitude toward books?
4. What is it, exactly, that Welty loved about books as a child?

5. Why did Welty's parents make sacrifices to buy books for the household? What were their hopes for their children? What kinds of books did the parents choose to buy and to read? What, if anything, do these choices tell us about the parents' characters?
6. For what reasons does the writer feel that learning the alphabet is so important? To what other learning processes does she compare it? Before she learned to recite her alphabet, why was it so important to her?
7. Explain in your own words what the writer considers to be the relation between physical sensations and learning words. According to the author why is it important for parents to read to their children?
8. What does Welty mean when she says a child's learning "Isn't steady. It's a pulse"?
9. Explain the significance of Welty's description of her experience of the moon at age 6.
10. What, if anything, do we learn from Herschel Brickell's advice?

Understanding the Writer's Techniques

1. What is the main idea of Welty's essay? Is there any point at which she directly states that main idea? Explain.
2. A *reminiscence* is a narrative account of a special memory. How does the writer use reminiscence in this essay?
3. The *tone* (see Glossary) of an essay is the expression of the writer's attitude toward the topic. State the tone of this essay. What specifically about the writing contributes to that tone?
4. Placing words in italics emphasizes them. Where does the author use italics in this essay? Why does she use them?
5. What does the writer mean by stating that the set of Dickens books "had been *through fire and water* before I was born" (par. 11)? How does the image contribute to the point she's making?
6. In paragraph 1, Welty employs a technique called *personification* (see Glossary) in stating that "the churning sobbed along with any story." Consider the effect of this technique, along with her description of her mother's reading style ("it was impossible not to know that she distrusted all cats") in the same paragraph. What does Welty seem to suggest about the connection between emotion (or expressiveness) and reading?

7. Why does Welty make a point of vividly describing books' physical characteristics, as in paragraphs 2, 10, and 15? What do her descriptions contribute to our understanding of her relationship to reading?
8. *Similes* (see Glossary) are imaginative comparisons using the word *like* or *as.* Use of similes often enlivens the writing and makes it memorable.

   In your own words, explain what is being compared in the following similes (in italics) drawn from Welty's essay, and tell how they contribute to the essay:
   a. . . . we were in her rocker together, which ticked in rhythm as we rocked, *as though we had a cricket accompanying the story.* (par. 1)
   b. . . . books were not natural wonders, coming up of themselves like grass. (par. 2)
   c. The word "moon" came into my mouth *as though fed to me out of a silver spoon.* (par. 18)
9. Welty makes a number of references to other writers, artists, and books, in addition to those listed in the "Building Vocabulary" section: for example, Nellie Melba, Enrico Caruso, Amelita Galli-Curci, and Geraldine Farrar; Sir Walter Scott, *Green Mansions,* and John Galsworthy; Walter Crane and Edward Lear—there are many others too.
   a. See if you can find some information on each of these references. When did the writers and artists live? When were the books written?
   b. Why do you think Welty makes these references? Do you think she expects her readers to recognize them? (Keep in mind that *One Writer's Beginnings* was first published in book form in 1984.) Do the references in any way contribute to your understanding of her piece, even if they were unfamiliar to you?

MIXING PATTERNS

Description helps the reader to "see" objects and scenes and to feel their importance through the author's eyes. *Narration*—the telling of a story—helps the reader follow a sequence of events. (See Chapters 3 and 4.) Both techniques rely on the writer's skill in choosing and presenting details. In what way does Welty make use of description and narration in this essay? How would you evaluate her use of details?

Exploring the Writer's Ideas

1. The writer believes that it is very important for parents to read to their children. Some specialists in child development even advocate reading to infants still in the womb and to babies before they've spoken their first words. For what reasons might such activities be important? Do you personally feel they are important or useful? Would you read to an unborn infant? Why or why not? If you would, *what* would you read?
2. Welty was born in 1909 and obviously belongs to a different generation from the vast majority of college students today. Do you feel that her type of love and advocacy of reading are as valid for the current generation, raised on television, video, CDs, cable, and MTV? Explain.
3. Welty describes her love of books as going beyond the words and stories they contain to their physical and visual attributes. What objects—not other people—do you love or respect with that intensity? Tell a little about why and how you have developed this feeling.

IDEAS FOR WRITING

Prewriting

In the visual and auditory age in which we live—we watch and listen to television, tune in the radio, see movies regularly—what is the proper role for reading? Talk to friends, teachers, and fellow students about the matter. Record their observations and try to classify their responses.

Guided Writing

Write an essay that describes your own attitude toward reading.

1. In order to set the stage for the discussion of your attitude, begin by recalling details about a moment with a parent or other adult.
2. Use dialogue as part of this scene.
3. Go as far back in your childhood as you can possibly remember, and narrate two or three incidents that help explain the formation of your current attitude toward reading.

4. Use sensory language (color, sound, smell, touch, and taste) to show how the environment of the home where you grew up helped shape your attitude.
5. Tell about a particular, special childhood fascination with something you *saw*—not read—in a book.
6. Try to describe the first time you were conscious of the *meaning* of a particular word.
7. Use at least one *simile* in your essay.
8. Create and keep a consistent *tone* throughout the essay.
9. End your essay with an explanation of how a particular book has been continually influential to you as well as to others of your generation.
10. Give your essay an unusual title that derives from some description in your essay.

Thinking and Writing Collaboratively

Form groups of three to five students, and read the essays you each prepared for the Guided Writing assignment. Together, make a list of the various attitudes expressed about reading by group members. Report to the class as a whole on the reading attitudes of your group.

Writing About the Text

This selection is written by someone whom many critics consider to be a great writer, a notch above the group of excellent, admirable, or fine writers. What qualities in Welty's writing support this high praise? How do these qualities square with the prescriptions for good writing offered in Chapter 1?

More Writing Projects

1. Enter in your journal early memories of people who read to you or of books that you read on your own. Try to capture the sensation and importance of these early reading experiences.
2. Return to question 2 in Exploring the Writer's Ideas, and write a one-paragraph response to it.
3. Write an essay on the person who most influenced your childhood education. Did this person read to you, give you books, make you do your homework? Assess the impact of this person on your life.

Volar

Judith Ortiz Cofer

A poet, novelist, and essayist, Judith Ortiz Cofer has explored the triumphs, discoveries, and costs of hyphenated Americanism in an impressive variety of highly regarded publications. Born in Puerto Rico and reared in Paterson, New Jersey, Ortiz Cofer identifies herself as "a daughter of the Puerto Rican diaspora," or dispersion, for whose writing nevertheless "a sense of place has been very important." Her collection of autobiographical essays, *Silent Dancing,* was awarded the 1990 Pushcart Prize for Non-Fiction, and her story "Nada" won the prestigious O'Henry Prize for the Short Story in 1994. Her books of poetry include *Peregrina* (1986) and *Terms of Survival* (1987). Other of her publications are *The Latin Deli: Prose and Poetry* (1993) and, most recently, *Woman in Front of the Sun: On Becoming a Writer* (2000). Ortiz Cofer received her B.A. from Augusta College, Georgia, in 1974 and is the Franklin Professor of English and the Director of the Creative Writing Program at the University of Georgia. In this selection, she recounts how reading—in this case, reading *Supergirl* comics—can feed a young person's hunger to live. This deftly structured essay also shows how art and life mysteriously—and often, ironically—flow into one another.

PREREADING: THINKING ABOUT THE ESSAY IN ADVANCE

What is "volar"? What expectations are raised by a title in Spanish? What sort of flying are we talking about?

Words to Watch

volar Spanish for "to fly"

aerodynamic (par. 1) relating to bodies in motion

supersonic (par. 1) speed greater than sound

ermine (par. 1) fur of a weasel, sometimes used to trim judge's robes as a symbol of honor and purity

incongruous (par. 1) not in harmony, unsuitable

dismal (par. 2) gloomy, depressing

1 At twelve I was an avid consumer of comic books—*Supergirl* being my favorite. I spent my allowance of a quarter a day on two twelve-cent comic books or a double issue for twenty-five. I had a

stack of *Legion of Super Heroes* and *Supergirl* comic books in my bedroom closet that was as tall as I. I had a recurring dream in those days: that I had long blond hair and could fly. In my dream I climbed the stairs to the top of our apartment building as myself, but as I went up each flight, changes would be taking place. Step by step I would fill out: my legs would grow long, my arms harden into steel, and my hair would magically go straight and turn a golden color. Of course I would add the bonus of breasts, but not too large; Supergirl had to be aerodynamic. Sleek and hard as a supersonic missile. Once on the roof, my parents safely asleep in their beds, I would get on tip-toe, arms outstretched in the position for flight and jump out my fifty-story-high window into the black lake of the sky. From up there, over the rooftops, I could see everything, even beyond the few blocks of our barrio; with my X-ray vision I could look inside the homes of people who interested me. Once I saw our landlord, whom I knew my parents feared, sitting in a treasure-room dressed in an ermine coat and a large gold crown. He sat on the floor counting his dollar bills. I played a trick on him. Going up to his building's chimney, I blew a little puff of my super-breath into his fireplace, scattering his stacks of money so that he had to start counting all over again. I could more or less program my Supergirl dreams in those days by focusing on the object of my current obsession. This way I "saw" into the private lives of my neighbors, my teachers, and in the last days of my childish fantasy and the beginning of adolescence, into the secret room of the boys I liked. In the mornings I'd wake up in my tiny bedroom with the incongruous—at least in our tiny apartment—white "princess" furniture my mother had chosen for me, and find myself back in my body; my tight curls still clinging to my head, skinny arms and legs and flat chest unchanged.

In the kitchen my mother and father would be talking softy 2
over a café con leche. She would come "wake me" exactly forty-five minutes after they had gotten up. It was their time together at the beginning of each day and even at an early age I could feel their disappointment if I interrupted them by getting up too early. So I would stay in my bed recalling my dreams of flight, perhaps planning my next flight. In the kitchen they would be discussing events in the barrio. Actually, he would be carrying that part of the conversation; when it was her turn to speak she would, more often than not, try shifting the topic toward her desire to see her *familia*

on the Island: *How about a vacation in Puerto Rico together this year, Querido? We could rent a car, go to the beach. We could . . .* And he would answer patiently, gently. *Mi amor, do you know how much it would cost for all of us to fly there? It is not possible for me to take the time off . . . Mi vida, please understand . . .* And I knew that soon she would rise from the table. Not abruptly. She would light a cigarette and look out the kitchen window. The view was of a dismal alley that was littered with refuse thrown from windows. The space was too narrow for anyone larger than a skinny child to enter safely, so it was never cleaned. My mother would check the time on the clock over her sink, the one with a prayer for patience and grace written. in Spanish. A birthday gift. She would see that it was time to wake me. She'd sigh deeply and say the same thing the view from her kitchen window always inspired her to say: *Ay, si yo pudiera volar.*

BUILDING VOCABULARY

Writing American English often involves using words from other languages, or words that originated in other languages but have been adopted (sometimes also adapted) into English. If you watch a Woody Allen movie, for example, you will hear characters use Yiddish words or expressions that have become commonplace in New York. This essay includes some words in Spanish. Translate these words into English. Which, if any, do you think have become commonplace, part of contemporary American usage.

- **a.** **barrio** (par. 1)
- **b.** **café con leche** (par. 2)
- **c.** **Querido** (par. 2)
- **d.** **Mi amor** (par. 2)
- **e.** **Mi vida** (par. 2)
- **f.** **Ay, si yo pudiera volar.** (par. 2)

THINKING CRITICALLY ABOUT THE ESSAY

Understanding the Writer's Ideas

1. How old was the writer at the time of the essay? What clues suggest roughly the calendar year in question?

2. What kinds of stories are found in the comics the writer "consumes"? How do the main characters in these stories differ from the writer?
3. In what kind of community does the writer live?
4. How does the writer use her fantastic powers to affect her everyday world?
5. Why does the writer describe her bedroom furniture as "incongruous" (par. 1)?
6. Why were the writer's parents "disappointed" if she woke too early (par. 2)?
7. What did the writer's father discuss over breakfast? The writer's mother?
8. Why does the writer say that when her mother rises from the breakfast table it is "Not abruptly" (par. 2)?
9. What did the writer's mother see outside the kitchen window?
10. What is the connection between the writer's dreams and what the view from the kitchen window "always inspired" her mother to say?

Understanding the Writer's Techniques

1. Does this essay have a thesis statement? If so, what is it? If not, express the essay's main idea in one or two sentences.
2. Compare and contrast the essay's two paragraphs—look, for example, at the similarities and differences in *setting, point of view,* and *theme.*
3. How does the writer achieve unity in a two-paragraph essay?
4. Show how *incongruity* serves as an organizing principle for each paragraph.
5. What is the role of *irony* in the essay?

Exploring the Writer's Ideas

1. The writer, at age 12, seems attracted to reading as a way of escaping the harsh reality of her barrio existence. What do you think is the adult writer's attitude toward her youthful habits? And what is your view: is reading or, say, watching television as an "escape" a good thing? A bad thing? Neither?
2. Do you think the essay aims to contrast two kinds of "flying"—that of daughter and mother; or does the essay want to

suggest *analogies* between the outlook of daughter and mother? Explain.

3. Is this an essay about a certain reaction to poverty, or does the essay have implications beyond the barrio? Explain.

IDEAS FOR WRITING

Prewriting

Think about what you read at age 12 or 13 that fed your fantasies. List a few book or magazine or comic book titles. Or, if you prefer, list movies or television shows that played this role.

Guided Writing

Write a two-paragraph essay that illustrates the differences between your reality at 12 or 13 and the fantasy life you led then, as stimulated by your reading or television or movie watching.

1. In the first paragraph identify the source of your fantasies.
2. In the same paragraph, describe how the fantasy imitates your reading or viewing and how you apply it to your life.
3. End the paragraph as you come back to reality and discover the incongruity between your fantasy and your true situation.
4. In the second paragraph, identify in a narrative fashion a situation that triggers your mother's or father's (or some other relative's) desire for escape, or that person's refusal to resort to escapism.
5. Conclude with a clinching last sentence that serves as a kind of punch line, linking your fantasizing and that of your relative or your fantasizing and your relative's lack of fantasizing.

Thinking and Writing Collaboratively

In a small group of three or four, explore the ways childhood reading and childhood fantasies work together. List some of the group members' favorite things to read as children that triggered childhood fantasies. On the basis of your discussion, write a paragraph or two about the kinds of things children like to read, and why.

Writing About the Text

Write an essay that shows how Ortiz Cofer achieves the essay's delicate and economical character portrayals—of herself, of her father, of her mother, of the family.

More Writing Projects

1. Are all fantasies of power benign? Pick up an assortment of comics that a young teenager might read and in your journal explore the kinds of fantasies these comics might induce.
2. Children's reading strongly tends toward imaginary worlds. Some of these imaginary worlds, as Ortiz Cofer shows, offer an escape from severe limits into unlimited power. But others are less directly escapist. In an extended paragraph, contrast the imaginary world invoked by *Supergirl* and the world invoked by a children's classic, such as *Winnie the Pooh* or *Alice in Wonderland* or *Little Women* or *The Little House on the Prairie.*
3. By doing some research into children's literature, expand into an essay the topic that is given in an extended paragraph in *Thinking and Writing Collaboratively.*

Prison Studies

Malcolm X

Born Malcolm Little in Omaha, Nebraska, Malcolm X (1925–1965) was a charismatic leader of the black power movement and founded the Organization of Afro-American Unity. In prison, he became a Black Muslim. (He split with this faith in 1963 to convert to orthodox Islam.) "Prison Studies" is excerpted from the popular and fascinating *Autobiography of Malcolm X,* which he cowrote with *Roots* author Alex Haley. The selection describes the writer's struggle to learn to read as well as the joy and power he felt when he won that struggle.

PREREADING: THINKING ABOUT THE ESSAY IN ADVANCE

Reflect on what you know about prison life. Could someone interested in reading and learning find a way to pursue these interests in such a setting? Why or why not?

Words to Watch

emulate (par. 2) imitate, especially from respect

motivation (par. 2) reason to do something

tablets (par. 3) writing notebooks

bunk (par. 9) small bed

rehabilitation (par. 10) the process of restoring to a state of usefulness or constructiveness

inmate (par. 10) prisoner

corridor (par. 13) hallway; walkway

vistas (par. 15) mental overviews

confers (par. 15) bestows; gives ceremoniously

alma mater (par. 15) the college that one has attended

1 Many who today hear me somewhere in person, or on television, or those who read something I've said, will think I went to school far beyond the eighth grade. This impression is due entirely to my prison studies.

2 It had really begun back in the Charlestown Prison, when Bimbi first made me feel envy of his stock of knowledge. Bimbi had always taken charge of any conversation he was in, and I had

tried to emulate him. But every book I picked up had few sentences which didn't contain anywhere from one to nearly all of the words that might as well have been in Chinese. When I just skipped those words, of course, I really ended up with little idea of what the book said. So I had come to the Norfolk Prison Colony still going through only book-reading motions. Pretty soon, I would have quit even these motions, unless I had received the motivation that I did.

I saw that the best thing I could do was get hold of a diction- 3
ary—to study, to learn some words. I was lucky enough to reason also that I should try to improve my penmanship. It was sad. I couldn't even write in a straight line. It was both ideas together that moved me to request a dictionary along with some tablets and pencils from the Norfolk Prison Colony school.

I spent two days just riffling uncertainly through the dictio- 4
nary's pages. I'd never realized so many words existed! I didn't know which words I needed to learn. Finally, to start some kind of action, I began copying.

In my slow, painstaking, ragged handwriting, I copied into my 5
tablet everything printed on that first page, down to the punctuation marks.

I believe it took me a day. Then, aloud, I read back, to myself, 6
everything I'd written on the tablet. Over and over, aloud, to myself, I read my own handwriting.

I woke up the next morning, thinking about those words—im- 7
mensely proud to realize that not only had I written so much at one time, but I'd written words that I never knew were in the world. Moreover, with a little effort, I also could remember what many of these words meant. I reviewed the words whose meanings I didn't remember. Funny thing, from the dictionary first page right now, that "aardvark" springs to my mind. The dictionary had a picture of it, a long-tailed, long-eared, burrowing African mammal, which lives off termites caught by sticking out its tongue as an anteater does for ants.

I was so fascinated that I went on—I copied the dictionary's 8
next page. And the same experience came when I studied that. With every succeeding page, I also learned of people and places and events from history. Actually the dictionary is like a miniature encyclopedia. Finally the dictionary's A section had filled a whole tablet—and I went on into the B's. That was the way I started copying what eventually became the entire dictionary. It went a lot

faster after so much practice helped me to pick up handwriting speed. Between what I wrote in my tablet, and writing letters, during the rest of my time in prison I would guess I wrote a million words.

9 I suppose it was inevitable that as my word-base broadened, I could for the first time pick up a book and read and now begin to understand what the book was saying. Anyone who has read a great deal can imagine the new world that opened. Let me tell you something; from then until I left that prison, in every free moment I had, if I was not reading in the library, I was reading on my bunk. You couldn't have gotten me out of books with a wedge. Between Mr. Muhammad's teachings, my correspondence, my visitors—usually Ella and Reginald—and my reading of books, months passed without my even thinking about being imprisoned. In fact, up to then, I never had been so truly free in my life. . . .

10 As you can imagine, especially in a prison where there was heavy emphasis on rehabilitation, an inmate was smiled upon if he demonstrated an unusually intense interest in books. There was a sizable number of well-read inmates, especially the popular debaters. Some were said by many to be practically walking encyclopedias. They were almost celebrities. No university would ask any student to devour literature as I did when this new world opened to me, of being able to read and *understand.*

11 I read more in my room than in the library itself. An inmate who was known to read a lot could check out more than the permitted maximum number of books. I preferred reading in the total isolation of my own room.

12 When I had progressed to really serious reading, every night at about ten P.M. I would be outraged with the "lights out." It always seemed to catch me right in the middle of something engrossing.

13 Fortunately, right outside my door was a corridor light that cast a glow into my room. The glow was enough to read by, once my eyes adjusted to it. So when "lights out" came, I would sit on the floor where I could continue reading in that glow.

14 At one-hour intervals the night guards paced past every room. Each time I heard the approaching footsteps, I jumped into bed and feigned sleep. And as soon as the guard passed, I got back out of bed onto the floor area of that light-glow, where I would read for another fifty-eight minutes—until the guard approached again. That went on until three or four every morning. Three or four

hours of sleep a night was enough for me. Often in the years in the streets I had slept less than that.

I have often reflected upon the new vistas that reading opened 15
to me. I knew right there in prison that reading had changed forever the course of my life. As I see it today, the ability to read awoke inside me some long dormant craving to be mentally alive. I certainly wasn't seeking any degree, the way a college confers a status symbol upon its students. My homemade education gave me, with every additional book that I read, a little bit more sensitivity to the deafness, dumbness, and blindness that was afflicting the black race in America. Not long ago, an English writer telephoned me from London, asking questions. One was, "What's your alma mater?" I told him, "Books." You will never catch me with a free fifteen minutes in which I'm not studying something I feel might be able to help the black man. . . .

Every time I catch a plane, I have with me a book that I want 16
to read—and that's a lot of books these days. If I weren't out here every day battling the white man, I could spend the rest of my life reading, just satisfying my curiosity—because you can hardly mention anything I'm not curious about. I don't think anybody ever got more out of going to prison than I did. In fact, prison enabled me to study far more intensively than I would have if my life had gone differently and I had attended some college. I imagine that one of the biggest troubles with colleges is there are too many distractions, too much panty-raiding, fraternities, and boola-boola and all of that. Where else but in prison could I have attacked my ignorance by being able to study intensely sometimes as much as fifteen hours a day?

BUILDING VOCABULARY

1. Throughout the selection, the writer uses *figurative* and *colloquial language* (see Glossary). As you know, figurative language involves imaginative comparisons, which go beyond plain or ordinary statements. Colloquial language involves informal or conversational phrases and expressions.

The following are examples of some of the figurative and colloquial usages in this essay. Explain each italicized word group in your own words.

a. *going through only book-reading motions* (par. 2)

b. I *was lucky enough* (par. 3)
c. *Funny thing* (par. 7)
d. can imagine *the new world that opened* (par. 9)
e. *You couldn't have gotten me out of books with a wedge* (par. 9)
f. an inmate was *smiled upon* (par. 10)
g. to be practically *walking encyclopedias* (par. 10)
h. ask any student *to devour literature* (par. 10)
i. changed forever *the course of my life* (par. 15)
j. *some long dormant craving to be mentally alive* (par. 15)
k. *the deafness, dumbness, and blindness that was afflicting* the black race in America (par. 15)
l. Every time I *catch a plane* (par. 16)
m. every day *battling the white man* (par. 16)
n. just *satisfying my curiosity* (par. 16)
o. *boola-boola and all of that* (par. 16)
p. I have *attacked my ignorance* (par. 16)

2. Find the following words in the essay. Write brief definitions for them without using a dictionary. If they are unfamiliar to you, try to determine their meaning based on the context in which they appear.
   a. riffling (par. 4)
   b. painstaking (par. 5)
   c. ragged (par. 5)
   d. burrowing (par. 7)
   e. inevitable (par. 9)
   f. emphasis (par. 10)
   g. distractions (par. 16)

THINKING CRITICALLY ABOUT THE ESSAY

Understanding the Writer's Ideas

1. What was the highest level of formal education that the writer achieved? How is this different from the impression most people got from him? Why?
2. Who was Bimbi? Where did Malcolm X meet him? How was Bimbi important to the writer?
3. What does the writer mean by stating that when he tried to read, most of the words "might as well have been in Chinese"? What

happened when he skipped over such words? What motivated him to change his way of reading?

4. Why did Malcolm X start trying to improve his handwriting? How was it connected to his desire to improve his reading ability? Briefly describe how he went about this dual process. How did he feel after the first day of this process? Why?
5. How is the dictionary "like a miniature encyclopedia"?
6. Judging from this essay and his description of his "homemade education," how much time did Malcolm X spend in prison? Does the fact that he was in prison affect your appreciation of his learning process? How?
7. What is a "word-base" (par. 9)? What happened once the author's word-base expanded? How did this give him a sense of freedom?
8. Who is "Mr. Muhammad"?
9. Why did the prison officials like Malcolm X? What special privileges came to him as a result of this favorable opinion?
10. Why was Malcolm X angered with the "lights out" procedure? How did he overcome it?
11. What does the following sentence tell you about Malcolm X's life: "Often in the years in the streets I had slept less than that" (par. 14)?
12. Characterize the writer's opinion of a college education. How does he compare his education to a college degree? How did his education influence his understanding of his place and role in American society?
13. In your own words, describe the writer's attitude toward American blacks. Toward the relation between blacks and whites?
14. To what main purpose in life does the writer refer? What was the relation between this purpose and his feelings about reading? Use one word to describe Malcolm X's attitude toward reading.
15. What does the conclusion mean?

Understanding the Writer's Techniques

1. What is the thesis? Where does the writer place it?
2. In Chapters 9 and 10, you will learn about the techniques of *process analysis* and *cause-and-effect analysis*. Briefly, process analysis tells the reader *how* something is done;

cause-and-effect analysis explains *why* one thing leads to or affects another.

For this essay, outline step by step the process whereby Malcolm X developed his ability to read and enthusiasm for reading. Next, for each step in your outline, explain why one step led to the next.

3. *Narration* (see Chapter 4) is the telling of a story or the orderly relating of a series of events. How does Malcolm X use narration in this essay? How does he order the events of his narration?
4. What is the effect of the words "Let me tell you something" in paragraph 9?
5. How is the writer's memory of the first page of the dictionary like a dictionary entry itself? What does this say about the importance of this memory to the author?
6. *Tone* (see Glossary) is a writer's attitude toward his or her subject. Characterize the tone of this essay. What elements of the writing contribute to that tone? Be specific.
7. Which paragraphs make up the conclusion of this essay? How does the writer develop his conclusion? How does he relate it to the main body of the essay? Do you feel that there is a change in tone (see question 6) in the conclusion? Explain, using specific examples.
8. What is Malcolm X's main purpose in writing this essay? For whom is it intended? How do you know?

Exploring the Writer's Ideas

1. Malcolm X writes about his newly found love of reading and ability to read: "In fact, up to then, I never had been so truly free in my life." Has learning any particular skill or activity ever given you such a feeling of freedom or joy? Explain.
2. What do you feel was the source of Malcolm X's attitude toward a college education? Do you think any of his points here are valid? Why? What are your opinions about the quality of the college education you are receiving?
3. The writer also implies that, in some ways, the educational opportunities of prison were superior to those he would have had at college. What is his basis for this attitude? Have you ever experienced a circumstance in which being restricted actually benefited you? Explain.

4. Malcolm X held very strong opinions about the relations between blacks and whites in America. Do some library research on him to try to understand his opinions. You might begin by reading *The Autobiography of Malcolm X,* from which this essay was excerpted. Do you agree or disagree with his feelings? Why?
5. Following Malcolm X's example, handwrite a page from a dictionary (a pocket dictionary will be fine), copying everything—including punctuation—exactly!

   How long did it take you? How did it make you feel? Did you learn anything from the experience?

IDEAS FOR WRITING

Prewriting

Brainstorm on a difficult activity that you learned how to perform. What problems did the activity present? Why did you want to learn how to do it?

Guided Writing

Write an essay in which you tell about an activity that you can now perform but that once seemed impossible to you.

1. Open your essay with an example in which you compare what most people assume about your skill or background in the activity to what the reality is.
2. Mention someone who especially influenced you in your desire to master this activity.
3. Tell what kept you from giving up on learning this activity.
4. Explain, step by step, the *process* by which you learned more and more about the activity. Explain how and why one step led to the next.
5. Use *figurative* and *colloquial* language where you think it appropriate in your essay.
6. Describe in some detail how you overcame an obstacle, imposed by others, which could have impeded your learning process.

7. Use your conclusion to express a deeply felt personal opinion and to generalize your learning of this skill to the population at large.

Thinking and Writing Collaboratively

Exchange a draft version of your Guided Writing essay with another writer in the class. After you read your partner's essay, make recommendations for helping the writer produce the next draft. Use the items numbered 1–7 above to guide your discussion.

Writing About the Text

In this essay, Malcolm X directly connects literacy and power, words and politics. Do you think that if Malcolm were alive today—in the era of the image, of TV and video—would he have been just as likely to have needed and have valued literacy? Write an essay that explores this question, drawing as much as seems appropriate on the selection.

More Writing Projects

1. Select any page of a standard dictionary and copy in your journal at least ten words, with definitions, that are new or somewhat unfamiliar to you. Then jot down some thoughts on the process.
2. Ask yourself formal, journalistic questions about Malcolm X's essay: *What* happened? *Who* was involved? *How* was it done? *Where* did it occur? *When* did it occur? *Why* did it happen? Write out answers to these questions, and then assemble them in a unified, coherent paragraph.
3. Form a group with three other classmates. Focus on the context of Malcolm X's essay and on his comment on "the deafness, dumbness, and blindness that was afflicting the black race in America" (par. 15). Discuss this issue and its connection to education. Then prepare a collaborative essay on the topic.

"See Spot Run": Teaching My Grandmother to Read

Ellen Tashie Frisina

Ellen Tashie Frisina writes about her "secret" project to teach her 70-year-old grandmother, who came to the United States from Greece in 1916, to read English. A reporter and editor as well as an Assistant Professor of Journalism and Media Studies at Hofstra University, Frisina reveals in her narrative the pleasures of reading and illustrates the importance of reading no matter what age the reader. This article first appeared in *Newsday,* a popular newspaper published in Long Island, New York.

PREREADING: THINKING ABOUT THE ESSAY IN ADVANCE

What do you think it would be like to be an adult who, living in America today, cannot read or write English? What problems would such a person face? Do you know or have you read about anyone who cannot read?

Words to Watch

differentiated (par. 1) separated from; distinguished from
stealthily (par. 2) secretly
monosyllabic (par. 3) one syllable; short in length
vehemently (par. 8) severely; intensely; angrily
phonetically (par. 14) pronounced by sound
afghan (par. 15) blanket or shawl
crocheting (par. 15) type of needlework

When I was 14 years old, and very impressed with my teenage status (looking forward to all the rewards it would bring), I set for myself a very special goal—a goal that so differentiated me from my friends that I don't believe I told a single one. As a teenager, I was expected to have deep, dark secrets, but I was not supposed to keep them from my friends. 1

My secret was a project that I undertook every day after school for several months. It began when I stealthily made my way into the local elementary school—horror of horrors should I be seen; I was now in junior high. I identified myself as a *graduate* of 2 the elementary school, and being taken under wing by a favorite fifth grade teacher, I was given a small bundle from a locked storeroom–a bundle that I quickly dropped into a bag, lest anyone see me walking home with something from the "little kids" school.

3 I brought the bundle home—proudly now, for within the confines of my home, I was proud of my project. I walked into the living room, and one by one, emptied the bag of basic reading books. They were thin books with colorful covers and large print. The words were monosyllabic and repetitive. I sat down to the secret task at hand.

4 "All right," I said authoritatively to my 70-year-old grandmother, "today we begin our first reading lesson."

5 For weeks afterward, my grandmother and I sat patiently side by side—roles reversed as she, with a bit of difficulty, sounded out every word, then read them again, piece by piece, until she understood the short sentences. When she slowly repeated the full sentence, we both would smile and clap our hands—I felt so proud, so grown up.

6 My grandmother was born in Kalamata, Greece, in a rocky little farming village where nothing much grew. She never had the time to go to school. As the oldest child, she was expected to take care of her brother and sister, as well as the house and meals, while her mother tended to the gardens, and her father scratched out what little he could from the soil.

7 So, for my grandmother, schooling was out. But she had big plans for herself. She had heard about America. About how rich you could be. How people on the streets would offer you a dollar just to smell the flower you were carrying. About how everyone lived in nice houses—not stone huts on the sides of mountains—and had nice clothes and time for school.

8 So my grandmother made a decision at 14—just a child, I realize now—to take a long and sickening 30-day sea voyage alone to the United States. After lying about her age to the passport officials, who would shake their heads vehemently at anyone under 16 leaving her family, and after giving her favorite gold earrings to her cousin, saying "In America, I will have all the gold I want," my young grandmother put herself on a ship. She landed in New York in 1916.

9 No need to repeat the story of how it went for years. The streets were not made of gold. People weren't interested in smelling flowers held by strangers. My grandmother was a foreigner. Alone. A young girl who worked hard doing piecework to

earn enough money for meals. No leisure time, no new gold earrings—and no school.

She learned only enough English to help her in her daily busi- 10
ness as she traveled about Brooklyn. Socially, the "foreigners"
stayed in neighborhoods where they didn't feel like foreigners.
English came slowly.

My grandmother had never learned to read. She could make 11
out a menu, but not a newspaper. She could read a street sign, but
not a shop directory. She could read only what she needed to read
as, through the years, she married, had five daughters, and helped
my grandfather with his restaurant.

So when I was 14—the same age that my grandmother was 12
when she left her family, her country, and everything she knew—
I took it upon myself to teach my grandmother something, something I already knew how to do. Something with which I could
give back to her some of the things she had taught me.

And it was slight repayment for all she taught me. How to 13
cover the fig tree in tar paper so it could survive the winter. How
to cultivate rose bushes and magnolia trees that thrived on her little piece of property. How to make baklava, and other Greek delights, working from her memory. ("Now we add some milk."
"How much?" "Until we have enough.") Best of all, she had
taught me my ethnic heritage.

First, we phonetically sounded out the alphabet. Then, we 14
talked about vowels—English is such a difficult language to learn.
I hadn't even begun to explain the different sounds "gh" could
make. We were still at the basics.

Every afternoon, we would sit in the living room, my grand- 15
mother with an afghan covering her knees, giving up her crocheting for her reading lesson. I, with the patience that can come only
from love, slowly coached her from the basic reader to the second-
grade reader, giving up my telephone gossiping.

Years later, my grandmother still hadn't learned quite enough 16
to sit comfortably with a newspaper or magazine, but it felt aw-
fully good to see her try. How we used to laugh at her pronuncia-
tion mistakes. She laughed more heartily than I. I never knew
whether I should laugh. Here was this old woman slowly and carefully sounding out each word, moving her lips, not saying anything aloud until she was absolutely sure, and then, loudly,
proudly, happily saying, "Look at Spot. See Spot run."

When my grandmother died and we faced the sad task of emp- 17
tying her home, I was going through her night-table drawer and

came upon the basic readers. I turned the pages slowly, remembering. I put them in a paper bag, and the next day returned them to the "little kids" school. Maybe someday, some teenager will request them again, for the same task. It will make for a lifetime of memories.

BUILDING VOCABULARY

Put the following phrases into your own words and explain what the writer means in the context of the essay.

a. "very impressed with my teenage status" (par. 1)
b. "No need to repeat the story of how it went for years." (par. 9) Why not? What is the implication of this sentence?
c. "doing piecework to earn enough money for meals." (par. 9) What was piecework?
d. "Best of all, she had taught me my ethnic heritage." (par. 13)
e. "First, we phonetically sounded out the alphabet." (par. 14)

THINKING CRITICALLY ABOUT THE ESSAY

Understanding the Writer's Ideas

1. The writer begins by saying that her project was a secret from her junior high school peers. Explain why a 14-year-old would not want to be seen carrying basic readers. What further reasons might the author have had for keeping her project a secret?
2. In paragraph 3, the writer uses the words "proudly" and "proud." Why has her attitude changed?
3. How does teaching her grandmother to read change the relation between the two? How does Frisina speak to her grandmother in paragraph 4?
4. What are the myths about America that cause the grandmother to make her difficult decision to leave her family in Greece? How does the real America live up to the stories the grandmother had heard before she arrived? How common are experiences like the grandmother's for other immigrants?
5. What does Frisina imply in paragraph 10 about the daily life of immigrants in the early twentieth century? How is language usually acquired? What limits the grandmother's ability to learn English?

6. The writer provides details of what her grandmother taught her for which the author is grateful. How do the specific details help the reader understand the kind of woman the grandmother was? What kind of life did the grandmother lead?
7. In paragraph 14, the writer describes how hard it is to learn English. What in particular makes English a hard language to read? What can you tell from paragraph 17 about how the grandmother felt about her reading? Why does the grandmother keep the schoolbooks in her night-table drawer? What does this tell you about how she felt about learning to read?

Understanding the Writer's Techniques

1. Where does the writer place her thesis statement? Why does she put it where she does? Explain the thesis in your own words.
2. *Diction* (see Glossary) refers to a writer's choice and use of words. We classify *levels of diction*—"informal," "academic," "low-class," "snobbish," "conversational," and so forth. How would you describe the general level of diction in this essay? Does the level suit the subject matter? Why?
3. Why does the writer rely on short paragraphs throughout her narrative? What does the paragraph length and diction tell you about the intended audience for this piece?
4. The writer assumes that the reader is familiar with the history of immigration in America in the early twentieth century. How do we know that she makes this assumption? Should she provide readers with more historical detail? Why or why not?
5. Describe the method the writer uses to teach her grandmother to read. Is this the way you remember learning to read? Describe the first book you remember reading. How did your experience compare with the grandmother's?

Exploring the Writer's Ideas

1. The writer uses the story of her grandmother's life to illustrate the experiences of many immigrants who came to America in the early twentieth century. How do those experiences compare with the arrival of immigrants to America today? Is it easier or more difficult to immigrate here now? What evidence can you provide to support your position?
2. Though the grandmother could barely read a newspaper, even her limited literacy seemed to give her pleasure. Why should

learning to read be so important to an adult who cannot read? In a world of television, movies, and other visual sources of information, is learning to read truly important for illiterate adults? Why or why not?

3. The effort to teach and learn reading helps bridge the gap between generations. Do you see any practical applications here for bringing old and young people together for more harmonious relations? How else can young people and old people be united?

IDEAS FOR WRITING

Prewriting

Teaching someone to do something—anything—is fraught with problems and, at the same time, alive with possibilities and rewards. What do you see as the positive and negative aspects of teaching someone to do something? Use free association to indicate as many pluses and minuses as you can.

Guided Writing

Write an essay titled "Teaching __________ to __________." Fill in the blanks after considering your own experience with teaching someone something. You might choose one of these topics:

Teaching my daughter/son to read
Reading English as a second language (about your own experience or someone else's)
Working as a volunteer in a neighborhood literacy program

1. Begin your essay with a general discussion about the expectations you had when you started this learning project and the feelings you had when you accomplished it.
2. Define yourself as a person with this skill, for example, as a reader. What age were you when you started the project? How did you practice the skill? How did you feel about this skill? Why?
3. Explain why you started the project of teaching someone this skill or of changing the level of your own reading skill. What situation encouraged or required you to change or act?

4. Use examples and illustrations to show how you began the task. Give examples of words and sentences you worked with. Give the steps you used to carry out your project.
5. Describe the moment when a change happened—for example, the first time your son or daughter read to you or the first time the skill became easy. Use dialogue to capture the moment.
6. Analyze how you changed as a result of this moment, and why you remember it so vividly.
7. Conclude by describing your present status with regard to this skill, or the skills level of the person you taught. Was the project worthwhile?

Thinking and Writing Collaboratively

Form groups of three students each, and read aloud drafts of each other's essays for the Guided Writing activity. Then discuss the essays. Was the writer's experience clear to you? Do you know why the writer started his or her teaching project? Do the illustrations show how the task was performed? Did the writer make clear the moment of change?

Writing About the Text

How would you describe the language in Frisina's essay? Is it simple or complex, scholarly or down to earth, spare or rich in detail? Write an essay in which you analyze Frisina's use of language. Provide specific examples from her essay to support your point. Keep in mind that she wrote this piece for a popular suburban newspaper in New York. How does her language suit the audience?

More Writing Projects

1. In your journal, write down your ideas about what the difference is between reading "See Spot Run" and reading a science textbook or a technical manual or a play by Shakespeare. Give steps by which a reader can increase his or her reading skills.
2. Write a paragraph in which you consider whether or not it is important to be a "good" reader to succeed in life.
3. Can teaching someone else, like a son or daughter, to read teach you to read better as well? Write an essay in which you discuss a parent's role in teaching his or her child to read. Consider what the child learns at school and what he or she learns at home about reading.

SUMMING UP: CHAPTER 2

1. In one way or another, all the writers in this chapter explain how reading has provided them with emotional ease or intellectual stimulation at some point in their lives. Which of these writers, alone or in combination, best reflects your own view of reading? Write an essay in which you address this question.
2. On the average, Americans are said to read less than one book per person annually. Take a survey of several people who are not students to find out how often and what kind of books they read. In an essay, analyze the results. Indicate the types of people you interviewed, and explain why your results either conformed to or differed from the norm. Indicate the types of books each person read.
3. List all the books you have read in the past six months. For each, write a brief two- or three-sentence reaction. Compare your list with those of your classmates. What reading trends do you notice? From these lists, what generalizations can you draw about college students' reading habits?
4. The United States ranks forty-ninth among nations in literacy. People often ask, "Why is there such a low rate of literacy in such an advanced nation?" What is your answer to this question? How do you think the writers in this chapter would respond to the question? Write an essay that explains your response by drawing on Welty, Ortiz Cofer, Malcolm X, and Frisina. Suggest some ways to improve the rate of literacy in this country. You might want to consider this fact: By the time the average American finishes high school, he or she has spent 18,000 hours in front of a television set as compared to 12,000 hours in the classroom.
5. Using Welty or Ortiz Cofer as an example, write an essay in which you reflect on your early memories of reading. Describe when you learned to read, when you experienced pleasure at being read to, or when you started appreciating a particular kind of reading. Call your essay "Reading When I Was Young."
6. The writers represented in this chapter each speak about reading in a distinctly personal way. In each case reading is vital to their sense of personal identity. But it is through the discovery of the world beyond the self, the great world found in books, that the writers find themselves. Write an essay that explores this paradox of reading.

7. Write a dialogue between Malcolm X and Eudora Welty on the subject of reading. Include at least one disagreement or argument in the dialogue.
8. Of the writers represented in this chapter, only Welty was born into a fairly comfortable home, and into a family that loved books. Do these facts separate her from the others, or does reading overcome differences of class and race? Explain your response.

FROM SEEING TO WRITING

Look at the photograph on the next page and write an essay in which you analyze the reasons that the Association of American Publishers chose to present such an advertisement in the national media. Why did the organization use a photograph of the baseball player Sammy Sosa reading Dr. Seuss? What does the tag line contribute to the intent of the ad? Why does the ad link celebrity and reading? Is this a good idea? Why or why not? Try to address these questions in your analysis.

The Association of American Publishers

CHAPTER 3

Description

WHAT IS DESCRIPTION?

Description is a technique for showing readers what the writer sees: objects, scenes, characters, ideas, and even emotions and moods. Good description relies on the use of *sensory language*—that is, language that evokes our five senses of sight, touch, taste, smell, and sound. In writing, description uses specific *nouns* and *adjectives* to create carefully selected vivid details. The word *vehicle* is neutral, but a "rusty, green 1959 Pontiac convertible" creates a picture. Description is frequently used to make abstract ideas more *concrete*. While the abstract word *liberty* may have a definition for each reader, a description of the Statue of Liberty gleaming in New York's harbor at twilight creates an emotional description of liberty. Description, then, is used by writers who want their readers to *see* what they are writing about. A writer like Annie Dillard uses description of the natural world to reflect on our life on earth. A physician, like Richard Selzer, uses description to re-create the experience of a dying patient. Maxine Hong Kingston uses vivid description of her mother's collection of turtles, catfish, pigeons, skunks, and other unexpected food sources to re-create for her readers a culture different from their own. Virginia Woolf relies on description to capture the reality of life and death. Each writer, then, uses description to help us, as readers, *see* the material about which he or she is writing. As writers, we can study their techniques to improve our own essays.

HOW DO WE READ DESCRIPTION?

Reading a descriptive essay requires us to

- Identify what the writer is describing, and ask why he or she is describing it.
- Look for the concrete nouns, supportive adjectives, or other sensory words that the writer uses to create vivid pictures.
- Find the perspective or angle from which the writer describes: Is it top to bottom, left to right, front to back? Or is it a mood description that relies on feelings? How has the writer *selected* details to create the mood?
- Determine how the writer has organized the description. Here we must look for a "dominant impression." This arises from the writer's focus on a single subject and the feelings that the writer brings to that subject. Each one should be identified.
- Identify the purpose of the description. What is the *thesis* of the writing?
- Determine what audience the writer is aiming toward. How do we know?

HOW DO WE WRITE DESCRIPTION?

After reading some of the selections of descriptive writing in this chapter, you should be ready to write your own description. Don't just read about Kingston's animals, though, or Woolf's moth. Think critically about how you can adapt their methods to your needs.

Select a topic and begin to write a thesis statement, keeping in mind that you will want to give the reader information about what you are describing and what angle you are taking on the topic.

Sample thesis sentence:

> For a first-time tourist in New York City, the subway trains can seem confusing and threatening, but the long-time resident finds the train system a clever, speedy network for traveling around the city.

Here, we see the thesis statement sets out a purpose and an audience. The purpose is to demonstrate the virtues of the New York transit system, and the audience is not the well-traveled New Yorker, but a visitor.

Collect a list of sensory words.

> New York City's subway trains are noisy and crowded, labeled with brightly colored letters, made of shiny corrugated stainless steel, travel at 90 miles per hour, display colorful graffiti and advertising signs, run on electricity.

Use the five senses:

What are subway sounds? Music by street musicians, the screech of brakes, conductors giving directions over scratchy loudspeakers, people talking in different languages.

What are subway smells? Pretzels roasting, the sweaty odor of human bodies crowded together on a hot summer day.

What are subway textures? Colored metal straps and poles for balance, the crisp corner of a newspaper you're reading.

What are subway tastes? A candy bar or chewing gum you buy at the newsstand.

What are subway sights? Crowds of people rushing to work; the colorful pillars freshly painted in each station; the drunk asleep on a bench; the police officer in a blue uniform; the litter on the ground; the subway system maps near each token booth; the advertising posters on the walls and trains.

Plan a dominant impression and an order for arranging details. You might look at the subway from a passenger's point of view and describe the travel process from getting onto the train to arriving at the destination. Your impression might be that to the uninitiated, the subway system seems confusing, but to the experienced New Yorker, trains are the fastest and safest way to get around town.

Express a *purpose* for the description. The purpose might be to prepare a visitor from out of town for her first subway ride by writing a letter to her before she arrives in New York.

Identify the audience: Who will read the essay?

If you were writing to the Commissioner of Transportation in New York, or to a cousin from Iowa whom you know well, you would write differently in each case. Awareness of audience can help you choose a level of diction and formality. Knowing your audience can also help you decide which details to include and which your readers might know. It is always best to assume that the audience knows less than you do and to include details even if they seem obvious to you.

For example, even if you, as a native New Yorker, know that subway trains run twenty-four hours a day, your cousin from Iowa would not be expected to know this, so you should include it as part of your description of how efficient the system is.

Writing the Draft

Use the thesis statement to set up an introductory paragraph. Then plan the body paragraphs so that they follow the order you decided on—from beginning the journey to arriving, from the top of a subway car to the bottom, or from the outside of the train to the inside. Include as many details in the first draft as possible; it is easier to take them out in a second or third draft than to add them later. Then plan the conclusion to help the reader understand what the purpose of the description has been.

Reading and Revising the Draft

Read your first draft, circling each description word. Then go back and add *another* description word after the ones already in the essay. If you can't think of any more words, use a *thesaurus* to find new words.

If possible, read your essay aloud to a classmate. Ask him or her to tell you if the details are vivid. Have your classmate suggest where more details are needed. Check to see that you have included some description in each sensory category: sight, sound, taste, touch, and smell.

Proofread your essay for correctness.
Make a clean, neat final copy.

A STUDENT PARAGRAPH: DESCRIPTION

Read the student paragraph below about the New York City subway. Look for descriptive elements that can help you write your own paper on description. Comments in the margin highlight important features of descriptive writing.

A first-time visitor to the New York City subway system will probably find the noise overwhelming, at least at first. The variety of sounds, and their sheer

Topic sentence announces purpose

volume, can send most unprepared tourists running for the exit; those who remain tend to slip into a state of deep shock. As I wait for the Number 4 train at the Lexington Avenue station, the passing express cars explode from the tunnel in a blur of red and gray. Sometimes as many as three trains roar by at the same time. A high-pitched squeal of brakes adds powerfully to the din. A few passengers heave sighs or mutter under their breath as the crackle and hiss of an unintelligible announcement coming over the public address system adds to the uproar. As I continue to wait for the local, I can hear fragments of the shouted exchanges between weary booth attendants and impatient customers trying to communicate through the bulletproof glass. Irritably, I watch one of the many subway musicians, an old bald man who sings "O Solo Mio" off-key as a battered tape recorder behind him plays warped-sounding violin music. Once in a while some goodhearted passenger tosses a crumpled dollar bill into an old straw hat at the singer's feet. Why are they encouraging these horrible sounds, I wonder to myself? I obviously haven't been here long enough to tune them out.

Supporting detail

Supporting detail

Supporting detail

Supporting detail

Concluding sentence returns to topic; providing *coherence*

In the Jungle

Annie Dillard

Essayist, novelist, and poet Annie Dillard, best known for her reflective, critically acclaimed writing about nature, was born in Pittsburgh, Pennsylvania, in 1945. She attended Hollins College in Virginia. Her book *Pilgrim at Tinker Creek* (1974), a collection of lyrical observations and meditations on the natural world of Virginia's Blue Ridge Mountains, was awarded the Pulitzer Prize for general nonfiction. Among Dillard's many books are *Teaching a Stone to Talk* (1982), a collection of essays; *An American Childhood* (1987), an autobiography; and *The Living* (1992), a novel. Her most recent book is *For the Time Being* (2000). Dillard is Writer in Residence and Adjunct Professor of English at Wesleyan University in Connecticut. This selection, from *Teaching a Stone to Talk,* illustrates Dillard's gift for evocative description that at the same time is a form of meditation on our residence on earth.

PREREADING: THINKING ABOUT THE ESSAY IN ADVANCE

What do you associate with the word *jungle?* What is nature like in the jungle? Do you expect to meet people in the jungle? If so, what sort of people? How do they live? Why might someone from the postmodern world of video and cities travel to a jungle?

Words to Watch

headwaters (par. 1) sources of a river
tributaries (par. 9) streams that feed larger streams
fronds (par. 14) large, fernlike leaves
boles (par. 14) trunks of trees
flanges (par. 14) supporting rims or ribs
iridescent (par. 14) shimmering with colors (as in a soap bubble)
dinghies (par. 14) small boats
reciprocate (par. 19) repay

1 Like any out-of-the-way place, the Napo River in the Ecuadorian jungle seems real enough when you are there, even central. Out of the way of *what?* I was sitting on a stump at the edge of a bankside palm-thatch village, in the middle of the night, on the headwaters

of the Amazon. Out of the way of human life, tenderness, or the glance of heaven?

A nightjar in a deep-leaved shadow called three long notes, 2
and hushed. The men with me talked softly in clumps: three North Americans, four Ecuadorians who were showing us the jungle. We were holding cool drinks and idly watching a hand-sized tarantula seize moths that came to the lone bulb on the generator shed beside us.

It was February, the middle of summer. Green fireflies spat- 3
tered lights across the air and illumined for seconds, now here, now there, the pale trunks of enormous, solitary trees. Beneath us the brown Napo River was rising, in all silence; it coiled up the sandy bank and tangled its foam in vines that trailed from the forest and roots that looped the shore.

Each breath of night smelled sweet, more moistened and 4
sweet than any kitchen, or garden, or cradle. Each star in Orion seemed to tremble and stir with my breath. All at once, in the thatch house across the clearing behind us, one of the village's Jesuit priests began playing an alto recorder, playing a wordless song, lyric, in a minor key, that twined over the village clearing, that caught in the big trees' canopies, muted our talk on the bankside, and wandered over the river, dissolving downstream.

This will do, I thought. This will do, for a weekend, or a sea- 5
son, or a home.

Later that night I loosed my hair from its braids and combed it 6
smooth—not for myself, but so the village girls could play with it in the morning.

We had disembarked at the village that afternoon, and I had 7
slumped on some shaded steps, wishing I knew some Spanish or some Quechua so I could speak with the ring of little girls who were alternately staring at me and smiling at their toes. I spoke anyway, and fooled with my hair, which they were obviously dying to get their hands on, and laughed, and soon they were all braiding my hair, all five of them, all fifty fingers, all my hair, even my bangs. And then they took it apart and did it again, laughing, and teaching me Spanish nouns, and meeting my eyes and each other's with open delight, while their small brothers in blue jeans climbed down from the trees and began kicking a volleyball around with one of the North American men.

Now, as I combed my hair in the little tent, another of the 8
men, a free-lance writer from Manhattan, was talking quietly. He

was telling us the tale of his life, describing his work in Hollywood, his apartment in Manhattan, his house in Paris. . . . "It makes me wonder," he said, "what I'm doing in a tent under a tree in the village of Pompeya, on the Napo River, in the jungle of Ecuador." After a pause he added, "It makes me wonder why I'm going *back*."

9 The point of going somewhere like the Napo River in Ecuador is not to see the most spectacular anything. It is simply to see what is there. We are here on the planet only once, and might as well get a feel for the place. We might as well get a feel for the fringes and hollows in which life is lived, for the Amazon basin, which covers half a continent, and for the life that—there, like anywhere else—is always and necessarily lived in detail: on the tributaries, in the riverside villages, sucking this particular white-fleshed guava in this particular pattern of shade.

10 What is there is interesting. The Napo River itself is wide (I mean wider than the Mississippi at Davenport) and brown, opaque, and smeared with floating foam and logs and branches from the jungle. White egrets hunch on shoreline deadfalls and parrots in flocks dart in and out of the light. Under the water in the river, unseen, are anacondas—which are reputed to take a few village toddlers every year—and water boas, stingrays, crocodiles, manatees, and sweet-meated fish.

11 Low water bares gray strips of sandbar on which the natives build tiny palm-thatch shelters, arched, the size of pup tents, for overnight fishing trips. You see these extraordinarily clean people (who bathe twice a day in the river, and whose straight black hair is always freshly washed) paddling down the river in dugout canoes, hugging the banks.

12 Some of the Indians of this region, earlier in the century, used to sleep naked in hammocks. The nights are cold. Gordon MacCreach, an American explorer in these Amazon tributaries, reported that he was startled to hear the Indians get up at three in the morning. He was even more startled, night after night, to hear them walk down to the river slowly, half asleep, and bathe in the water. Only later did he learn what they were doing: they were getting warm. The cold woke them; they warmed their skins in the river, which was always ninety degrees; then they returned to their hammocks and slept through the rest of the night.

13 The riverbanks are low, and from the river you see an unbroken wall of dark forest in every direction, from the Andes to the

Atlantic. You get a taste for looking at trees: trees hung with the swinging nests of yellow troupials, trees from which ant nests the size of grain sacks hang like black goiters, trees from which seven-colored tanagers flutter, coral trees, teak, balsa and breadfruit, enormous emergent silk-cotton trees, and the pale-barked *samona* palms.

When you are inside the jungle, away from the river, the trees vault out of sight. It is hard to remember to look up the long trunks and see the fans, strips, fronds, and sprays of glossy leaves. Inside the jungle you are more likely to notice the snarl of climbers and creepers round the trees' boles, the flowering bromeliads and epiphytes in every bough's crook, and the fantastic silk-cotton tree trunks thirty or forty feet across, trunks buttressed in flanges of wood whose curves can make three high walls of a room—a shady, loamy-aired room where you would gladly live, or die. Butterflies, iridescent blue, striped, or clear-winged, thread the jungle paths at eye level. And at your feet is a swath of ants bearing triangular bits of green leaf. The ants with their leaves look like a wide fleet of sailing dinghies—but they don't quit. In either direction they wobble over the jungle floor as far as the eye can see. I followed them off the path as far as I dared, and never saw an end to ants or to those luffing chips of green they bore. 14

Unseen in the jungle, but present, are tapirs, jaguars, many species of snake and lizard, ocelots, armadillos, marmosets, howler monkeys, toucans and macaws and a hundred other birds, deer, bats, peccaries, capybaras, agoutis, and sloths. Also present in this jungle, but variously distant, are Texaco derricks and pipelines, and some of the wildest Indians in the world, blowgun-using Indians, who killed missionaries in 1956 and ate them. 15

Long lakes shine in the jungle. We traveled one of these in dugout canoes, canoes with two inches of freeboard, canoes paddled with machete-hewn oars chopped from buttresses of silk-cotton trees, or poled in the shallows with peeled cane or bamboo. Our part-Indian guide had cleared the path to the lake the day before; when we walked the path we saw where he had impaled the lopped head of a boa, open-mouthed, on a pointed stick by the canoes, for decoration. 16

The lake was wonderful. Herons, egrets, and ibises plodded the sawgrass shores, kingfishers and cuckoos clattered from sunlight to shade, great turkeylike birds fussed in dead branches, and hawks lolled overhead. There was all the time in the world. A 17 turtle slid into the water. The boy in the bow of my canoe slapped stones at birds with a simple sling, a rubber throng and leather pad. He aimed brilliantly at moving targets, always, and always missed; the birds were out of range. He stuffed his sling back in his shirt. I looked around.

18 The lake and river waters are as opaque as rain-forest leaves; they are veils, blinds, painted screens. You see things only by their effects. I saw the shoreline water roil and the sawgrass heave above a thrashing *paichi,* an enormous black fish of these waters; one had been caught the previous week weighing 430 pounds. Piranha fish live in the lakes, and electric eels. I dangled my fingers in the water, figuring it would be worth it.

19 We would eat chicken that night in the village, and rice, yucca, onions, beets, and heaps of fruit. The sun would ring down, pulling darkness after it like a curtain. Twilight is short, and the unseen birds of twilight wistful, uncanny, catching the heart. The two nuns in their dazzling white habits—the beautiful-boned young nun and the warm-faced old—would glide to the open cane-and-thatch schoolroom in darkness, and start the children singing. The children would sing in piping Spanish, high-pitched and pure; they would sing "Nearer My God to Thee" in Quechua, very fast. (To reciprocate, we sang for them "Old MacDonald Had a Farm"; I thought they might recognize the animal sounds. Of course they thought we were out of our minds.) As the children became excited by their own singing, they left their log benches and swarmed around the nuns, hopping, smiling at us, everyone smiling, the nuns' faces bursting in their cowls, and the clear-voiced children still singing, and the palm-leafed roofing stirred.

20 The Napo River: it is not out of the way. It is *in* the way, catching sunlight the way a cup catches poured water; it is a bowl of sweet air, a basin of greenness, and of grace, and, it would seem, of peace.

BUILDING VOCABULARY

1. An important tool of description is *diction,* the word choices a writer makes. In the sentences below, substitute your own words for those in italics:
   a. Beneath us the brown Napo River was rising . . . it *coiled* up the *sandy* bank and *tangled* its *foam* in vines that

trailed from the forest and roots that *looped* the shore (par. 3).

b. [O]ne of the village's Jesuit priests began playing . . . a wordless song, lyric, in a minor key, that *twined* over the village clearing, that *caught* in the big trees' *canopies, muted* our talk on the *bankside,* and *wandered* over the river, *dissolving* downstream (par. 4)

2. One way the writer suggests the jungle is out of the way is to name its inhabitants. Look up the animal or plant names you don't know that appear in pars. 13, 14, 15, and 17.

THINKING CRITICALLY ABOUT THE ESSAY

Understanding the Writer's Ideas

1. The writer begins by saying that the jungle is out of the way. Out of the way of what? She ends however, by saying that the jungle river is "*in* the way." Of what? What is the implication of these apparently opposite points of view?
2. Why does the writer go to the jungle?
3. Where is the jungle that Dillard writes about?
4. At what time of year, and in what season, does the writer visit the jungle?
5. Who inhabits the village where the writer disembarks?
6. What does the writer mean when she says, "This will do" (par. 5)? Who else that is there evidently agrees with her?
7. The writer says that what she finds in the jungle is "interesting." How is it interesting for her?
8. What does the writer mean by saying "it would be worth it" when she dangles her fingers in water that is supposed to contain piranha—flesh eating jungle fish?
9. Are the writer and her companions at home in the jungle? How are they viewed by the natives?
10. The writer concludes by saying that Napo River is a place "of grace, and, it would seem, of peace." What evidence can you find in the essay to support this conclusion? What evidence is there that seems to support a different conclusion? Does the writer simply ignore this contrary evidence, or does she incorporate it into her view of the jungle? Explain.

Understanding the Writer's Techniques

1. What is the main idea of this essay? Where is it stated?
2. What is the effect of the opening paragraph of the essay? What is the relation of the opening paragraph to the thesis of the essay?
3. How does the writer establish that the jungle is "out of the way"?
4. The essay's introduction takes up five paragraphs. In what ways does the rest of the essay amplify the introduction?
5. How does the writer convey her attitude toward the natives?
6. What is the connection between the concluding sentence of par. 17—"I looked around"—and the theme of the essay? Why do you think this sentence appears at this point of the essay?
7. What aspects of the final two paragraphs contribute to an effective conclusion for the essay?

Exploring the Writer's Ideas

1. The writer ends her introduction with this sentence: "This will do, for a weekend, for a season, for a home." Do you find this progression of commitments believable—that is, are you persuaded that the writer is actually considering making the Napo River her home? If so, what evidence in the essay supports such a reading? If not, what evidence do you find to the contrary?
2. The writer says that, since we are "on the planet only once," we "might as well get a feel for the place." Does the writer persuade you that going to the jungle offers a significantly different "feel for the place" than staying at home (wherever home may be)? The nineteenth-century poet Emily Dickinson, who is considered one of the greatest American poets, is said almost never to have left her home village—Amherst, Massachusetts. What do you think she might have said to the writer about the pointlessness of travelling to the jungle? What might Dillard have said to persuade Emily Dickinson to come along to the Napo River?
3. The natives of this region, the writer reports, have eaten people in the past. One native boy in her party aims at birds with stones, and the part-native guide puts a snake's head on a pole

for decoration. What is Dillard's attitude towards these "out-of-the-way" behaviors? Do you share her attitude? If so, why? If not, why not?

IDEAS FOR WRITING

Prewriting

Think about an experience of yours that was "out-of-the-way" and whose "strangeness" seemed full of lessons or richness of experience. Write down some of the things you particularly remember about that experience.

Guided Writing

Write an essay describing a place or experience that is as "out-of-the-way" of your usual lifestyle as possible, but which you can show as "interesting" in itself and instructive about what to value in your usual everyday life. (You might think of a neighborhood completely different from your own, or, say, a meal—Thanksgiving dinner at the soup kitchen—completely different from what to you is "usual.")

1. Begin, as Dillard does, by identifying where you are, and catching yourself thinking what an out-of-the-way place or experience this is.
2. Give a graphic description of the place—but not yet of the people who inhabit it.
3. Suggest, through more description, how this place has features deeper, richer, more intense than the places where you usually spend your days.
4. Now pause to reflect: hmm, is this a place where I might want to live?
5. Describe the people in this place through your interaction with them.
6. Write about what you notice in the place upon better acquaintance, maybe later in the day or just before leaving.
7. End by thinking back, now that you have returned to your routine, about how the out-of-the-way place is *in* the way of . . .

Thinking and Writing Collaboratively

In small groups discuss your impressions of places you have been that are different from those you are used to and people you have known who are completely different from you. What qualities of these other places and other people most impress you? What do other places and people make you miss most about your usual life? What do they make you want most to add to your usual life?

Writing About the Text

Dillard tells us, through many details, about the jungle. She contrasts the jungle with an implicit picture of the non-jungle where she lives. Write an essay that looks at those implicit contrasts and that explores her essay not in terms of *description* but rather in terms of *argument* or *persuasion.* Is the jungle a place rich in things and values that are absent from the non-jungle? Does Dillard "romanticize" the jungle? Does Dillard make you want to go to the jungle? If yes, why? If not, why not?

More Writing Projects

1. In your journal write an essay about travelling as a nuisance, a bore, a rip-off . . . .
2. Spend a day in a place that is as close to being wild as you can find near where you live. For at least an hour of that day, sit still in one spot. Write a descriptive paragraph about your day.
3. Who are the nuns and priests in the jungle? Why do the boys wear blue jeans? On the basis of some outside reading, or online research, write an essay that discusses some aspect of the encounter, in the Amazon, between the old and new worlds and between the "first world" and the "third."

Catfish in the Bathtub

Maxine Hong Kingston

Born in 1940 in Stockton, California, Maxine Hong Kingston is the daughter of Chinese immigrants. Her first language was Say Yup, a dialect of Cantonese. She was named "Maxine" after a lucky blonde gambler who frequented the gambling house where her scholarly father was forced to find work. She received a B.A. from the University of California at Berkeley, and is married to the actor Earll Kingston. Her first book, *The Woman Warrior* (1976), vividly depicts her experience growing up as a girl and young woman in the United States but within an intensely Chinese-American home and culture. *China Men* (1980) is a sequel to *The Woman Warrior,* exploring the experience of being Chinese-American males. Kingston has also published a collection of prose writing about her residence in Hawaii—*Hawaii One Summer* (1987)—and the novel *Tripmaster Monkey: His Fake Book* (1989). This selection from *The Woman Warrior* is one of many vignettes in that book about Kingston's mother, a larger-than-life figure. Through a colorful evocation of the strange food her mother served up, Kingston portrays a world of difference that is at once rich and weird, powerful and repelling. She brings that world to life by means of a style that is characteristically fierce, poetic, and tender all at the same time.

PREREADING: THINKING ABOUT THE ESSAY IN ADVANCE

What unusual foods have you eaten? What unusual dish can you remember one of your relatives preparing when you were a child? How did you feel about eating this food?

Words to Watch

dromedaries (par. 1) one-humped camels
sensibility (par. 1) ability to receive sensations
perched (par. 1) resting on a bird's roost
scowls (par. 1) expressions of displeasure
dismembering (par. 1) taking apart bodily limbs and innards
sprains (par. 2) sudden twists of joints such as ankles or wrists
unsettle (par. 3) make uneasy or uncomfortable

tufts (par. 4) forms into small patches of hair
awobble (par. 6) unsteady; teetering
toadstools (par. 7) mushrooms
revulsion (par. 8) a strong reaction away from something

1 My mother has cooked for us: raccoons, skunks, hawks, city pigeons, wild ducks, wild geese, black-skinned bantams, snakes, garden snails, turtles that crawled about the pantry floor and sometimes escaped under refrigerator or stove, catfish that swam in the bathtub. "The emperors used to eat the peaked hump of purple dromedaries," she would say. "They used chopsticks made from rhinoceros horn, and they ate ducks' tongues and monkeys' lips." She boiled the weeds we pulled up in the yard. There was a tender plant with flowers like white stars hiding under the leaves, which were like the flower petals but green. I've not been able to find it since growing up. It had no taste. When I was as tall as the washing machine, I stepped out on the back porch one night, and some heavy, ruffling, windy, clawed thing dived at me. Even after getting chanted back to sensibility, I shook when I recalled that perched everywhere there were owls with great hunched shoulders and yellow scowls. They were a surprise for my mother from my father. We children used to hide under the beds with our fingers in our ears to shut out the bird screams and the thud, thud of the turtles swimming in the boiling water, their shells hitting the sides of the pot. Once the third aunt who worked at the laundry ran out and bought us bags of candy to hold over our noses; my mother was dismembering skunk on the chopping block. I could smell the rubbery odor through the candy.

2 In a glass jar on a shelf my mother kept a big brown hand with pointed claws stewing in alcohol and herbs. She must have brought it from China because I do not remember a time when I did not have the hand to look at. She said it was a bear's claw, and for many years I thought bears were hairless. My mother used the tobacco, leeks, and grasses swimming about the hand to rub our sprains and bruises.

3 Just as I would climb up to the shelf to take one look after another at the hand, I would hear my mother's monkey story. I'd take my fingers out of my ears and let her monkey words enter my brain. I did not always listen voluntarily, though. She would begin telling the story, perhaps repeating it to a homesick villager, and

I'd overhear before I had a chance to protect myself. Then the monkey words would unsettle me; a curtain flapped loose inside my brain. I have wanted to say, "Stop it. Stop it," but not once did I say, "Stop it."

"Do you know what people in China eat when they have the money?" my mother began. "They buy into a monkey feast. The eaters sit around a thick wood table with a hole in the middle. Boys bring in the monkey at the end of a pole. Its neck is in a collar at the end of the pole, and it is screaming. Its hands are tied behind it. They clamp the monkey into the table; the whole table fits like another collar around its neck. Using a surgeon's saw, the cooks cut a clean line in a circle at the top of its head. To loosen the bone, they tap with a tiny hammer and wedge here and there with a silver pick. Then an old woman reaches out her hand to the monkey's face and up to its scalp, where she tufts some hairs and lifts off the lid of the skull. The eaters spoon out the brains." 4

Did she say, "You should have seen the faces the monkey made"? Did she say, "The people laughed at the monkey screaming"? It was alive? The curtain flaps closed like merciful black wings. 5

"Eat! Eat!" my mother would shout at our heads bent over bowls, the blood pudding awobble in the middle of the table. 6

She had one rule to keep us safe from toadstools and such: "If it tastes good, it's bad for you," she said. "If it tastes bad, it's good for you." 7

We'd have to face four- and five-day-old leftovers until we ate it all. The squid eye would keep appearing at breakfast and dinner until eaten. Sometimes brown masses sat on every dish. I have seen revulsion on the faces of visitors who've caught us at meals. 8

"Have you eaten yet?" the Chinese greet one another. 9

"Yes, I have," they answer whether they have or not. "And you?" 10

I would live on plastic. 11

BUILDING VOCABULARY

1. Go through this essay again and list every animal mentioned. Then, write a short description of each, using the dictionary or encyclopedia if necessary.
2. Use any five of the Words to Watch in sentences of your own.

THINKING CRITICALLY ABOUT THE ESSAY

Understanding the Writer's Ideas

1. What is Kingston saying about her childhood? How does her opening catalogue of foods that her mother prepared, combined with further descriptions of foods, support this point? What are some of the "strange" foods that she ate but that are not mentioned in this first paragraph?
2. Who are "the emperors" mentioned in paragraph 1? What were some of their more unusual dishes?
3. What attacks and frightens the young Kingston on her back porch? Where did they come from? How do we know that she was a young girl at the time? Explain the meaning of "even after getting chanted back to sensibility."
4. At the end of the first paragraph, the writer mentions methods that she and her siblings used to shut out unpleasant sensory input. What were they?
5. For what purpose did her mother keep a bear's claw in a glass jar? Where did Kingston think it came from? Why?
6. What are the "monkey words"? Summarize the "monkey words" in your own language. Kingston says that she wanted to say "Stop it" to the monkey words, but didn't. Why didn't she?
7. What was Kingston's mother's attitude toward the taste of things in relation to their healthfulness?
8. Why would there sometimes be "revulsion on the faces of visitors" who watched the author's family eating?
9. What is the traditional Chinese greeting?
10. What is the writer's overall attitude toward her mother? Explain.

Understanding the Writer's Techniques

1. Does Kingston ever make a direct *thesis statement?* Why or why not?
2. In this essay, Kingston seems to shift in and out of various tenses deliberately. For example, in paragraph 3, she writes: ". . . a curtain *flapped* loose inside my brain. I *have wanted* to say. . . ." Why do you think that Kingston uses such a technique? List three other examples of such tense shifts.

3. Comment on Kingston's use of transitions. How do they contribute to the overall *coherence* (see Glossary) of the essay?
4. How does Kingston use the five senses to create descriptive imagery? Give examples of her use of sounds, tastes, smells, sights, and feelings. Which are the most effective?
5. Eliminating the specific references to China, how do we know that the writer is of Chinese background? Which details or references contribute to this understanding?
6. Evaluate the use of *dialogue* (records of spoken words or conversations) in this essay. What effect does it have on the flow of the writing? On our understanding of Kingston's main point?
7. In paragraph 1, why does the writer give so much attention to the white flower stars with no taste? Is she merely describing yet another thing she ate, or does she have some other purpose? Explain.
8. Although other incidents or ideas are described rather briefly, Kingston devotes a full, detailed paragraph to a description of the monkey feast. Why?
9. Throughout the essay, Kingston combines very realistic description (the bear's claw, the turtles thudding against the cook pot, the monkey feast) with various *similes* and *metaphors* (see Glossary). Explain the meaning of the following uses of *figurative language* (see Glossary):
   - **a.** a curtain flapped loose inside my brain (par. 3)
   - **b.** The curtain flaps closed like merciful black wings. (par. 5)
   - **c.** Sometimes brown masses sat on every dish. (par. 8)
10. What is the effect of the series of questions in paragraph 5? Why are some in quotations and others not?
11. Explain the meaning of the last sentence. How does it relate to Kingston's *purpose* (see Glossary) in this essay?

Exploring the Writer' Ideas

1. Kingston certainly describes some "strange" foods and eating habits in this essay. But what makes particular foods "strange"? What are some of the strangest foods you have ever eaten? Where did they come from? Why did you eat them? How did you react to them? What foods or eating habits that are common to your everyday life might be considered strange by people from other cultures?

2. In this essay, Kingston concentrates on her mother, mentioning her father only once. Speculate on why she excludes her father in this way, but base your speculation on the material of the essay.
3. As we all know, different cultures have very different customs. In this essay, for example, the writer describes the Chinese way of greeting one another as well as the monkey feast, both of which are quite foreign to American culture. Describe different cultural customs that you have observed in your school, among your friends, in places around your city or town. How do you feel when you observe customs different from the ones you are familiar with? Do you believe that any particular custom is "right" or "wrong"? Why? Which custom among your own culture's would you most like to see changed? Why?
4. Describe your reaction to the monkey feast description.
5. For what reason do you think the Chinese greet each other with the words "Have you eaten yet?" Attempt to do further research on this custom. List as many different ways as you know of people greeting one another.

IDEAS FOR WRITING

Prewriting

Write the words *Family Food* on top of a sheet of paper and write everything that comes to mind about the topic. Give yourself about five minutes or so. Do not edit your writing: put as many of your ideas as you can on paper.

Guided Writing

Write an essay entitled "Food" in which you describe its importance to you, your family, and your cultural background.

1. Begin with a list of important foods related to your family's lifestyle.
2. Show the role of your parents or other relatives in relation to these foods.
3. Briefly tell about an incident involving food that affected you deeply.

4. Create strong sensory imagery. Attempt to use at least one image for each of the five senses.
5. If possible, relate food customs to your family's ethnic or cultural background.
6. Use dialogue in your essay, including some of the dialogue of your "inner voice."
7. Use transitions to make the parts of your essay cohere.
8. Mention how outsiders experienced this custom.
9. End your essay with a direct statement to summarize your current attitude toward the food you have described and those times in your life.

Thinking and Writing Collaboratively

Read a draft of the Guided Writing essay by one of your classmates. Then, write a paragraph to indicate what you learned about the importance of food to the writer and to his or her family and cultural background. What parts of the essay stand out most in your mind? Where do you think the writer might have included further details?

Writing About the Text

The power of Kingston's writing derives in part from the power of her descriptions. These are often startling, even bizarre. Write an essay that takes a close, careful look at some of her descriptions. Aim to weigh the question of whether she has painted an exaggerated picture in order to shock, or whether her pictures reflect a complex reality, one aspect of which is indeed shocking.

More Writing Projects

1. In your journal, write a description of an interesting custom or activity that you witnessed, a custom coming from outside your own cultural or social background. Include vivid sensory details.
2. Write a paragraph describing in detail the most wonderful meal you have ever eaten.
3. Research and write a short report about the food and eating customs of a culture other than your own.

The Discus Thrower

Richard Selzer

Born in 1928 in Troy, New York, Richard Selzer is a graduate of the Albany Medical College and of Yale, where he also taught until 1985 as Assistant Clinical Professor of Surgery. His father was a family doctor, and his mother a singer. Selzer fulfilled the ambitions of both parents for their son by becoming a writer as well as a surgeon. His first book was a collection of short stories, *Rituals of Surgery* (1973). Other works from Selzer's considerable output include *Confessions of a Knife* (1979), a book of 24 essays, most about surgery, and *Imagine a Woman* (1990), a collection of five novellas. In 1991 Selzer contracted Legionnaire's disease but fortunately, after 23 days in a coma, recovered to write *Raising the Dead: A Doctor's Encounter with His Own Mortality* (1994). Selzer's writing brings a sense of acute perception, both of things seen and of moral nuance, to the often-hidden world of medicine with its triumphs but also its suffering, pain, and death. This selection, from *Confessions of a Knife,* dramatically describes a patient's last day of life.

PREREADING: THINKING ABOUT THE ESSAY IN ADVANCE

What experiences have you had with hospital patients? Have you ever visited anyone in a hospital? What was the experience like? What did the patient look like?

Words to Watch

furtive (par. 1) sly

pruned (par. 2) cut back; trimmed

facsimile (par. 2) an exact copy

forceps (par. 19) an instrument used in operations for holding or pulling

shard (par. 19) a broken piece; fragment

athwart (par. 20) across

probes (par. 32) investigates thoroughly

hefts (par. 32) tests the weight of by lifting; heaves

1 I spy on my patients. Ought not a doctor to observe his patients by any means and from any stance, that he might the more fully assemble evidence? So I stand in the doorways of hospital rooms

and gaze. Oh, it is not all that furtive an act. Those in bed need only look up to discover me. But they never do.

From the doorway of Room 542 the man in the bed seems 2
deeply tanned. Blue eyes and close-cropped white hair give him the appearance of vigor and good health. But I know that his skin is not brown from the sun. It is rusted, rather, in the last stage of containing the vile repose within. And the blue eyes are frosted, looking inward like the windows of a snowbound cottage. This man is blind. This man is also legless—the right leg missing from midthigh down, the left from just below the knee. It gives him the look of a bonsai, roots and branches pruned into the dwarfed facsimile of a great tree.

Propped on pillows, he cups his right thigh in both hands. 3
Now and then he shakes his head as though acknowledging the intensity of his suffering. In all of this he makes no sound. Is he mute as well as blind?

The room in which he dwells is empty of all possessions—no 4
get-well cards, small, private caches of food, day-old flowers, slippers, all the usual kick-shaws of the sickroom. There is only the bed, a chair, a nightstand, and a tray on wheels that can be swung across his lap for meals.

"What time is it?" he asks. 5

"Three o'clock." 6

"Morning or afternoon?" 7

"Afternoon." 8

He is silent. There is nothing else he wants to know. 9

"How are you?" I say. 10

"Who is it?" he asks. 11

"It's the doctor. How do you feel?" 12

He does not answer right away. 13

"Feel?" he says. 14

"I hope you feel better," I say. 15

I press the button at the side of the bed. 16

"Down you go," I say. 17

"Yes, down," he says. 18

He falls back upon the bed awkwardly. His stumps, un- 19
weighted by legs and feet, rise in the air, presenting themselves. I unwrap the bandages from the stumps, and begin to cut away the black scabs and the dead, glazed fat with scissors and forceps. A shard of white bone comes loose. I pick it away. I wash the wounds with disinfectant and redress the stumps. All this while, he

does not speak. What is he thinking behind those lids that do not blink? Is he remembering a time when he was whole? Does he dream of feet? Of when his body was not a rotting log?

20 He lies solid and inert. In spite of everything, he remains impressive, as though he were a sailor standing athwart a slanting deck.

21 "Anything more I can do for you?" I ask.

22 For a long moment he is silent.

23 "Yes," he says at last and without the least irony. "You can bring me a pair of shoes."

24 In the corridor, the head nurse is waiting for me.

25 "We have to do something about him," she says. "Every morning he orders scrambled eggs for breakfast, and, instead of eating them, he picks up the plate and throws it against the wall."

26 "Throws his plate?"

27 "Nasty. That's what he is. No wonder his family doesn't come to visit. They probably can't stand him any more than we can."

28 She is waiting for me to do something.

29 "Well?"

30 "We'll see," I say.

31 The next morning I am waiting in the corridor when the kitchen delivers his breakfast. I watch the aide place the tray on the stand and swing it across his lap. She presses the button to raise the head of the bed. Then she leaves.

32 In time the man reaches to find the rim of the tray, then on to find the dome of the covered dish. He lifts off the cover and places it on the stand. He fingers across the plate until he probes the eggs. He lifts the plate in both hands, sets it on the palm of his right hand, centers it, balances it. He hefts it up and down slightly, getting the feel of it. Abruptly, he draws back his right arm as far as he can.

33 There is the crack of the plate breaking against the wall at the foot of his bed and the small wet sound of the scrambled eggs dropping to the floor.

34 And then he laughs. It is a sound you have never heard. It is something new under the sun. It could cure cancer.

35 Out in the corridor, the eyes of the head nurse narrow.

36 "Laughed, did he?"

37 She writes something down on her clipboard.

38 A second aide arrives, brings a second breakfast tray, puts it on the nightstand, out of his reach. She looks over at me shaking

her head and making her mouth go. I see that we are to be accomplices.

"I've got to feed you," she says to the man. 39

"Oh, no you don't," the man says. 40

"Oh, yes I do," the aide says, "after the way you just did. 41
Nurse says so."

"Get me my shoes," the man says. 42

"Here's oatmeal," the aide says. "Open." And she touches the 43
spoon to his lower lip.

"I ordered scrambled eggs," says the man. 44

"That's right," the aide says. 45

I step forward. 46

"Is there anything I can do?" I say. 47

"Who are you?" the man asks. 48

In the evening I go once more to that ward to make my 49
rounds. The head nurse reports to me that Room 542 is deceased. She has discovered this quite by accident, she says. No, there had been no sound. Nothing. It's a blessing, she says.

I go into his room, a spy looking for secrets. He is still there in 50
his bed. His face is relaxed, grave, dignified. After a while, I turn to leave. My gaze sweeps the wall at the foot of the bed, and I see the place where it has been repeatedly washed, where the wall looks very clean and very white.

BUILDING VOCABULARY

1. In this essay, Selzer uses a few words that derive from languages other than English. Look up the following words and tell what language they come from. Then, write a definition for each.
   a. bonsai (par. 2)
   b. caches (par. 4)
   c. kick-shaws (par. 4)
2. Use these words from the essay in complete sentences of your own.
   a. vile (par. 2)
   b. repose (par. 2)
   c. dwarfed (par. 2)
   d. glazed (par. 19)
   e. inert (par. 20)
   f. accomplices (par. 38)

THINKING CRITICALLY ABOUT THE ESSAY

Understanding the Writer's Ideas

1. What reason does Selzer give for a doctor's spying on his patients?
2. What does the man in Room 542 look like? Why is his skin brown? How does Selzer know he is blind? Why does Selzer think the patient may be mute? When do we know that he is not mute?
3. What is the writer's meaning of the phrase "vile repose" (par. 2)?
4. How do we know that this patient does not receive many visitors?
5. Aside from wanting to know the time of day, what is the patient's one request? Do you think he is serious about his request? Why?
6. Why does the patient hurl his food tray against the wall?
7. For what reason does the head nurse complain about the patient?
8. What does Selzer feel and think about the patient? How do you know?

Understanding the Writer's Techniques

1. What is the writer's thesis? Where is it stated?
2. Throughout the essay, Selzer asks a number of questions. Locate at least three of these questions that are not a part of the dialogue. To whom do you think they are addressed? What is their effect on the reader?
3. Selzer heightens the description by making vivid and unusual comparisons. Locate and explain in your own words three comparisons that you feel are especially descriptive and intriguing.
4. Selzer uses some very short sentences interspersed among longer ones. Locate at least four very short sentences. How do they draw your attention to the description?
5. Locate in Selzer's essay at least five examples of vivid description (imagery) relating to illness. What is their emotional effect on the reader?
6. How does Selzer use *dialogue* to reveal the personality of the patient? of the doctor? of the head nurse?

7. In paragraph 23, Selzer states that the patient delivers his request "without the least irony." *Irony* (see Glossary) is saying what is opposite to what one means. Why might Selzer have expected irony from the patient? Why might someone in the sick man's condition use irony? What do you think the man means by his request "You can bring me a pair of shoes"—if, in fact, the remark is not an ironical one?
8. What does the title of the essay mean? What is a discus thrower? Why has Selzer chosen an ancient image of an athlete as the title of this essay? In what way is the title ironic?
9. Why does Selzer use such an unusual word as *kick-shaws* (par. 4)?
10. *Double entendre* is a French expression that indicates that something has a double meaning, each equally valid. What might be the two meanings of the nurse's words "It's a blessing"?
11. In this essay, the author uses a *framing* device: that is, he opens and closes the essay with a similar image or idea. What is that idea? Why is it effective? What are the differences in the use of this idea in the opening and closing paragraphs?
12. The heart of this essay is the patient's insistence upon throwing his breakfast plate at the wall, and yet Selzer does not attempt to explain the man's reasons for such an act. Why do you think the man hurls his breakfast across the room each morning—and why does he laugh? Why does Selzer not provide an analysis of the action? How does the title help us see Selzer's attitude toward the man's act?

Exploring the Writer's Ideas

1. In the beginning of the essay Selzer asks, "Ought not a doctor to observe his patients by any means from any stance, that he might the more fully assemble evidence?" Do you feel that a doctor should have this right? Why? What rights do you believe patients should have in a hospital?
2. The head nurse in Selzer's description seems fed up with the patient in Room 542. Why do you think she feels this way? Do you think that a person in her position has the right to express this feeling on his or her job? Why or why not?
3. The patient's attitude is influenced by his physical state and his nearness to death. How have physical ailments or handi-

caps changed the attitudes of people you have known? Has an illness influenced your thoughts at any time?

IDEAS FOR WRITING

Prewriting

How can you tell when a person is ill or under stress? Make a list of the behavioral qualities that tell you that the person is not him- or herself.

Guided Writing

Describe a person you have observed who was seriously ill, in danger, or under great stress.

1. Base your description on close observation of the person during a short but concentrated span of time: a morning or afternoon, an hour or two, even a few minutes.
2. Begin with a short, direct paragraph in which you introduce the person and the critical situation he or she faces.
3. Include yourself ("I") in the description.
4. Describe the vantage point from which you are "spying" or observing, and focus on the particular subject of the scene.
5. Throughout your essay, ask key questions.
6. Use imagery and original comparisons to highlight the description of your subject.
7. Include some dialogue with either the subject or another person.
8. Describe at least one very intense action performed by your subject.
9. Tell how the subject and scene had changed when you next saw them.

Thinking and Writing Collaboratively

Assisted suicide for terminally ill patients has received a great deal of attention in the national press recently. Form discussion groups of about five students and consider the issue. Then, have the group write a paragraph summarizing its views on a patient's "right to die."

Writing About the Text

Life and death—how frequently we juxtapose the two, how often the words are bound together ("It was a life-and-death situation"). The head nurse finds the patient irritating and at best pathetic. But Selzer, recognizing the reasons for this view, sees something different, and finds both dignity and power in this dreadfully maimed dying man. Write an essay that tries to show how Selzer achieves this, perhaps surprising, effect.

More Writing Projects

1. In your journal, describe a hospital room in which you stayed or visited some other person. Focus on your sensory perceptions of the place.
2. Describe in an extended paragraph an interaction you had with a person who was blind or deaf or was disabled in some other way. In your description, focus closely on the person's features. Write about your reactions during and after the interaction.
3. Using both description and commentary, analyze the people you observe in one of the following situations: a bus or train during rush hour; breakfast at a diner or restaurant; a sports event or concert. Incorporate the description and observation into a five-paragraph essay.

The Death of the Moth

Virginia Woolf

Virginia Woolf (1882–1941) is one of the handful of major figures who developed the modern English novel. The daughter of a leading Victorian man-of-letters, Leslie Stephen, and Julia Duckworth, of a prominent publishing family, Woolf was raised in the heart of late-nineteenth-century intellectual London. She was mainly educated at home, however, and did not attend a university, a fact that she bitterly resented all her life. Her adolescence and young adulthood were shadowed by the deaths of her mother (in 1895), half-sister (in 1897), her father (in 1904), and finally her beloved brother Thoby (in 1906). In addition, she was plagued by mental illness all her life, exhibiting classic manic-depressive symptoms and suffering serious mental breakdowns at the ages of 13, 22, 28, and 30.

After the death of her father, Woolf, her sister Vanessa, who was to become an important English painter, and her brothers Thoby and Adrian moved into a house in the mainly commercial Bloomsbury district of London. They began to entertain friends on Thursday evenings, a practice that led to the "Bloomsbury Group," a loose but nonetheless highly influential modernist circle that came to include the biographer Lytton Strachey, the leading twentieth-century economist John Maynard Keynes, the art critic Roger Fry, and occasionally figures such as the poet T. S. Eliot and the novelist E. M. Forster.

In 1912 Woolf married the editor and political writer Leonard Woolf. In her writing Virginia Woolf rejected the realist conventions of the Victorian novel, seeking instead to capture the rush of sensations—physical, emotional, spiritual—that she believed actually constitute our inner reality. Her major works include the novels *Mrs. Dalloway* (1925) and *To The Lighthouse* (1927) as well as *A Room of One's Own* (1929), a classic extended essay on the condition of women. This selection is representative of Woolf's experimental narratives, which draw profound truths from fleeting impressions or the rush of thought and sensation of a "moment." Woolf drowned herself in the River Ouse near her home in Sussex towards the end of March 1941.

PREREADING: THINKING ABOUT THE ESSAY IN ADVANCE

Moths are usually unseen and, unless we catch them eating holes in our sweaters, insignificant. Does pausing to notice a moth seem therefore a waste of time, or at least an eccentric activity? Death may also, like a moth, be unseen, but we attribute to it enormous significance. What does the association of death and a moth suggest? What kind of an essay do you anticipate? A zoological reflection? A technical description? A comic piece?

Words to Watch

hybrid (par. 1) mixed, originating in more than one source

benignant (par. 1) kindly, gentle

share (par. 1) plough

down (par. 1) a treeless, undulating upland

rook (par. 1) a common English bird, related to the American crow

vociferation (par. 1) shouting

circumspection (par. 3) tact

mean (par. 5) small

Moths that fly by day are not properly to be called moths; they do not excite that pleasant sense of dark autumn nights and ivy-blossom which the commonest yellow underwing asleep in the shadow of the curtain never fails to rouse in us. They are hybrid creatures, neither gay like butterflies nor sombre like their own species. Nevertheless the present specimen, with his narrow hay-coloured wings, fringed with a tassel of the same colour, seemed to be content with life. It was a pleasant morning, mid-September, mild, benignant, yet with a keener breath than that of the summer months. The plough was already scoring the field opposite the window, and where the share had been, the earth was pressed flat and gleamed with moisture. Such vigour came rolling in from the fields and the down beyond that it was difficult to keep the eyes strictly turned upon the book. The rooks too were keeping one of their annual festivities; soaring round the tree-tops until it looked as if a vast net with thousands of black knots in it has been cast up into the air; which, after a few moments sank slowly down upon the trees until every twig seemed to have a knot at the end of it. Then, suddenly, the net would be thrown into the air again in a wider circle this time, with the utmost clamour and vociferation, as though to be thrown into the air and settle slowly down upon the tree-tops were a tremendously exciting experience. 1

The same energy which inspired the rooks, the ploughmen, the horses, and even, it seemed, the lean bare-backed downs, sent the moth fluttering from side to side of his square of the windowpane. One could not help watching him. One was, indeed, conscious of a 2 queer feeling of pity for him. The possibilities of pleasure seemed that morning so enormous and so various that to have only a moth's part in life, and a day moth's at that, appeared a hard fate, and his zest in enjoying his meagre opportunities to the full, pathetic. He flew vigorously to one corner of his compartment, and, after waiting there a second, flew across to the other. What remained for him but to fly to a third corner and then to a fourth? That was all he could do, in spite of the size of the downs, the width of the sky, the far-off smoke of houses, and the romantic voice, now and then, of a steamer out at sea. What he could do he did. Watching him, it seemed as if a fibre, very thin but pure, of the enormous energy of the world had been thrust into his frail and diminutive body. As often as he crossed the pane, I could fancy that a thread of vital light became visible. He was little or nothing but life.

3 Yet, because he was so small, and so simple a form of the energy that was rolling in at the open window and driving its way through so many narrow and intricate corridors in my own brain and in those of other human beings, there was something marvelous as well as pathetic about him. It was as if someone had taken a tiny bead of pure life and decking it as lightly as possible with down and feathers, had set it dancing and zigzagging to show us the true nature of life. Thus displayed one could not get over the strangeness of it. One is apt to forget all about life, seeing it humped and bossed and garnished and cumbered so that it has to move with the greatest circumspection and dignity. Again, the thought of all that life might have been had he been born in any other shape caused one to view his simple activities with a kind of pity.

4 After a time, tired by his dancing apparently, he settled on the window ledge in the sun, and the queer spectacle being at an end, I forgot about him. Then, looking up, my eye was caught by him. He was trying to resume his dancing, but seemed either so stiff or so awkward that he could only flutter to the bottom of the window-pane; and when he tried to fly across it he failed. Being intent on other matters I watched these futile attempts for a time without thinking, unconsciously waiting for him to resume his flight, as one waits for a machine, that has stopped momentarily, to start again without considering the reason for its failure. After perhaps a seventh attempt he slipped from the wooden ledge and fell, fluttering his wings, on to his back on the window-sill. The helplessness of his attitude roused me. It flashed upon me that he was

in difficulties; he could no longer raise himself, his legs struggled vainly. But, as I stretched out a pencil, meaning to help him to right himself, it came over me that the failure and awkwardness were the approach of death. I laid the pencil down again.

5 The legs agitated themselves once more. I looked as if for the enemy against which he struggled. I looked out of doors. What had happened there? Presumably it was midday, and work in the fields had stopped. Stillness and quiet had replaced the previous animation. The birds had taken themselves off to feed in the brooks. The horses stood still. Yet the power was there all the same, massed outside indifferent, impersonal, not attending to anything in particular. Somehow it was opposed to the little hay-coloured moth. It was useless to try to do anything. One could only watch the extraordinary efforts made by those tiny legs against an oncoming doom which could, had it chosen, have submerged an entire city, not merely a city, but masses of human beings; nothing, I knew, had any chance against death. Nevertheless after a pause of exhaustion the legs fluttered again. It was superb this last protest, and so frantic that he succeeded at last in righting himself. One's sympathies, of course, were all on the side of life. Also, when there was nobody to care or to know, this gigantic effort on the part of an insignificant little moth, against a power of such magnitude, to retain what no one else valued or desired to keep, moved one strangely. Again, somehow, one saw life, a pure bead. I lifted the pencil again, useless though I knew it to be. But even as I did so, the unmistakable tokens of death showed themselves. The body relaxed, and instantly grew stiff. The struggle was over. The insignificant little creature now knew death. As I looked at the dead moth, this minute wayside triumph of so great a force over so mean an antagonist filled me with wonder. Just as life had been strange a few minutes before, so death was now as strange. The moth having righted himself now lay most decently and uncomplainingly composed. O yes, he seemed to say, death is stronger than I am.

BUILDING VOCABULARY

British and American English often diverge subtly, especially in certain kinds of usage. Rewrite the following in a more contemporary, American English.

a. One was, indeed, conscious of a queer feeling of pity for him (par. 2).
b. As he crossed the pane, I could fancy that a thread of vital light became visible (par. 2).
c. One is apt to forget all about life, seeing it humped and bossed and garnished and cumbered so that it has to move with the greatest circumspection and dignity (par. 3).
d. It flashed upon me that he was in difficulties . . . (par. 4).

THINKING CRITICALLY ABOUT THE ESSAY

Understanding the Writer's Ideas

1. What is the connection between the September day outside and the moth at Woolf's window?
2. At first Woolf feels pity for the moth. Why?
3. How does the writer's attitude change as she watches the moth further?
4. Why does Woolf think we forget about life (par. 3)?
5. After ignoring him for a time, the writer looks up to notice the moth again. What has changed? What is the writer's reaction to the change?
6. Why does the writer look outdoors as the moth struggles? What does she see outdoors?
7. What is "superb" (par. 5) about the moth's final effort to live?
8. What fills the writer with wonder at the conclusion of her essay?

Understanding the Writer's Techniques

1. This selection is composed of five fairly equal paragraphs. Write an outline of the essay using no more than one sentence to capture the essence of each paragraph.
2. Does this essay have a thesis statement? If so, where is it to be found? If not, how does the writer communicate her main point?
3. The writer's observation of the moth occupies at most a couple of hours. How does she make the passing of time apparent to the reader? How does she achieve a sense of continuous progression from the beginning to the end of the essay?

4. A key aspect of description is depiction of vivid and compelling images. Choose two or three of Woolf's images and explain what makes them especially effective.
5. Discuss Woolf's use of the contrast between indoors and outdoors. What other structural or rhetorical devices help the writer achieve her effects?
6. Is the *tone* of the essay consistent throughout? What is the *tone* of the conclusion? How is the conclusion a highly compressed summary of the essay as a whole?

MIXING PATTERNS

Description is the basic mode of development in this essay, but Woolf also uses narrative and illustration. In what ways do these strategies help advance her point? For example, Woolf's essay can be seen as an extended illustration of the human condition. How does Woolf use the moth to illustrate larger themes?

Exploring the Writer's Ideas

1. Often in this essay Woolf attributes feelings to the moth. He "seemed content with life" (par. 1); ". . . tired by his dancing apparently . . ." (par. 4); "The helplessness of his attitude roused me" (par. 4)—and so forth. Is Woolf describing what she sees? Or is she imposing feelings and attitudes on the moth for the sake of her essay? Does it matter? Explain.
2. Consider the implications of the essay's title. What would be different if it were called "Death of a Moth"?
3. What is the writer's attitude toward death? Does she confront death as the moth does, or differently? Explain.
4. If you had been in Woolf s position, do you think you would have noticed the moth? Would you have written about the moth? Virginia Woolf tried to kill herself more than once, and she finally ended her life by drowning herself in a river near her home. Do you think this essay in any way hints at her suicide; or, in retrospect, can we learn anything about Woolf s attitude toward, or attraction toward, the moth from the fact of her suicide?

IDEAS FOR WRITING

Prewriting

Locate some small living creature, say, a spider or an ant, a dog or a cat, or perhaps even a baby. Observe the creature you have chosen for fifteen minutes or longer (long enough to have observed what seems to you an evocative fifteen minutes). Note carefully what it does, and note carefully what ideas the creature's actions prompt in you.

Guided Writing

Write an essay called "Fifteen Minutes in the Life of . . ." and choose something small but alive to write about—an ant, a dog or cat, or a human or animal baby. Observe your subject carefully, over a matter of days so that you can identify the most evocative fifteen minutes of the creature's life to write about.

1. Begin by identifying your subject and by setting your subject in a possibly contrastive context—if you are inside, for example, identify the weather and activities outside, or if you are looking at an anthill, mention the busy human street nearby.
2. Describe the main activity of your subject, as well as the emotions and thoughts that the subject evokes in you.
3. Describe the difficulties of watching something small for an extended period of time, and what, if anything, distracts you.
4. Describe how you are once more caught up in watching your subject; capture what is happening in the context, too.
5. Bring the activity of the subject to a crucial point or crisis—the achievement of something, such as capturing a fly for a spider, or turning over for a baby, or . . . This can be an actual achievement, or a frustrated effort, or a defeat.
6. Discuss your thoughts on the crisis.
7. Bring the essay to a close with an appropriate concluding sentence or two.

Thinking and Writing Collaboratively

We are surrounded by living and dying that usually we don't notice. In small groups of five or six, discuss those occasions where you have suddenly encountered a life you usually are wholly unaware of—say, when you have hit an animal on the road, or found a spider in your bath. What were your reactions to these unexpected encounters?

Writing About the Text

Woolf uses a number of devices to capture the odd interconnection between herself and the moth. Sometimes that interaction distances the moth from the human world; sometimes that interaction reaches across the divide between the moth and Woolf. You might say her temptation to use her pencil to help the moth falls into the latter category, the pencil being not only a useful implement but what Woolf uses to write—presumably, too, to write "The Death of the Moth." Write an essay that explores these devices and considers how they help Woolf get her point across.

More Writing Projects

1. Is Woolf's essay about the insect world, the world of nonhuman creatures all around us; or is it about humans? In your journal, explain what the death of the moth reveals about human beings.
2. Write a paragraph that explores the way various aspects of this scene seem to draw Woolf away from her everyday habits despite herself. Look, for instance, at passages like these: ". . . it was difficult to keep the eyes turned upon the book" (par. 1); "One could not help watching him" (par. 2); ". . . my eye was caught by him" (par. 4); and so forth.
3. Write an essay that interprets "The Death of the Moth" by focusing on the nuances of the final sentence.

SUMMING UP: CHAPTER 3

1. As you have discovered in this chapter, one of the keys to writing effective description is the selection and creation of vivid and relevant images. How do the writers in this chapter use imagery? Which writer's images do you find most concrete, original, vivid, and creative? For each of the four essays of description in this chapter, write a paragraph in which you evaluate the writer's use of imagery.
2. All the writers in this chapter provide vivid descriptions of people, places, and objects. What general guidelines for describing people, places, and objects do you derive from these writers? Write a short essay called "How to Write Description," basing your observations on at least two of the writers' techniques.
3. The essays by Woolf and Selzer are, each in its own way, meditations on life and death. What did you learn about life and death from these two writers?
4. Both Dillard and Woolf write about the relation between the human and nonhuman worlds. Compare and contrast their observations and discoveries, as revealed in their essays here. How do you think their outlook on nature affects the way they write?
5. A common complaint about fiction is often phrased something like this: "Oh, I skipped that part—there was too much description." How would you use evidence from these essays to encourage the imaginary speaker of this sentence to reconsider his or her view of description?
6. As these essays show, description is rarely an end in itself. The writer usually uses description to make a general point concrete, or to advance an argument through something vivid and tangible, or to offer an example that can help the reader better to understand something. Yet it seems that the *purpose* of a description is often best achieved when the writer—and hence the reader—enjoys the description itself. A dull description is a lot worse than no description at all. Find examples in these essays where you sense that the writer is enjoying the writing of a descriptive passage, and discuss what qualities in the writing make this or that description especially effective because of the nature of the description itself.

7. Compare and contrast the way Amy Tan (pp. 29–34) and Maxine Hong Kingston (pp. 113–114) describe their mothers.

FROM SEEING TO WRITING

Examine the photograph of the busy marketplace and write a descriptive essay about it, drawing on sensory impressions implied by the scene. Remember to avoid description for its own sake. Develop a thesis about what you see in the photograph and present descriptive details to support that thesis.

Michael Dwyer/Stock Boston

CHAPTER 4

Narration

WHAT IS NARRATION?

Narration is the telling of a story. As a technique in essay writing, it normally involves a discussion of events that are "true" or real, events that take place over a period of time. Narration helps a writer explain things and, as such, it is an important skill for the kind of writing often required of you.

Narration often includes the use of *description* in order to make the *purpose* of the story clear. A good narrative, then, must have a *thesis.* The thesis tells the reader that the narrative goes beyond just telling a story for entertainment. Like description, the narrative has a purpose, and an audience. The writer puts forth a main idea through the events and details of the story. For example, a writer might decide to *narrate* the events that led her to leave her native country and come to the United States as an immigrant. She would establish her thesis—her main point—quickly, and then use the body of the essay to tell about the event itself. She would use narration as the means to an end—to make a significant statement about the important decision that changed her life.

Writer Elizabeth Wong uses narrative to explore the pitfalls of divorcing herself from her cultural heritage as she tells about events in her youth with the purpose of pointing out the dangers of becoming "All-American." In his comic narrative "Salvation," Langston Hughes reveals his disillusionment as he cannot find Jesus as his family expects him to. The renowned writer George Orwell narrates events at a hanging he witnessed in Burma to call attention to how all too often we can take the value of life for granted. The novelist Grace Paley uses the narrative of two trips to the American South to raise questions about both race relations and memory. Each writer, then, whose work you will read in this chapter, uses narrative to tell a story of events that take place over a period of time, but also to put forward a thesis or main idea that comes directly out of events in the story.

HOW DO WE READ NARRATIVE?

Reading narrative requires us to look for more than the story, but not to overlook the story. So, as we read, we should ask ourselves:

- What are the main events in the narrative or story?
- What is the writer's purpose in telling us about these events, as stated in the thesis?
- How is the story organized? Is it chronological? Does the writer use *flashback* (see Glossary)? How much time is covered in the narrative?
- Does the author use description to make the narrative more vivid for a reader?
- What point of view does the author use? Are events told through his or her own eyes, or from a detached and objective point of view? Why did the writer make this choice about point of view? How would altering the point of view alter the purpose of the narrative?
- What transitions of time does the writer use to connect events? Look for expressions that link events: *next, soon after, a day later, suddenly, after two years.* These expressions act like bridges to connect the various moments in the narrative pattern.
- Does the writer use dialogue? What is the effect of dialogue in the narrative?
- What audience is the author aiming at? How do we know?

HOW DO WE WRITE NARRATIVE?

After reading the selections of narrative writing in this chapter, you should be ready to try narrative writing on your own. Fortunately, most individuals have a basic storytelling ability and know how to develop stories that make a point. Once you master narration as a writing pattern, you will be able to use it in a variety of situations.

Select the event you want to tell a story about. Begin with a thesis statement that gives the reader the purpose of the narrative.

Sample thesis statement:

> My year studying abroad in Paris was an adventure that taught me not only skills in a foreign language but also a new respect for people with cultural values different from my own.

Decide which point of view you will use: first person? third person? Think about who your audience is, and choose the point of view best suited for that audience. If you are writing to a friend, first person may be more informal. If you are writing to address a wider public audience, as Orwell is, third person might be more effective.

First person: I saw a man hanged, and the experience changed my views on capital punishment.

Third person: Spending a day at a Planned Parenthood clinic would help opponents of abortion understand the other side's fervent commitment to choice.

Determine the purpose of the narrative in relation to your audience. If you were writing for a Roman Catholic newspaper, for instance, your audience would be different from the audience you'd address in a feminist magazine like *Ms.*: the purpose would be different as well. In one case, you might be trying to get readers to change their views through your description. In another case, you might be showing how weak the opposition was by the way you described them.

Plan the scope of the piece: How much time will events cover? Can you describe all the events within the required length of the essay?

Plan to include dialogue. For example, you might include a few fragments of conversation between lost or confused freshmen to give a "first day at school" story real-life flavor:

"Did you buy your books yet?"

"No, I couldn't find the bookstore!"

"Well, I already spent $125, and that was only for two courses. I'm going to have to ask my Mom for more money."

"Yeah, I'm thinking maybe I'm going to need a part-time job."

"Yeah, maybe we can work in the bookstore and get a discount."

Make a list of *transitions* that show the passage of time and use (without overusing) as many as you need to help your reader follow the narrative sequence. Check that there are transitions between events: *after that, a few hours later, by the time the day ended.*

State your *thesis.* Write out the thesis statement so that you know the *subject* and the *purpose* of the essay. Then make a list of the major events in the story. You might begin with why you chose the college you did, and how you felt when you got accepted. Or you might begin with your arrival on the first day of classes, and go through the main events of the day—going to class, buying books, meeting other new students, evaluating teachers, having lunch, and so forth.

Plan an arrangement of events. Most narratives benefit from a clear chronological sequence. All the writers here pay careful attention to the march of events over time, and you should follow their lead. As in Orwell's focused narrative, integrate commentary, analysis, or assessment, but keep your eye on the order of events.

Writing the Draft

Once you have structured your essay, build your ideas by including descriptive details. Insert as many descriptive words as possible to help a reader *see* the campus, the students, the cafeteria, and so on:

the bright-colored sofas in the student lounge, filled with cigarette burns

the smells of French fries from the cafeteria, with its long rows of orange tables

the conversations of the biology majors at the next table, who were talking about cutting up frogs

the large, imposing library, with its rows of blue computer terminals and its hushed whispered sounds

Discuss how these events made you feel about your decision. Did you choose the right college?

Write a conclusion that reinforces the purpose of the essay. Make a direct statement of the way the events in the narrative changed you, or how your expectations for the day compare with what really happened.

Reading and Revising the Draft

Read the essay aloud to a classmate who is also a new freshman. Ask your listener if his or her day was the same as yours. Did you put the events in a logical sequence? Can your listener suggest more ideas to add? Have you included enough details so that a reader who was not a member of the college community could see the events as you saw them?

Proofread carefully for correctness and make a neat final copy.

A STUDENT PARAGRAPH: NARRATION

In preparation for the essay on narration, one student wrote a narrative paragraph to tell part of the story of his first day on campus. Look at the selection and the annotations, which highlight important elements of narrative writing.

It was my first official day as a student here at State; the September morning had hardly begun, and I was already in a sweat. The crisp, colorful map I'd picked up shortly after passing through the iron gates had collapsed into a moist crumpled ball in my fist. Now I was flushed, panting, and miserable, as I tried to decide which seemingly endless line of students I needed to join next in order to fix the financial mess the university's computers had put me in. Standing in the middle of the quad, hemmed in on all sides by towering brick and marble buildings, I gazed helplessly around me. Suddenly, I caught a glimpse of a familiar face: Dan Merritt, a tall, skinny kid with bright red hair who had quit the Westmont High football team in his sophomore year, a few weeks before I did. Springing into action, I virtually tackled the poor guy, frantic lest he should escape and leave me alone with my rapidly disappearing self-confidence. I felt a real jolt of pleasure, though, when I saw relief flood his face. "Boy, am I glad to see you," Dan said. "I was beginning to think I wouldn't get out of here alive."

Topic sentence

Statement of time and place helps set narrative scene

"I" sets narrative point of view (first person)

Supporting detail

Transitions ("now," "next") promote chronological sequence

Supporting detail

Supporting detail

Dialogue adds real-life flavor

The Struggle to Be an All-American Girl

Elizabeth Wong

Elizabeth Wong is an award-winning Chinese-American playwright. *Letters to a Student Revolutionary* (1991), her best-known work, has been produced around the world. Her other plays include *Kimchee and Chitlins* (1990), about relations between Korean-Americans and African-Americans, and, most recently, *The Happy Prince* (1997). Wong was a staff writer for the ABC sitcom *All-American Girl,* the first network series to feature an Asian-American woman as its central character. In this selection, which originally appeared in the *Los Angeles Times,* Wong effectively blends concrete description and imaginative comparisons. She uses her storytelling gifts to give the reader a vivid look into the life of a child who felt that she had a Chinese exterior but an American interior.

PREREADING: THINKING ABOUT THE ESSAY IN ADVANCE

America prides itself on its ability to assimilate cultures, yet the process of assimilation is not without difficulties, particularly for children. What problems do you foresee for a child of one cultural background growing up in the midst of another culture?

Words to Watch

stoically (par. 1) without showing emotion

dissuade (par. 2) to talk out of doing something

ideographs (par. 7) Chinese picture symbols used to form words

disassociate (par. 8) to detach from association

vendors (par. 8) sellers of goods

gibberish (par. 9) confused, unintelligible speech or language

pidgin (par. 10) simplified speech that is usually a mixture of two or more languages

It's still there, the Chinese school on Yale Street where my brother and I used to go. Despite the new coat of paint and the high wire fence, the school I knew 10 years ago remains remarkably, stoically the same. 1

Every day at 5 P.M., instead of playing with our fourth- and fifth-grade friends or sneaking out to the empty lot to hunt ghosts and animal bones, my brother and I had to go to Chinese school. 2

No amount of kicking, screaming, or pleading could dissuade my mother, who was solidly determined to have us learn the language of our heritage.

3 Forcibly, she walked us the seven long, hilly blocks from our home to school, depositing our defiant tearful faces before the stern principal. My only memory of him is that he swayed on his heels like a palm tree, and he always clasped his impatient twitching hands behind his back. I recognized him as a repressed maniacal child killer, and knew that if we ever saw his hands we'd be in big trouble.

4 We all sat in little chairs in an empty auditorium. The room smelled like Chinese medicine, an imported faraway mustiness. Like ancient mothballs or dirty closets. I hated that smell. I favored crisp new scents. Like the soft French perfume that my American teacher wore in public school.

5 There was a stage far to the right, flanked by an American flag and the flag of the Nationalist Republic of China, which was also red, white and blue but not as pretty.

6 Although the emphasis at the school was mainly language—speaking, reading, writing—the lessons always began with an exercise in politeness. With the entrance of the teacher, the best student would tap a bell and everyone would get up, kowtow, and chant, "Sing san ho," the phonetic for "How are you, teacher?"

7 Being ten years old, I had better things to learn than ideographs copied painstakingly in lines that ran right to left from the tip of a *moc but,* a real ink pen that had to be held in an awkward way if blotches were to be avoided. After all, I could do the multiplication tables, name the satellites of Mars, and write reports on "Little Women" and "Black Beauty." Nancy Drew, my favorite book heroine, never spoke Chinese.

8 The language was a source of embarrassment. More times than not, I had tried to disassociate myself from the nagging loud voice that followed me wherever I wandered in the nearby American supermarket outside Chinatown. The voice belonged to my grandmother, a fragile woman in her seventies who could outshout the best of the street vendors. Her humor was raunchy, her Chinese rhythmless, patternless. It was quick, it was loud, it was unbeautiful. It was not like the quiet, lilting romance of French or the gentle refinement of the American South. Chinese sounded pedestrian. Public.

9 In Chinatown, the comings and goings of hundreds of Chinese on their daily tasks sounded chaotic and frenzied. I did not want to

be thought of as mad, as talking gibberish. When I spoke English, people nodded at me, smiled sweetly, said encouraging words. Even the people in my culture would cluck and say that I'd do well in life. "My, doesn't she move her lips fast," they would say, meaning that I'd be able to keep up with the world outside Chinatown.

My brother was even more fanatical than I about speaking English. He was especially hard on my mother, criticizing her, often cruelly, for her pidgin speech—smatterings of Chinese scattered like chop suey in her conversation. "It's not 'What it is,' Mom," he'd say in exasperation. "It's 'What *is* it, what *is* it, what *is* it!' Sometimes Mom might leave out an occasional "the" or "a," or perhaps a verb of being. He would stop her in mid-sentence: "Say it again, Mom. Say it right." When he tripped over his own tongue, he'd blame it on her: "See, Mom, it's all your fault. You set a bad example." 10

What infuriated my mother most was when my brother cornered her on her consonants, especially "r." My father had played a cruel joke on Mom by assigning her an American name that her tongue wouldn't allow her to say. No matter how hard she tried, "Ruth" always ended up "Luth" or "Roof." 11

After two years of writing with a *moc but* and reciting words with multiples of meanings, I finally was granted a cultural divorce. I was permitted to stop Chinese school. 12

I thought of myself as multicultural. I preferred tacos to egg rolls; I enjoyed Cinco de Mayo more than Chinese New Year. 13

At last, I was one of you; I wasn't one of them. 14

Sadly, I still am. 15

BUILDING VOCABULARY

For each of the words in italics, choose the letter of the word or expression that most closely matches its meaning.

1. the *stern* principal (par. 3)
   a. military
   b. very old
   c. immoral
   d. strict
2. *repressed* maniacal child killer (par. 3)
   a. quiet
   b. ugly

- **c.** held back
- **d.** retired

3. an imported faraway *mustiness* (par. 4)

- **a.** country
- **b.** moth balls
- **c.** chair
- **d.** staleness

4. a *fragile* woman (par. 8)

- **a.** elderly
- **b.** frail
- **c.** tall
- **d.** inconsistent

5. her humor was *raunchy* (par. 8)

- **a.** obscene
- **b.** unclear
- **c.** childish
- **d.** very funny

6. quiet *lilting* romance of French (par. 8)

- **a.** musical
- **b.** tilting
- **c.** loving
- **d.** complicated

7. thought of as *mad* (par. 9)

- **a.** foreign
- **b.** angry
- **c.** stupid
- **d.** crazy

8. what *infuriated* my mother most (par. 11)

- **a.** angered
- **b.** humiliated
- **c.** made laugh
- **d.** typified

THINKING CRITICALLY ABOUT THE ESSAY

Understanding the Writer's Ideas

1. What did Elizabeth Wong and her brother do every day after school? How did that make them different from their friends? What was their attitude toward what they did? How do you know?

2. What does Wong mean when she says of the principal "I recognized him as a repressed maniacal child killer"? Why were she and her brother afraid to see his hands?
3. What was the main purpose of going to Chinese school? What did Wong feel she had learned at "regular" American school? Which did she feel was more important? What are *Little Women, Black Beauty,* and Nancy Drew?
4. In the first sentence of paragraph 8, what language is "the language"?
5. What was Wong's grandmother like? What was Wong's attitude toward her? Why?
6. When Wong spoke English in Chinatown, why did the others think it was good that she moved her lips quickly?
7. What was her brother's attitude toward speaking English? How did he treat their mother when she tried to speak English? Why was it unfortunate that the mother had the American name *Ruth?* Who gave her that name? Why?
8. Explain the expression "he tripped over his own tongue" (par. 10).
9. In paragraph 13, Wong states, "I thought of myself as multicultural." What does that mean? What are tacos, egg rolls, and Cinco de Mayo? Why is it surprising that Wong includes those items as examples of her multiculturalism?
10. Who are the "you" and "them" of paragraph 14? Explain the significance of the last sentence. What does it indicate about Wong's attitude toward Chinese school from the vantage point of being an adult?

Understanding the Writer's Techniques

1. Wong does not state a thesis directly in a thesis sentence. How does her title imply a thesis? If you were writing a thesis sentence of your own for this essay, what would it be?
2. What is Wong's purpose in writing this narrative? Is the technique of narration an appropriate one to her purpose? Why or why not?
3. This narrative contains several stories. The first one ends after paragraph 7 and tells about Wong's routine after 5 P.M. on school days. Paragraphs 8 and 9, 10 and 11, and 12 and 13 offer other related narratives. Summarize each of these briefly. How does Wong help the reader shift from story to story?

4. The writer of narration will present *time* in a way that best fulfills the purpose of the narration. This presentation may take many forms: a single, personal event; a series of related events; a historical occurrence; an aging process. Obviously Wong chose a series of related events. Why does she use such a narrative structure to make her point? Could she have chosen an alternative plan, do you think? Why or why not?
5. Writers of narration often rely upon descriptive details to flesh out their stories. Find examples of sensory language here that makes the scene come alive for the reader.
6. Writers often use figurative comparisons to enliven their writing and to make it more distinctive. A *simile* is an imaginative form of figurative comparison using "like" or "as" to connect two items. One thing is similar to another in this figure. A *metaphor* is a figure of speech in which the writer compares two items not normally thought of as similar, but unlike in a simile, the comparison is direct—that is, it does not use "like" or "as." In other words, one thing is said to be the other thing, not merely to be like it. For example, if you wanted to compare love to a rose, you might use these two comparisons:

   Simile:
   My love is *like* a red, red rose.
   Metaphor:
   My love *is* a red, red rose.

   In Wong's essay, find the similes and metaphors in paragraphs 2, 3, 4, 10, and 12. For each, name the two items compared and explain the comparison in your own words.
7. Narratives often include lines of spoken language—that is, one person in the narrative talking alone or to another. Wong uses quoted detail sparsely here. Why did she choose to limit the dialogue? How effective is the dialogue that appears here? Where do you think she might have used more dialogue to advance the narrative?
8. The last two paragraphs are only one sentence each. Why do you think the author chose this technique?
9. What is the *irony* (see Glossary) in the last sentence of the essay? How would the meaning of the last sentence change if you eliminated the word "sadly"? What is the irony in the title of the essay?

10. What is the *tone* (see Glossary) of this essay? How does Wong create that tone?

Exploring the Writer's Ideas

1. Wong and her brother deeply resented being forced to attend Chinese school. When children very clearly express displeasure or unhappiness, should parents force them to do things anyway? Why or why not?
2. On one level this essay is about a clash of cultures, here the ancient Chinese culture of Wong's ancestry and the culture of twentieth-century United States. Is it possible for someone to maintain connections to his or her ethnic or cultural background and at the same time to become an All-American girl or boy? What do people of foreign backgrounds gain when they become completely Americanized? What do they lose?
3. Because of their foreign ways, the mother and grandmother clearly embarrassed the Wong children. Under what other conditions that you can think of do parents embarrass children? Children, parents?

IDEAS FOR WRITING

Prewriting

Do timed writing—that is, write nonstop for fifteen or twenty minutes without editing or correcting your work—on the topic of your grade school or high school. What experience stands out most in your mind? What moment taught you most about yourself?

Guided Writing

Write a narration in which you tell about some difficult moment that took place in grade school or high school, a moment that taught you something about yourself, your needs, or your cultural background.

1. Provide a concrete description of the school.
2. Tell in correct sequence about the event.
3. Identify people who play a part in this moment.
4. Use concrete, sensory description throughout your essay.

5. Use original similes and metaphors to make your narrative clearer and more dramatic.
6. Use dialogue (or spoken conversation) appropriately in order to advance the narrative.
7. In your conclusion, indicate what your attitude toward this moment is now that you are an adult.
8. Write a title that implies your thesis.

Thinking and Writing Collaboratively

In groups of two or three, read aloud drafts of each other's essays, looking particularly at the use of concrete sensory detail and figures of speech—metaphors and similes. Which images strike you as most clear, original, and easy to visualize?

Writing About the Text

Write an essay that explores the ambivalence of the concluding two sentences. Why is Wong sad? Is the mixed emphasis of these final sentences, for example, felt throughout the essay? Is the ending a surprise?

More Writing Projects

1. Did you have any problems in grade school or high school because of your background or ancestry? Did you know someone who had such problems? Record a specific incident in your journal.
2. Write a narrative paragraph explaining some basic insights about your heritage or culture.
3. Get together with other classmates in a small group and brainstorm or bounce ideas off one another on troubling ethnic, racial, or cultural issues on campus. Write down all the incidents. Then write a narrative essay tracing one episode or connecting a series of them.

Salvation

Langston Hughes

One of the great American writers of the twentieth century, Langston Hughes was born in 1902 in Joplin, Missouri. His parents divorced while he was still an infant, and he was reared by his maternal grandmother, Mary Langston. His grandmother, whose first husband died in the raid on Harpers Ferry as a follower of John Brown, was an abiding influence on Hughes. Nonetheless, he suffered from parental absence; he later said that it was childhood loneliness that led him to books "and the wonderful world in books." Hughes studied for a year at Columbia University and later completed his college education at the historically black Lincoln University in Pennsylvania.

In 1926 Hughes published "The Negro Artist and the Racial Mountain," an essay that served as a manifesto for the Harlem Renaissance, of which he was a leading figure—as a poet, an essayist, a novelist, and a playwright. His poetry brilliantly employed the sounds of African-American speech and of jazz, as suggested by the titles of two of his books of poems, *The Weary Blues* (1926) and *Montage of a Dream Deferred* (1951). In 1942 Hughes began to write a weekly column for the *Chicago Defender.* For two decades the column featured an offbeat Harlem character, Jesse B. Simple, Hughes's best-known and most-loved creation. Simple appears in five collections that Hughes edited, beginning with *Simple Speaks His Mind* (1950). This selection, from Hughes's autobiography, *The Big Sea* (1940), tells the story of his "conversion" to Christ. Salvation was a key event in the life of his community, but Hughes tells comically, and poignantly, of how he bowed to pressure by permitting himself to be "saved from sin." Hughes died in 1967.

PREREADING: THINKING ABOUT THE ESSAY IN ADVANCE

What is the role of religion today in the lives of most Americans? What role does religion play in your life? In what ways do the religious values of your family compare and contrast with your own?

Words to Watch

dire (par. 3) terrible; disastrous

gnarled (par. 4) knotty; twisted

rounder (par. 6) watchman; policeman

deacons (par. 6) members of the clergy or laypersons who are appointed to help the minister

serenely (par. 7) calmly; tranquilly

knickerbockered (par. 11) dressed in short, loose trousers that are gathered below the knees

1 I was saved from sin when I was going on thirteen. But not really saved. It happened like this. There was a big revival at my Auntie Reed's church. Every night for weeks there had been much preaching, singing, praying, and shouting, and some very hardened sinners had been brought to Christ, and the membership of the church had grown by leaps and bounds. Then just before the revival ended, they held a special meeting for children, "to bring the young lambs to the fold." My aunt spoke of it for days ahead. That night I was escorted to the front row and placed on the mourners' bench with all the other young sinners, who had not yet been brought to Jesus.

2 My aunt told me that when you were saved you saw a light, and something happened to you inside! And Jesus came into your life! And God was with you from then on! She said you could see and hear and feel Jesus in your soul. I believed her. I had heard a great many old people say the same thing and it seemed to me they ought to know. So I sat there calmly in the hot, crowded church, waiting for Jesus to come to me.

3 The preacher preached a wonderful rhythmical sermon, all moans and shouts and lonely cries and dire pictures of hell, and then he sang a song about the ninety and nine safe in the fold, but one little lamb was left out in the cold. Then he said: "Won't you come? Won't you come to Jesus? Young lambs, won't you come?" And he held out his arms to all us young sinners there on the mourners' bench. And the little girls cried. And some of them jumped up and went to Jesus right away. But most of us just sat there.

4 A great many old people came and knelt around us and prayed, old women with jet-black faces and braided hair, old men with work-gnarled hands. And the church sang a song about the lower lights are burning, some poor sinners to be saved. And the whole building rocked with prayer and song.

5 Still I kept waiting to *see* Jesus.

6 Finally all the young people had gone to the altar and were saved, but one boy and me. He was a rounder's son named Westley. Westley and I were surrounded by sisters and deacons praying.

It was very hot in the church, and getting late now. Finally Westley said to me in a whisper: "God damn! I'm tired o' sitting here.
Let's get up and be saved." So he got up and was saved.

Then I was left all alone on the mourners' bench. My aunt 7
came and knelt at my knees and cried, while prayers and songs
swirled all around me in the little church. The whole congregation
prayed for me alone, in a mighty wail of moans and voices. And I
kept waiting serenely for Jesus, waiting, waiting—but he didn't
come. I wanted to see him, but nothing happened to me. Nothing!
I wanted something to happen to me, but nothing happened.

I heard the songs and the minister saying: "Why don't you 8
come? My dear child, why don't you come to Jesus? Jesus is waiting for you. He wants you. Why don't you come? Sister Reed,
what is this child's name?"

"Langston," my aunt sobbed. 9

"Langston, why don't you come? Why don't you come and be 10
saved? Oh, Lamb of God! Why don't you come?"

Now it was really getting late. I began to be ashamed of my- 11
self, holding everything up so long. I began to wonder what God
thought about Westley, who certainly hadn't seen Jesus either, but
who was now sitting proudly on the platform, swinging his
knickerbockered legs and grinning down at me, surrounded by
deacons and old women on their knees praying. God had not
struck Westley dead for taking his name in vain or for lying in the
temple. So I decided that maybe to save further trouble, I'd better
lie, too, and say that Jesus had come, and get up and be saved.

So I got up. 12

Suddenly the whole room broke into a sea of shouting, as they 13
saw me rise. Waves of rejoicing swept the place. Women leaped in
the air. My aunt threw her arms around me. The minister took me
by the hand and led me to the platform.

When things quieted down, in a hushed silence, punctuated by 14
a few ecstatic "Amens," all the new young lambs were blessed in
the name of God. Then joyous singing filled the room.

That night, for the last time in my life but one—for I was a big 15
boy twelve years old—I cried. I cried, in bed alone, and couldn't
stop. I buried my head under the quilts, but my aunt heard me. She
woke up and told my uncle I was crying because the Holy Ghost
had come into my life, and because I had seen Jesus. But I was really crying because I couldn't bear to tell her that I had lied, that I
had deceived everybody in the church, that I hadn't seen Jesus,

and that now I didn't believe there was a Jesus any more, since he didn't come to help me.

BUILDING VOCABULARY

1. Throughout this essay, Hughes selects words dealing with religion to emphasize his ideas. Look up the following words in a dictionary. Then tell what *connotations* (see Glossary) the words have for you.
   a. sin (par. 1)
   b. mourner (par. 1)
   c. lamb (par. 3)
   d. salvation (title)
2. Locate additional words that deal with religion.
3. When Hughes talks about lambs in the fold—and lambs in general—he is using a figure of speech, a comparison (see Chapter 6). What is being compared? How does religion enter into the comparison? Why is it useful as a figure of speech?

THINKING CRITICALLY ABOUT THE ESSAY

Understanding the Writer's Ideas

1. According to Hughes's description, what is a revival meeting like? What is the effect of the "preaching, singing, praying, and shouting" on the "sinners" and the "young lambs"?
2. Why does Westley "see" Jesus? Why does Langston Hughes come to Jesus?
3. How does the author feel after his salvation? Does Hughes finally believe in Christ after his experience? How do you know?

Understanding the Writer's Techniques

1. Is there a thesis statement in the essay? Where is it located?
2. How does the first paragraph serve as an introduction to the narrative?
3. What is the value of description in this essay? List several instances of vivid description that contribute to the narrative.

4. Where does the main narration begin? How much time passes in the course of the action?
5. In narration, it is especially important to have effective *transitions*—or word bridges—from stage to stage in the action. Transitions help the reader shift easily from idea to idea, event to event. List several transition words that Hughes uses.
6. A piece of writing has *coherence* if all its parts relate clearly and logically to one another. Each sentence grows naturally from the sentence before it; each paragraph grows naturally from the paragraph before it. Is Hughes's essay coherent? Which transitions help advance the action and relate the parts of a single paragraph to one another? Which transitions help connect paragraphs together? How does the way Hughes organized this essay help establish coherence?
7. A story (whether it is true or fiction) has to be told from the first-person ("I, we"), second-person ("you"), or third-person ("he, she, it, they") *point of view.* Point of view in narration sets up the author's position in regard to the action, making the author either a part of the action or an observer of it.
   a. What is the point of view in "Salvation"—is it first, second, or third person?
   b. Why has Hughes chosen this point of view instead of any other? Can you think of any advantages to this point of view?
8. What is your opinion about the last paragraph, the conclusion of this selection? What does it suggest about the mind of a twelve-year-old boy? What does it say about adults' misunderstanding of the activities of children?
9. What does the word "conversion" mean? What conversion really takes place in this piece? How does that compare with what people usually mean when they use "conversion" in a religious sense?

Exploring the Writer's Ideas

1. Hughes seems to suggest that we are forced to do things because of social pressures. Do you agree with his suggestion? Do people do things because their friends or families expect them to? To what extent are we part of the "herd"? Is it possi-

ble for a person to retain individuality under pressure from a group? When did you bow to group pressures? When did you resist?

2. Do you find the religious experience in Hughes's essay unusual or extreme? Why or why not? How do *you* define religion?
3. Under what circumstances might a person lie in order to satisfy others? Try to recall a specific episode in which you or someone you know was forced to lie in order to please others.

IDEAS FOR WRITING

Prewriting

Write a few sentences to define *group pressure.* Then give an example or two of a time when you gave in to group pressure or were forced to lie in order to impress others.

Guided Writing

Narrate an event in your life where you (or someone you know) gave in to group pressure or were forced to lie in order to please those around you.

1. Start with a thesis statement.
2. Set the stage for your narrative in the opening paragraph by telling where and when the incident took place. Use specific names for places.
3. Try to keep the action within as brief a time period as possible. If you can write about an event that took no more than a few minutes, so much the better.
4. Use description to sketch in the characters around you. Use colors, actions, sounds, smells, sensations of touch to fill in details of the scene.
5. Use effective transitions of time to link sentences and paragraphs.
6. Use the last paragraph to explain how you felt immediately after the incident.

Thinking and Writing Collaboratively

Exchange drafts of your Guided Writing essay with one other person in the class. Then, write out a brief outline of the events the writer has presented in the narrative. Is the sequence clear? Do the introduction and thesis set the stage appropriately for the sequence of events? Do the transitions link paragraphs and sentences effectively? Return the paper with your written response.

Writing About the Text

Write an essay that speculates about whether, as an adult, Hughes did—or didn't—discover a meaning in his life through religion. Use evidence from this essay, written, after all, when Hughes was an adult.

More Writing Projects

1. Explain in a journal entry an abstract word like "salvation," "sin," "love," or "hatred" by narrating an event that reveals the meaning of the word to you.
2. Write an extended paragraph on an important event that affected your relationship with family, friends, or your community during your childhood.
3. Make a list of all the important details that you associate with some religious occasion in your life. Then write a narrative essay on the experience.

A Hanging

George Orwell

George Orwell (the pen name of Eric Blair) was born in Bengal, India in 1903. His parents were members of the British Civil Service in India, and Orwell followed in their footsteps when as a young man he joined the Imperial Police in Burma. But ironically Orwell's experience as a policeman in Burma turned him against British colonialism, as he recounts in a famous essay, "Shooting an Elephant." Indeed, he became a committed socialist but a fiercely antiautocratic one. In the mid-1930s, like many left-wing intellectuals and writers, he went to Spain to fight with the International Brigade in support of the recently elected Popular Front government, then under military attack by Fascist forces led by the ultimately victorious General Franco. Orwell was seriously wounded in the Spanish Civil War, and when the Spanish Communists, under orders from Moscow, attempted to wipe out their allies on the left, he fought against them, finally fleeing for his life.

Orwell became famous in the early years of the Cold War for two prophetic, satirical books fed by his experiences with Communism, books that brilliantly attack totalitarian forms of government. The first, *Animal Farm* (1945), tells the story of the terror tactics and deception that pigs use to take over a farm—but it is an allegorical fable aimed against Stalinism. The second, *Nineteen Eighty-Four* (1949), is a "dystopian" novel, a futuristic novel that portrays the future as dreadful rather than an amazing improvement on life as we have known it (as "utopian" works do). It is to *Nineteen Eighty-Four* that we owe the idea and the expression, "Big Brother is watching you." This selection is one of a group of enormously influential essays by Orwell that employ personal narrative to explore issues of broad concern, in particular social and political issues. In "Politics and the English Language," Orwell maintained that muddy writing, obscurity, inaccuracy, pretentiousness are closely related to a flawed political outlook, and that democracy and equality are strengthened by clear, honest, and direct writing. Saying things clearly, writing to be understood, were, for Orwell, *political* virtues. Orwell died of tuberculosis in 1950.

PREREADING: THINKING ABOUT THE ESSAY IN ADVANCE

The number of people executed through the system of justice in the United States has increased dramatically over the past few years. How do you explain this increase in the number of executions by lethal injection or the electric chair? Why does U.S. society continue to use capital punishment? Under what circumstances is a person sentenced to capital punishment?

Words to Watch

sodden (par. 1) heavy with water
absurdly (par. 2) ridiculously
desolately (par. 3) gloomily; lifelessly; cheerlessly
prodding (par. 3) poking or thrusting at something
Dravidian (par. 4) any member of a group of intermixed races of southern India and Burma
pariah (par. 6) outcast; a member of a low caste of southern India and Burma
servile (par. 11) slavelike; lacking spirit or independence
reiterated (par. 12) repeated
abominable (par. 13) hateful; disagreeable; unpleasant
timorously (par. 15) fearfully
oscillated (par. 16) moved back and forth between two points
garrulously (par. 20) in a talkative manner
refractory (par. 22) stubborn
amicably (par. 24) in a friendly way; peaceably

It was in Burma, a sodden morning of the rains. A sickly light, like yellow tinfoil, was slanting over the high walls into the jail yard. We were waiting outside the condemned cells, a row of sheds fronted with double bars, like small animal cages. Each cell measured about ten feet by ten and was quite bare within except for a plank bed and a pot of drinking water. In some of them brown silent men were squatting at the inner bars, with their blankets draped round them. These were the condemned men, due to be hanged within the next week or two. 1

One prisoner had been brought out of his cell. He was a Hindu, a puny wisp of a man, with a shaven head and vague liquid eyes. He had a thick, sprouting moustache, absurdly too big for his body, rather like the moustache of a comic man on the films. Six tall Indian warders were guarding him and getting him ready for the gallows. Two of them stood by with rifles with fixed bayonets, while the others handcuffed him, passed a chain through his handcuffs 2 and fixed it to their belts, and lashed his arms tight to his sides. They crowded very close about him, with their hands always on him in a careful, caressing grip, as though all the while feeling him to make sure he was there. It was like men handling a fish which is still alive and may jump back into the water. But he stood quite unresisting, yielding his arms limply to the ropes, as though he hardly noticed what was happening.

3 Eight o'clock struck and a bugle call, desolately thin in the wet air, floated from the distant barracks. The superintendent of the jail, who was standing apart from the rest of us, moodily prodding the gravel with his stick, raised his head at the sound. He was an army doctor, with a grey toothbrush moustache and a gruff voice. "For God's sake hurry up, Francis," he said irritably. "The man ought to have been dead by this time. Aren't you ready yet?"

4 Francis, the head jailer, a fat Dravidian in a white drill suit and gold spectacles, waved his black hand. "Yes sir, yes sir," he bubbled. "All iss satisfactorily prepared. The hangman iss waiting. We shall proceed."

5 "Well, quick march, then. The prisoners can't get their breakfast till this job's over."

6 We set out for the gallows. Two warders marched on either side of the prisoner, with their files at the slope; two others marched close against him, gripping him by arm and shoulder, as though at once pushing and supporting him. The rest of us, magistrates and the like, followed behind. Suddenly, when we had gone ten yards, the procession stopped short without any order or warning. A dreadful thing had happened—a dog, come goodness knows whence, had appeared in the yard. It came bounding among us with a loud volley of barks, and leapt round us wagging its whole body, wild with glee at finding so many human beings together. It was a large woolly dog, half Airedale, half pariah. For a moment it pranced round us, and then, before anyone could stop it, it had made a dash for the prisoner, and jumping up tried to lick his face. Everyone stood aghast, too taken aback even to grab at the dog.

7 "Who let that bloody brute in here?" said the superintendent angrily. "Catch it, someone!"

8 A warder, detached from the escort, charged clumsily after the dog, but it danced and gambolled just out of his reach, taking everything as part of the game. A young Eurasian jailer picked up a handful of gravel and tried to stone the dog away, but it dodged the stones and came after us again. Its yaps echoed from the jail

walls. The prisoner, in the grasp of the two warders, looked on incuriously, as though this was another formality of the hanging. It was several minutes before someone managed to catch the dog. Then we put my handkerchief through its collar and moved off once more, with the dog still straining and whimpering.

It was about forty yards to the gallows. I watched the bare brown back of the prisoner marching in front of me. He walked clumsily with his bound arms, but quite steadily, with that bobbing gait of the Indian who never straightens his knees. At each step his muscles slid neatly into place, the lock of hair on his scalp danced up and down, his feet printed themselves on the wet gravel. And once, in spite of the men who gripped him by each shoulder, he stepped slightly aside to avoid a puddle on the path. 9

It is curious, but till that moment I had never realised what it means to destroy a healthy, conscious man. When I saw the prisoner step aside to avoid the puddle, I saw the mystery, the unspeakable wrongness, of cutting a life short when it is in full tide. This man was not dying, he was alive just as we were alive. All the organs of his body were working—bowels digesting food, skin renewing itself, nails growing, tissues forming—all toiling away in solemn foolery. His nails would still be growing when he stood on the drop, when he was falling through the air with a tenth of a second to live. His eyes saw the yellow gravel and the grey walls, and his brain still remembered, foresaw, reasoned—reasoned even about puddles. He and we were a party of men walking together, seeing, hearing, feeling, understanding the same world; and in two minutes, with a sudden snap, one of us would be gone—one mind less, one world less. 10

The gallows stood in a small yard, separate from the main grounds of the prison, and overgrown with tall prickly weeds. It was a brick erection like three sides of a shed, with planking on top, and above that two beams and a crossbar with the rope dangling. The hangman, a grey-haired convict in the white uniform of the prison, was waiting beside his machine. He greeted us with a servile crouch as we entered. At a word from Francis the two warders, gripping the prisoner more closely than ever, half led, half pushed him to the gallows and helped him clumsily up the ladder. Then the hangman climbed up and fixed the rope round the prisoner's neck. 11

We stood waiting, five yards away. The warders had formed in a rough circle round the gallows. And then, when the noose was 12 fixed, the prisoner began crying out on his god. It was a high, reiterated cry of "Ram! Ram! Ram! Ram!", not urgent and fearful like a prayer or a cry for help, but steady, rhythmical, almost like the tolling of a bell. The dog answered the sound with a whine. The hangman, still standing on the gallows, produced a small cotton bag like a flour bag and drew it down over the Prisoner's face. But the sound, muffled by the cloth, still persisted, over and over again: "Ram! Ram! Ram! Ram! Ram!"

13 The hangman climbed down and stood ready, holding the lever. Minutes seemed to pass. The steady, muffled crying from the prisoner went on and on, "Ram! Ram! Ram!" never faltering for an instant. The superintendent, his head on his chest, was slowly poking the ground with his stick; perhaps he was counting the cries, allowing the prisoner a fixed number—fifty, perhaps, or a hundred. Everyone had changed colour. The Indians had gone grey like bad coffee, and one or two of the bayonets were wavering. We looked at the lashed, hooded man on the drop, and listened to his cries—each cry another second of life; the same thought was in all our minds: oh, kill him quickly, get it over, stop that abominable noise!

14 Suddenly the superintendent made up his mind. Throwing up his head he made a swift motion with his stick. "Chalo!" he shouted almost fiercely.

15 There was a clanking noise, and then dead silence. The prisoner had vanished, and the rope was twisting on itself. I let go of the dog, and it galloped immediately to the back of the gallows; but when it got there it stopped short, barked, and then retreated into a corner of the yard, where it stood among the weeds, looking timorously out at us. We went round the gallows to inspect the prisoner's body. He was dangling with his toes pointed straight downwards, very slowly revolving, as dead as a stone.

16 The superintendent reached out with his stick and poked the bare body; it oscillated, slightly. "*He's* all right," said the superintendent. He backed out from under the gallows, and blew out a deep breath. The moody look had gone out of his face quite suddenly. He glanced at his wristwatch. "Eight minutes past eight. Well, that's all for this morning, thank God."

17 The warders unfixed bayonets and marched away. The dog, sobered and conscious of having misbehaved itself, slipped after them. We walked out of the gallows yard, past the condemned cells with their waiting prisoners, into the big central yard of the

prison. The convicts, under the command of warders armed with lathis, were already receiving their breakfast. They squatted in long rows, each man holding a tin pannikin, while two warders with buckets marched round ladling out rice; it seemed quite a homely, jolly scene, after the hanging. An enormous relief had come upon us now that the job was done. One felt an impulse to sing, to break into a run, to snigger. All at once everyone began chattering gaily.

The Eurasian boy walking beside me nodded towards the way 18
we had come, with a knowing smile: "Do you know, sir, our friend (he meant the dead man), when he heard his appeal had been dismissed, he pissed on the floor of his cell. From fright—Kindly take one of my cigarettes, sir. Do you not admire my new silver case, sir? From the boxwallah, two rupees eight annas. Classy European style."

Several people laughed—at what, nobody seemed certain. 19

Francis was walking by the superintendent, talking garru- 20
lously: "Well, sir, all hass passed off with the utmost satisfactoriness. It wass all finished—flick! like that. It iss not always so—oah, no! I have known cases where the doctor wass obliged to go beneath the gallows and pull the prisoner's legs to ensure decease. Most disagreeable!"

"Wriggling about, eh? That's bad," said the superintendent. 21

"Ach, sir, it iss worse when they become refractory! One man, 22
I recall, clung to the bars of hiss cage when we went to take him out. You will scarcely credit, sir, that it took six warders to dislodge him, three pulling at each leg. We reasoned with him. My dear fellow, we said, think of all the pain and trouble you are causing to us! But no, he would not listen! Ach, he wass very troublesome!"

I found that I was laughing quite loudly. Everyone was laugh- 23
ing. Even the superintendent grinned in a tolerant way. "You'd better all come out and have a drink," he said quite genially. "I've got a bottle of whisky in the car. We could do with it."

We went through the big double gates of the prison, into the 24
road. "Pulling at his legs!" exclaimed a Burmese magistrate suddenly, and burst into a loud chuckling. We all began laughing again. At that moment Francis's anecdote seemed extraordinarily funny. We all had a drink together, native and European alike, quite amicably. The dead man was a hundred yards away.

BUILDING VOCABULARY

1. Use *context clues* (see Glossary) to make an "educated guess" about the definitions of the following words in italics. Before you guess, look back to the paragraph for clues. Afterward, check your guess in a dictionary.
   - **a.** *condemned* men (par. 1)
   - **b.** puny *wisp* of a man (par. 2)
   - **c.** Indian *warders* (par. 2)
   - **d.** careful, *caressing* grip (par. 2)
   - **e.** stood *aghast* (par. 6)
   - **f.** it danced and *gambolled* (par. 8)
   - **g.** *solemn* foolery (par. 10)
   - **h.** armed with *lathis* (par. 17)
   - **i.** a tin *pannikin* (par. 17)
   - **j.** quite *genially* (par. 23)
2. What are definitions for the words below? Look at words within them, which you may be able to recognize.
   - **a.** moodily
   - **b.** dreadful
   - **c.** Eurasian
   - **d.** incuriously
   - **e.** formality

THINKING CRITICALLY ABOUT THE ESSAY

Understanding the Writer's Ideas

1. The events in the essay occur in a country in Asia, Burma (also called Myanmar, since 1989). Describe in your own words the specific details of the action.
2. Who are the major characters in this essay? Why might you include the dog as a major character?
3. In a narrative essay the writer often tells the events in chronological order. Examine the following events from "A Hanging." Arrange them in the order in which they occurred.
   - **a.** A large woolly dog tries to lick the prisoner's face.
   - **b.** A Eurasian boy talks about his silver case.
   - **c.** The superintendent signals "Chalo!" to the hangman.
   - **d.** One prisoner, a Hindu, is brought from his cell.

e. Francis discusses with the superintendent a prisoner who had to be pulled off the bars of his cage.
f. The prisoner steps aside to avoid a puddle as he marches to the gallows.

4. What is the author's opinion of *capital punishment* (legally killing someone who has disobeyed the laws of society)? How does the incident with the puddle suggest that opinion, even indirectly?

Understanding the Writer's Techniques

1. What is the main point that the writer wishes to make in this essay? Which paragraph tells the author's thesis most clearly? Which sentence in that paragraph best states the main idea of the essay?
2. In the first paragraph of the essay, we see clear images such as "brown silent men were squatting at the inner bars, with their blankets draped around them." The use of color and action makes an instant appeal to our sense of sight.
   - **a.** What images in the rest of the essay do you find most vivid?
   - **b.** Which sentence gives the best details of sound?
   - **c.** What word pictures suggest action and color?
   - **d.** Where do you find words that describe a sensation of touch?
3. In order to make their images clearer, writers use *figurative language* (see Glossary). "A Hanging" is especially rich in *similes,* which are comparisons using the word "like" or "as."
   - **a.** What simile does Orwell use in the first paragraph in order to let us see how the light slants over the jail yard walls? How does the simile make the scene clearer?
   - **b.** What other simile does Orwell use in the first paragraph?
   - **c.** Discuss the similes in the paragraphs listed below. What are the things being compared? Are the similes, in your opinion, original? How do they contribute to the image the author intends to create?
     - **(1)** It was like men handling a fish (par. 2)
     - **(2)** a thick sprouting moustache . . . rather like the moustache of a comic man on the films (par. 2)
     - **(3)** It was a high, reiterated cry . . . like the tolling of a bell. (par. 12)

(4) The Indians had gone grey like bad coffee (par. 13)
(5) He was dangling with his toes pointed straight downwards, slowly revolving, as dead as a stone. (par. 15)

4. You know that an important feature of narration is the writer's ability to look at a brief span of time and to expand that moment with specific language.
   a. How has Orwell limited the events in "A Hanging" to a specific moment in time and place?
   b. How does the image "a sodden morning of the rains" in paragraph 1 set the mood for the main event portrayed in the essay? What is the effect of the image "brown silent men"? Why does Orwell describe the prisoner as "a puny wisp of a man, with a shaven head and vague liquid eyes" (par. 2)? Why does the author present him in almost a comic way?
   c. What is the effect of the image about the bugle call in paragraph 3? Why does Orwell create the image of the dog trying to lick the prisoner's face (par. 6)? How does it contribute to his main point? In paragraph 12, Orwell tells us that the dog whines. Why does he give that detail? Discuss the value of the images about the dog in paragraphs 15 and 17.
   d. Why does Orwell offer the image of the prisoner stepping aside "to avoid a puddle on the path"? How does it advance the point of the essay? What is the effect of the image of the superintendent poking the ground with his stick (par. 13)?
   e. What is the importance of the superintendent's words in paragraph 3? What is the value of the Eurasian boy's conversation in paragraph 18? How does the dialogue in paragraphs 20 to 24 contribute to Orwell's main point?
   f. Why has Orwell left out information about the crime the prisoner committed? How would you feel about the prisoner if you knew he were, say, a rapist, a murderer, a molester of children, or a heroin supplier?
5. Analyze the point of view in the essay. Is the "I" narrator an observer, a participant, or both? Is he neutral or involved? Support your opinion.
6. In "A Hanging," Orwell skillfully uses several forms of *irony* to support his main ideas. Irony, in general, is the use of language to suggest the opposite of what is said. First, there is

verbal irony, which involves a contrast between what is said and what is actually meant. Second, there is *irony of situation,* where there is a contrast between what is expected or thought appropriate and what actually happens. Then, there is *dramatic irony,* in which there is a contrast between what a character says and what the reader (or the audience) actually knows or understands.

a. In paragraph 2, why does Orwell describe the prisoner as a *comic* type? Why does he emphasize the prisoner's *smallness?* Why does Orwell write that the prisoner "hardly noticed what was happening"? Why might this be called ironic?

b. When the dog appears in paragraph 6, how is its behavior described? How do the dog's actions contrast with the situation?

c. What is the major irony that Orwell analyzes in paragraph 10?

d. In paragraph 11, how does the fact that one prisoner is being used to execute another prisoner strike you?

e. Why is the superintendent's remark in paragraph 16—"*He's* all right"—a good example of verbal irony?

f. After the hanging, the men engage in seemingly normal actions. However, Orwell undercuts these actions through the use of irony. Find at least two examples of irony in paragraphs 17 to 24.

MIXING PATTERNS

"Description," we say in the introduction to Chapter 3, "is frequently used to make abstract ideas more *concrete.*" In this essay, basically a narrative, how does Orwell use description to make an abstract idea—capital punishment is wrong—concrete? Identify three or four examples.

Exploring the Writer's Ideas

1. Orwell is clearly against capital punishment. Why might you agree or disagree with him? Are there any crimes for which capital punishment is acceptable to you? If not, what should society do with those convicted of serious crimes?

2. Do you think the method used to perform capital punishment has anything to do with the way we view it? Is death by hanging or firing squad worse than death by gas or by the electric chair? Or are they all the same? Socrates—a Greek philosopher convicted of conspiracy—was forced to drink *hemlock,* a fast-acting poison. Can you accept that?
3. Orwell shows a variety of reactions people have to an act of execution. Can you believe the way the people behave here? Why? How do you explain the large crowds that gathered to watch public executions in Europe in the sixteenth and seventeenth centuries?

IDEAS FOR WRITING

Prewriting

Make two columns on a sheet of paper that you have headed *Capital Punishment.* In one column, jot down all the reasons you can think of in favor of capital punishment. In the other column, indicate all the reasons you can think of against it.

Guided Writing

Write a narrative essay in which you tell about a punishment you either saw or received. Use sensory language, selecting your details carefully. At one point in your paper—as Orwell does in paragraph 10—state your opinion or interpretation of the punishment clearly.

1. Use a number of images that name colors, sounds, smells, and actions.
2. Try to write at least three original similes. Think through your comparisons carefully. Make sure they are logical. Avoid overused comparisons like "He was white as a ghost."
3. Set your narrative in time and place. Tell the season of the year and the place in which the event occurred.
4. Fill in details of the setting. Show what the surroundings look like.
5. Name people by name. Show details of their actions. Quote some of their spoken dialogue.
6. Use the first-person point of view.

Thinking and Writing Collaboratively

In small groups, read drafts of each other's essays for the Guided Writing activity. Look especially at the point at which the writer states an opinion about or interprets the punishment received. Does the writer adequately explain the event? What insights has the writer brought to the moment by analyzing it? How could either the narrative itself or the interpretation be made clearer or more powerful?

Writing About the Text

Write an essay in which you consider why Orwell chose to include the dog in this essay. How would the essay be different without the dog? Do you think the dog was *actually* present at the scene of the hanging, or do you suspect that Orwell made him up?

More Writing Projects

1. Narrate in your journal an event that turned out differently from what you expected—a blind date, a picnic, a holiday. Try to stress the irony of the situation.
2. Write a narrative paragraph that describes a vivid event in which you hid your true feelings about the event, such as a postelection party, the wedding of someone you disliked, a job interview, a visit to the doctor.
3. Write an editorial for your college newspaper supporting or attacking the idea of capital punishment. Communicate your position through the use of real or hypothetical narration of a relevant event.

Travelling

Grace Paley

Grace Paley, often identified as "a bard of Jewish New York," was born in the Bronx in 1922. She is the author of three revered collections of short fiction—*The Little Disturbances of Man* (1959), *Enormous Changes at the Last Minute* (1974), and *Later the Same Day* (1985). Her work is known for its subtlety, its thoughtful exploration of human relations, and its intimate tone. She regards herself as a "somewhat combative pacifist and cooperative anarchist" and has been active all her life in liberal and left-wing causes such as Women's Pentagon Action and the Greenwich Village Peace Center. In 1987 Paley received a Senior Fellowship from the National Endowment for the Arts in recognition of her lifetime contribution to literature. Currently Paley is writer-in-residence at City College of the City University of New York and also teaches at Sarah Lawrence College. This selection, originally published in *The New Yorker,* tells two stories about travelling into the American South by bus during the time of racial segregation. In recounting these stories about her mother and herself, Paley also asks: Why do we remember some things and not others? She probes this question as a writer and a daughter, weaving the meanings of private and public journeys into her account.

PREREADING: THINKING ABOUT THE ESSAY IN ADVANCE

What stories in your family make up the family saga, the tales that identify you as a family group? How do you know that these stories are "true"? Are there stories in your family about the days of racial segregation?

Words to Watch

fatigues (par. 10) clothing worn by soldiers in training
ebbed (par. 12) flowing of tide back to the sea
Gentile (par. 16) any person not a Jew
anti-Semitism (par. 16) prejudice against Jews
adamant (par. 20) unyielding

1 My mother and sister were travelling South. The year was 1927. They had begun their journey in New York. They were going to

visit my brother, who was studying at the Medical College of Virginia, in Richmond. Their bus was an express and had stopped only in Philadelphia, Wilmington, and now Washington. Here the darker people who had got on in Philadelphia or New York rose from their seats, put their bags and boxes together, and moved to the back of the bus. People who boarded in Washington knew where to seat themselves. My mother had heard that something like this would happen. My sister had heard of it, too. They had not lived in it. This reorganization of passengers by color happened in silence. My mother and sister remained in their seats, which were about three-quarters of the way back.

When everyone was settled, the bus driver began to collect tickets. My sister saw him coming. She pinched my mother—"Ma! Look!" Of course, my mother saw him, too. What frightened my sister was the quietness. The white people in front, the black people in back—silent. 2

The driver sighed, said, "You can't sit here, ma'am. It's for them—waving over his shoulder at the Negroes, among whom they were now sitting. "Move, please." 3

My mother said, "No." 4

He said, "You don't understand, ma'am. It's against the law. You have to move to the front." 5

My mother said, "No." 6

When I first tried to write this scene, I imagined my mother saying, "That's all right, mister. We're comfortable. I can't change my seat every minute." I read this invention to my sister. She said it was nothing like that. My mother did not try to be friendly or pretend innocence. While my sister trembled in the silence, my mother said for the third time—quietly—"No." 7

Somehow, finally, they were in Richmond. There was my brother, in school among so many American boys. After hugs and my mother's anxious looks at her young son, my sister said, "Vic, you know what Mama did?" 8

My brother remembers thinking, What? Oh! She wouldn't move? He had a classmate, a Jewish boy like him, but from Virginia, who had had a public confrontation with a Negro man. He had punched that man hard, knocked him down. My brother couldn't believe it. He was stunned. He couldn't imagine a Jewish boy wanting to knock anyone down. He had never wanted to. But he thought, looking back, that he had been set down to work and study in a nearly foreign place, and had had to get used to it. Then 9 he told me about the Second World War, when the disgrace of black soldiers forced to sit behind white German P.O.W.s shook him. Shamed him.

10 About fifteen years later, in 1943, in early summer, I rode the bus for about three days from New York to Miami Beach, where my husband and hundreds of other boys in sweaty fatigues were trudging up and down the streets and beaches to prepare themselves for war.

11 By late afternoon of the second long day, we were well into the South, beyond Richmond, maybe in South Carolina or Georgia. My excitement about travel in the wide world was damaged a little by a sudden fear that I might not recognize Jess, or he me. We hadn't seen each other for two months. I took a photograph out of my pocket; yes, I would know him.

12 I had been sleeping, waking, reading, writing, dozing, waking. So many hours, the movement of the passengers was like a tide that sometimes ebbed and now seemed to be noisily rising. I opened my eyes to the sound of people brushing past my aisle seat. And looked up to see a colored woman holding a large sleeping baby, who, with the heaviness of sleep, his arms tight around her neck, seemed to be pulling her head down. I looked around and noticed that I was in the last white row. The press of new travellers had made it impossible for her to move farther back. She seemed so tired, and I had been sitting and sitting for a day and a half at least. Not thinking, or maybe refusing to think, I offered her my seat.

13 She looked to the right and left as well as she could. Softly, she said, "Oh, no." I became fully awake. A white man was standing right beside her, but on the other side of the invisible absolute racial border. Of course, she couldn't accept my seat. Her sleeping child hung mercilessly from her neck. She shifted a little to balance the burden. She whispered to herself, "Oh, I just don't know." So I said, "Well, at least give me the baby." First, she turned, barely looking at the man beside her. He made no move. Then, to my surprise, but obviously out of sheer exhaustion, she disengaged the child from her body and placed him on my lap. He was deep in child-sleep. He stirred, but not enough to bother himself or me. I liked holding him, aligning him along my twenty-year-old young woman's shape. I thought ahead to that holding, that breathing together that would happen in my life if this war would ever end. I was so comfortable under his nice weight. I closed my eyes

for a couple of minutes, but suddenly opened them to look up into the face of a white man talking. In a loud voice, he addressed me: "Lady, I wouldn't of touched that thing with a meat hook."

I thought, Oh, this world will end in ice. I could do nothing but look straight into his eyes. I did not look away from him. Then I held that little boy a little tighter, kissed his curly head, pressed him even closer, so that he began to squirm. So sleepy, he reshaped himself inside my arms. His mother tried to narrow herself away from that dangerous border, too frightened at first to move at all. After a couple of minutes, she leaned forward a little, placed her hand on the baby's head, and held it there until the next stop. I couldn't look up into her mother face. 14

I write this remembrance more than fifty years later. I look back at that mother and child. I see how young she is. Her hand on his head is quite small, though she tries by spreading her fingers wide to hide him from the white man. But the child I'm holding, his little face as he turns toward me, is the dark-brown face of my *own* grandson, my daughter's boy, the open mouth of the sleeper, the full lips, the thick little body of a child who runs wildly from one end of the yard to the other, leaps from dangerous heights with experienced caution, muscling his body, his mind, for coming realities. 15

Of course, when my mother and sister returned from Charlottesville the family at home wanted to know: How was Vic doing in school among all those Gentiles? Was the long bus ride hard? Was the anti-Semitism really bad or just normal? What happened on the bus? I was probably present at that supper, the attentive listener and total forgetter of information that immediately started to form me. 16

Then, last year, my sister, casting the net of old age (through which recent experience easily slips), brought up that old story. First, I was angry. How come you never told me about your bus ride with Mama? I mean, really, so many years ago. 17

I don't know, she said. Anyway, you were only about four years old and, besides, maybe I did. 18

I asked my brother why we'd never talked about that day. He said he thought now that it had had a great effect on him; he had tried unravelling its meaning for years—then life, family, work happened. So I imagined him, a youngster, really, a kid from the Bronx in Virginia in 1927—why, he was a stranger there himself. 19

20 In the next couple of weeks, we continued to talk about our mother, the way she was principled, adamant, and at the same time so shy. What else could we remember . . . Well, I said, I have a story about those buses, too. Then I told them: how it happened on just such a journey, when I was still quite young, that I first knew my grandson, first held him close but could protect him for only about twenty minutes fifty years ago.

BUILDING VOCABULARY

Use the following words in sentences of your own:

a. confrontation (par. 9)
b. absolute (par. 13)
c. remembrance (par. 15)
d. principled (par. 20)

THINKING CRITICALLY ABOUT THE ESSAY

Understanding the Writer's Ideas

1. What is the effect of the writer's reference to some of the passengers as "the darker people"?
2. After the writer's mother utters her dramatic "No" the essay seems to shift (par. 7) to a new subject. What is that subject? What is the connection between this subject and the apparent subject of the first six paragraphs? Why does the writer connect these two subjects?
3. What do we learn from her brother's recollection of her mother's trip?
4. Compare and contrast the writer's experience riding a bus into the South in 1943 and her mother's experience fifteen years earlier.
5. What does the writer mean by "Oh, this world will end in ice" (par. 14)?
6. Why does the writer say, at the end of par. 14, "I couldn't look up into her mother face"?
7. What do we learn in the concluding paragraphs of the essay, paragraphs located in the present?

Understanding the Writer's Techniques

1. An essay in the form of *narrative* may not follow the conventions of a more argumentative essay. For instance, the essay does not have an explicit thesis statement but rather is written to answer two related questions. What are these questions?
2. A narrative by its nature is likely to make its points differently from a less literary kind of essay. A narrative, for example, may stress emotion more than reason. What techniques does the writer use to build an *emotional* argument?
3. This essay has four main sections (par. 1–par. 6; par. 7–par. 14; par. 15; and par. 16–par. 20). Indicate briefly the purpose of each section and note how the writer connects these sections.
4. This essay has at least two focuses—one on specific incidents in the context of racism, one on recollection. How does the writer keep the time frame of the various incidents of the story clearly before the reader? How does the writer weave the process of recollecting into the narrating of the actual incidents?
5. Narration allows a writer to suggest or evoke meanings rather than to specify or to hone in for greater precision. Can you find examples in the essay where instead of clear-cut statements meaning is suggested or evoked?
6. Why are the details of the essay's last section (par. 16 on) left to the end?

Exploring the Writer's Ideas

1. The writer emphasizes the process of remembering as perilous, incomplete, open to reverie. Do you agree? Can you give examples from your own experience that confirm or refute Paley's view of memory?
2. The stories the writer tells about her mother and herself portray them both as principled people doing the right thing. What evidence does the essay provide to support the view of Paley and her mother as people of rectitude? Or do you find evidence that in fact Paley has exaggerated what happened?
3. Do you think the experience of "seeing before the fact" that Paley narrates (see par. 15) is true to life, or colored for the purposes of storytelling? Defend your view.

IDEAS FOR WRITING

Prewriting

Write a few sentences telling something about an especially "principled, adamant" member of your family.

Guided Writing

Narrate an incident or related incidents that (a) show you or a member of your family doing something "principled"; and (b) make the process of remembering a part of your essay.

1. Begin with the account of an incident—without indicating that you are writing out of second-hand knowledge or recollection.
2. Then suggest an alternative way you may have narrated the incident.
3. Indicate how you concluded what was true to the incident and belonged in your narration.
4. Write a paragraph that reflects on the incident(s) and ties its meaning to the process of recollection.
5. End by offering some matter-of-fact details about the process of remembering that fill in some of the blanks of "what actually happened."

Thinking and Writing Collaboratively

In a small group of four or five students, share your Guided Writing essays with each other. Then attempt alternative narrative lines for each essay, suggesting different possible openings, sequences of events, emphases, and endings. Ask each other which versions you prefer, and why. Discuss the problems of trying to recapture "what really happened" in the past in an essay.

Writing About the Text

Write an essay about the function of memory in this piece, "Travelling." Consider the *organization* of Paley's essay as part of your discussion.

More Writing Projects

1. Write a journal entry about your personal experience of relations among white and African-American people.
2. In a paragraph, explore the narrative possibilities of an incident in your life that could be interpreted as "foreseeing" a future event, just as Paley's encounter with the black baby on the bus "foretold" her acquaintance with her grandchild.
3. Talk with two or three members of your family about an important incident in the family's history. Write an account that weighs these different recollections, and what each person thinks to be most important.

SUMMING UP: CHAPTER 4

1. Orwell's essay has remained one of the outstanding essays of the century, widely anthologized and frequently taught in English writing classes. How do you account for its popularity? Would you consider it the best essay in this chapter or in the four chapters you have read so far? Why or why not? Write an essay in which you analyze and evaluate "A Hanging."
2. Elizabeth Wong and Grace Paley both challenge cultural assumptions. Use their narratives as a starting point, and write an essay about a particular time in your childhood when you tried to accept, ignore, or defy a given cultural or social expectation.
3. You are Richard Selzer (author of "The Discus Thrower," pages 199–122) and you have been asked by a local newspaper to write a short review of George Orwell's "A Hanging." Basing your insights on the philosophy of "The Discus Thrower," write the review. Or, if you choose, be George Orwell and write a review of Selzer's "The Discus Thrower."
4. What have you learned about writing strong narratives from the writers in this chapter? What generalizations can you draw? What "rules" can you derive? Write an essay called "How to Write Narratives" based on what you have learned from Wong, Hughes, Orwell, and (or) Paley. Make specific references to the writer(s) of your choice.
5. Hughes's essay highlights the role of religion in life. Write an essay in which you narrate an important religious experience that you remember. You might want to narrate the story of your own "conversion."
6. Narrative is often used to recreate a memory—as is the case in the essays in this chapter. But our memories, especially of emotionally charged happenings—and especially of emotionally charged happenings that occurred long ago—are notoriously unreliable. How do the writers in this chapter deal with the problem of the possible unreliability of memory? How much would it matter if some of the incidents narrated here were *in*accurately recalled by the writer, or even altered to make a better essay?

7. Compare and contrast the importance of an attitude toward language for Amy Tan (pp. 28–34) and Elizabeth Wong.
8. Hughes, Orwell, and Paley explore the ambiguities of thinking or feeling things that distinguish you from most of the people around you—such as being a colonial policeman who is opposed to colonialism, or being a white woman opposed to segregation and traveling in a segregated society. Compare and contrast how these writers treat the situation of the person who does not conform to society's values and beliefs.

FROM SEEING TO WRITING

Write a narrative essay in which you tell what you think is the story of the picture reprinted here. Develop your thesis, present lively details to hold your reader's attention, and introduce your details in a sequence that is easy to follow.

James Carroll/Stock Boston

CHAPTER 5

Illustration

WHAT IS ILLUSTRATION?

One convenient way for writers to present and to support a point is through *illustration*—that is, by means of several examples to back up an idea. Illustration (or *exemplification*) helps a writer put general or abstract thoughts into specific examples. As readers, we often find that we are able to understand a writer's point more effectively because we respond to the concrete examples. We are familiar with illustration in everyday life. If a police officer is called a racist, the review board will want *illustrations* of the racist behavior. The accuser will have to provide concrete examples of racist language, or present arrest statistics that show the officer was more likely to arrest Korean-Americans, for instance, than white Americans.

Writing that uses illustration is most effective if it uses *several* examples to support the thesis. A single, isolated example might not convince anyone easily, but a series of examples builds up a stronger case. Writers can also use an *extended example,* which is one example that is developed at length.

For instance, you might want to illustrate your thesis that American patchwork quilts are an important record of women's history. Since your reader might not be familiar with quilts, you would have to illustrate your argument with examples such as these:

- Baltimore album quilts were given to Eastern women heading West in the nineteenth century, and contain signatures and dates stitched in the squares to mark the event.
- Women used blue and white in quilt patterns to show their support for the temperance movement that opposed sale of alcohol.

- Women named patterns after geographic and historical events, creating such quilts as Rocky Road to Kansas and Abe Lincoln's Platform.
- African-American quilters adapted techniques from West Africa to make blankets for slave quarters.
- One quilter from Kentucky recorded all the deaths in her family in her work. The unusual quilt contains a pattern of a cemetery and coffins with names for each family member!

If you visited a museum and there was only one painting on the wall, you would probably feel that you hadn't gotten your money's worth. You expect a museum to be a *collection* of paintings, so that you can study a variety of types of art or several paintings by the same painter. In the same way, through the accumulation of illustrations, the writer builds a case for the thesis.

In this chapter, writers use illustration forcefully to make their points. Brent Staples, an African-American journalist, shows how some people perceive his mere presence on a street at night as a threat. Barbara Ehrenreich uses irony to illustrate, from a feminist perspective, what women can learn from men. Amartya Sen uses examples from history to debunk current ideas about "clashing civilizations." Finally, Lewis Thomas uses examples from his experience as a surgeon to illustrate how death is a natural part of the life cycle. Each writer knows that one example is insufficient to create a case, but that multiple examples yield a convincing essay.

HOW DO WE READ ILLUSTRATION?

Reading illustration requires us to ask ourselves these questions:

- What is the writer's thesis? What is the *purpose* of the examples?
- What audience is the writer addressing? How do we know?
- What other techniques is the writer using? Is there narration? Description? How are these used to help the illustration?
- In what order has the writer arranged the examples? Where is the most important example placed?
- How does the writer use *transitions?* Often, transitions in illustration essays enumerate: *first, second, third; one, another.*

HOW DO WE WRITE WITH ILLUSTRATIONS?

Read the selections critically to see the many ways in which writers can use illustrations to support an idea.

Select your topic and write a thesis that tells the reader what you are going to illustrate and what your main idea is about the subject.

Sample thesis statement:

> Many people have long cherished quilts for their beautiful colors and patterns, but few collectors recognize the history stitched into the squares.

Make a list of *examples* to support the thesis.

Examples by quilt types: Baltimore album quilts, political quilts, suffrage quilts, slave quilts, graveyard quilts

Examples by quilt pattern names: Radical Rose; Drunkard's Path; Memory Blocks; Old Maid's Puzzle; Wheel of Mystery; Log Cabin; Rocky Road to Kansas; Slave Chain; Underground Railroad; Delectable Mountains; Union Star; Jackson Star; Old Indian Trail; Trip around the World

Determine who the audience will be: a group of experienced quilters? museum curators? a PTA group? Each is a different audience with different interests and needs.

Plan an arrangement of the examples. Begin with the least important and build up to the most important. Or arrange the examples in chronological order.

Plan to use other techniques (such as description), especially if your audience is unfamiliar with your subject. If you are writing the quilt paper and using the example of the Baltimore album quilt, you would then have to *describe* it for readers who do not know what such a quilt looks like.

Be sure that the *purpose* of the illustrations is clearly stated, especially in the conclusion. In the quilt essay, for instance, different quilt patterns might be illustrated in order to encourage readers to preserve and study quilts.

Writing and Revising the Draft

Use the first paragraph to introduce the subject and to set up a clear thesis. You might introduce an *abstract* idea, such as forgotten history, that will be *illustrated* in the examples.

Plan the body to give the reader lots of examples, and to develop the examples if necessary. Use narration, description, and dialogue to enhance the illustrations. Write a conclusion that returns to the abstract idea you began with in the introduction.

Write a second draft for reading aloud.

Revise, based on your listener's comments. Proofread the essay carefully. Check spelling and grammar. Make a final copy.

A STUDENT PARAGRAPH: ILLUSTRATION

This paragraph from a student's illustration paper on quiltmaking shows how the use of examples advances the thesis of the essay. The thesis, which you examined on page 179, asserts that, the colors and patterns of quilts aside, "few collectors recognize the history stitched into the squares."

Reference to essay thesis, "history stitched into squares"

Transition ("one of the most significant examples") asserts order according to significance

Reference to other points in essay provides unity

Kinsale's work is main illustration developed in the paragraph

Supporting detail

Supporting detail

Closing sentence connects to essay's thesis

We can find a significant example of the historical, recordkeeping function of quiltmaking in Mary Kinsale's needlework. Kinsale lived in Kentucky in the mid-nineteenth century. Unlike the political quilts discussed earlier, and the various quilts that document "official" history, Kinsale's quilts deal only with the history of her family. Specifically, Kinsale set out to document the precise dates of death of all her family members, illustrating the squares with coffins, open graves, and other symbols of death. What we might call morbid or tasteless today probably struck members of Kinsale's community as natural and proper; the American culture had not yet restricted images of gaunt, grinning skulls, mossy tombstones, and other symbols of death to horror movies. In fact, Kinsale's images served an important religious and social purpose by reminding family and friends to reform their lives while there was still time. Kinsale decided to record the vital dates of her dearly departed, and remind the living of their duty in life, by stitching a quilt, rather than simply writing an entry in the family Bible, or leaving the task to the government. Her quiltmaking illustrates nineteenth-century society's old-fashioned attitude towards death, as well as their understanding of the role ordinary individuals could play in recording history.

Night Walker

Brent Staples

Brent Staples is an editorial writer for the *New York Times* and holds a Ph.D. in psychology from the University of Chicago. Yet, since his youth, he has instilled fear and suspicion in many just by taking nighttime walks to combat his insomnia. In this essay, which appeared in the *Los Angeles Times* in 1986, Staples explains how others perceive themselves as his potential victim simply because he is a black man in "urban America."

PREREADING: THINKING ABOUT THE ESSAY IN ADVANCE

Imagine this scene: you are walking alone at night in your own neighborhood and you hear footsteps behind you that you believe are the footsteps of someone of a different race from yours. How do you feel? What do you do? Why?

Words to Watch

affluent (par. 1) wealthy
discreet (par. 1) showing good judgment; careful
quarry (par. 2) prey; object of a hunt
dismayed (par. 2) discouraged
taut (par. 4) tight; tense
warrenlike (par. 5) like a crowded tenement district
bandolier (par. 5) gun belt worn across the chest
solace (par. 5) relief; consolation; comfort
retrospect (par. 6) review of past event
ad hoc (par. 7) unplanned; for the particular case at hand
labyrinthine (par. 7) like a maze
skittish (par. 9) nervous; jumpy
constitutionals (par. 10) regular walks

1 My first victim was a woman—white, well dressed, probably in her early 20s. I came upon her late one evening on a deserted street in Hyde Park, a relatively affluent neighborhood in an otherwise mean, impoverished section of Chicago. As I swung onto the avenue behind her, there seemed to be a discreet, uninflammatory

distance between us. Not so. She cast back a worried glance. To her, the youngish black man—a broad six feet two inches with a beard and billowing hair, both hands shoved into the pockets of a bulky military jacket—seemed menacingly close. She picked up her pace and was soon running in earnest. Within seconds she disappeared into a cross street.

That was more than a decade ago. I was 22 years old, a graduate student newly arrived at the University of Chicago. It was in the echo of that terrified woman's footfalls that I first began to know the unwieldy inheritance I'd come into—the ability to alter public space in ugly ways. It was clear that she thought herself the quarry of a mugger, a rapist, or worse. Suffering a bout of insomnia, however, I was stalking sleep, not defenseless wayfarers. As a softy who is scarcely able to take a knife to a raw chicken—let alone hold one to a person's throat—I was surprised, embarrassed, and dismayed all at once. Her flight made me feel like an accomplice in tyranny. It also made it clear that I was indistinguishable from the muggers who occasionally seeped into the area from the surrounding ghetto. I soon gathered that being perceived as dangerous is a hazard in itself: Where fear and weapons meet—and they often do in urban America—there is always the possibility of death. 2

In that first year, my first away from my hometown, I was to become thoroughly familiar with the language of fear. At dark, shadowy intersections, I could cross in front of a car stopped at a traffic light and elicit the *thunk, thunk, thunk, thunk* of the driver—black, white, male, female—hammering down the door locks. On less traveled streets after dark, I grew accustomed to but never comfortable with people crossing to the other side of the street rather than pass me. Then there were the standard unpleasantries with policemen, doormen, bouncers, cabdrivers, and others whose business it is to screen out troublesome individuals *before* there is any nastiness. 3

I moved to New York nearly two years ago and I have remained an avid night walker. In central Manhattan, the near-constant crowd covers the tense one-on-one street encounters. Elsewhere, things can get very taut indeed. 4

After dark, on the warrenlike streets of Brooklyn where I live, I often see women who fear the worst from me. They seem to have set their faces on neutral, and with their purse straps strung across their chests bandolier-style, they forge ahead as though bracing 5 themselves against being tackled. I understand, of course, that the danger they perceive is not a hallucination. Women are particularly vulnerable to street violence, and young black males are drastically overrepresented among the perpetrators of that violence. Yet these truths are no solace against the alienation that comes of being ever the suspect, an entity with whom pedestrians avoid making eye contact.

6 It is not altogether clear to me how I reached the ripe old age of 22 without being conscious of the lethality nighttime pedestrians attributed to me. Perhaps it was because in Chester, Pa., the small, angry industrial town where I came of age in the 1960s, I was scarcely noticeable against a backdrop of gang warfare, street knifings, and murders. I grew up one of the good boys, had perhaps a half-dozen fistfights. In retrospect, my shyness of combat has clear sources. As a boy, I saw countless tough guys locked away; I have since buried several, too. They were babies, really—a teen-age cousin, a brother of 22, a childhood friend in his mid-20s—all gone down in episodes of bravado played out in the streets. I chose, perhaps unconsciously, to remain a shadow—timid, but a survivor.

7 The fearsomeness mistakenly attributed to me in public places often has a perilous flavor. The most frightening of these confusions occurred in the late 1970s and early 1980s, when I worked as a journalist in Chicago. One day, rushing into the office of a magazine I was writing for with a deadline story in hand, I was mistaken for a burglar. The office manager called security and, with an ad hoc posse, pursued me through the labyrinthine halls, nearly to my editor's door. I had no way of proving who I was. I could only move briskly toward the company of someone who knew me.

8 Relatively speaking, however, I never fared as badly as another black male journalist. He went to nearby Waukegan, Ill., a couple of summers ago to work on a story about a murderer who was born there. Mistaking the reporter for the killer, police officers hauled him from his car at gunpoint and but for his press credentials would probably have tried to book him. Such episodes are not uncommon. Black men trade tales like this all the time.

9 Over the years, I learned to smother the rage I felt at so often being mistaken for a criminal. Not to do so would surely have led to madness. I now take precautions to make myself less threatening. I move about with care, particularly late in the evening. I give a wide berth to nervous people on subway platforms during the

wee hours. If I happen to be entering a building behind some people who appear skittish, I may walk by, letting them clear the lobby before I return, so as not to seem to be following them. I have been calm and extremely congenial on those rare occasions when I've been pulled over by the police.

10 And on late-evening constitutionals I employ what has proved to be an excellent tension-reducing measure: I whistle melodies from Beethoven and Vivaldi and the more popular classical composers. Even steely New Yorkers hunching toward nighttime destinations seem to relax, and occasionally they even join in the tune. Virtually everybody seems to sense that a mugger wouldn't be warbling bright, sunny selections from Vivaldi's "Four Seasons." It is my equivalent of the cowbell that hikers wear when they are in bear country.

BUILDING VOCABULARY

1. Use context clues to determine the meaning of each word in italics. Return to the appropriate paragraph in the essay for more clues. Then, if necessary, check your definitions in a dictionary and compare the dictionary meaning with the meaning you derived from the context.
   - **a.** seemed *menacingly* close (par. 1)
   - **b.** I was *indistinguishable* from the muggers who occasionally *seeped* into the area (par. 2)
   - **c.** I have remained an *avid* night walker (par. 4)
   - **d.** they *forge* ahead (par. 5)
   - **e.** Women are particularly *vulnerable* to street violence (par. 5)
   - **f.** the *lethality* nighttime pedestrians attributed to me (par. 6)
   - **g.** episodes of *bravado* played out in the streets (par. 6)
   - **h.** I learned to *smother* the rage I felt . . . so often (par. 9)
   - **i.** I now take *precautions* to make myself less threatening (par. 9)
   - **j.** Even *steely* New Yorkers *hunching* toward nighttime destinations (par. 10)
2. Reread paragraph 1. List all the words suggesting action and all the words involving emotion. What is the cumulative effect?

THINKING CRITICALLY ABOUT THE ESSAY

Understanding the Writer's Ideas

1. How does Staples describe himself in paragraph 1? What point is he making by such a description?
2. Explain in your own words the incident Staples narrates in paragraph 1. Where does it take place? When? How old was the author at the time? What was he doing? During the incident, why did the woman "cast back a worried glance"? Was she really his "victim"? Explain. What was Staples's reaction to the incident?
3. What is the "unwieldy inheritance" mentioned in paragraph 2? What is Staples's definition of it? What is the implied meaning?
4. How would you describe Staples's personality? What does he mean when he describes himself as "a softy"? How does he illustrate the fact that he is "a softy"? Why did he develop this personality?
5. Explain the meaning of the statement, "I soon gathered that being perceived as dangerous is a hazard in itself" (par. 2).
6. What is "the language of fear" (par. 3)? What examples does Staples provide to illustrate this "language"?
7. Why did car drivers lock their doors when the author walked in front of their cars? How did Staples feel about that?
8. Where did Staples grow up? Did he experience the same reactions there to his nighttime walks as he did in Chicago? Why? How was Manhattan different from Chicago for the author? How was Brooklyn different from Manhattan?
9. What has been Staples's reaction to the numerous incidents of mistaken identity? How has he dealt with that reaction? What "precautions" does he take to make himself "less threatening"?
10. Summarize the example Staples narrates about the black journalist in Waukegan.
11. What has been the author's experiences with the police? Explain.
12. Does the author feel that all the danger people attribute to him when he takes night walks is unfair or unwarranted? Explain.
13. Why does his whistling selections from Beethoven and Vivaldi seem to make people less afraid of the author?

Understanding the Writer's Techniques

1. What is Staples's thesis in this essay?
2. How do the title and opening statement of this essay grasp and hold the reader's interest?
3. Reread the first paragraph. What *mood* or *tone* does Staples establish here? How? Does he sustain that mood? Is there a shift in tone? Explain.
4. How does the author use *narration* in paragraph 1 as a way to illustrate a point? What point is illustrated? Where else does he use narration?
5. What is the effect of the two-word sentence "Not so" in paragraph 1?
6. Staples uses *description* in this essay. Which descriptions serve as illustrations? Explain what ideas they support.
7. *Onomatopoeia* is the use of words whose sounds suggest their sense or action. Where in the essay does Staples use this technique? What action does the sound represent? Why does the author use this technique instead of simply describing the action?
8. What examples from Staples's childhood illustrate why he developed his particular adult personality?
9. Explain the meaning of the final sentence in the essay.
10. *Stereotypes* are oversimplified, uncritical judgments about people, races, issues, events, and so forth. Where in this essay does the author present stereotypes? For what purpose?
11. For whom was this article intended? Why do you think so? Is it written primarily for a white or black audience? Explain.

Exploring the Writer's Ideas

1. In this essay, Staples gives not only examples of his own experiences but also those of other black men. It is interesting, however, that he does not include examples of the experiences of black women. Why do you think he omitted these references? How do you feel about the omission? Are there any recent news stories, either in your city or in others, which might be included as such illustrations?
2. What prejudices and stereotypes about different racial and cultural groups do people in your community hold? Where do

these prejudices and stereotypes come from? Do you think any are justified?

3. What everyday situations do you perceive as most dangerous? Why do you perceive them as such? How do you react to protect yourself? Do you feel your perceptions and reactions are realistic? Explain.

IDEAS FOR WRITING

Prewriting

Write down a few of your personality traits, and then jot down ways in which people identify those traits. Also, indicate how people misperceive you—that is, how they reach wrong conclusions about your personality.

Guided Writing

Write an essay that illustrates how something about your personality has been incorrectly perceived at some time or over a period of time.

1. Begin your essay by narrating a single incident that vividly illustrates the misperception. Begin this illustration with a statement.
2. Explain the time context of this incident as it fits into your life or into a continuing misperception.
3. Describe and illustrate "who you really are" in relation to this misperception.
4. Explain how this misperception fits into a larger context outside your immediate, personal experience of it.
5. Write a series of descriptive illustrations to explain how this misperception has continued to affect you over time.
6. Explain how you first became aware of the misperception.
7. If possible, offer illustrations of others who have suffered the same or similar misperceptions of themselves.
8. Write about your emotional reaction to this overall situation.
9. Illustrate how you have learned to cope with the situation.
10. Give your essay a "catchy" title.

Thinking and Writing Collaboratively

Form groups of four or five, and recommend productive ways to solve the key problems raised by Staples in his essay. Take notes, and then as a group write down the problems and their possible solutions. Share the group's writing with the rest of the class.

Writing About the Text

To advance his thesis, Staples relies on language that suggests anger, fear, and violence. Write an essay in which you examine this language in "Night Walker." Which words seem to express those elements? How do they relate to Staples's thesis? In what ways, if at all, is Staples angry, fearful, or violent? The people around him?

More Writing Projects

1. Usually stereotypes are thought of as negative. Illustrate at least three *positive* stereotypes in your latest journal entry.
2. Write a paragraph in which you illustrate your family's or friends' misconceptions about your girlfriend/boyfriend, wife/husband, or best friend.
3. What tension reducing measures do you use in situations that might frighten you or in which you might frighten others? Write an essay to address the issue.

What I've Learned from Men

Barbara Ehrenreich

In this essay from *Ms.* magazine, the feminist author and historian Barbara Ehrenreich illustrates the qualities that have made her one of our most-read voices of dissent. Among these qualities is a sense of humor—though she can use her humor to deadly effect, as readers of her regular contributions to *The Nation* magazine, a weekly devoted to left-liberal commentary, can attest. Her work has been characterized by the *New York Times* as "elegant, trenchant, savagely angry, morally outraged and outrageously funny." Ehrenreich is the author of numerous essays and books, including *Fear of Falling: The Inner Life of the Middle Class* (1989), *The Snarling Citizen* (1995), and, most recently, *Nickel and Dimed: On (Not) Getting By in America* (2001). *Nickel and Dimed* is the account of three month-long episodes in different American cities where Ehrenreich lived entirely on earnings from jobs paying $7 or $8 per hour. She is the recipient of a National Magazine Award for Excellence in Reporting and of a Guggenheim Fellowship. In this selection, Ehrenreich shows that sometimes you can learn the most important things from your enemies, in this case, men. Aside from being able to catch the eye of a waiter, a not inconsiderable attribute, men have one wrongly maligned quality that women would do well to learn from, Ehrenreich argues: how to be tough.

PREREADING: THINKING ABOUT THE ESSAY IN ADVANCE

What have you learned from the opposite sex? What expectations are raised by a woman saying she has learned something from men?

Words to Watch

euthanasia (par. 1) mercy killing
lecherous (par. 3) lewd
unconscionable (par. 3) beyond reasonable bounds
servility (par. 4) attitude appropriate to servants
AWOL (par. 4) used in military for Absent Without Leave
veneer (par. 4) mere outside show
rueful (par. 4) regretful

aura (par. 6) distinctive air
self-deprecation (par. 6) putting oneself down
brazenly (par. 6) shamelessly
taciturn (par. 9) silent
purveyors (par. 10) providers
emulating (par. 11) imitating
basso profundo (par. 11) deep bass voice
blandishments (par. 12) allurements

For many years I believed that women had only one thing to learn from men: how to get the attention of a waiter by some means short of kicking over the table and shrieking. Never in my life have I gotten the attention of a waiter, unless it was an off-duty waiter whose car I'd accidentally scraped in a parking lot somewhere. Men, however, can summon a maître d' just by thinking the word "coffee," and this is a power women would be well advised to study. What else would we possibly want to learn from them? How to interrupt someone in mid-sentence as if you were performing an act of conversational euthanasia? How to drop a pair of socks three feet from an open hamper and keep right on walking? How to make those weird guttural gargling sounds in the bathroom? 1

But now, at mid-life, I am willing to admit that there are some real and useful things to learn from men. Not from all men—in fact, we may have the most to learn from some of the men we like the least. This realization does not mean that my feminist principles have gone soft with age: what I think women could learn from men is how to get *tough.* After more than a decade of consciousness-raising, assertiveness training, and hand-to-hand combat in the battle of the sexes, we're still too ladylike. Let me try that again—we're just too *damn* ladylike. 2

Here is an example from my own experience, a story that I blush to recount. A few years ago, at an international conference held in an exotic and luxurious setting, a prestigious professor invited me to his room for what he said would be an intellectual discussion on matters of theoretical importance. So far, so good. I showed up promptly. But only minutes into the conversation—held in all-too-adjacent chairs—it emerged that he was interested in something more substantial than a meeting of minds. I was disgusted, but not enough to overcome 30-odd years of programming in ladylikeness. Every time his comments took a lecherous turn, 3

I chattered distractingly; every time his hand found its way to my knee, I returned it as if it were something he had misplaced. This went on for an unconscionable period (as much as 20 minutes); then there was a minor scuffle, a dash for the door, and I was out—with nothing violated but my self-esteem. I, a full-grown feminist, conversant with such matters as rape crisis counseling and sexual harassment at the workplace, had behaved like a ninny—or, as I now understand it, like a lady.

4 The essence of ladylikeness is a persistent servility masked as "niceness." For example, we (women) tend to assume that it is our responsibility to keep everything "nice" even when the person we are with is rude, aggressive, or emotionally AWOL. (In the above example, I was so busy taking responsibility for preserving the veneer of "niceness" that I almost forgot to take responsibility for myself.) In conversations with men, we do almost all the work: sociologists have observed that in male-female social interactions it's the woman who throws out leading questions and verbal encouragements ("So how did you *feel* about that?" and so on) while the man, typically, says "Hmmmm." Wherever we go, we're perpetually smiling—the on-cue smile, like the now-outmoded curtsy, being one of our culture's little rituals of submission. We're trained to feel embarrassed if we're praised, but if we see a criticism coming at us from miles down the road, we rush to acknowledge it. And when we're feeling aggressive or angry or resentful, we just tighten up our smiles or turn them into rueful little moues. In short, we spend a great deal of time acting like wimps.

5 For contrast, think of the macho stars we love to watch. Think, for example, of Mel Gibson facing down punk marauders in "The Road Warrior" . . . John Travolta swaggering his way through the early scenes of "Saturday Night Fever" . . . or Marlon Brando shrugging off the local law in "The Wild One." Would they simper their way through tight spots? Chatter aimlessly to keep the conversation going? Get all clutched up whenever they think they might—just might—have hurt someone's feelings? No, of course not, and therein, I think, lies their fascination for us.

6 The attraction of the "tough guy" is that he has—or at least seems to have—what most of us lack, and that is an aura of power and control. In an article, feminist psychiatrist Jean Baker Miller writes that "a Woman's using self-determined power for herself is equivalent to selfishness [and] destructiveness"—an equation that makes us want to avoid even the appearance of power. Miller cites

cases of women who get depressed just when they're on the verge of success—and of women who do succeed and then bury their achievement in self-deprecation. As an example, she describes one company's periodic meetings to recognize outstanding salespeople: when a woman is asked to say a few words about her achievement, she tends to say something like, "Well, I really don't know how it happened. I guess I was just lucky this time." In contrast, the men will cheerfully own up to the hard work, intelligence, and so on, to which they owe their success. By putting herself down, a woman avoids feeling brazenly powerful and potentially "selfish"; she also does the traditional lady's work of trying to make everyone else feel better ("She's not really so smart, after all, just lucky").

So we might as well get a little tougher. And a good place to start is by cutting back on the small acts of deference that we've been programmed to perform since girlhood. Like unnecessary smiling. For many women—waitresses, flight attendants, receptionists—smiling is an occupational requirement, but there's no reason for anyone to go around grinning when she's not being paid for it. I'd suggest that we save our off-duty smiles for when we truly feel like sharing them, and if you're not sure what to do with your face in the meantime, study Clint Eastwood's expressions—both of them. 7

Along the same lines, I think women should stop taking responsibility for every human interaction we engage in. In a social encounter with a woman, the average man can go 25 minutes saying nothing more than "You don't say?" "Izzat so?" and, of course, "Hmmmm." Why should we do all the work? By taking so much responsibility for making conversations go well, we act as if we had much more at stake in the encounter than the other party—and that gives him (or her) the power advantage. Every now and then, we deserve to get more out of a conversation than we put into it: I'd suggest not offering information you'd rather not share ("I'm really terrified that my sales plan won't work") and not, out of sheer politeness, soliciting information you don't really want ("Wherever did you get that lovely tie?"). There will be pauses, but they don't have to be awkward for *you*. 8

It is true that some, perhaps most, men will interpret any decrease in female deference as a deliberate act of hostility. Omit the 9 free smiles and perky conversation-boosters and someone is bound to ask, "Well, what's come over *you* today?" For most of us, the first impulse is to stare at our feet and make vague references to a terminally ill aunt in Atlanta, but we should have as much right to be taciturn as the average (male) taxi driver. If you're taking a vacation from smiles and small talk and some fellow is moved to inquire about what's "bothering" you, just stare back levelly and say, the international debt crisis, the arms race, or the death of God.

10 There are all kinds of ways to toughen up—and potentially move up—at work, and I leave the details to the purveyors of assertiveness training. But Jean Baker Miller's study underscores a fundamental principle that anyone can master on her own. We can stop acting less capable than we actually are. For example, in the matter of taking credit when credit is due, there's a key difference between saying "I was just lucky" and saying "I had a plan and it worked." If you take the credit you deserve, you're letting people know that you were confident you'd succeed all along, and that you fully intend to do so again.

11 Finally, we may be able to learn something from men about what to do with anger. As a general rule, women get irritated: men get *mad.* We make tight little smiles of ladylike exasperation; they pound on desks and roar. I wouldn't recommend emulating the full basso profundo male tantrum, but women do need ways of expressing justified anger clearly, colorfully, and, when necessary, crudely. If you're not just irritated, but *pissed off,* it might help to say so.

12 I, for example, have rerun the scene with the prestigious professor many times in my mind. And in my mind, I play it like Bogart. I start by moving my chair over to where I can look the professor full in the face. I let him do the chattering, and when it becomes evident that he has nothing serious to say, I lean back and cross my arms, just to let him know that he's wasting my time. I do not smile, neither do I nod encouragement. Nor, of course, do I respond to his blandishments with apologetic shrugs and blushes. Then, at the first flicker of lechery, I stand up and announce coolly, "All right, I've had enough of this crap." Then I walk out—slowly, deliberately, confidently. Just like a man.

13 Or—now that I think of it—just like a woman.

BUILDING VOCABULARY

1. The writer uses a number of words ascribed to "ladies" for ironic effect. Try the same in sentences of your own that use the following:
   - **a.** curtsy
   - **b.** simper
   - **c.** chatter
2. The writer is comfortable using a mixture of formal and informal words, as the essay requires. Use the following combinations of words in sentences or paragraphs of your own:
   - **a.** prestigious (par. 3) *and* hand-to-hand combat (par. 2)
   - **b.** theoretical (par. 3) *and* clutched up (par. 5)
   - **c.** deliberate (par. 9) *and* perky (par. 9)

THINKING CRITICALLY ABOUT THE ESSAY

Understanding the Writer's Ideas

1. What does the writer's opening paragraph tell us about her attitude toward men?
2. The writer contrasts "being tough" and "being ladylike." What are the attitudes and behaviors that she associates with these opposing ways of being?
3. Why does the writer risk embarrassing herself by telling the story of her encounter with the "prestigious professor" of paragraph 3?
4. According to Ehrenreich, why are women reluctant to exert power?
5. The writer advocates two alternative strategies women should pursue "to get tough." The first is to stop doing things that are subservient; the second is to begin to act differently. What does she recommend women should stop doing, and why? What does she recommend women should start doing, and why?

Understanding the Writer's Techniques

1. *Tone* (see Glossary) expresses a writer's attitude toward his or her subject. What is the tone of the opening paragraph? What

does the tone of this paragraph suggest we can expect in the rest of the essay?

2. Why does the author delay her thesis statement until close to the end of the second paragraph?
3. One key to a smooth, graceful essay is effective use of transitions. Explain how the writer establishes effective transitions between paragraphs 3 and 4, 4 and 5, and 6 and 7.
4. Writers sometimes seek to strengthen their arguments by quoting supporting views from authorities. For what reasons does the writer quote Jean Baker Miller?
5. Why does the writer mix informal and formal diction in this essay? What does this choice of diction suggest about the writer's intended audience?
6. Why does the writer "rerun" the scene with the "prestigious professor" to conclude her essay?

Exploring the Writer's Ideas

1. Perhaps it is in the nature of waiters—who are often busy and pestered by customers—to make it hard for you to catch their attention, regardless of your gender. In that case, was Ehrenreich's envy of "men's" sway over waiters another case of a feminine inferiority complex, or is Ehrenreich simply using a rhetorical ploy to grab your attention at the start of her essay? Explain.
2. Ehrenreich seems to want us to distinguish between the servile characteristics of what is ladylike and the more robust qualities of women. Do you believe her portrait of a lady is fair and accurate? Why?
3. Is it a moral failing of the essay that the writer acknowledges only one possible character for all men, and that is the unattractive character of the "macho" male? Ought the essay to have provided us with a positive example of male character too? Does the absence of positive male role models weaken the essay's argument about women? Why, or why not?
4. Ehrenreich's argument proceeds by building one generalization on another. She quotes Jean Baker Miller, for example, to make the point that *for all women* the exercise of power is associated with selfishness and destructiveness. If you can think of exceptions to her main general statements, does this undermine her argument for you, or do you remain persuaded of her

generalizations despite the exceptions. Discuss in relation to one or two examples.

5. You are likely to have heard someone described as "one tough lady." How are the attributes of such a person the same as or different from those that Ehrenreich advocates for all women?

IDEAS FOR WRITING

Prewriting

Make a list of character traits generally associated with men, and another of traits generally associated with women. Then make a second list of those traits men might wish to adapt from women, and women from men.

Guided Writing

Write an essay titled "What I've Learned from . . ." Fill in the blank with a word of your choice. Your essay should illustrate how you came to realize you could learn something positive from those you had long ago given up on as sources of wisdom. Some possible titles might be "What I've Learned from Parents," "What I've Learned from Professional Wrestlers," or "What I've Learned from the Boss."

1. Begin your essay by indicating why you long ago abandoned the idea that you could learn anything from "________."
2. But then explain why you have realized that the very thing that made "__________" so unattractive, might be instructive after all.
3. Provide an example from your own behavior where having a little more of that something undesirable you always disliked in "_________" might have been a good thing.
4. Now explain how that nice quality of your own character that is just the opposite of the undesirable "_________" might actually reflect a weakness or flaw in your character.
5. If possible, quote an authoritative source to underscore how your apparently good quality masks a serious weakness (as in the flaws of being a lady).

6. Now illustrate how adopting some of "________" behaviors would be a good thing.
7. Conclude by showing how this quality in "________," when adopted by you and those like you, actually brings out better what you are truly like.

Thinking and Writing Collaboratively

In small groups, discuss the lists of attributes of men and women you had drawn up in your Prewriting exercise. Do the qualities listed compose stereotypes, or do they reflect abiding truths about the differences between the sexes? Compare the lists made up by the students in your group—what can you conclude from the similarities and differences among these lists?

Writing About the Text

Many words in this essay are "man" words, that is, words that our culture often uses to describe and identify males. Similarly, many "woman" words appear here too. How does Ehrenreich use "man" and "woman" language to advantage here? Identify several words that she uses in each gender category and explore their effect on the essay.

More Writing Projects

1. For a journal entry, write about a quality, usually associated with the opposite sex, that you secretly admire, or wish you could say was a quality of your own.
2. In an essay, explore a quality in yourself or in people more generally that is commonly viewed as good—such as kindness—for its possibly "weak" or self-defeating underside (in the case of kindness, for example, always doing for others and never thinking of yourself).
3. Write an essay on the dangers of stereotyping, that is, of thinking of individuals as necessarily having the characteristics of a group.

A World Not Neatly Divided

Amartya Sen

Amartya Sen, born in Santiniketan, India, in 1933, was awarded the Nobel Prize in Economics (1998) for his groundbreaking contributions to "welfare economics." Concerned with poverty and inequality, Sen has clarified the nature of decision making and analysis with respect to poverty, not only creating more useful indexes of poverty but also providing an intellectual foundation for the practical application of group values to individual instances of need or distress. His major works include *Collective Choice and Social Welfare* (1970), *On Economic Inequality* (1973), and *Poverty and Famines: An Essay on Entitlement and Deprivation* (1981). Educated at Presidency College, Calcutta, and Trinity College, Cambridge, England, in 1998 Sen left his professorships in economics and philosophy at Harvard University to become Master of Trinity College, Cambridge. In this selection, which appeared in the *New York Times* on November 23, 2001, Sen uses extensive examples to show how blanket generalizations about "civilizations" grossly oversimplify the complex reality of all cultures.

PREREADING: THINKING ABOUT THE ESSAY IN ADVANCE

When you think of the world as being "neatly divided," what kinds of divisions come to mind? Does the idea of broad classifications—into, for example, "Western civilization," "the Islamic world," and so on—seem to you important in understanding contemporary history? Or do such classifications seem arbitrary and misleading?

Words to Watch

thesis (par. 1) proposition, a developed argumentative position

befuddling (par. 2) confusing

singular (par. 2) unique, single

futile (par. 2) useless

atheists (par. 2) those who do not believe in the existence of God

agnostics (par. 2) those who are skeptical that whether God does or does not exist can be known

homogeneous (par. 4) consisting of similar parts or elements

excommunicating (par. 4) excluding from membership in a church; expelling
discrete (par. 5) composed of distinct parts
imperious (par. 5) arrogant
plurality (par. 7) being numerous
flammable (par. 7) easily ignited

1 When people talk about clashing civilizations, as so many politicians and academics do now, they can sometimes miss the central issue. The inadequacy of this thesis begins well before we get to the question of whether civilizations must clash. The basic weakness of the theory lies in its program of categorizing people of the world according to a unique, allegedly commanding system of classification. This is problematic because civilizational categories are crude and inconsistent and also because there are other ways of seeing people (linked to politics, language, literature, class, occupation or other affiliations).

2 The befuddling influence of a singular classification also traps those who dispute the thesis of a clash: To talk about "the Islamic world" or "the Western world" is already to adopt an impoverished vision of humanity as unalterably divided. In fact, civilizations are hard to partition in this way, given the diversities within each society as well as the linkages among different countries and cultures. For example, describing India as a "Hindu civilization" misses the fact that India has more Muslims than any other country except Indonesia and possibly Pakistan. It is futile to try to understand Indian art, literature, music, food or politics without seeing the extensive interactions across barriers of religious communities. These include Hindus and Muslims, Buddhists, Jains, Sikhs, Parsees, Christians (who have been in India since at least the fourth century, well before England's conversion to Christianity), Jews (present since the fall of Jerusalem), and even atheists and agnostics. Sanskrit has a larger atheistic literature than exists in any other classical language. Speaking of India as a Hindu civilization may be comforting to the Hindu fundamentalist, but it is an odd reading of India.

3 A similar coarseness can be seen in the other categories invoked, like "the Islamic world." Consider Akbar and Aurangzeb, two Muslim emperors of the Mogul dynasty in India. Aurangzeb tried hard to convert Hindus into Muslims and instituted various policies in that direction, of which taxing the non-Muslims was

only one example. In contrast, Akbar reveled in his multiethnic court and pluralist laws, and issued official proclamations insisting that no one "should be interfered with on account of religion" and that "anyone is to be allowed to go over to a religion that pleases him."

If a homogeneous view of Islam were to be taken, then only one of these emperors could count as a true Muslim. The Islamic fundamentalist would have no time for Akbar; Prime Minister Tony Blair, given his insistence that tolerance is a defining characteristic of Islam, would have to consider excommunicating Aurangzeb. I expect both Akbar and Aurangzeb would protest, and so would I. A similar crudity is present in the characterization of what is called "Western civilization." Tolerance and individual freedom have certainly been present in European history. But there is no dearth of diversity here, either. When Akbar was making his pronouncements on religious tolerance in Agra, in the 1590's, the Inquisitions were still going on; in 1600, Giordano Bruno was burned at the stake, for heresy, in Campo dei Fiori in Rome. 4

Dividing the world into discrete civilizations is not just crude. It propels us into the absurd belief that this partitioning is natural and necessary and must overwhelm all other ways of identifying people. That imperious view goes not only against the sentiment that "we human beings are all much the same," but also against the more plausible understanding that we are diversely different. For example, Bangladesh's split from Pakistan was not connected with religion, but with language and politics. 5

Each of us has many features in our self-conception. Our religion, important as it may be, cannot be an all-engulfing identity. Even a shared poverty can be a source of solidarity across the borders. The kind of division highlighted by, say, the so-called "antiglobalization" protesters—whose movement is, incidentally, one of the most globalized in the world—tries to unite the underdogs of the world economy and goes firmly against religious, national or "civilizational" lines of division. 6

The main hope of harmony lies not in any imagined uniformity, but in the plurality of our identities, which cut across each other and work against sharp divisions into impenetrable civilizational camps. Political leaders who think and act in terms of sectioning off humanity into various "worlds" stand to make the world more flammable—even when their intentions are very different. They also end up, in the case of civilizations defined by religion, lending authority to religious leaders seen as spokesmen for 7 their "worlds." In the process, other voices are muffled and other concerns silenced. The robbing of our plural identities not only reduces us; it impoverishes the world.

BUILDING VOCABULARY

This selection addresses the many ethnicities and religious views of the world's civilizations. Identify the following:

a. Hindus (par. 2)
b. Muslims (par. 2)
c. Buddhists (par. 2)
d. Jains (par. 2)
e. Sikhs (par. 2)
f. Parsees (par. 2)
g. Mogul (par. 3)

THINKING CRITICALLY ABOUT THE ESSAY

Understanding the Writer's Ideas

1. What, in your own words, is the inadequacy that Sen attributes to the view that the world is today divided among "clashing civilizations" (par. 1)?
2. What does Sen mean by "singular classification" (par. 2)?
3. How is a "singular classification" of civilizations inaccurate?
4. How does Sen show that "the Islamic world" is much more diverse than the term suggests?
5. How does Sen show that "Western civilization" is not "homogeneous"?
6. Why does Sen think that "dividing the world into discrete civilizations" (par. 5) is "imperious"?
7. What features of societies other than religion can influence identity?
8. According to Sen where does the "main hope for harmony" in the world lie?

Understanding the Writer's Techniques

1. Sen opens his essay by arguing against a point of view different from his own. What is that point of view?

2. The writer presents his own view by asserting the "inadequacy" of the opposing view. How would you restate Sen's view in your own words?
3. Sen's essay exposes the inadequacies of the opposing view by citing illustrations that undermine it. What are three such illustrations?
4. Sen uses illustrations to refute a "thesis." How does he achieve a coherent development of ideas in the essay?
5. What examples of effective transitions can you identify in the essay? Why are they effective?
6. Which illustration do you find especially useful in refuting the thesis of clashing civilizations?
7. How does Sen's use of illustration provide adequate evidence for his point that the "main hope of harmony" lies in the "plurality of our identities"?
8. How effective is Sen's closing paragraph? Explain your answer.

MIXING PATTERNS

Illustration is a major rhetorical strategy that Sen uses here, but classification (see Chapter 8) also figures strongly in advancing his thesis. And both illustration and classification work along with argumentation (see Chapter 11). How do these three writing techniques interact? How do illustration and classification help develop the argument, which stresses logic and valid evidence?

Exploring the Writer's Ideas

1. Everyday conversation frequently uses a form of "singular classification" of nations, groups, or civilizations. We say, "New Yorkers are always on the go," or, "The British . . ." and so forth. Are these categorizations inexcusably "befuddling" or do they usually contain at least a grain of truth? Explain your answer.
2. Even if we accept Sen's view that civilizations are not "homogeneous," does it follow that they can't be characterized in some overall or "singular" way? Is it wrong to think that what distinguishes "the West" and, say, the Middle East is mainly religion? Why or why not?

3. Sen is concerned that imposing uniform categories on civilizations encourages division and conflict. But does he offer sufficient support for the idea that the opposite point of view—that our identities are plural—is likely to create harmony?
4. In what ways does Sen's essay provide useful insights about the September 11, 2001 terrorist tragedy at the World Trade Center in New York City?

IDEAS FOR WRITING

Prewriting

Sen says that "singular classification" belies the complexity and diversity of every civilization. Can you think of other cases where the same argument could be made—that is, where we impose a "singular" interpretation on something or someone or some group when the reality is more complex or diverse?

Guided Writing

Write an essay that, through illustration, challenges what you see as an oversimplified or inadequate division of people, objects, or ideas. You might want to challenge the classification of people as honest or untruthful, or gay or straight; or the classification of movies as adult or children's, or as fantasy or realism; or the classification of countries as dictatorships or democracies, or as rich or poor.

1. Begin by identifying the "thesis" or view that you intend to question, and indicate the main ways in which you think the thesis is inadequate (indicate at least three major inadequacies)
2. Define and identify the classifications you are challenging.
3. Illustrate the inadequacies you see in three separate paragraphs. Think carefully about the order of your illustrations so that your view is developed. Be sure to use effective transitions from one paragraph, and illustration, to the next.
4. Draw your three illustrations together into a view of human affairs that sees things differently from the thesis you are refuting.

5. Conclude by suggesting the main harm done by following the simplified or inadequate division you are challenging.
6. In your final sentence restate your strongest point.

Thinking and Writing Collaboratively

In small groups, choose a popular example of "singular classification"—say, "Yankee fans" or "Republicans" or "lawyers"—and list qualities that are usually attributed to that "singular classification" as well as those that contradict it. Share your list with the class, and as a class discuss the pros and cons of singular classification.

Writing About the Text

Sen makes many references to historical, cultural, and religious figures and events in order to make his point. Write an essay in which you identify and analyze the use of the most important such references in the essay. How do they advance Sen's thesis?

More Writing Projects

1. Write a journal entry about your own identity, using three to five illustrations to support your self-portrait.
2. Write a paragraph that Sen might add to his essay, illustrating yet further the inadequacy of "singular classification" of civilizations.
3. Assume that a publisher of a brief encyclopedia asks you to write a 500-word entry on "Western civilization." Write two versions of an essay: one that attempts a "singular classification" and one that stresses diversity.

Death in the Open

Lewis Thomas

Lewis Thomas (1913–1993) was a distinguished physician and the leading interpreter of science for the lay public. The son of a surgeon, Thomas was born in Flushing, New York, and educated at Princeton and Harvard. He served as dean of the medical schools of New York University and Yale, and from 1973 to 1983 headed the world's foremost cancer hospital, the Memorial Sloan-Kettering Cancer Center in New York City. But he is likely to be remembered for his memorable essays, written from 1971 for his column, "Notes of a Biology Watcher," in the authoritative *New England Journal of Medicine*. These essays were published as *The Lives of a Cell* (1974) and *The Medusa and the Snail* (1979), both winners of the National Book Award. His last published book was *The Fragile Species* (1992). Thomas's essays display his unusual gift for describing complex scientific topics in vivid and accessible ways. In a dispassionate but humane voice, Thomas was able to convey the wonder, and sometimes the terror, of science, as well as its dazzling, humbling, and poignant implications for the human animal. This selection, from *Lives of a Cell,* is a fine example of Thomas at work, probing the "natural marvel" of death.

PREREADING: THINKING ABOUT THE ESSAY IN ADVANCE

A familiar phenomenon that many of us have witnessed is an animal's dead body—a squirrel, a mouse, a bird, a cat or dog—on a street or highway, dead either as roadkill or from natural causes. Reflect a moment on such a phenomenon. What do you think of and feel when you witness such a scene?

Words to Watch

voles (par. 1) the members of any one of several species of small rodents

impropriety (par. 2) an improper action or remark

progeny (par. 4) descendants or offspring

mutation (par. 4) a sudden genetic change

amebocytes (par. 4) one-celled organisms

stipulated (par. 6) made a special condition for

incongruity (par. 6) something which is not consistent with its environment

conspicuous (par. 7) very obvious

inexplicably (par. 7) unexplainably

anomalies (par. 10) irregularities

notion (par. 11) an idea

detestable (par. 11) hateful

synchrony (par. 11) simultaneous occurrence

Most of the dead animals you see on highways near the cities are dogs, a few cats. Out in the countryside, the forms and coloring of the dead are strange; these are the wild creatures. Seen from a car window they appear as fragments, evoking memories of woodchucks, badgers, skunks, voles, snakes, sometimes the mysterious wreckage of a deer. 1

It is always a queer shock, part a sudden upwelling of grief, part unaccountable amazement. It is simply astounding to see an animal dead on a highway. The outrage is more than just the location; it is the impropriety of such visible death, anywhere. You do not expect to see dead animals in the open. It is the nature of animals to die alone, off somewhere, hidden. It is wrong to see them lying out on the highway; it is wrong to see them anywhere. 2

Everything in the world dies, but we only know about it as a kind of abstraction. If you stand in a meadow, at the edge of a hillside, and look around carefully, almost everything you can catch sight of is in the process of dying, and most things will be dead long before you are. If it were not for the constant renewal and replacement going on before your eyes, the whole place would turn to stone and sand under your feet. 3

There are some creatures that do not seem to die at all; they simply vanish totally into their own progeny. Single cells do this. The cell becomes two, then four, and so on, and after a while the last trace is gone. It cannot be seen as death; barring mutation, the descendants are simply the first cell, living all over again. The cycles of the slime mold have episodes that seem as conclusive as death, but the withered slug, with its stalk and fruiting body, is plainly the transient tissue of a developing animal; the free-swimming amebocytes use this organ collectively in order to produce more of themselves. 4

There are said to be a billion billion insects on the earth at any moment, most of them with very short life expectancies by our 5 standards. Someone has estimated that there are 25 million assorted insects hanging in the air over every temperate square mile, in a column extending upward for thousands of feet, drifting through the layers of the atmosphere like plankton. They are dying steadily, some by being eaten, some just dropping in their tracks, tons of them around the earth, disintegrating as they die, invisibly.

6 Who ever sees dead birds, in anything like the huge numbers stipulated by the certainty of the death of all birds? A dead bird is an incongruity, more startling than an unexpected live bird, sure evidence to the human mind that something has gone wrong. Birds do their dying off somewhere, behind things, under things, never on the wing.

7 Animals seem to have an instinct for performing death alone, hidden. Even the largest, most conspicuous ones find ways to conceal themselves in time. If an elephant missteps and dies in an open place, the herd will not leave him there; the others will pick him up and carry the body from place to place, finally putting it down in some inexplicably suitable location. When elephants encounter the skeleton of an elephant out in the open, they methodically take up each of the bones and distribute them, in a ponderous ceremony, over neighboring acres.

8 It is a natural marvel. All of the life of the earth dies, all of the time, in the same volume as the new life that dazzles us each morning, each spring. All we see of this is the odd stump, the fly struggling on the porch floor of the summer house in October, the fragment on the highway. I have lived all my life with an embarrassment of squirrels in my backyard, they are all over the place, all year long, and I have never seen, anywhere, a dead squirrel.

9 I suppose it is just as well. If the earth were otherwise, and all the dying were done in the open, with the dead there to be looked at, we would never have it out of our minds. We can forget about it much of the time, or think of it as an accident to be avoided, somehow. But it does make the process of dying seem more exceptional than it really is, and harder to engage in at the times when we must ourselves engage.

10 In our way, we conform as best we can to the rest of nature. The obituary pages tell us of the news that we are dying away, while the birth announcements in finer print, off at the side of the page, inform us of our replacements, but we get no grasp from this of the enormity of scale. There are 3 billion of us on the earth, and all 3 billion must be dead, on a schedule, within this lifetime. The

vast mortality, involving something over 50 million of us each year, takes place in relative secrecy. We can only really know of the deaths in our households, or among our friends. These, detached in our minds from all the rest, we take to be unnatural events, anomalies, outrages. We speak of our own dead in low voices; struck down, we say, as though visible death can only occur for cause, by disease or violence, avoidably. We send off for flowers, grieve, make ceremonies, scatter bones, unaware of the rest of the 3 billion on the same schedule. All of that immense mass of flesh and bone and consciousness will disappear by absorption into the earth, without recognition by the transient survivors.

11 Less than a half century from now, our replacements will have more than doubled the numbers. It is hard to see how we can continue to keep the secret, with such multitudes doing the dying. We will have to give up the notion that death is catastrophe, or detestable, or avoidable, or even strange. We will need to learn more about the cycling of life in the rest of the system, and about our connection to the process. Everything that comes alive seems to be in trade for something that dies, cell for cell. There might be some comfort in the recognition of synchrony, in the information that we all go down together, in the best of company.

BUILDING VOCABULARY

1. Thomas makes imaginative and often unique use of adjectival expressions. Explain the meaning of each adjective in the phrases below:
   - **a.** *queer* shock (par. 2)
   - **b.** *unaccountable* amazement (par. 2)
   - **c.** *visible* death (pars. 2 and 10)
   - **d.** *transient* tissue (par. 4)
   - **e.** *ponderous* ceremony (par. 7)
   - **f.** *neighboring* acres (par. 7)
   - **g.** *natural* marvel (par. 8)
   - **h.** *vast* mortality (par. 10)
   - **i.** *relative* secrecy (par. 10)
   - **j.** *transient* survivors (par. 10)
2. An *idiom* is an expression that has a special meaning only when taken as a whole; taken separately, the words may not make sense. What are the meanings of the following idioms?

a. upwelling of grief (par. 2)
b. catch sight of (par. 3)
c. on the wing (par. 6)
d. in time (par. 7)
e. no grasp . . . of (par. 10)
f. for cause (par. 10)

THINKING CRITICALLY ABOUT THE ESSAY

Understanding the Writer's Ideas

1. Why does Thomas feel that it is strange to see dead animals in the countryside? How are dead animals more varied in the country than in the city? According to Thomas, for what reason is it a shock to see a dead animal on the road?
2. In paragraph 3, Thomas suggests that death is often an "abstraction." What does he mean by this statement? How does he suggest we can make death something more real? In your own words, for what reasons does he suggest we accept the life-death cycle as a more concrete idea?
3. Why, according to Thomas, do single cells seem not to die?
4. What is the meaning of the question at the beginning of paragraph 6? How does it relate to the theme of the essay? To what does the writer compare seeing a dead bird? Why does he call it an "incongruity"? How is it "sure evidence . . . that something has gone wrong"?
5. Explain the process of death among elephants as Thomas describes it.
6. Explain the meaning of "the odd stump" in paragraph 8. What two examples of "the odd stump" does Thomas offer?
7. What example from personal experience does Thomas give to show that dead animals seem "to disappear"?
8. Explain the meaning of the first sentence of paragraph 9. In your own words, tell why Thomas feels the way he does.
9. What is the "secret" in paragraph 11?
10. In paragraph 10 Thomas says, "In our way, we conform as best we can to the rest of nature." What does he mean? What supporting examples does he offer? What is the result? What examples does Thomas give of our reactions to the death of other human beings?

11. Why does Thomas say we must change our attitude toward death? How does he suggest that we do so?

Understanding the Writer's Techniques

1. What is Thomas's thesis in this essay? In what way does the concluding paragraph reinforce it?
2. Study the introductory paragraphs. Why does the author offer several examples? Why is "the mysterious wreckage of a deer" an especially effective example?
3. Are there any clear illustrations in paragraph 2? Why or why not? What is the effect? Explain the connection between paragraphs 2 and 3.
4. Paragraphs 4 to 8 use illustrations to support a series of generalizations or topic sentences. Put a check mark by the topic sentence in these paragraphs and identify the generalization. Then analyze the illustrations used to support each one. Which examples are the most specific? the most visual? the most personal? Are there any extended examples?
5. How does paragraph 9 serve as a transition to the topic of paragraph 10? Why does Thomas use statistics in paragraph 10? How do they drive his point home?
6. Examine the author's use of pronouns in this essay. First, trace the use of first-person pronouns ("I," "we," "my," "our"). Why does Thomas use such pronouns? Why is their use in paragraph 8 especially effective? Next, consider Thomas's frequent use of the pronoun *it.* (Beginning writers are often instructed to minimize their use of such pronouns as *it, this,* and *that* because they are not specific and may leave the reader confused.) Explain what the word *it* stands for in paragraphs 2, 4, 8, and 9. Why does Thomas use a word whose meaning may be confusing?
7. Thomas uses *figurative language* (see Glossary) in this essay, particularly *similes* and *metaphors* (see Glossary). Explain in your own words the meanings of the following similes and metaphors:
   a. *the mysterious wreckage* of a deer (par. 1)
   b. episodes that seem *as conclusive as death* (par. 4)
   c. drifting through the layers of the atmosphere *like plankton* (par. 5)

8. We may say that the expression "dropping in their tracks" in paragraph 5 is a kind of pun. (A *pun* is a humorous use of a word or an expression that suggests two meanings.) What is the popular expression using the words *dropping* and *flies* that Thomas's phrase puns on?
9. Thomas makes use of a technique called "repetition with a difference"—that is, saying *almost* the same thing for added emphasis. Explain how repetition with a difference adds effectiveness to the sentences in which each of the following expressions is used:
   a. alone, hidden (par. 7)
   b. each morning, each spring (par. 8)
   c. unnatural events, anomalies, outrages (par. 10)
   d. catastrophe, or detestable, or avoidable, or even strange (par. 11)
10. *Parallelism* (see Glossary) is a type of sentence structure within a paragraph that creates a balance in the presentation of ideas and adds emphasis. It often uses a repeating pattern of subjects and verbs, prepositional phrases, questions, and so on. How does Thomas use parallelism in paragraph 3? paragraph 10? paragraph 11?

Exploring the Writer's Ideas

1. We might say that Thomas's title, "Death in the Open," is a double entendre (that is, has a double meaning). In what two ways may we interpret the phrase "in the open" as it relates to the contents of the essay? How do the two meanings relate to the philosophical points Thomas makes, especially in the two opening paragraphs and in the conclusion? Do you feel it is important to be more "open" about death? Why?
2. In paragraph 10, Thomas writes, "We speak of our own dead in low voices; struck down, we . . . ."Struck down" is used here as a *euphemism* (see Glossary) in place of other words that might be upsetting or distasteful. What other euphemisms do we have for death? Euphemisms for dying are often used to explain death to children. Do you think it is right, or necessary, to use such "guarded language" with youngsters? Why? For what other words or expressions do we commonly use euphemisms?

3. At the end of the essay, Thomas suggests that we might be more comfortable with death if we understood it as a natural, common occurrence. What are your feelings about this philosophy?
4. According to Thomas's views in paragraph 9, because we don't often see dead animals "in the open," we are less prepared when we do encounter death. Do you think this reasoning is correct? Why or why not?
5. In paragraph 7 Thomas explains the process of death among elephants. What is your impression of the elephant herd's behavior at the death of one of its members? Why does Thomas call it "a natural marvel"? Have you ever heard the expression "the elephant dying grounds"? What does it mean?

IDEAS FOR WRITING

Prewriting

Brainstorm for five to ten minutes on the phrase "in the open." What does it mean? What does it mean to you? What various ways can you apply it to elements in your life? What other acts "in the open" surprise, puzzle, stir, or shock you?

Guided Writing

Write an essay in which you illustrate "__________ in the Open." Fill in the blank with a word of your choice, a word that reflects some phenomenon, emotion, or idea whose features are often hard to understand. You might write about birth in the open, concerts in the open, love in the open, fear in the open, or war in the open, for example.

1. Develop an introduction with general examples that are relevant to your topic.
2. Add one or two paragraphs in which you speculate or philosophize on the phenomenon you are writing about.
3. Point out how the topic is most common throughout nature, society, or the world.
4. Give at least three extended examples that illustrate your topic.

5. Use the first-person pronouns "I" and "we": to add emphasis.
6. Illustrate ways in which people are generally unaware of certain features of the topic or tend to hide these features.
7. Try to include at least one statistic in your essay.
8. Use some idiomatic expressions in your essay.
9. Conclude your essay with some examples of how and why we can become more "open" about the topic.

Thinking and Writing Collaboratively

Form small groups, and read the drafts of each other's Guided Writing essays. After general comments about how to take the essay to the next draft, concentrate on the conclusions in each piece. Does the writer give appropriate examples in the conclusion? Do you see how and why the writer feels that we can become more open about the topic at hand?

Writing About the Text

Thomas wrote this essay originally for a medical journal and its specialized audience of physicians. Why would the essay appeal to medical practitioners? What elements also would appeal to a general audience? Write an essay that answers these questions, providing specific examples from the text.

More Writing Projects

1. For a journal entry, use examples to tell of your first experiences with death. You may want to write about the death of a relative, a friend, an acquaintance, a celebrity, or a pet.
2. Visit a place in the countryside (or a park) for one hour. Make a written record as you walk around detailing all evidence of natural death that you come across. Then write an illustrative paragraph on natural death as you observed it.
3. In your library, explore various burial practices among different races, religions, or ethnic groups and write an essay in which you illustrate several of these practices.

SUMMING UP: CHAPTER 5

1. Richard Selzer ("The Discus Thrower," pages 119–122), Lewis Thomas ("Death in the Open," pages 207–210), and George Orwell ("A Hanging," pages 157–163) all deal with death and dying. Write your own essay about the issue, drawing on points from these three authors to illustrate your own position.
2. From this chapter select the essay that you think best uses the mode of illustration. Write an essay in which you analyze the writer's techniques and strategies. Make specific references to the text.
3. The world of the night, the environment of Staples's "Night Walker," challenges our senses and our perceptions, simply because it is so different from the typical daytime worlds we usually inhabit. What unusual nighttime experiences have you had? How do you feel about the night? Write an essay of illustration to address these questions.
4. Staples and Sen both write about how stereotypes can prevent us from seeing a more diverse truth. What ideas and examples from Sen's essay would support Staples's thesis? What ideas and examples from Staples's essay would support Sen's thesis?
5. The writers in this chapter all use illustration to challenge a widely held view. The view, these essays suggest, is held by many people, maybe by most people. Most white women are made nervous by black men walking behind them on dark deserted streets. Most feminists think the last people they have anything to learn from are men. And so forth. How is illustration an effective method for these writers to achieve their purposes? What other rhetorical means could these writers have used? Write an essay that argues for or against the view that illustration is the most effective tool for poking holes in a commonly held point of view.
6. You could easily overhear the following sentence in a casual conversation: "I don't know about that—give me an example." The sentence implies that the speaker has heard something she's skeptical about; she wants to hear an example to see if there's anything to support it. A political scientist might say skeptically to Sen, "India isn't a Hindu civilization? I don't believe it. Give me an example." Or any one of us might say to Thomas, "What do you mean we know about death

only as an abstraction? Give me an example." In these cases, do the examples, in your view, overcome the skepticism of the imaginary questioner? Are the examples provided strong enough? Explain your answer in an essay.

FROM SEEING TO WRITING

Look at the photograph of the destruction caused by Hurricane Andrew when it swept through southern Florida in 1992. Develop a thesis about the picture that you can support through the strategies of illustration explored in this chapter. Then, write an essay in which you draw on features of the photographic image to support your thesis. Make specific references to what you see in the picture.

Lionel Delevingne/Stock Boston

CHAPTER 6

Comparison and Contrast

WHAT IS COMPARISON AND CONTRAST?

When we compare two things, we look for similarities. When we contrast, we look for differences. The comparison-contrast writing strategy, then, is a way of analyzing likenesses and differences between two or more subjects. Usually, the purpose is to evaluate or judge which is superior. Thus we might appreciate soccer if we compare it with football; we understand Roman Catholicism better if we see it in light of Buddhism.

Writers who use the comparison-contrast technique know that careful planning is required to *organize* the likenesses and differences into logical patterns. Some authors might use only *comparison,* to look at the similarities between subjects. Others might use only *contrast.* Often, writers combine the two in a carefully structured essay that balances one with the other.

Like many of the writing and reading strategies you have learned, comparison and contrast is familiar from everyday life. If you were about to buy a new car, for instance, you would look at several models before you made a choice. You might consider price, size, horsepower, options, safety features, status, and dependability before you spent such a large amount of money. If you were deciding whether to send your daughter to a public school or a private school, you would compare and contrast the features of each type of institution: cost, teacher quality, class size, location, curriculum, and composition of the student body might all be considered. If you were an art historian, you might compare and contrast an early picture by Matisse with one he completed late in life in order to understand his development as an artist.

Writing a comparison-contrast essay requires more careful planning, however, than the everyday life application technique. Both call for common sense. You wouldn't compare parochial schools with an Oldsmobile, for instance; they simply don't relate. But you would compare The Dalton School with Public School 34, or a Cutlass Supreme with a Volvo, a Matisse with a Cezanne. Clearly, any strong pattern of comparison and contrast treats items that are in the same category or class. Moreover, there always has to be a basis for comparison; in other words, you compare or contrast two items in order to try to deal with all-important aspects of the objects being compared before arriving at a final determination. These commonsense characteristics of comparison and contrast apply to our pattern of thought as well as our pattern of writing.

Author Rachel Carson, for instance, contrasts two visions of the future for planet Earth: a flourishing environment or a devastated landscape. Thus she has a common category: the condition of the global ecology. She can use *contrast* because she has a common ground for her analysis. Ellen Goodman looks at friendships, Katha Pollitt at what explains why boys don't play with dolls, and Michele Ingrassia at the different body images of black girls and white girls. Each author sets up a formal pattern for contrasting and comparing subjects within a related class. One side of the pattern helps us understand the other. Finally, we may establish a preference for one or the other subject.

HOW DO WE READ COMPARISON AND CONTRAST?

Reading comparison and contrast requires us to ask ourselves these questions:

- What subjects has the author selected? Are they from a similar class or category?
- What is the basis for the comparison or contrast? What is the writer's *thesis?*
- What is the arrangement of topics? How has the writer organized each paragraph? Notice where transitional expressions (*on the one hand, on the other hand, similarly, in contrast*) help the reader follow the writer's train of thought.
- Is the writer fair to each subject, devoting an equal amount of space to each side? Make an outline of one of the reading selections to see how the writer has balanced the two subjects.

- Has the writer used narration, description, or illustration to develop the comparison? What other techniques has the author used?
- Does the conclusion show a preference for one subject over the other? Is the conclusion justified by the evidence in the body?

HOW DO WE WRITE COMPARISON AND CONTRAST?

After reading the professional writers in this chapter, you will be better prepared to organize your own essay. Begin by clearly identifying the subjects of your comparison and by establishing the basis for it. The thesis sentence performs this important function for you.

Sample thesis statement:

> Living in a small town is better than living in a big city because life is safer, friendlier, and cheaper.

Plan a strategy for the comparison and contrast. Writers can use one of three main techniques: block, alternating, or combination. The *block method* requires that the writer put all the points about one side (the small town in this case) in one part of the essay, and all the points about the other side (big-city life) together in another part of the essay. In the *alternating method,* the writer explains one point about small-town life and then immediately gives the contrasting point about big-city life. The *combination* pattern allows the writer to use both alternating and block techniques.

Make a careful outline. For each point about one side, try to find a balancing point about the other. If, for instance, you write about the housing available in a small town, write about housing in the big city. Although it may be impossible to manage exact matches, try to be as fair as possible to each side.

Writing and Revising the Draft

Set up a purpose for the comparison and contrast in the thesis sentence.

Write an outline using paragraph blocks to indicate subject A and subject B. For instance, if you were going to write in the block form, your outline would look like this:

Introduction (with thesis)

Block A: Small Town
1. housing
2. jobs
3. social life

Block B: Big City
1. housing
2. jobs
3. social life

Conclusion

If you were going to use the alternating form, the outline would look as follows:

Introduction (with thesis)

Block A: Housing
1. big city
2. small town

Block B: Jobs
1. big city
2. small town

Block C: Social Life
1. big city
2. small town

Conclusion

Use transitional devices, especially with the alternating form. Each time you shift from one subject to the other, use a transition as needed: *like, unlike, on the one hand, on the other hand, in contrast, similarly.*

In the conclusion, offer your view of the two subjects.

Proofread carefully. Check the draft for clarity and correctness and make a final copy.

A STUDENT PARAGRAPH: COMPARISON AND CONTRAST

Here is a body paragraph from a student essay comparing small town life and city life. Using the alternating method described above, the student concentrates here on housing, presenting the efforts she made first to find an apartment in her home town and then to find a place to live in Chicago.

Topic statement

Alternating method of contrast: Quincy first

Supporting detail

Transition reminds reader of previous point and flows smoothly into next point to produce *coherence*

Alternating method: Chicago second

Supporting detail

"Quincy closet" connects to previous point

Supporting detail

Supporting detail

Closing sentence clinches paragraph's main point

Finding an apartment back home in Quincy was easy, but Chicago was a whole different ball game. In Quincy, I found an affordable one-bedroom place with the help of a friendly local real estate agent. The apartment consisted of three huge, sunny, high-ceilinged rooms that looked out over a stretch of velvety green lawn—and it was all just for me, no roommates, since I could easily pay the rent out of my weekly paycheck. When I moved to the big city, however, my luck ran out. The phonebook's long list of realtors looked too intimidating, so I first scoured the classified ads in the Chicago Tribune. After visiting all the places I could afford, I realized that in the language of the classifieds, "cozy" meant the size of a Quincy closet, and "fixer-upper" meant that slamming a door would bring the place tumbling down over my ears. I decided to try an apartment-finding service instead. When I admitted how little I had to spend on rent, a grim-faced woman who worked there offered me a list of apartments to share. The first potential roomie I met this way opened the door flushed, sweating, and dressed in blue Spandex from head to toe. Bad 1980s dance music blared from the living room. She looked put out that I had interrupted her aerobics routine and handed me a list of rules that specified, among other things, that I could bring only fat-free food into the kitchen. Another required an oath to engage only in "healthy thoughts" while on the premises. I excused myself as politely as I could and called home to Quincy to see if I could get my old place back.

A Fable for Tomorrow

Rachel Carson

Rachel Carson (1907–1964), "the mother of the modern environmental movement," was raised in a simple farmhouse outside the river town of Springdale in western Pennsylvania. The first woman to take and pass the civil service exam, Carson worked for the Bureau of Fisheries from 1936 to 1952, rising to be the editor-in-chief of publications for the U.S. Fish and Wildlife Service. In 1951 she published *The Sea Around Us,* a ground-breaking book on life under the sea based on her years of work as a marine biologist. Her most famous book, *Silent Spring* (1962), raised the alarm about the use of pesticides and other chemicals in the production of food. The book was one of the earliest popular works alerting Americans to the dangers facing our natural environment. *Silent Spring* impressed President Kennedy, who ordered testing of and research into the substances Carson brought under scrutiny in the book. In this selection from *Silent Spring,* Carson establishes contrasts for an imaginary town as part of a literary strategy to call attention to the implications of today's practices for tomorrow. A concerned citizen and an informed advocate for a clean environment, Carson here makes her argument not through statistics or other facts, but through a "fable." A fable is a story, usually fictitious, intended to point to a moral. Why does Carson choose to make her argument through a fable?

PREREADING: THINKING ABOUT THE ESSAY IN ADVANCE

What dangers do you see affecting our environment over the next decades? How can we as a society address these environmental problems?

Words to Watch

migrants (par. 2) people, animals, or birds that move from one place to another

blight (par. 3) a disease or condition that kills or checks growth

maladies (par. 3) illnesses

moribund (par. 4) dying

pollination (par. 5) the transfer of pollen (male sex cells) from one part of the flower to another

granular (par. 7) consisting of grains

specter (par. 9) a ghost; an object of fear or dread
stark (par. 9) bleak; barren; standing out in sharp outline

There was once a town in the heart of America where all life seemed to live in harmony with its surroundings. The town lay in the midst of a checkerboard of prosperous farms, with fields of grain and hillsides of orchards where, in spring, white clouds of bloom drifted above the green fields. In autumn, oak and maple and birch set up a blaze of color that flamed and flickered across a backdrop of pines. Then foxes barked in the hills and deer silently crossed the fields, half hidden in the mists of the fall mornings. 1

Along the roads, laurel, viburnum and alder, great ferns and wildflowers delighted the traveler's eye through much of the year. Even in winter the roadsides were places of beauty, where countless birds came to feed on the berries and on the seed heads of the dried weeds rising above the snow. The countryside was, in fact, famous for the abundance and variety of its bird life, and when the flood of migrants was pouring through in spring and fall people traveled from great distances to observe them. Others came to fish the streams, which flowed clear and cold out of the hills and contained shady pools where trout lay. So it had been from the days many years ago when the first settlers raised their houses, sank their wells, and built their barns. 2

Then a strange blight crept over the area and everything began to change. Some evil spell had settled on the community: mysterious maladies swept the flocks of chickens; the cattle and sheep sickened and died. Everywhere was a shadow of death. The farmers spoke of much illness among their families. In the town the doctors had become more and more puzzled by new kinds of sickness appearing among their patients. There had been several sudden and unexplained deaths not only among adults but even among children, who would be stricken suddenly while at play and die within a few hours. 3

There was a strange stillness. The birds, for example—where had they gone? Many people spoke of them, puzzled and disturbed. The feeding stations in the backyards were deserted. The few birds seen anywhere were moribund; they trembled violently and could not fly. It was a spring without voices. On the mornings that had once throbbed with the dawn chorus of robins, catbirds, doves, jays, wrens, and scores of other bird voices there was now no sound; only silence lay over the fields and woods and marsh. 4

5 On the farms the hens brooded, but no chicks hatched. The farmers complained that they were unable to raise any pigs—the litters were small and the young survived only a few days. The apple trees were coming into bloom but no bees droned among the blossoms, so there was no pollination and there would be no fruit.

6 The roadsides, once so attractive, were now lined with browned and withered vegetation as though swept by fire. These, too, were silent, deserted by all living things. Even the streams were now lifeless. Anglers no longer visited them, for all the fish had died.

7 In the gutters under the eaves and between the shingles of the roofs, a white granular powder still showed a few patches; somc weeks before it had fallen like snow upon the roofs and the lawns, the fields and streams.

8 No witchcraft, no enemy action had silenced the rebirth of new life in this stricken world. The people had done it themselves.

9 This town does not actually exist, but it might easily have a thousand counterparts in America or elsewhere in the world. I know of no community that has experienced all the misfortunes I describe. Yet every one of these disasters has actually happened somewhere, and many real communities have already suffered a substantial number of them. A grim specter has crept upon us almost unnoticed, and this imagined tragedy may easily become a stark reality we all shall know.

BUILDING VOCABULARY

1. In the second paragraph, find at least five concrete words that relate to trees, birds, and vegetation. How many of these objects could you identify? Look in a dictionary for the meanings of those words you do not know.
2. Try to identify the italicized words through the *context clues* (see Glossary) provided by the complete sentence.
   - **a.** half-hidden in the *mists* (par. 1)
   - **b.** when the first settlers *raised* their houses (par. 2)
   - **c.** *stricken* suddenly while at play (par. 3)
   - **d.** the hens *brooded,* but no chicks hatched (par. 5)
   - **e.** *Anglers* no longer visited them, for all the fish had died. (par. 6)

THINKING CRITICALLY ABOUT THE ESSAY

Understanding the Writer's Ideas

1. What is the quality of the world that Carson describes in her opening paragraph? If you had to describe it in just one or two words, which would you use?
2. What are some of the natural objects that Carson describes in her first two paragraphs? Why does she not focus on simply one aspect of nature—like animals, trees, or flowers?
3. How does Carson describe the "evil spell" that settles over the countryside?
4. What does Carson mean when she declares, "It was a spring without voices" (par. 4)? Why does she show that the critical action takes place in the springtime?
5. What do you think is the "white granular powder" that Carson refers to in paragraph 7? Why does she not explain what it is or where it came from?
6. In paragraph 9, the author states her basic point. What is it? Does she offer a solution to the problem that she poses?

Understanding the Writer's Techniques

1. A *fable* is a story with a moral; in other words, a fable is a form of teaching narrative. How does Carson structure her narrative in this essay? What is the "moral" or thesis?
2. What is the purpose of the description in this essay? Why does the writer use such vivid and precise words?
3. Where in this essay does Carson begin to shift from an essentially optimistic tone to a negative one?
4. Does Carson rely on comparison or contrast in this essay?
5. In the *block method* of comparison and contrast, the writer presents all information about one subject, and then all information about a second subject, as in the following:

A

B

   a. How does Carson use this pattern in her essay?
   b. Are there actually two subjects in this essay, or two different aspects of one subject? How does chronology relate to the block structure?

   c. Are the two major parts of Carson's essay equally weighted? Why or why not?
   d. In the second part of the essay, does Carson ever lose sight of the objects introduced in the first part? What new terms does she introduce?
6. How can you explain paragraphs 8 and 9—which do not involve narration, description, or comparison and contrast—in relation to the rest of the essay? What is the nature of Carson's conclusion?

Exploring the Writer's Ideas

1. Today chemicals are used to destroy crop insects, to color and preserve food, and to purify our water, among other things. Would Carson term this "progress"? Would you? Do you think that there are inadequate safeguards and controls in the use of chemicals? What recent examples of chemical use have made the news?
2. Why would you agree or disagree that factories and corporations should protect the environment that they use? Should a company, for example, be forced to clean up an entire river that it polluted? What about oil spills?
3. Have there been any problems with the use of chemicals and the environment in your own area? Describe them. How do local citizens feel about these problems?
4. Do you think that it will be possible in the future for Americans to "live in harmony" with their natural surroundings? Why do you believe what you do?

IDEAS FOR WRITING

Prewriting

Define the word *fable.* List the various elements that you think contribute to successful fables.

Guided Writing

Write a fable (an imaginary story with a moral) in which you contrast one aspect of the life of a person, community, or nation with another.

1. Begin with a phrase similar to Carson's "There was once . . ." so that the reader knows you are writing a narrative fable.
2. Relate your story to an American problem.
3. Use the block method in order to establish your contrast. Write first about one aspect of the topic and then about the other.
4. Use sensory detail in order to make your narrative clear and interesting.
5. Make certain that you establish an effective transition as you move into the contrast.
6. In the second part of your essay, be sure to refer to the same points you raised in the first part.
7. Use the conclusion to establish the "moral" of your fable.

Thinking and Writing Collaboratively

Exchange Guided Writing essays with another member of the class. Has the writer produced a successful fable? Why or why not? Is the moral clear? Is the American problem well defined? Finally, discuss the structure of the essay. Has the writer used the block method of development appropriately? Does an effective transition link the contrast with the stated problem?

Writing About the Text

Write an essay arguing *either* that Carson's fable changed your view of the responsibility of corporations to protect the environment *or* that Carson's fable was too imaginary to influence your thinking one way or another.

More Writing Projects

1. In a journal entry, describe a place you know well, one that has changed for better or worse. Contrast the place as it once was with the way it is now. Use concrete images that appeal to color, action, sound, smell, taste, and touch.
2. Examine in two block paragraphs the two sides of a specific ecological issue today—for instance, acid rain, the global warming trend, or the use of nuclear energy.
3. Using the block method, compare and contrast Carson's fable with the fable you wrote in Guided Writing.

Why Boys Don't Play with Dolls

Katha Pollitt

Katha Pollitt's column, "Subject to Debate," appears in *The Nation,* a left-leaning weekly magazine of opinion. A vigorous polemicist, Pollitt is known for her provocative analyses of hot-button contemporary issues such as family values and teenage motherhood. Pollitt is a poet as well as an essaysist. Her volume of poetry *Antarctic Traveler* won the National Book Critics Circle Award in 1982. Ten years later, a "Subject to Debate" piece on the culture wars, entitled "Why We Read: Canon to the Right of Me . . . ," received the National Magazine Award for essays and criticism. A native of New York City, she is author of *Reasonable Creatures: Essays on Women and Feminism* (1994) and *Subject to Debate: Sense and Dissents on Women, Politics, and Culture* (2001). In this selection, through a series of pointed comparisons and contrasts, Pollitt builds an entertaining, irritated case against recent arguments that account for gender differences by reference to "innate" biological tendencies. Notice, for example, how she uses comparison and contrast both to explore opposing explanations of why boys and girls behave differently and to cast a critical eye on the differences, in the matter of child rearing, between what parents preach and what they do. Consider, too, what Pollitt assumes about the values and opinions of her audience—the essay originally appeared in the *New York Times,* October 8, 1995.

PREREADING: THINKING ABOUT THE ESSAY IN ADVANCE

Gender roles are something we all know from personal experience and therefore something we may feel we know inside out. What is *your* answer to the question that the essay, according to its title, will be answering? Is your answer based just on experience? In what ways, if at all, is it based on knowledge obtained from reading or research? Are you open to hearing views other than your own on this subject?

Words to Watch

prenatal (par. 1)   before birth

hormonal (par. 1) having to do with hormones, that is, those chemical substances that are created by living cells and trigger activity elsewhere in the body

cognitive (par. 2) having to do with mental processes

innate (par. 4) inborn, something we are born with

index (par. 4) indication

ambivalently (par. 7) with mixed feelings

hierarchical (par. 13) arranged in order of rank, status, or importance

determinist (par. 13) the view that acts or attributes are wholly caused by preexisting factors, such as genes

inculcating (par. 16) instilling

It's twenty-eight years since the founding of now, and boys still like trucks and girls still like dolls. Increasingly, we are told that the source of these robust preferences must lie outside society—in prenatal hormonal influences, brain chemistry, genes—and that feminism has reached its natural limits. What else could possibly explain the love of preschool girls for party dresses or the desire of toddler boys to own more guns than Mark from Michigan? 1

True, recent studies claim to show small cognitive differences between the sexes: He gets around by orienting himself in space; she does it by remembering landmarks. Time will tell if any deserve the hoopla with which each is invariably greeted, over the protests of the researchers themselves. But even if the results hold up (and the history of such research is not encouraging), we don't need studies of sex-differentiated brain activity in reading, say, to understand why boys and girls still seem so unalike. 2

The feminist movement has done much for some women, and something for every woman, but it has hardly turned America into a playground free of sex roles. It hasn't even got women to stop dieting or men to stop interrupting them. 3

Instead of looking at kids to "prove" that differences in behavior by sex are innate, we can look at the ways we raise kids as an index to how unfinished the feminist revolution really is, and how tentatively it is embraced even by adults who fully expect their daughters to enter previously male-dominated professions and their sons to change diapers. 4

I'm at a children's birthday party. "I'm sorry," one mom silently mouths to the mother of the birthday girl, who has just torn 5 open her present—Tropical Splash Barbie. Now, you can love Barbie or you can hate Barbie, and there are feminists in both camps. But *apologize* for Barbie? Inflict Barbie, against your own convictions, on the child of a friend you know will be none too pleased?

6 Every mother in that room had spent years becoming a person who had to be taken seriously, not least by herself. Even the most attractive, I'm willing to bet, had suffered over her body's failure to fit the impossible American ideal. Given all that, it seems crazy to transmit Barbie to the next generation. Yet to reject her is to say that what Barbie represents—being sexy, thin, stylish—is unimportant, which is obviously not true, and children know it's not true.

7 Women's looks matter terribly in this society, and so Barbie, however ambivalently, must be passed along. After all, there are worse toys. The Cut and Style Barbie styling head, for example, a grotesque object intended to encourage "hair play." The grown-ups who give that probably apologize, too.

8 How happy would most parents be to have a child who flouted sex conventions? I know a lot of women, feminists, who complain in a comical, eyeball-rolling way about their sons' passion for sports: the ruined weekends, obnoxious coaches, macho values. But they would not think of discouraging their sons from participating in this activity they find so foolish. Or do they? Their husbands are sports fans, too, and they like their husbands a lot.

9 Could it be that even sports-resistant moms see athletics as part of manliness? That if their sons wanted to spend the weekend writing up their diaries, or reading, or baking, they'd find it disturbing? Too anti-social? Too lonely? Too gay?

10 Theories of innate differences in behavior are appealing. They let parents off the hook—no small recommendation in a culture that holds moms, and sometimes even dads, responsible for their children's every misstep on the road to bliss and success.

11 They allow grown-ups to take the path of least resistance to the dominant culture, which always requires less psychic effort, even if it means more actual work: Just ask the working mother who comes home exhausted and nonetheless finds it easier to pick up her son's socks than make him do it himself. They let families buy for their children, without *too* much guilt, the unbelievably sexist junk that the kids, who have been watching commercials since birth, understandably crave.

But the thing the theories do most of all is tell adults that the *adult* world—in which moms and dads still play by many of the old rules even as they question and fidget and chafe against them—is the way it's supposed to be. A girl with a doll and a boy with a truck "explain" why men are from Mars and women are from Venus, why wives do housework and husbands just don't understand. 12

The paradox is that the world of rigid and hierarchical sex roles evoked by determinist theories is already passing away. Three-year-olds may indeed insist that doctors are male and nurses female, even if their own mother is a physician. Six-year-olds know better. These days, something like half of all medical students are female, and male applications to nursing school are inching upward. When tomorrow's three-year-olds play doctor, who's to say how they'll assign the roles? 13

With sex roles, as in every area of life, people aspire to what is possible, and conform to what is necessary. But these are not fixed, especially today. Biological determinism may reassure some adults about their present, but it is feminism, the ideology of flexible and converging sex roles, that fits our children's future. And the kids, somehow, know this. 14

That's why, if you look carefully, you'll find that for every kid who fits a stereotype, there's another who's breaking one down. Sometimes it's the same kid—the boy who skateboards *and* takes cooking in his afterschool program; the girl who collects stuffed animals *and* A-pluses in science. 15

Feminists are often accused of imposing their "agenda" on children. Isn't that what adults always do, consciously and unconsciously? Kids aren't born religious, or polite, or kind, or able to remember where they put their sneakers. Inculcating these behaviors, and the values behind them, is a tremendous amount of work, involving many adults. We don't have a choice, really, about *whether* we should give our children messages about what it means to be male and female—they're bombarded with them from morning till night. 16

BUILDING VOCABULARY

The writer engaged in contemporary debate assumes that her reader will naturally understand topical allusions or other kinds of references, especially insofar as they are political. Define or identify the following topical terms or phrases:

a. NOW (par. 1)
b. feminism (par. 1), feminist revolution (par. 4)
c. the Cut and Style Barbie styling head (par. 7)
d. macho values (par. 8)
e. men are from Mars and women are from Venus (par. 12)

THINKING CRITICALLY ABOUT THE ESSAY

Understanding the Writer's Ideas

1. What is the implication of Pollitt's opening sentence?
2. What does the writer say that we are told explains the continued preference of boys for trucks and girls for dolls?
3. According to the writer, instead of innate qualities, what "index" should we look to in order to explain differences in behavior by sex?
4. Why does the writer say you should not apologize for Barbie? What does she mean by this?
5. What do you think is the writer's answer to the question that opens paragraph 8?
6. What reasons does Pollitt give to account for why innate differences in behavior are appealing?
7. Why does the writer think that the era of rigid, hierarchical sex roles is at an end?
8. "People aspire," the writer says in the opening sentence of paragraph 14, "to what is possible, and conform to what is necessary." What does this statement mean? What would you say the writer thinks is possible, and what does she think is necessary when it comes to sex roles?

Understanding the Writer's Techniques

1. What are the various comparisons and contrasts that appear in the essay?
2. What is the thesis statement of this essay?
3. Offer one or two examples of how the various comparisons and contrasts in the essay support the writer's thesis statement.

4. One provocative rhetorical device is the question that is actually a statement, either directly or by implication. Consider, for example, the question that opens paragraph 8. The question implies an argument—the argument that, while in principle most parents might reject as "sexist" our society's sex-role conventions, in practice most parents do not want their children to deviate from these conventions. Where else in the essay does Pollitt use questions to make an argument?
5. What is the *tone* of this essay? Are there places where the tone changes?
6. Explain why you find the essay's conclusion effective or ineffective.

MIXING PATTERNS

In comparing and contrasting the preferences of boys and girls, Pollitt attempts to answer the question *why* it seems that boys continue to prefer trucks and that girls continue to prefer dolls. In other words, she attempts to explain the *causes* of behavior. (See Chapter 10.) How does Pollitt explain the causes of the persistence of children's preferences in toys?

Exploring the Writer's Ideas

1. The "nature/nurture" debate—are we who we are because of something inborn or genetic or preprogrammed, or are we the way we are because of the society in which we are reared?—is an old one. Pollitt opens her essay by alluding to new evidence to support the deterministic (nature) side, but she clearly intends to argue against a deterministic view of sex roles. However, aside from a dismissive reference in the next paragraph, she does not tell us anything about what this new evidence might be. Why? How, if at all, does this omission affect her essay?
2. What kinds of evidence does Pollitt use to make her case? Is her evidence "scientific"? Is her evidence sufficient to refute deterministic views? Why does she never address deterministic arguments directly? Which piece of the writer's evidence do you find especially persuasive, if any? Which piece of evidence do you find least persuasive? Why?

3. What do you think Pollitt means when she says that feminism is "the ideology of flexible and converging sex roles" (par. 14)? Is feminism an ideology? What are flexible sex roles? Can you be a feminist and a determinist too? Can you be skeptical about determinist views about sex roles and yet not be a feminist? Is Pollitt's association of one position with another—antideterminism and feminism—justified and necessary, or arbitrary and opinionated?

IDEAS FOR WRITING

Prewriting

List some examples of "flexible" or "converging" sex roles that children exhibit or might see in adults today in contrast to the past. Try to draw examples from all areas of life—the home, the school, the workplace, public life. Make your examples specific (e.g., boys and girls play sports together).

Guided Writing

Write an essay that contrasts sex roles in the past and in the present, stressing the emergence of new, more flexible roles among children.

1. Begin with a sentence similar to Pollitt's but that stresses the differences between today and yesterday.
2. Indicate that these changes illustrate the power of nurture over nature.
3. Give two or three examples, devoting a short paragraph to each. Compare and contrast the past or present, and, using causal analysis, suggest why "nature" or conventional stereotypes might have made us doubt the emergence of the new roles you are discussing.
4. Show that these new roles are emerging despite the discomfort of adults about stepping beyond the bounds of conventional sex roles.
5. Conclude by restating your opening point, but from a future-oriented perspective.

Thinking and Writing Collaboratively

In small groups of four or five, do a Web search for new developments (one or two new findings in biological or psychological research) in the nature/nurture debate. Think about whether the evidence you discover seems to support or refute Pollitt's main argument, and share you conclusions with the rest of the class.

Writing About the Text

Write an essay based on questions 2 or 3 in Exploring the Writer's Ideas.

More Writing Projects

1. In your journal explore the ways in which, upon reflection, you can see that you have been "shaped" by parents/genes/society.
2. Write an extended paragraph that explores your personal experience of sex roles. Compare and contrast what you may have wanted to do and what you felt was expected of you.
3. Write an essay that explores the contrast between what people say and what they do. Include in your discussion a plausible defense of why people might say one thing and do another.

The Tapestry of Friendships

Ellen Goodman

Ellen Goodman is a columnist and associate editor of the *Boston Globe,* where she began working in 1967 as a writer on the women's pages. After the birth of her daughter Katie in 1969, Goodman became one of the few working mothers on the *Globe*'s staff. Her writing was instrumental in expanding the coverage of the *Globe*'s women's pages from food and fashion to include the full array of contemporary women's issues. She began writing her weekly column in 1971, and in 1976 her column became syndicated; today it appears in over 400 newspapers across the United States. Born Ellen Holtz in Newton, Massachusetts, on April 11, 1941, Goodman was educated at Radcliffe College. She has published five collections of her columns, dealing with a broad range of topics such as family, politics, abortion, and of course the ever-changing status of women. This selection is from her first collection, *Close to Home* (1979). In 1980 Ellen Goodman's columns were awarded the Pulitzer Prize for Distinguished Commentary. Here she presents a thought-provoking comparison of two categories of human relationships. Notice especially how she blends personal experience with a clipped, direct journalistic style to examine the ways in which "friends" and "buddies" relate to one another.

PREREADING: THINKING ABOUT THE ESSAY IN ADVANCE

How do you define "friendship"? Does this definition apply to both your female and male friends? Is there a difference between your male and female friendships, and if so, how do you explain it?

Words to Watch

slight (par. 1) not having much substance
fragility (par. 2) condition of being easily broken or harmed
resiliency (par. 2) the ability to recover easily from misfortune
binge (par. 4) spree; indulgence
atavistic (par. 5) manifesting a throwback to the past
culled (par. 5) chosen from
palpably (par. 8) in a way that can be touched or felt
loathsome (par. 10) detestable; hateful

wretched (par. 13) miserable; woeful

claustrophobic (par. 16) uncomfortable at being confined in small places

It was, in many ways, a slight movie. Nothing actually happened. There was no big-budget chase scene, no bloody shoot-out. The story ended without any cosmic conclusions. 1

Yet she found Claudia Weill's film *Girlfriends* gentle and affecting. Slowly, it panned across the tapestry of friendship—showing its fragility, its resiliency, its role as the connecting tissue between the lives of two young women. 2

When it was over, she thought about the movies she'd seen this year—*Julia, The Turning Point* and now *Girlfriends.* It seemed that the peculiar eye, the social lens of the cinema, had drastically shifted its focus. Suddenly the Male Buddy movies had been replaced by the Female Friendship flicks. 3

This wasn't just another binge of trendiness, but a kind of *cinéma vérité.* For once the movies were reflecting a shift, not just from men to women but from one definition of friendship to another. 4

Across millions of miles of celluloid, the ideal of friendship had always been male—a world of sidekicks and "pardners," of Butch Cassidys and Sundance Kids. There had been something almost atavistic about these visions of attachments—as if producers culled their plots from some pop anthropology book on male bonding. Movies portrayed the idea that only men, those direct descendants of hunters and Hemingways, inherited a primal capacity for friendship. In contrast, they portrayed women picking on each other, the way they once picked berries. 5

Well, that duality must have been mortally wounded in some shoot-out at the You're OK, I'm OK Corral. Now, on the screen, they were at least aware of the subtle distinction between men and women as buddies and friends. 6

About 150 years ago, Coleridge had written, "A woman's friendship borders more closely on love than man's. Men affect each other in the reflection of noble or friendly acts, whilst women ask fewer proofs and more signs and expressions of attachment." 7

Well, she thought, on the whole, men had buddies, while women had friends. Buddies bonded, but friends loved. Buddies faced adversity together, but friends faced each other. There was something palpably different in the way they spent their time. Buddies seemed to "do" things together; friends simply "were" together. 8

9 Buddies came linked, like accessories, to one activity or another. People have golf buddies and business buddies, college buddies and club buddies. Men often keep their buddies in these categories, while women keep a special category for friends.

10 A man once told her that men weren't real buddies until they'd been "through the wars" together—corporate or athletic or military. They had to soldier together, he said. Women, on the other hand, didn't count themselves as friends until they'd shared three loathsome confidences.

11 Buddies hang tough together; friends hang onto each other.

12 It probably had something to do with pride. You don't show off to a friend; you show need. Buddies try to keep the worst from each other; friends confess it.

13 A friend of hers once telephoned her lover, just to find out if he were home. She hung up without a hello when he picked up the phone. Later, wretched with embarrassment, the friend moaned, "Can you believe me? A thirty-five-year-old lawyer, making a chicken call?" Together they laughed and made it better.

14 Buddies seek approval. But friends seek acceptance.

15 She knew so many men who had been trained in restraint, afraid of each other's judgment or awkward with each other's affection. She wasn't sure which. Like buddies in the movies, they would die for each other, but never hug each other.

16 She'd reread *Babbitt* recently, that extraordinary catalogue of male grievances. The only relationship that gave meaning to the claustrophobic life of George Babbitt had been with Paul Riesling. But not once in the tragedy of their lives had one been able to say to the other: You make a difference.

17 Even now men shocked her at times with their description of friendship. Does this one have a best friend? "Why, of course, we see each other every February." Does that one call his most intimate pal long distance? "Why, certainly, whenever there's a real reason." Do those two old chums ever have dinner together? "You mean alone? Without our wives?"

18 Yet, things were changing. The ideal of intimacy wasn't this parallel playmate, this teammate, this trenchmate. Not even in Hollywood. In the double standard of friendship, for once the female version was becoming accepted as the general ideal.

19 After all, a buddy is a fine life-companion. But one's friends, as Santayana once wrote, "are that part of the race with which one can be human."

BUILDING VOCABULARY

1. The first six paragraphs of this essay use many words and expressions related to film. Explain the meaning or connotation of each of the following words and expressions. Pay special attention to their context in Goodman's article.
   a. big-budget chase scene (par. 1)
   b. bloody shoot-out (par. 1)
   c. it panned (par. 2)
   d. the peculiar eye (par. 3)
   e. the social lens of the cinema (par. 3)
   f. shifted its focus (par. 3)
   g. flicks (par. 3)
   h. *cinéma vérité* (par. 4)
   i. millions of miles of celluloid (par. 5)
   j. plots (par. 5)
   k. on the screen (par. 6)
2. Write an *antonym* (word with an opposite meaning) for each of the following words from the Words to Watch section. Then use each antonym in a sentence.
   a. slight
   b. fragility
   c. resiliency
   d. atavistic
   e. palpably
   f. loathsome
   g. wretched

THINKING CRITICALLY ABOUT THE ESSAY

Understanding the Writer's Ideas

1. What does the author mean when she writes that the movie "ended without any cosmic conclusions" (par. 1)? Is she being critical or descriptive in this statement? Explain.
2. Who is the "she" first mentioned at the beginning of paragraph 2 and referred to throughout the essay?
3. What pattern of change does the author note in the same-year releases of the films *Julia, The Turning Point,* and *Girlfriends?* Does she feel this is a superficial or real change? How do you know?

4. What is the author's main complaint about the ways in which movies have traditionally portrayed friendships? What example does she offer? Explain the meaning of the sentence, "Movies portrayed the idea that only men, those direct descendants of hunters and Hemingways, inherited a primal capacity for friendship" (par. 5). What is "male bonding"?
5. What two allusions does Goodman combine to produce the expression "the You're OK, I'm OK Corral"? Explain the full meaning of the sentence in which that expression appears.
6. According to Goodman, what is the main difference between male and female friendships? Which type do you think she prefers? Why?
7. What quality of friendships is suggested by the title?
8. What is meant by "the double standard of friendship"?
9. How does Goodman's conclusion support her preference for male or female types of friendships?

Understanding the Writer's Techniques

1. What is the main idea of this essay? Which sentence serves as the thesis statement? What two subjects form the basis for comparison in this essay?
2. Like most well-constructed essays, this one has three clear sections: introduction, body, conclusion. Specify which paragraphs make up each section. Does this seem a good balance? Explain.
3. How would you describe the effect of the writing in the opening paragraph? Does it give you a clear idea of the subject of this essay? Is that important in this essay? Why?
4. In the beginning, Goodman uses a number of *metaphors* (see Glossary), including the title. Explain the following metaphors in your own words:
   a. The Tapestry of Friendships (title and par. 2)
   b. The connecting tissue between the lives of two young women (par. 2)

   In what ways do the two metaphors convey similar ideas? Which do you prefer? Why?
5. What is the effect of the use of the pronoun "she" throughout the essay? Why do you suppose Goodman chose to use "she" rather than "I"?
6. Among the main purposes of a comparison-contrast essay are (a) *to explain* something unfamiliar in terms of something

already familiar, (b) *to understand* better two things already known by comparing them point for point, (c) *to evaluate* the relative value of two things. Which of these objectives most closely describes Goodman's purpose? Explain.

7. Which of the three methods of writing comparison essays—block, alternating, or combination—dominates in this essay? Explain.
8. Who is the intended audience for this essay? Why?
9. There are four literary *allusions* (see Glossary) in this essay: (a) Hemingway, (b) Coleridge, (c) *Babbitt,* and (d) Santayana. Identify each and explain why Goodman chose to include it.
10. Throughout the essay, Goodman uses short, direct sentences and relatively short paragraphs. What is her purpose for that? Does it allow for adequate development of this subject matter? Why or why not?
11. At what points does Goodman make use of relatively *extended illustrations?*
12. Goodman chooses to point out the contrasts between her two subjects in short, directly opposing sentences or clauses, beginning with paragraph 8: ". . . men had buddies, while women had friends. Buddies bonded, but friends loved."
    Go through the essay and list all such opposing statements. How do these statements affect your reading of the essay?
13. How does Goodman use *repetition* as a transitional device in the essay?
14. What is the effect of the series of questions that comprise paragraph 17? How is it like a dialogue? Why are some of the questions in quotation marks and others not?
15. A good conclusion for an essay of comparison or contrast will either (a) restate the main idea, (b) offer a solution, or (c) set a new frame of reference by generalizing from the thesis. Which approach or combination of approaches does Goodman use? How effective is her conclusion? Why?

Exploring the Writer's Ideas

1. Do you agree with Goodman's basic distinction between female and male friendships? Why or why not? How closely does it relate to your own experiences? Do you have any friendships that don't fit into either of the two categories she describes?

2. In the beginning of this essay, Goodman refers to the "binge of trendiness" toward pop anthropology and psychology. Such periodicals, books, and syndicated columns as *Psychology Today, Men Are from Mars, Women Are from Venus,* and Dr. Joyce Brothers—to name just a few—are widely read. What's more, radio call-in shows offering on-the-air advice are nationally syndicated and immensely popular.
   What are your feelings about such media presentations? Do you think they are useful? Are there instances when they might be harmful? Why do you think they are so popular?
3. Why does Goodman avoid any discussion of friendship between men and women? Do you feel this omission in any way affects the forcefulness or completeness of her essay? Explain.

IDEAS FOR WRITING

Prewriting

Draw a line down a sheet of paper, labeling the left side *Women* and the right side *Men.* Then identify a topic—for example, dating—that you think men and women approach differently. Next, jot down a few points of contrast that help to explain the precise nature of the differences you plan to investigate.

Guided Writing

Write an essay that contrasts the ways in which men and women perceive or approach some aspect of interpersonal relationships. You might choose, for example, dating, parenting, expressing affection, or divorce.

1. Begin with a description of some depiction of the subject in the contemporary media (for example, a film, TV program, book, video, commercial).
2. Staying with the same medium, give other examples that illustrate how the medium is shifting away from the old, established ways of viewing the subject. Use language specific to that medium.
3. In the rest of your introductory section, use a few metaphors.
4. As a transitional device, cite a statement from a well-known authority (not necessarily on the particular subject).

5. State the main idea of your essay at the beginning of the body section.
6. Develop your contrast using short, direct, opposing statements that summarize the different approaches of men and women.
7. Develop at least two of these opposing statements through extended personal examples.
8. Make your preference for either approach *implicit* (subtle) rather than *explicit* (obvious) throughout.
9. Make the last paragraph of the body of your essay a series of questions that form an internal dialogue.
10. Conclude with a statement that generalizes the main differences and your evaluation of the two approaches.

Thinking and Writing Collaboratively

Working in groups of four, examine the opening paragraphs of your Guided Writing essays. Which of the four introductory paragraphs encourage you to read more of the essay? Which, if any, need revision for stronger effect? Suggest specific ways to improve each introductory paragraph. Revise your own introduction based on readers' responses.

Writing About the Text

Write an essay in which you analyze Goodman's use of comparison and contrast strategies. You might want to use as guideposts for developing your essay some of the questions in the Understanding the Writer's Techniques section on pages 241–242. (Remember that *figurative language* in general and metaphor in particular are also comparison and contrast techniques.)

More Writing Projects

1. Compare and contrast in a journal entry two films or books, plays, or television programs that portray contrasting views of friendship, love, or marriage.
2. Compare in one or two paragraphs the ways you relate to two close friends.
3. Write an essay that compares and/or contrasts what was considered physically attractive in two different time periods in America. You may either focus your essay on one sex or attempt to discuss both.

The Body of the Beholder

Michele Ingrassia

Journalist Michele Ingrassia, in an essay that originally appeared in *Newsweek,* takes a look at a study that shows why white girls dislike their bodies, but black girls are proud of theirs. Why do some find that being fat can also mean being fit?

PREREADING: THINKING ABOUT THE ESSAY IN ADVANCE

Look in the mirror. What do you see? How do you feel about your body? Why do you feel that way?

Words to Watch

dissect (par. 1) to cut apart or separate (tissue), especially for anatomical study

anthropologist (par. 3) a scientist who studies the origin, behavior, and physical, social, and cultural development of human beings

superwaif (par. 4) a slang phrase meaning a model who makes a lot of money because she looks gaunt, like an orphaned child (waif)

magnetism (par. 5) unusual power to attract, fascinate, or influence

1 When you're a teenage girl, there's no place to hide. Certainly not in gym class, where the shorts are short, the T shirts revealing and the adolescent critics eager to dissect every flaw. Yet out on the hardwood gym floors at Morgan Park High, a largely African-American school on Chicago's Southwest Side, the girls aren't talking about how bad their bodies are, but how good. Sure, all of them compete to see how many sit-ups they can do—Janet Jackson's washboard stomach is their model. But ask Diane Howard about weight, and the African-American senior, who carries 133 pounds on her 5-foot 7½-inch frame, says she'd happily add 15 pounds—if she could ensure they'd land on her hips. Or La'Taria Stokes, a stoutly built junior who takes it as high praise when boys remark, "Your hips are screaming for twins!" "I know I'm fat," La'Taria says. "I don't care."

2 In a society that worships at the altar of supermodels like Claudia, Christy and Kate, white teenagers are obsessed with staying thin. But there's growing evidence that black and white girls

view their bodies in dramatically different ways. The latest findings come in a study to be published in the journal *Human Organization* this spring by a team of black and white researchers at the University of Arizona. While 90 percent of the white junior-high and high-school girls studied voiced dissatisfaction with their weight, 70 percent of African-American teens were satisfied with their bodies.

In fact, even significantly overweight black teens described themselves as happy. That confidence may not carry over to other areas of black teens' lives, but the study suggests that, at least here, it's a lifelong source of pride. Asked to describe women as they age, two thirds of the black teens said they get more beautiful, and many cited their mothers as examples. White girls responded that their mothers may have been beautiful—back in their youth. Says anthropologist Mimi Nichter, one of the study's coauthors, "In white culture, the window of beauty is so small." 3

What is beauty? White teens defined perfection as 5 feet 7 and 100 to 110 pounds—superwaif Kate Moss's vital stats. African-American girls described the perfect size in more attainable terms—full hips, thick thighs, the sort of proportions about which Hammer ("Pumps and a Bump") and Sir Mix-Alot ("Baby Got Back") rap poetic. But they said that true beauty—"looking good"—is about more than size. Almost two thirds of the black teens defined beauty as "the right attitude." 4

The disparity in body images isn't just in kids' heads. It's reflected in fashion magazines, in ads, and it's out there, on TV, every Thursday night. On NBC, the sitcom "Friends" stars Courteney Cox, Jennifer Aniston and Lisa Kudrow, all of them white and twentysomething, classically beautiful and reed thin. Meanwhile, Fox Television's "Living Single," aimed at an African-American audience, projects a less Hollywood ideal—its stars are four twentysomething black women whose bodies are, well, *real*. Especially the big-boned, bronze-haired rapper Queen Latifah, whose size only adds to her magnetism. During a break at the Lite Nites program at the Harlem YMCA, over the squeal of sneakers on the basketball court, Brandy Wood, 14, describes Queen Latifah's appeal: "What I like about her is the way she wears her hair and the color in it and the clothes she wears." 5

Underlying the beauty gap are 200 years of cultural differences. "In white, middle-class America, part of the great American 6

Dream of making it is to be able to make yourself over," says Nichter. "In the black community, there is the reality that you might not move up the ladder as easily. As one girl put it, you have to be realistic—if you think negatively about yourself, you won't get anywhere." It's no accident that Barbie has long embodied a white-adolescent ideal—in the early days, she came with her own scale (set at 110) and her own diet guide ("How to Lose Weight: Don't Eat"). Even in this postfeminist era, Barbie's tight-is-right message is stronger than ever. Before kindergarten, researchers say, white girls know that Daddy eats and Mommy diets. By high school, many have split the world into physical haves and have-nots, rivals across the beauty line. "It's not that you hate them [perfect girls]," says Sarah Immel, a junior at Evanston Township High School north of Chicago. "It's that you're kind of jealous that they have it so easy, that they're so perfect-looking."

7 In the black community, size isn't debated, it's taken for granted—a sign, some say, that after decades of preaching black-is-beautiful, black parents and educators have gotten across the message of self-respect. Indeed, black teens grow up equating a full figure with health and fertility. Black women's magazines tend to tout NOT TRYING TO BE SIZE 8, not TEN TIPS FOR THIN THIGHS. And even girls who fit the white ideal aren't necessarily comfortable there. Supermodel Tyra Banks recalls how, in high school in Los Angeles, she was the envy of her white girlfriends. "They would tell me, 'Oh, Tyra, you look so good,'" says Banks. "But I was like, 'I want a booty and thighs like my black girlfriends.'"

8 Men send some of the strongest signals. What's fat? "You got to be *real* fat for me to notice," says Muhammad Latif, a Harlem 15-year-old. White girls follow what they *think* guys want, whether guys want it or not. Sprawled across the well-worn sofas and hard-back chairs of the student lounge, boys at Evanston High scoff at the girls' idealization of Kate Moss. "Sickly," they say, "gross." Sixteen-year-old Trevis Milton, a blond swimmer, has no interest in dating Kate wanna-bes. "I don't want to feel like I'm going to break them." Here, perfection is a hardbody, like Linda Hamilton in "Terminator II." "It's not so much about eating broccoli and water as running," says senior Kevin Mack.

9 And if hardbodies are hot, girls often need to diet to achieve them, too. According to the Arizona study, which was funded by the National Institute of Child Health and Human Development,

62 percent of the white girls reported dieting at least once in the past year. Even those who say they'd rather be fit than thin get caught up. Sarah Martin, 16, a junior at Evanston, confesses she's tried forcing herself to throw up but couldn't. She's still frustrated: ". . . have a big appetite, and I feel so guilty when I eat."

Black teens don't usually go to such extremes. Anorexia and 10
bulimia are relatively minor problems among African-American girls. And though 51 percent of the black teens in the study said they'd dieted in the last year, follow-up interviews showed that far fewer were on sustained weight-and-exercise programs. Indeed, 64 percent of the black girls thought it was better to be "a little" overweight than underweight. And while they agreed that "very overweight" girls should diet, they defined that as someone who "takes up two seats on the bus."

The black image of beauty may seem saner, but it's not neces- 11
sarily healthy. Black women don't obsess on size, but they do worry about other white cultural ideals that black men value. "We look at Heather Locklear and see the long hair and the fair, pure skin," says *Essence* magazine senior editor Pamela Johnson. More troubling, the acceptance of fat means many girls ignore the real dangers of obesity. Dieting costs money—even if it's not a fancy commercial program; fruits, vegetables and lean meats are pricier than high-fat foods. Exercise? Only one state—Illinois—requires daily physical education for every kid. Anyway, as black teenagers complain, exercise can ruin your hair—and, if you're plunking down $35 a week at the hairdresser, you don't want to sweat out your 'do in the gym. "I don't think we should obsess about weight and fitness, but there is a middle ground," says the well-toned black actress Jada Pinkett. Maybe that's where Queen Latifah meets Kate Moss.

BUILDING VOCABULARY

These words have medical denotations. What are they? Check a medical dictionary.

a. anorexia (par. 10)
b. bulimia (par. 10)
c. obsess (par. 11)

THINKING CRITICALLY ABOUT THE ESSAY

Understanding the Writer's Ideas

1. What does the writer mean when she says teenage girls generally have "no place to hide" (par. 1)?
2. What did the findings of a study by the journal *Human Organization* reveal about the way young girls see their bodies?
3. How did black and white teens view the bodies of their mothers?
4. How does superwaif Kate Moss serve as a role model for teenage girls?
5. Television seems to reflect the different attitudes about body image of black and white teenage girls. How?
6. What may account for the differing views of beauty for black and white girls?
7. How are full-figured black women viewed in their community? Why?
8. Dieting is an American obsession. But is this true for black teens? Explain.
9. Are attitudes about black women's bodies potentially harmful, leading to an increase in obesity in black girls?

Understanding the Writer's Techniques

1. Where does the writer state her thesis? How does the statement make the essay's plan clear?
2. How are the essay's paragraphs ordered around the comparison-contrast structure?
3. How does the writer use statistics to support the comparison-contrast paragraph technique?
4. What audience does the writer have in mind? Do you think this essay is written for men or women? Explain.
5. What makes the transition sentences in paragraph 4 different from the others?
6. Do all the paragraphs (including par. 4) have a topic sentence? Give examples.
7. In the concluding paragraph of the comparison-contrast essay, it is common to bring the two subjects together for a final observation. How does this writer follow that strategy?

Exploring the Writer's Ideas

1. Do you agree with the writer's premise that white girls are mostly obsessed with being thin? Explain.
2. Given the reported differences in the way black and white girls see their bodies, whose view do you prefer and why?
3. Is there a connection between how girls see their mothers' bodies and how they see their own, as the essay suggests? What is your feeling?
4. Television is blamed for many of society's ills. Should television be more responsible for the body types it chooses if it influences the way young girls see their own bodies? Explain.
5. In the black community, "there is the reality that you might not move up the ladder as easily." How do you feel about this statement? What does it mean and how does it relate to body image?
6. If the "black-is-beautiful" movement helped black women avoid negative body images, do white women need a similar movement? Give examples in your response.
7. How do men in your community communicate what they think constitutes a beautiful body? What is a beautiful man's body?
8. Despite the positive aspects of liking yourself (even if you are heavy), can an acceptance of weight lead to ill health? Why or why not? What do you propose?

IDEAS FOR WRITING

Prewriting

Make a list of your body features, explaining what you like or dislike about yourself (and/or others).

Guided Writing

Compare your attitudes about your body to those examined in Ingrassia's essay.

1. Begin with a description that shows how your attitudes about your body are shared (or not) by your community.

2. Make sure your thesis reflects the comparison your essay plans to make between your body image and those discussed in the above essay.
3. Focus on how your ideas of beauty differ from (or are the same as) the ideas in the essay. Try to make at least three comparisons (paragraphs).
4. Tell how your culture has historically looked at beauty.
5. How (and what) do men make clear about feminine (or masculine) beauty in your community?
6. Conclude by evaluating what the ideal body type should be for you (and/or men and women).

Thinking and Writing Collaboratively

Working in a group of four, use what you know about body image and the ways it can hurt some people, and research ways society can change to make people of all body types feel more comfortable with themselves. Then write an essay using what the group has gathered to compare ways society can change to help all people develop a positive body image.

Writing About the Text

Write an essay that probes Ingrassia's analysis by looking at how white and black women think of their bodies in similar ways. What instances can you find in Ingrassia's essay in which gender may be more important than race?

More Writing Projects

1. Watch television commercials for women's and men's products. Reflect in your journal on what beauty messages the television commercials are communicating.
2. Look at the body images of men and women in magazine ads. Then write a paragraph that compares the beauty messages you find in television commercials and magazine ads.
3. Write an essay that compares the images of men and women in television commercials and magazine ads. Take a position on which ones are acceptable or not acceptable. Consider which ones have the most harmful effects on young people or society in general.

SUMMING UP: CHAPTER 6

1. In the essays you have read thus far in this book, you have learned much about the personal lives of many of the authors. Select two whose lives seem very different, and write an essay in which you contrast their lives. In your essay, use only illustrations that you can cite or derive from the selections; that is, do not do research or use other outside information about the authors.
2. In this chapter, Rachel Carson deals with a very old fictional form: the fable. Check the definition of this term. Then, write an essay in which you explore the author's use of the word.
3. Which writer in this chapter do you think most successfully uses the comparison-contrast form? Write an essay in which you analyze the best comparison-contrast essay as you see it. Indicate the techniques and strategies that you feel work best. Make specific references to the essay that you have chosen as a model.
4. In the manner of Rachel Carson, write your own "Fable for Tomorrow," in which you show how today's indifference to the environment will affect the future. Remember: *Silent Spring* was written in 1962, and many scholars believe that the way people abuse the environment today is even more serious than it was then.
5. Examine the essays by Katha Pollitt ("Why Boys Don't Play with Dolls"), Ellen Goodman ("The Tapestry of Friendships"), and Michele Ingrassia ("The Body of the Beholder"). Compare and contrast the ways in which they discuss boys and girls, men and women, and white and black Americans, respectively.
6. Katha Pollitt says children are bombarded with messages about what it means to be male and female (par. 16). Take notes on the ads in one evening's viewing of one television channel, and write an essay comparing and contrasting the messages about men and women that are transmitted.
7. Compare and contrast Ann Quindlen's ideas about female friendships (pp. 237–239) and Ellen Goodman's. Include in your comparison and contrast a consideration of the *tone* in which each essay is written.

Top photo: Culver Pictures; Bottom photo: John Boykin/Photo Edit

FROM SEEING TO WRITING

Examine these two photographs and identify the elements of "play" they have in common. Next, formulate a thesis statement about the importance or nature of play and establish three points of comparison and/or contrast that you plan to develop. Make certain you refer to the photographs to support your ideas. Use either the block or point-by-point method to structure your comparative essay.

CHAPTER 7

Definition

WHAT IS DEFINITION?

We are used to opening a dictionary when we want to *define* a word. Often, however, the dictionary definition is brief, and does not fully explain the meaning of a word as an individual writer sees it. An *extended definition* is necessary when a writer wishes to convey the full meaning of a word that is central to the writer's or a culture's thought. When an entire essay focuses on the meaning of a key word or group of related words, extended definition becomes the primary method of organization.

Definition can look at the *denotation* of a word, which is its literal meaning, or at the *connotations,* which are the variety of meanings associated with the word through common use (see Glossary). Denotation is generally available in the dictionary. Connotation, on the other hand, requires that the writer examine not only the denotation but also the way the word is used. In defining, a writer can also explore levels of *diction* (see Glossary), such as standard English, colloquial expressions, and slang. The word "red," for example, denotes a primary color. The connotations, however, are varied: In the early twentieth century Communists were called "Reds" because of the color of the Russian flag. We also associate red with the color of Valentine's cards, with passion and romance. "Redneck" derives from the sunburned skin of a white person who works outdoors and connotes a lifestyle associated with outdoor living and conservative political views. "Redskin" was a pejorative term used by European settlers to describe Native Americans.

We need extended definition to help us fully understand the complexity of our language. Most often, we use definition when words are abstract, controversial, or complex. Terms like "freedom," "pornography," "affirmative action," "bisexual," and "feminism" demand extended definition because they are often confused with some other word or term; because they are so easily misunderstood; or because they are of special importance to the writer, who chooses to redefine the term for his or her own purposes.

Although we can, of course, offer an extended definition just for the sake of definition, we usually go through the trouble of defining because we have strong opinions about complex and controversial words; consequently, we try to provide an extended definition for the purpose of illuminating a thesis for readers. Writer Alice Walker, for instance, once wrote an essay about feminism and African-American women. In her extended definition, she said that the meaning of "feminism" was restricted to white, upper- and middle-class women. As a result, the word did not apply to black women. She created the term "womanist," and wrote her essay to define it. Because of the controversial nature of her definition of "feminist," Walker relied on extended definition to support her thesis that the women's movement needed to pay more attention to women of color.

It *is* possible to give an objective definition of "feminism," with the writer tracing its history, explaining its historic applications, and describing its various subdivisions, such as "radical feminism." However, most of the time, writers have strong opinions. They would want to develop a thesis about the term, perhaps covering much of the same ground as the objective account but taking care that the reader understands the word as they do. It is normal for us to have our own opinions about any word, but in all instances we must make the reader understand fully what we mean by it.

In this chapter Gloria Naylor, an African-American woman, uses extended definition to confront the hate word "nigger." Her many *illustrations* of how and where the word is used show how definition is often determined by context. Janice Castro, with Dan Cook and Cristina Garcia, tackles the issue of what is English as they define a new American language, "Spanglish." Suzanne Britt Jordan has fun defining "fun," and David Brooks defines the new elite.

HOW DO WE READ DEFINITION?

Reading definition requires us to ask ourselves these questions:

- What is the writer's thesis? Determine if the definition is *objective* or *subjective* (see Glossary).
- Does the writer state the definition directly, or expect the reader to understand it from the information the writer gives? When you finish reading the essay, write out a one-sentence definition of the term the writer has defined.
- What are the various techniques the writer uses, such as illustration with examples, description, narration, comparison and contrast? The writer may also use *negation,* a technique of defining a word by what it does *not* mean. In addition, a writer may use a strategy of defining some general group to which the subject belongs (for instance, an orange is a member of the larger group of citrus), and to show how the word differs from all other words in the general group (by its color, acid content, size, and so forth).
- What is the writer's tone? Is the definition comic or serious? Does it rely on *irony* (see Glossary)?

HOW DO WE WRITE A DEFINITION?

Reading the variety of *definitions* in this chapter will prepare you to write your own. The skill required in good definition writing is to make abstract ideas concrete. Writing good definitions allows you to practice many of the other writing strategies you already know, including narration, description, and illustration.

The thesis for your definition does not have to appear in the introduction, but it is helpful to write it out for yourself before you begin.

- Select the word: for example, *multiculturalism.*
- Place it in a class: Multiculturalism is a *belief,* or *system of values,* or *philosophy.*
- Distinguish it from other members of that class: Multiculturalists favor recognition and celebration of differences among various social groups instead of seeking similarities.
- Use negation: Multiculturalism is not the "melting pot" metaphor of how American society is constituted.

By arranging these pieces, and revising the language, you can create a working thesis.

Sample thesis statement:

> Multiculturalism supports the preservation and celebration of differences among people of diverse cultures rather than urging them to replace their ethnic identities with one single "American" identity.

Select support to illustrate, narrate, and describe the term. The selection of evidence can demonstrate the writer's *point of view* on the term. Is multiculturalism splitting the nation into separate groups, or is it affirming the identity of both minority and majority citizens? Look at how the term is used in a variety of settings, such as education, government, social services agencies, and religious institutions.

You might want to visit the library to see how a reference book's definition compares with your own. Libraries have a variety of dictionaries. Depending on the kind of word you are researching, you might want to look at a dictionary of slang, or even a dictionary of quotations to read some famous opinions about abstract words like "love," "hope," and "truth."

What is the *purpose* of the definition? Decide whether you want to show support for the policy or argue against its effectiveness.

Who is the audience? The writer would choose different language for addressing a PTA meeting than for writing to Congress.

Plan an arrangement of the supporting evidence. Unlike comparison and contrast, for instance, definition does not require a formal method of outlining. Examples can be arranged to suit the kind of word being defined, and the mood of the writer. Because so many methods can be applied effectively in an essay of extended definition, you should be able to organize and develop this type of composition easily.

Review the *transitions* you have used in other essays and see which ones apply here. You might want to focus on transitions that show addition: *another, in addition, furthermore.*

Writing and Revising the Draft

Think about where to put the thesis. What is the effect of placing it at the end rather than at the beginning?

Plan your strategy. Arrange the examples so that they most effectively create the extended definition you want. Your essay should have *coherence.* Avoid an unrelated collection of definitions.

Read your essay to a classmate who has defined a similar word. Decide whose definition is more successful, and why.

Revise. Revision may require that you reorganize, moving the examples and other supporting evidence to different sentences and paragraphs to make your argument more effective for a reader.

Proofread for correctness and make a final copy of your work.

A STUDENT PARAGRAPH: DEFINITION

Look at this introductory paragraph of a student's definition essay on multiculturalism and examine the comments in the margin to help you see the various elements of writing definitions.

Introduction of word to be defined

Comparison-contrast to aid definition: *melting pot* and *multiculturalism*

Supporting detail: dictionary citation

Detail helps reader see "melting pot" metaphor

Transition "on the other hand" signals shift to topic *multiculturalism*

Essay thesis; body paragraphs will offer support

Some people these days use the term "multiculturalism" as a kind of insult, as if the idea of the American "melting pot" is the only valid way to define a culture of different peoples. The American Heritage Dictionary defines "melting pot" as "a place where immigrants of different cultures or races form an integrated society." "Melting pot," of course is a metaphor. The image suggests that different cultures are like different kinds of metals that meld to form a new alloy—an alloy that is stronger and more versatile than the original metals. This "alloy," of course, is the integrated society, in which everybody gives up his or her own distinctive cultural heritage to make a new (and, by implication, "better," "stronger") culture. "Multiculturalism," on the other hand, makes a very different point. Without rejecting the idea of an integrated society, it rejects the idea of a homogenous one. The idea is more along the lines of different vegetables in a big cauldron, imparting their various flavors to make the perfect soup, while still retaining much of their distinctive shape and color. Those who criticize the term "multicultural" are actually criticizing the diversity that enriches our American culture. Multiculturalism celebrates the differences among people of diverse cultures rather than urging them to replace their ethnic identities with an "American" identity.

Spanglish

Janice Castro with Dan Cook and Cristina Garcia

Janice Castro, a native of California, is a senior editor of *Time,* where she has worked since 1973. She was a principal writer of *Time*'s 1991 Special Issue on Women, and she frequently writes on health policy. Her book *The American Way of Health: How Medicine Is Changing, and What It Means to You* appeared in 1994. In this selection, which Castro wrote with *Time* staffers Dan Cook and Cristina Garcia, the authors explore the free-form blend of English and Spanish known as "Spanglish." They survey this hybrid language's growing influence on American English. The essay originally appeared in *Time* in 1988.

PREREADING: THINKING ABOUT THE ESSAY IN ADVANCE

Some people think America should be an English-only country. For example, they object to government tax forms or road signs in languages like Spanish or Chinese. What do you think?

Words to Watch

bemused (par. 1) caused to be bewildered; confused

melting pot (par. 3) a place where immigrants of different cultures or races form an integrated society

transplanted (par. 5) transferred from one place or residence to another; resettled or relocated

luxuriant (par. 10) excessively elaborate

mangled (par. 10) butchered; deformed

1 In Manhattan a first-grader greets her visiting grandparents, happily exclaiming, "Come here, *siéntate!*" Her bemused grandfather, who does not speak Spanish, nevertheless knows she is asking him to sit down. A Miami personnel officer understands what a job applicant means when he says, "*Quiero un* part time." Nor do drivers miss a beat reading a billboard alongside a Los Angeles street advertising CERVEZA—SIX-PACK!

2 This free-form blend of Spanish and English, known as
3 Spanglish, is common linguistic currency wherever concentrations

of Hispanic Americans are found in the U.S. In Los Angeles, where 55% of the city's 3 million inhabitants speak Spanish, Spanglish is as much a part of daily life as sunglasses. Unlike the broken-English efforts of earlier immigrants from Europe, Asia and other regions, Spanglish has become a widely accepted conversational mode used casually—even playfully—by Spanish-speaking immigrants and native-born Americans alike.

Consisting of one part Hispanicized English, one part Americanized Spanish and more than a little fractured syntax, Spanglish is a bit like a Robin Williams comedy routine: a crackling line of cross-cultural patter straight from the melting pot. Often it enters Anglo homes and families through the children, who pick it up at school or at play with their young Hispanic contemporaries. In other cases, it comes from watching TV; many an Anglo child watching *Sesame Street* has learned *uno dos tres* almost as quickly as one two three. 4

Spanglish takes a variety of forms, from the Southern California Anglos who bid farewell with the utterly silly "*hasta la* bye-bye" to the Cuban-American drivers in Miami who *parquean* their *carros.* Some Spanglish sentences are mostly Spanish, with a quick detour for an English word or two. A Latino friend may cut short a conversation by glancing at his watch and excusing himself with the explanation that he must "*ir al* supermarket." 5

Many of the English words transplanted in this way are simply handier than their Spanish counterparts. No matter how distasteful the subject, for example, it is still easier to say "income tax" than *impuesto sobre la renta.* At the same time, many Spanish-speaking immigrants have adopted such terms as VCR, microwave and dishwasher for what they view as largely American phenomena. Still other English words convey a cultural context that is not implicit in the Spanish. A friend who invites you to *lonche* most likely has in mind the brisk American custom of "doing lunch" rather than the languorous afternoon break traditionally implied by *almuerzo.* 6

Mainstream Americans exposed to similar hybrids of German, Chinese or Hindi might be mystified. But even Anglos who speak little or no Spanish are somewhat familiar with Spanglish. Living among them, for one thing, are 19 million Hispanics. In addition, more American high school and university students sign up for Spanish than for any other foreign language. 7

Only in the past ten years, though, has Spanglish begun to turn into a national slang. Its popularity has grown with the explosive 8 increases in U.S. immigration from Latin American countries. English has increasingly collided with Spanish in retail stores, offices and classrooms, in pop music and on street corners. Anglos whose ancestors picked up such Spanish words as *rancho, bronco, tornado* and *incommunicado,* for instance, now freely use such Spanish words as *gracias, bueno, amigo* and *por favor.*

9 Among Latinos, Spanglish conversations often flow easily from Spanish into several sentences of English and back.

10 Spanglish is a sort of code for Latinos: the speakers know Spanish, but their hybrid language reflects the American culture in which they live. Many lean to shorter, clipped phrases in place of the longer, more graceful expressions their parents used. Says Leonel de la Cuesta, an assistant professor of modern languages at Florida International University in Miami: "In the U.S., time is money, and that is showing up in Spanglish as an economy of language." Conversational examples: *taipiar* (type) and *winshi-wiper* (windshield wiper) replace *escribir a m quina* and *limpiaparabrisas.*

11 Major advertisers, eager to tap the estimated $134 billion in spending power wielded by Spanish-speaking Americans, have ventured into Spanglish to promote their products. In some cases, attempts to sprinkle Spanish through commercials have produced embarrassing gaffes. A Braniff airlines ad that sought to tell Spanish-speaking audiences they could settle back *en* (in) luxuriant *cuero* (leather) seats, for example, inadvertently said they could fly without clothes (*encuero*). A fractured translation of the Miller Lite slogan told readers the beer was "Filling, and less delicious." Similar blunders are often made by Anglos trying to impress Spanish-speaking pals. But if Latinos are amused by mangled Spanglish, they also recognize these goofs as a sort of friendly acceptance. As they might put it, *no problema.*

BUILDING VOCABULARY

The words below all refer to language use. Write definitions for the words. Then use each word in a sentence.

a. linguistic (par. 2)
b. syntax (par. 3)
c. patter (par. 3)
d. implicit (par. 5)
e. hybrids (par. 6)
f. gaffes (par. 10)

THINKING CRITICALLY ABOUT THE ESSAY

Understanding the Writer's Ideas

1. A street advertisement "CERVEZA—SIX PACK," is an example of what type of language?
2. How do many youngsters (Hispanics and Anglos) pick up cross-cultural speech?
3. What are the different forms of Spanglish?
4. Why is Spanglish sometimes handier for Hispanics than their Spanish language?
5. What makes Spanglish easier to understand for most Americans than, say, a hybrid of English and Hindi?
6. For Anglos, Spanglish can result in some embarrassing gaffes. Why and how? Give an example.

Understanding the Writer's Techniques

1. What is the thesis of the essay?
2. How does the title reflect the essay's thesis?
3. These writers give a clear definition of Spanglish. Where and what is it, precisely?
4. What statistics do the writers present to help inform readers about Spanglish? What effect does the use of statistics have on the essay? Would this essay be as instructive without them? Explain.
5. In the essay the writer makes use of many of the other expository techniques. Explain where the writer uses these techniques: illustration; process; comparison and contrast.
6. Some information in this essay is highlighted by the use of italics. Why is the material set off from the main text of the essay? Explain.
7. Is this essay written for English or Spanish speakers? Why?

Exploring the Writer's Ideas

1. What attitudes do Americans have about those who speak "broken" English?
2. Do you believe Spanglish, as this essay suggests, is more accepted by Americans who studied a foreign language in school, especially Spanish?

3. What in your high school experience was the language most studied? Was it Spanish? Why or why not?
4. What is your experience with a hybrid language? Describe. What is your feeling about hybrid languages? Are they a threat to the purity of our national language—English? Explain.
5. In what ways are many transplanted English words "simply handier than their Spanish counterparts"? Why is "handiness" an element in language use? How might societal values affect the need for handy expressions?

IDEAS FOR WRITING

Prewriting

Freewrite for fifteen minutes about whatever comes to mind when you think of the word "language." Consider social, political, and cultural elements as well as the obvious linguistic elements.

Guided Writing

Write an extended definition of the term "language," focusing on the key element or elements that you think are most important for someone to understand about the word. Address social, political, or cultural features that help explain the importance of language as a human phenomenon.

1. Begin with a short anecdote from personal experience to introduce the concept of language.
2. Write a thesis sentence to link language with the concept you are addressing. For example, you might write, "Because the idea of language is so connected to cultural identity, understanding a culture can help us understand why certain groups resist learning the language of a new country." Or you might write, "Teenagers have a distinct language all their own."
3. Define "language" from your particular perspective, drawing on the element you have chosen for your focus.
4. Give some examples of the language element that you are focusing on.
5. Explain how people understand or do not understand the element you are exploring. What problems are created because people do not understand or appreciate that element?

6. Propose the results if, in fact, people did come to understand the language feature you are dealing with.
7. Give your essay a lively title that blends the elements you are considering in the way that Castro has blended them in her title "Spanglish."

Thinking and Writing Collaboratively

In groups of three, read drafts of each other's essays and write a one-paragraph critique for each of the two papers you have read. What language element does the writer focus on? Does the thesis sentence explain the writer's position clearly? Do the examples illustrate the point effectively? Then, read the critiques of your own essay, and use them to help you think your essay through before you do your next revision.

Writing About the Text

Teachers often tell students to learn proper English in order to get a job. According to this essay, advertisers and people in business have found it worthwhile to use Spanglish to sell their products. Why do schools emphasize proper language when businesses are trying to learn and use hybrid languages? What is going on? Write an essay to explore this issue.

More Writing Projects

1. In your journal, reflect on the possible advantages and problems that result when cultures come in close contact with each other.
2. Write a paragraph to define the word "slang."
3. Select any cultural group that you think has had a major impact on American culture, and write an essay to examine that impact. Consider linguistic, social, and economic contributions.

Fun, Oh Boy. Fun. You Could Die from It.

Suzanne Britt Jordan

A native of Winston-Salem, North Carolina, Suzanne Britt Jordan has published widely in popular magazines and newspapers. Her books include a collection of essays, *Show and Tell* (1982), *Skinny People Are Dull and Crunchy like Carrots* (1982), and *A Writer's Rhetoric* (1988), a college composition textbook. In this selection, which originally appeared in 1979, Jordan offers an extended definition of the word *fun* by pointing out what it is *not.*

PREREADING: THINKING ABOUT THE ESSAY IN ADVANCE

What expectations do you bring to an article entitled "Fun, Oh Boy. Fun. You Could Die from It"? Can "fun" actually harm or kill you? In what ways? Do you think that we are too much of a "fun" culture? Why or why not?

Words to Watch

puritan (par. 3) one who practices or preaches a stricter moral code than that which most people now follow

selfless (par. 4) unselfish; having no concern for oneself

fetish (par. 5) something regarded with extravagant trust or respect

licentiousness (par. 9) a lack of moral restraints

consumption (par. 9) act of taking in or using up a substance; eating or drinking

epitome (par. 11) an ideal; a typical representation

capacity (par. 12) the ability to hold something

damper (par. 13) something that regulates or that stops something from flowing

reverently (par. 13) respectfully; worshipfully

blaspheme (par. 13) to speak of without reverence

weary (par. 14) tired; worn-out

horizon (par. 14) the apparent line where the earth meets the sky

scan (par. 14) to examine something carefully

Fun is hard to have. 1

Fun is a rare jewel. 2

Somewhere along the line people got the modern idea that fun 3 was there for the asking, that people deserved fun, that if we didn't have a little fun every day we would turn into (sakes alive!) puritans.

"Was it fun?" became the question that overshadowed all 4 other questions: good questions like: Was it moral? Was it kind? Was it honest? Was it beneficial? Was it generous? Was it necessary? And (my favorite) was it selfless?

When the pleasure got to be the main thing, the fun fetish was 5 sure to follow. Everything was supposed to be fun. If it wasn't fun, then by Jove, we were going to make it fun, or else.

Think of all the things that got the reputation of being fun. 6 Family outings were supposed to be fun. Sex was supposed to be fun. Education was supposed to be fun. Work was supposed to be fun. Walt Disney was supposed to be fun. Church was supposed to be fun. Staying fit was supposed to be fun.

Just to make sure that everybody knew how much fun we 7 were having, we put happy faces on flunking test papers, dirty bumpers, sticky refrigerator doors, bathroom mirrors.

If a kid, looking at his very happy parents traipsing through 8 that very happy Disney World, said, "This ain't fun, ma," his ma's heart sank. She wondered where she had gone wrong. Everybody told her what fun family outings to Disney World would be. Golly gee, what was the matter?

Fun got to be such a big thing that everybody started to look 9 for more and more thrilling ways to supply it. One way was to step up the level of danger or licentiousness or alcohol or drug consumption so that you could be sure that, no matter what, you would manage to have a little fun.

Television commercials brought a lot of fun and fun-loving 10 folks into the picture. Everything that people in those commercials did looked like fun: taking Polaroid snapshots, swilling beer, buying insurance, mopping the floor, bowling, taking aspirin. We all wished, I'm sure, that we could have half as much fun as those rough-and-ready guys around the locker room, flicking each other with towels and pouring champagne. The more commercials people watched, the more they wondered when the fun would start in their own lives. It was pretty depressing.

11 Big occasions were supposed to be fun. Christmas, Thanksgiving and Easter were obviously supposed to be fun. Your wedding day was supposed to be fun. Your wedding night was supposed to be a whole lot of fun. Your honeymoon was supposed to be the epitome of fundom. And so we ended up going through every Big Event we ever celebrated, waiting for the fun to start.

12 It occurred to me, while I was sitting around waiting for the fun to start, that not much is, and that I should tell you just in case you're worried about your fun capacity.

13 I don't mean to put a damper on things. I just mean we ought to treat fun reverently. It is a mystery. It cannot be caught like a virus. It cannot be trapped like an animal. The god of mirth is paying us back for all those years of thinking fun was everywhere by refusing to come to our party. I don't want to blaspheme fun anymore. When fun comes in on little dancing feet, you probably won't be expecting it. In fact, I bet it comes when you're doing your duty, your job, or your work. It may even come on a Tuesday.

14 I remember one day, long ago, on which I had an especially good time. Pam Davis and I walked to the College Village drug store one Saturday morning to buy some candy. We were about 12 years old (fun ages). She got her Bit-O-Honey. I got my malted milk balls, chocolate stars, Chunkys, and a small bag of M & M's. We started back to her house. I was going to spend the night. We had the whole day to look forward to. We had plenty of candy. It was a long way to Pam's house but every time we got weary Pam would put her hand over her eyes, scan the horizon like a sailor and say, "Oughta reach home by nightfall," at which point the two of us would laugh until we thought we couldn't stand it another minute. Then after we got calm, she'd say it again. You should have been there. It was the kind of day and friendship and occasion that made me deeply regretful that I had to grow up.

15 It was fun.

BUILDING VOCABULARY

1. *Trite language* refers to words and expressions that have been overused and, consequently, have lost much of their effectiveness. People do rely on trite language in their conversations, but writers usually avoid overused expressions. However, a

good writer will be able to introduce such vocabulary at strategic points. Examples of trite language in Jordan's essay appear below. Explain in your own words what they mean.

   a. a rare jewel (par. 2)
   b. by Jove (par. 5)
   c. his ma's heart sank (par. 8)
   d. golly gee (par. 8)

2. For each of the following words drawn from Jordan's essay, write a denotative definition. Then list four *connotations* (see Glossary) that each word has for you.

   a. overshadowed (par. 4)
   b. flunking (par. 7)
   c. traipsing (par. 8)
   d. swilling (par. 10)
   e. mirth (par. 13)

3. Select five words from the Words to Watch section and use them in sentences of your own.

THINKING CRITICALLY ABOUT THE ESSAY

Understanding the Writer's Ideas

1. What are some of the things Jordan says fun is not?

2. What does Jordan suggest we did to something if it wasn't already fun? Identify some of the things she says are "supposed" to be fun.

3. In paragraph 6, Jordan lists some familiar things that seem empty of fun. How does she say people made them fun anyway?

4. What are some of the ways people make fun even more thrilling?

5. What does Jordan list as looking like fun on television commercials?

6. Discuss the relationship between big occasions and the experience of fun. Explain the meaning of the statement, "It may even come on a Tuesday" (par. 13).

7. Describe Jordan's attitude concerning how much in life really is fun. According to Jordan, how should we treat fun? Why? Is it something she says can be experienced only at special times?

8. How old was Jordan at the time she remembers having an especially good time with her friend Pam? Describe in your own words why she had such a good time that day. What are some of the candies she remembers buying? Why was it especially funny when Pam would say, "Oughta reach home by nightfall"?
9. For what reason does Jordan feel regretful at the end of the essay? Although she is regretful, do you think she is actually sad? Why?

Understanding the Writer's Techniques

1. What is the author's thesis? Where is it in the essay?
2. Does Jordan ever offer a single-sentence definition of "fun"? Where? Is that sentence sufficient to define the concept? Why?
3. Jordan employs the technique of *negation*—defining a term through showing what it is *not*—so strongly in this essay that the writing verges on *irony.* Irony is using language to suggest the opposite of what is said (see Glossary). Explain the irony in paragraphs 9, 10, and 11.
4. Why does the author continually point out things that are supposed to be fun? What is she trying to tell us about these things?
5. Writers usually avoid vague language such as "everything" and "everybody" in their writing, yet Jordan uses these words frequently in her essay. Explain her purpose in deliberately avoiding concrete terms.
6. What is the *tone* (see Glossary) of this essay? Is it fun? How does Jordan create the tone? Much of the writing in this essay has a very conversational quality to it, as though the author were speaking directly to the reader. Locate five words or phrases that have this quality.
7. Why does Jordan use so many examples and illustrations in this essay? Which paragraphs use multiple illustrations with special effectiveness?
8. There is a definite turning point in this essay where Jordan switches from an ironic to an affirmative point of view and begins to explain what fun *can be* rather than what it *is not.* One paragraph in particular serves as the transition between the two attitudes. Which one is it? Which is the first paragraph to be mostly affirmative? What is the result of this switch?

9. Jordan uses specific brand names in the essay. Locate at least four of them. Why do you think she uses these brand names instead of names that simply identify the object?
10. What is the function of narration in the development of this essay? Where does the author *narrate* an imagined incident? Where does she use a real incident? Why does Jordan use narration in this paper?
11. Compare the effects of the two simple, direct statements that begin and end the essay. Why does Jordan not develop a more elaborate introduction and conclusion?

Exploring the Writer's Ideas

1. Jordan begins her essay by stating, "Fun is hard to have." At one point she indicates, "Fun got to be such a big thing that everybody started looking for more and more thrilling ways to supply it" (par. 9). Do you think that fun is hard to have? Why or why not? What relationship does the epidemic use of drugs and alcohol have to our difficulties in having fun today?
2. The author raises the question of how at big events we are sometimes left "waiting for the fun to start" (par. 11). What functions do events or occasions such as holidays, weddings, or birthdays play in our society? Why is there an emphasis placed on having fun at those events? Do you think there should be such an emphasis? Why?
3. This essay appeared as a guest editorial in the *New York Times*. We do not usually think of the *New York Times* as a "fun" newspaper, but rather as one that deals with serious issues of international significance. Jordan's article might be considered popular writing or light reading. Do you feel there is a place in the media—newspapers, magazines, radio, television—for a mixture of "heavy" and "light" attitudes? What well-respected newspapers or magazines that you know include articles on popular topics? What subjects do you think would currently be most appealing to popular audiences?
4. At the end of the essay, Jordan seems to imply that it is easier for children to have fun than it is for grownups. Do you agree? Is the basic experience of fun any different for kids or for adults? Do you feel it was any easier for people to have fun in days past than it is now? Why?

IDEAS FOR WRITING

Prewriting

Words like "fun," "love," and "prejudice" have strong connotations—many shades of meaning—associated with them. Select your own highly connotative word, and then make a list of words and phrases that help to define it.

Guided Writing

Select one of the following highly connotative terms for various types of experiences and write an extended definition about it: love, creativity, alienation, prejudice, fidelity.

1. Prepare for your essay by consulting a good dictionary for the lexical definition (denotation) of the term. However, instead of beginning with this definition, start with some catchy, interesting opening statements related to the definition.
2. Write a thesis sentence that names the word you will define and that tells the special opinion, attitude, or point of view you have about the word.
3. Attempt to establish the importance of your subject by considering it in terms of our current understanding of fun.
4. Use the technique of negation (see page 256) by providing various examples and illustrations of what your topic *is not* in order to establish your own viewpoint of what it *is*.
5. Use other strategies—description, narration, comparison and contrast, and so forth—to aid in clearly establishing an extended definition of your topic.
6. At the end of your essay dramatize through narration at least one personal experience that relates the importance of the topic to your life.

Thinking and Writing Collaboratively

Exchange a draft version of your Guided Writing definition essay with another class member, and review your partner's paper carefully. Does it follow the recommendations in the Guided Writing exercise? Which strategies for writing an extended definition have been used? Does the essay incorporate personal experience? Write a one-paragraph evaluation of your classmate's essay.

Writing About the Text

Concentrating on the implied judgments about "modern" life in this essay (see, for example, par. 3), write an essay that takes issue with Jordan and celebrates the "right" to fun.

More Writing Projects

1. Go to a place on campus where you can observe people having fun. Record in your journal their behavior—actions, gestures, noises, and so forth. Then turn these notes into a definition of "campus fun."
2. Write a brief one-paragraph definition of a "funny person." Use vivid details to create this portrait.
3. From a book of popular quotations (*Bartlett's Familiar Quotations,* the *Oxford Dictionary of Quotations*) check under the heading "fun" and select a number of statements about fun by professional writers. Then write an essay in which you expand one of those definitions. Draw upon your own experiences or readings to support the definition you choose to expand.

A Word's Meaning

Gloria Naylor

Gloria Naylor was born in New York City on January 25, 1950. When she was thirteen, her mother joined Jehovah's Witnesses; Naylor herself was baptized and became a Jehovah's Witnesses minister in 1968. She proselytized for Jehovah's Witnesses in New York, North Carolina, and Florida over a period of years, supporting herself as a switchboard operator. In 1975 she left Jehovah's Witnesses, suffered a nervous breakdown, and entered Medgar Evers College to study nursing. After reading Toni Morrison's *The Bluest Eye,* Naylor began to think of writing herself. In 1981 she graduated from Brooklyn College with a B.A. in English. The following year she published *The Women of Brewster Place,* still her best-known novel. She has also published *Mama Day* (1986), *Bailey's Cafe* (1992), and *The Men of Brewster Place* (1998). In 1990 Naylor established One Way Productions, her own multimedia production company. As an African-American woman and a writer, Naylor has found that words can change their meaning, depending on who defines them. Telling of a confrontation with an angry classmate who called her a "nigger" in the third grade, Naylor develops an extended definition of the word and its multiple meanings. As you read, think about other words that depend on context for their meaning.

PREREADING: THINKING ABOUT THE ESSAY IN ADVANCE

Naylor suggests that different words—even offensive words—mean different things to different people. Would you agree or disagree, and why? Can you think of a word that you personally find very offensive but others might find acceptable?

Words to Watch

transcendent (par. 1) rising above
fleeting (par. 1) moving quickly
intermittent (par. 2) alternate; repeated
consensus (par. 2) agreement
verified (par. 3) confirmed
gravitated (par. 4) moved toward
inflections (par. 5) pitch or tone of voice
endearment (par. 9) expression of affection

disembodied (par. 9) separated from the body
unkempt (par. 10) messy
social stratum (par. 14) status

Language is the subject. It is the written form with which I've 1
managed to keep the wolf away from the door and, in diaries, to keep my sanity. In spite of this, I consider the written word inferior to the spoken, and much of the frustration experienced by novelists is the awareness that whatever we manage to capture in even the most transcendent passages falls far short of the richness of life. Dialogue achieves its power in the dynamics of a fleeting moment of sight, sound, smell and touch.

I'm not going to enter the debate here about whether it is lan- 2
guage that shapes reality or vice versa. That battle is doomed to be waged whenever we seek intermittent reprieve from the chicken and egg dispute. I will simply take the position that the spoken word, like the written word, amounts to a nonsensical arrangement of sounds or letters without a consensus that assigns "meaning." And building from the meanings of what we hear, we order reality. Words themselves are innocuous; it is the consensus that gives them true power.

I remember the first time I heard the word nigger. In my third- 3
grade class, our math tests were being passed down the rows, and as I handed the papers to a little boy in back of me, I remarked that once again he had received a much lower mark than I did. He snatched his test from me and spit out that word. Had he called me a nymphomaniac or a necrophiliac, I couldn't have been more puzzled. I didn't know what a nigger was, but I knew that whatever it meant, it was something he shouldn't have called me. This was verified when I raised my hand, and in a loud voice repeated what he had said and watched the teacher scold him for using a "bad" word. I was later to go home and ask the inevitable questions that every black parent must face—"Mommy, what does 'nigger' mean?"

And what exactly did it mean? Thinking back, I realize that 4
this could not have been the first time the word was used in my presence. I was part of a large extended family that had migrated from the rural South after World War II and formed a close-knit network that gravitated around my maternal grandparents. Their ground-floor apartment in one of the buildings they owned in Harlem was a weekend mecca for my immediate family, along with countless aunts, uncles and cousins who brought along

assorted friends. It was a bustling and open house with assorted neighbors and tenants popping in and out to exchange bits of gossip, pick up an old quarrel or referee the ongoing checkers game in which my grandmother cheated shamelessly. They were all there to let down their hair and put up their feet after a week of labor in the factories, laundries and shipyards of New York.

5 Amid the clamor, which could reach deafening proportions—two or three conversations going on simultaneously, punctuated by the sound of a baby's crying somewhere in the back rooms or out on the street—there was still a rigid set of rules about what was said and how. Older children were sent out of the living room when it was time to get into the juicy details about "you-know-who" up on the third floor who had gone and gotten herself "p-r-e-g-n-a-n-t!" But my parents, knowing that I could spell well beyond my years, always demanded that I follow the others out to play. Beyond sexual misconduct and death, everything else was considered harmless for our young ears. And so among the anecdotes of the triumphs and disappointments in the various workings of their lives, the word nigger was used in my presence, but it was set within contexts and inflections that caused it to register in my mind as something else.

6 In the singular, the word was always applied to a man who had distinguished himself in some situation that brought their approval for his strength, intelligence or drive:

7 "Did Johnny *really* do that?"

8 "I'm telling you, that nigger pulled in $6,000 of overtime last year. Said he got enough for a down payment on a house."

9 When used with a possessive adjective by a woman—"my nigger"—it became a term of endearment for husband or boyfriend. But it could be more than just a term applied to a man. In their mouths it became the pure essence of manhood—a disembodied force that channeled their past history of struggle and present survival against the odds into a victorious statement of being: "Yeah, that old foreman found out quick enough—you don't mess with a nigger."

10 In the plural, it became a description of some group within the community that had overstepped the bounds of decency as my family defined it: Parents who neglected their children, a drunken couple who fought in public, people who simply refused to look for work, those with excessively dirty mouths or unkempt households were all "trifling niggers." This particular circle could forgive hard times, unemployment, the occasional bout of depression—

they had gone through all of that themselves—but the unforgivable sin was a lack of self-respect.

A woman could never be a "nigger" in the singular, with its 11
connotation of confirming worth. The noun "girl" was its closest equivalent in that sense, but only when used in direct address and regardless of the gender doing the addressing. "Girl" was a token of respect for a woman. The one-syllable word was drawn out to sound like three in recognition of the extra ounce of wit, nerve or daring that the woman had shown in the situation under discussion.

"G-i-r-l, stop. You mean you said that to his face?" 12

But if the word was used in a third-person reference or short- 13
ened so that it almost snapped out of the mouth, it always involved some element of communal disapproval. And age became an important factor in these exchanges. It was only between individuals of the same generation, or from an older person to a younger (but never the other way around), that "girl" would be considered a compliment.

I don't agree with the argument that use of the word nigger at 14
this social stratum of the black community was an internalization of racism. The dynamics were the exact opposite: the people in my grandmother's living room took a word that whites used to signify worthlessness or degradation and rendered it impotent. Gathering there together, they transformed "nigger" to signify the varied and complex human beings they knew themselves to be. If the word was to disappear totally from the mouths of even the most liberal of white society, no one in that room was naïve enough to believe it would disappear from white minds. Meeting the word head-on, they proved it had absolutely nothing to do with the way they were determined to live their lives.

So there must have been dozens of times that the "nigger" was 15
spoken in front of me before I reached the third grade. But I didn't "hear" it until it was said by a small pair of lips that had already learned it could be a way to humiliate me. That was the word I went home and asked my mother about. And since she knew that I had to grow up in America, she took me in her lap and explained.

BUILDING VOCABULARY

1. In paragraph 3, Naylor says the word *nigger* is as puzzling to her as "nymphomaniac" and "necrophiliac." Using a dictionary, find both the meanings of these two terms and their etymology, or roots.

2. In paragraph 14, Naylor writes, "I don't agree with the argument that use of the word nigger at this social stratum of the black community was an internalization of racism." Put Naylor's idea into your own words. Use the context of the sentence to understand key terms such as "social stratum" and "internalization."

THINKING CRITICALLY ABOUT THE ESSAY

Understanding the Writer's Ideas

1. What is the original situation in which Naylor recognizes that *nigger* can be a hate word? What clues from outside the dictionary meaning of the word help her to recognize this meaning? What confirms her suspicion that the word is "bad"?
2. In paragraph 4, Naylor gives us information about her family and background. In your own words, what kind of family did Naylor come from? Where did she grow up? What economic and social class did her family come from? How do you know?
3. In paragraph 5, Naylor explains the values of her group. What was considered appropriate and what was inappropriate for children to hear? What kind of behavior was condemned by the group?
4. Naylor defines at least five contexts in which the word *nigger* might be used. Make a list giving the five contexts, and write a sentence putting the use of the word into your own definition.
5. Explain one context in which Naylor says *nigger* was never used (par. 11). How are age and gender important in determining how the word was used?
6. When Naylor says in paragraph 14 that blacks' use of the word *nigger* about themselves rendered the word "impotent," what does she mean? How do they "transform" the meaning of the word?
7. In the last paragraph, Naylor recalls her mother's reaction to the experience of hearing a third-grade classmate use the word to humiliate her. What do you think the mother explained?

Understanding the Writer's Techniques

1. Where is the thesis statement of Naylor's essay? How do you know?

2. Why does Naylor begin with two paragraphs about language, in a very general or theoretical way? Explain what these two paragraphs tell us about the writer's authority to define words. How does she use her introduction to make herself sound like an expert on the problem of defining words?
3. In paragraph 3, the author shifts tone. She moves from the formal language of the introduction to the personal voice as she retells her childhood experience. What is the effect of this transition on the reader? Why?
4. Look closely at the examples of usage Naylor provides in paragraphs 8, 9, 10, and 11. Why does she give dialogue to illustrate the various contexts in which she heard the word *nigger* used? In what way is this variety of speakers related to her thesis statement?
5. Naylor uses grammatical terms to clarify differences in meaning, such as "in the singular" (par. 6), "possessive adjective" (par. 9), "plural" (par. 10), and "third-person reference" (par. 13). Why does she use these technical terms? What does it reveal about the audience for whom she is writing? What does it reveal about Naylor's understanding of that audience?
6. What do you think about the last sentence of the essay? Why does the author return to the simple and direct language of her childhood experience in order to conclude rather than using the theoretical and technical language of other parts of the essay?

Exploring the Writer's Ideas

1. Naylor chooses to define a difficult and controversial word in her essay. How does the way that she defines it make you think again about the meaning of the word *nigger?* Have you used the word in any of the ways she defines? How have contemporary rap musicians used the word in ways to suggest that Naylor's definition is accurate?
2. Naylor argues that the definition of words emerges from consensus. So, if the third-grader used *nigger* to humiliate his classmate, we must draw the conclusion that that little boy's society consented to the racism he intended by using the word. How does Naylor reinforce this idea in the last paragraph of the essay? What attitude toward racism does the mother seem to reveal when she picks up her daughter? Does Naylor's definition essay offer any solutions to the negative meaning the word carries? In what ways?

3. The classic American novel *The Adventures of Huckleberry Finn* by Mark Twain uses the word *nigger* almost 200 times. For this reason, some school libraries want to ban the book. In what ways does Naylor's definition essay engage in this censorship debate?

IDEAS FOR WRITING

Prewriting

Select an objectionable or offensive word, and for five minutes freewrite on the subject, trying to cover as many ways in which the word is used as possible.

Guided Writing

Choose a word that you have recently heard used that offended you because it was sexist, racist, homophobic, or otherwise objectionable. Write a definition essay in which you define the word, show examples of its power to offend, and conclude by offering alternate words.

1. Use an anecdote to show whom you heard using the word, where it was used, and how you felt when you heard it used. Explain who you are, and who the other speaker was in your introduction.
2. In your thesis give the word and give an expanded definition of what the word means to you.
3. Explain the background of the word's negative use. Who uses it? What is the dictionary meaning of the word? How do you think the word got corrupted?
4. Give examples to expand your thesis that the word has negative meanings. Show who uses it, and for what purpose. Draw your examples from people at work, the media, or historical figures.
5. Use another example to show how the word can change meaning if the speaker deliberately uses it in order to mock its usual meaning or "render it impotent" as Naylor says.
6. If possible, try to define the word by negation—that is, by what it does not mean.

7. Connect your paragraphs with transitions that relate one idea thoughtfully to the next.
8. In your conclusion, place the term in a broader perspective, one that goes beyond the specific word to the power of language to shape reality or control behavior.

Thinking and Writing Collaboratively

Many colleges and universities are trying to find ways to discourage or prevent hate speech by writing codes of conduct. In groups of five or six, discuss possible approaches to this issue, and then draft a policy statement that defines what unacceptable language is and how your campus will respond to it.

Writing About the Text

In what way does Naylor's discussion of language raise issues similar to those discussed by Amy Tan in "Mother Tongue" (pages 28–34)? Although Tan is dealing with language among immigrants and Naylor is addressing the varieties of meaning of words to native speakers of English, both writers deal with the politics of language. How does each writer define the relationship between language and power?

More Writing Projects

1. In your journal, record an incident in which someone addressed you or someone you know with an offensive word. Explain how you reacted and why.
2. Write a one-paragraph definition of a word or phrase by which you would feel comfortable being labeled. Are you a single parent? an Italian-American? an honor student? Write a sharp thesis to define the term, and then expand the definition with examples.
3. The term "multicultural" refers to a perspective on society that values the differences among people of varying ethnic origin, religious belief, sexual preference, and social class. In an essay, write an extended definition of the term "multicultural society." Draw upon your own experiences and (or) your readings to support your definition.

The Organization Kid

David Brooks

The journalist David Brooks is a senior editor at the *Weekly Standard,* is a contributing editor at *Newsweek,* and writes the "Machine Age" column for the *New York Times* Magazine. Prior to joining the *Weekly Standard,* Brooks worked on the *Wall Street Journal* as op-ed page editor. A graduate of the University of Chicago, Brooks writes on a broad range of topics (he has worked as a foreign correspondent and as a movie critic) but is best known as a conservative commentator. He has edited *Backward and Upward: The New Conservative Writing*. Most recently, he has published *Bobos in Paradise: The New Upper Class and How They Got There* (2000). In this selection, which has been excerpted from an article that first appeared in the *Atlantic Monthly* in April 2001, Brooks explores the coming elite (students at Ivy League colleges) their hyperorganized lives and their feelings about the remarkable demands and expectations that they seem happily to have placed on themselves.

PREWRITING: THINKING ABOUT THE ESSAY IN ADVANCE

The title of this selection alludes to an influential study by William H. Whyte, called *The Organization Man* (1956). Whyte wanted to understand people who not only worked for "The Organization," but also "belonged" to it. What do you anticipate might be the characteristics of an organization *kid?* For the adult, the organization is the place of work, the corporation: what might be the organization for a kid?

Words to Watch

a capella (par. 2) literally, in the chapel style—that is, singing without instrumental accompaniment

pejoratively (par. 7) disparagingly

prudential (par. 9) cautious, avoiding risk

sacrosanct (par. 11) holy, untouchable

lament (par. 11) to say regretfully

mandatory (par. 12) obligatory

euthanasia (par. 12) mercy killing

demographic (par. 13) statistical information about society
frenetic (par. 14) hectic
nihilism (par. 16) rejection of accepted beliefs and values
alienation (par. 19) sense of being cut off from mainstream social life
beneficent (par. 19) good

A few months ago I went to Princeton University to see what the young people who are going to be running our country in a few decades are like. Faculty members gave me the names of a few dozen articulate students, and I sent them e-mails, inviting them out to lunch or dinner in small groups. I would go to sleep in my hotel room at around midnight each night, and when I awoke, my mailbox would be full of replies—sent at 1:15 A.M., 2:59 A.M., 3:23 A.M. 1

In our conversations I would ask the students when they got around to sleeping. One senior told me that she went to bed around two and woke up each morning at seven; she could afford that much rest because she had learned to supplement her full day of work by studying in her sleep. As she was falling asleep she would recite a math problem or a paper topic to herself; she would then sometimes dream about it, and when she woke up, the problem might be solved. I asked several students to describe their daily schedules, and their replies sounded like a session of Future Workaholics of America: crew practice at dawn, classes in the morning, resident-adviser duty, lunch, study groups, classes in the afternoon, tutoring disadvantaged kids in Trenton, a cappella practice, dinner, study, science lab, prayer session, hit the StairMaster, study a few hours more. One young man told me that he had to schedule appointment times for chatting with his friends. I mentioned this to other groups, and usually one or two people would volunteer that they did the same thing. "I just had an appointment with my best friend at seven this morning," one woman said. "Or else you lose touch." 2

There are a lot of things these future leaders no longer have time for. I was on campus at the height of the election season, and I saw not even one Bush or Gore poster. I asked around about this and was told that most students have no time to read newspapers, follow national politics, or get involved in crusades. One senior told me she had subscribed to *The New York Times* once, but the papers had just piled up unread in her dorm room. "It's a basic question of hours in the day," a student journalist told me. "People 3 are too busy to get involved in larger issues. When I think of all that I have to keep up with, I'm relieved there are no bigger compelling causes." Even the biological necessities get squeezed out. I was amazed to learn how little dating goes on. Students go out in groups, and there is certainly a fair bit of partying on campus, but as one told me, "People don't have time or energy to put into real relationships." Sometimes they'll have close friendships and "friendships with privileges" (meaning with sex), but often they don't get serious until they are a few years out of college and meet again at a reunion—after their careers are on track and they can begin to spare the time.

4 I went to lunch with one young man in a student dining room that by 1:10 had emptied out, as students hustled back to the library and their classes. I mentioned that when I went to college, in the late 1970s and early 1980s, we often spent two or three hours around the table, shooting the breeze and arguing about things. He admitted that there was little discussion about intellectual matters outside class. "Most students don't like that that's the case," he told me, "but it is the case." So he and a bunch of his friends had formed a discussion group called Paidea, which meets regularly with a faculty guest to talk about such topics as millennialism, postmodernism, and Byzantine music. If discussion can be scheduled, it can be done.

5 The students were lively conversationalists on just about any topic—except moral argument and character-building, about which more below. But when I asked a group of them if they ever felt like workaholics, their faces lit up and they all started talking at once. One, a student-government officer, said, "Sometimes we feel like we're just tools for processing information. That's what we call ourselves—power tools. And we call these our tool bags." He held up his satchel. The other students laughed, and one exclaimed, "You're giving away all our secrets."

6 But nowhere did I find any real unhappiness with this state of affairs; nowhere did I find anybody who seriously considered living any other way. These super-accomplished kids aren't working so hard because they are compelled to. They are facing, it still appears, the sweetest job market in the nation's history. Investment banks flood the campus looking for hires. Princeton also offers a multitude of post-graduation service jobs in places like China and Africa. Everyone I spoke to felt confident that he or she could get a good job after graduation. Nor do these students seem driven by

some Puritan work ethic deep in their cultural memory. It's not the stick that drives them on, it's the carrot. Opportunity lures them. And at a place like Princeton, in a rich information-age country like America, promises of enjoyable work abound—at least for people as smart and ambitious as these. "I want to be this busy," one young woman insisted, after she had described a daily schedule that would count as slave-driving if it were imposed on anyone.

The best overall description of the students' ethos came from a professor in the politics department and at the Woodrow Wilson School of Public and International Affairs, Jeffrey Herbst. "They are professional students," he said. "I don't say that pejoratively. Their profession for these four years is to be a student." 7

That doesn't mean that these leaders-in-training are money mad (though they are certainly career-conscious). It means they are goal-oriented. An activity—whether it is studying, hitting the treadmill, drama group, community service, or one of the student groups they found and join in great numbers—is rarely an end in itself. It is a means for self-improvement, rèsumè-building, and enrichment. College is just one step on the continual stairway of advancement, and they are always aware that they must get to the next step (law school, medical school, whatever) so that they can progress up the steps after that. 8

One day I went to lunch with Fred Hargadon, who has been the dean of admissions at Princeton for thirteen years and was the dean of admissions at Stanford before that. Like all the administrators and faculty members I spoke with, Hargadon loves these students, and he is extraordinarily grateful for the opportunity to be around them. "I would trust these kids with my life," he told me. But he, like almost all the other older people I talked to, is a little disquieted by the achievement ethos and the calm acceptance of established order that prevails among elite students today. Hargadon said he had been struck by a 1966 booklet called "College Admissions and the Public Interest," written by a retired MIT admissions director named Brainerd Alden Thresher. Thresher made a distinction between students who come to campus in a "poetic" frame of mind and those who come in a "prudential" frame of mind. "Certainly more kids are entering in a prudential frame of mind," Hargadon said. "Most kids see their education as a means to an end." 9

10 They're not trying to buck the system; they're trying to climb it, and they are streamlined for ascent. Hence they are not a disputatious group. I often heard at Princeton a verbal tic to be found in model young people these days: if someone is about to disagree with someone else in a group, he or she will apologize beforehand, and will couch the disagreement in the most civil, nonconfrontational terms available. These students are also extremely respectful of authority, treating their professors as one might treat a CEO or a division head at a company meeting.

11 "Undergrads somehow got this ethos that the faculty is sacrosanct," Dave Wilkinson, a professor of physics, told me. "You don't mess with the faculty. I cannot get the students to call me by my first name." Aaron Friedberg, who teaches international relations, said, "It's very rare to get a student to challenge anything or to take a position that's counter to what the professor says." Robert Wuthnow, a sociologist, lamented. "They are disconcertingly comfortable with authority. That's the most common complaint the faculty has of Princeton students. They're eager to please, eager to jump through whatever hoops the faculty puts in front of them, eager to conform."

12 For the generation of runners of things which came to power in the Clinton years, at least a modest degree of participation in college-years protest was very nearly mandatory. The new elite does not protest. Young achievers vaguely know that they are supposed to feel guilty about not marching in the street for some cause. But they don't seem to feel guilty. When the controversial ethicist Peter Singer was hired by Princeton, there were protests over his views on euthanasia. But it was mostly outsiders who protested, not students. Two years ago the administration outlawed the Nude Olympics, a raucous school tradition. Many of the students were upset, but not enough to protest. "It wasn't rational to buck authority once you found out what the penalties were," one student journalist told me. "The university said they would suspend you from school for a year." A prudential ethos indeed.

13 Part of this is just Princeton. It has always been the preppiest of the Ivy League schools. It has earned a reputation for sending more graduates into consulting and investment banking than into academia or the arts. But this is also what life is like at other competitive universities today. In the months since I spoke with the Princeton students, I've been at several other top schools. Students,

faculty members, and administrators at those places describe a culture that is very similar to the one I found at Princeton. This culture does not absolutely reflect or inform the lives and values of young Americans as a whole, but it does reflect and inform the lives and values of an important subset of this generation: the meritocratic elite. It is this elite that I am primarily reporting on in this article, rather than the whole range of young people across the demographic or SAT spectrum. It should also be said, though, that the young elite are not entirely unlike the other young; they are the logical extreme of America's increasingly efficient and demanding sorting-out process, which uses a complex set of incentives and conditions to channel and shape and rank our children throughout their young lives.

It will surprise no one who has kids to discover that social-science 14
statistics support that description. Not just Princetonians lead a frenetic, tightly packed existence. Kids of all stripes lead lives that are structured, supervised. and stuffed with enrichment. Time-analysis studies done at the University of Michigan's Institute for Social Research provide the best picture of the trend: From 1981 to 1997 the amount of time that children aged three to twelve spent playing indoors declined by 16 percent. The amount of time spent watching TV declined by 23 percent. Meanwhile, the amount of time spent studying increased by 20 percent and the amount of time spent doing organized sports increased by 27 percent. Drive around your neighborhood. Remember all those parks that used to have open fields? They have been carved up into neatly trimmed soccer and baseball fields crowded with parents in folding chairs who are watching their kids perform. In 1981 the association U.S. Youth Soccer had 811,000 registered players. By 1998 it had nearly three million.

Today's elite kids are likely to spend their afternoons and 15
weekends shuttling from one skill-enhancing activity to the next. By the time they reach college, they take this sort of pace for granted, sometimes at a cost. In 1985 only 18 percent of college freshmen told the annual University of California at Los Angeles freshman norms survey that they felt "overwhelmed." Now 28 percent of college freshmen say they feel that way.

But in general they are happy with their lot. Neil Howe and 16
William Strauss surveyed young people for their book *Millennials*

Rising (2000); they found America's young to be generally a hardworking, cheerful, earnest, and deferential group. Howe and Strauss listed their respondents' traits, which accord pretty well with what I found at Princeton: "They're optimists . . . They're cooperative team players . . . They accept authority . . . They're rule followers." The authors paint a picture of incredibly wholesome youths who will correct the narcissism and nihilism of their Boomer parents.

17 Not only at Princeton but also in the rest of the country young people today are more likely to defer to and admire authority figures. Responding to a 1997 Gallup survey, 96 percent of teenagers said they got along with their parents, and 82 percent described their home life as "wonderful" or "good." Roughly three out of four said they shared their parents' general values. When asked by Roper Starch Worldwide in 1998 to rank the major problems facing America today, students aged twelve to nineteen most frequently named as their top five concerns selfishness, people who don't respect law and the authorities, wrongdoing by politicians, lack of parental discipline, and courts that care too much about criminals' rights. It is impossible to imagine teenagers a few decades ago calling for stricter parental discipline and more respect for authority. In 1974 a majority of teenagers reported that they could not "comfortably approach their parents with personal matters of concern." Forty percent believed they would be "better off not living with their parents."

18 Walk through any mall in America. Browse through the racks at Old Navy and Abercrombie & Fitch and the Gap. The colors are bright and chipper. The sales staff is peppy. The look is vaguely retro—upbeat 1962 pre-assassination innocence. The Gap's television ads don't show edgy individualists; they show perky conformists, a bunch of happy kids all wearing the same clothes and all swing-dancing the same moves.

19 In short, at the top of the meritocratic ladder we have in America a generation of students who are extraordinarily bright, morally earnest, and incredibly industrious. They like to study and socialize in groups. They create and join organizations with great enthusiasm. They are responsible, safety-conscious, and mature. They feel no compelling need to rebel—not even a hint of one. They not only defer to authority; they admire it. "Alienation" is a word one almost never hears from them. They regard the universe

as beneficent, orderly, and meaningful. At the schools and colleges where the next leadership class is being bred, one finds not angry revolutionaries, despondent slackers, or dark cynics but the Organization Kid.

BUILDING VOCABULARY

This selection, aiming at a definition of a social group, assumes a general familiarity with sociological concepts or terms. Define the following:

- **a.** goal-oriented (par. 8)
- **b.** end in itself (par. 8
- **c.** meritocratic elite (par. 13)
- **d.** Boomer parents (par. 16)
- **e.** Gallup survey (par. 17)
- **f.** retro-upbeat 1962 pre-assassination innocence (par. 18)

THINKING CRITICALLY ABOUT THE ESSAY

Understanding the Writer's Ideas

1. What do the e-mail messages that the writer receives from students tell him about "what the young people who are going to be running our country in a few decades are like"?
2. What do these "future leaders" no longer have time for? What do these students think about what they no longer have time for? What does the writer think?
3. Why do these students call themselves "power tools"?
4. What does the writer identify as the main motivation for these students' "frenetic" pace (par. 6)?
5. How do these students view the "goal-oriented" activities in which they participate?
6. How do these students view "the established order"? What examples does the writer use to illustrate their attitude toward the established order?
7. What aspects of their upbringing does the writer identify as contributing to their goal-oriented outlook?
8. How do these students differ from "the generation of runners of things which came to power in the Clinton years" (par. 12)?

Understanding the Writer's Techniques

1. What is the thesis in this piece?
2. How would you describe the writer's stance in advancing his definition. What is his attitude toward his subject? Is he an objective investigator reporting sociological facts? Is he an *engaged observer?* Is he advancing any particular point of view? Offer two examples to support your answer.
3. In what ways does the writer see his student subjects as unusual or typical, or both? What evidence does Brooks offer to support the view that these students are an atypical elite? What evidence does he offer to support the view that they are representative of their generation?
4. The writer frequently structures his definition by means of contrasts—"The students were lively conversationalists . . . except . . ." (par. 5); "That doesn't mean that these leaders-in-training are money mad . . . It means . . ." (par. 8). Why do you think Brooks uses contrast so frequently? Do you find his contrasts effective? Why?
5. What kind of evidence does the writer rely on in the first part of his piece (up to par. 4))? In the rest of it? Why does he switch from one form of evidence to the other?
6. Does the final paragraph establish a good conclusion? Why, or why not?

MIXING PATTERNS

The writer uses at least three rhetorical techniques other than definition to examine this "organization" generation: illustration, comparison, and analysis. Identify two examples of each.

Exploring the Writer's Ideas

1. One technique the writer uses to build his thesis is to compare the organization generation with past generations. In what ways is the portrait of the past that Brooks paints consistent and coherent? What aspects of the experience and values of past generations do you think the writer views as better than the experience and values of the present generation? What aspects do you think he sees as worse?

2. The writer says that many people at Princeton are "disquieted by . . . [these students'] calm acceptance of established order" (par. 9). Why do people find this quality disquieting? Does the writer find it disquieting? Do you? Why or why not?
3. As a student, does this portrait of students seem to you convincing? Why or why not? What did you find most recognizable? What did you think was inaccurate? Explain your answers. What did you learn about the current generation of students that you did not already know?

IDEAS FOR WRITING

Prewriting

Organization can imply many things—keeping good order, keeping things in check, being on top of things, being the prisoner of external demands, and so on. We speak of "organizing" a union; we ask, "How organized is too organized?" Jot down a few characteristics of organization, separating your list into good and bad qualities.

Guided Writing

Write an essay titled "How Organized Is Too Organized?" Your essay will assume that you have done some field work observing and interviewing students in a local junior high or high school. You can choose actually to interview students; or you can make up the interviews.

1. Begin with a paragraph that both introduces the reader to your project and captures its most distinctive feature through an apt illustration. (For example, "I had been told that the tenth graders at Tompkins School were a highly motivated bunch, super-organized, but the first time I tried to meet them no one showed up on time.")
2. Draw out the implications of your illustration for your theme—let's say the tenth graders were late because they were so engrossed in astronomy that . . .
3. Now offer a kind of summary-thesis, stating the issue you are exploring and its significance.

4. In the next two paragraphs state some of the positive and then negative features of the super-organized life of the tenth graders (or whatever your sample may be).
5. Indicate your own response to their lifestyle.
6. Indicate their responses—are they happy, secure, uncertain, stressed-out?
7. Draw an appropriate conclusion, snapping the essay shut on an apt tag that might identify this group, just as Brooks did for the college students he observed.

Thinking and Writing Collaboratively

In small groups talk about whether Brooks's portrait rings true, whether it describes *you* and your classmates as college students. What would you add to Brooks's portrait? What would you take out, if anything, as exaggerated or misleading? On the basis of the views gathered in the discussion, write notes for a letter to Brooks about his essay.

Writing About the Text

All writing makes conscious or unconscious assumptions. In this essay, for example, the writer assumes (par. 4) that students *want* time for intellectual bull sessions and that these are a good thing. Write an analysis of Brooks's essay in which you uncover his assumptions in order to arrive at a statement of his view of education.

More Writing Projects

1. In your journal, make a list of elements that you would consider in writing an essay called "The Organization Woman."
2. Turn your notes from the Thinking and Writing Collaboratively activity into an actual letter to the writer (aim at a letter of a paragraph or two).
3. The writer offers with little comment features of the life of the undergraduates he met that might strike the reader as coldly amoral (the concept of "friendships with privileges," for example). Write an essay that probes the moral implications of the super-organized life. Is an intense goal-orientation likely to distort a person's values and feelings for others? Why or why not?

SUMMING UP: CHAPTER 7

1. In her essay on fun, Suzanne Britt Jordan defines a term we all understand but might have difficulty explaining. One way she approaches this definition is through negation—that is, explaining what fun *is not*. Write an essay that defines by negation a similar understood but difficult-to-explain term—for example "privacy," "the blues," "class," "happiness," or "success."
2. Both Gloria Naylor and Janice Castro define words that relate to values placed on language within an ethnic community. Think of a word that has troubled you or been used against you in your early life. It might be a word you associate, for example, with ethnicity, economic status, or personal appearance. Write an essay in which you define this word, considering both how the people who aimed it meant it to be interpreted and how an outsider might define it.
3. Gloria Naylor argues that a word is defined by "consensus." That is, a community agrees among its members on how the word will be used, despite outside definitions. On your campus find examples of current words, defined by "consensus" in the college community, whose meanings would be surprising to outsiders like your parents.
4. Look back over the titles of all the essays in this chapter and previous chapters of this book. Choose one term from any title (for example, "All-American Girl," "Salvation," or "Night Walker"), and write an essay defining that term *subjectively* (from a personal viewpoint).
5. What do you think the students David Brooks portrays would say about Suzanne Britt Jordan's essay?
6. Amy Tan (pp. 28–34) discovers that she has as a resource many "Englishes." Janice Castro defines the qualities of one such English, "Spanglish." But both essays are written in standard English. Why is that?

FROM SEEING TO WRITING

Think about this 1934 photograph of a street scene in Harlem, the section of New York City that is famous as a center of African-American culture. Use the photograph as the basis for an extended definition of a key term or concept—for example, "community," "culture," "city," or "race." In writing your essay, refer specifically to elements in the photograph that support your thesis. Use those writing strategies that serve best to develop your extended definition.

Culver Pictures

CHAPTER 8

Classification

WHAT IS CLASSIFICATION?

Classification is the arrangement of information into groups or categories in order to make clear the relations among members of the group. In a supermarket, the soups are together in one aisle, the frozen foods in another. In a record, tape, and disc store, all the jazz is in one section while the rap music is in a separate section. You wouldn't expect to find a can of tomato soup next to the butter pecan ice cream any more than you'd look for a CD of George Gershwin's *An American in Paris* in the same section as a CD by Ice-T.

Writers need to classify, because it helps them present a mass of material by means of some orderly system. Related bits of information seem clearer when presented together as parts of a group. Unlike writing narrative, for example, developing classification requires a different level of analysis and planning. The writer not only presents a single topic or event, but also places the subject into a complex network of relations. In a narrative, we can tell the story of a single event from start to finish, such as the time we saw a Van Gogh painting in an art museum. In classification, we have to think beyond the personal experience to try to place that Van Gogh painting in a wider context. Where does Van Gogh "fit" in the history of painting? Why is he different from other painters? How does his style relate to other work of the same period? In pursuing these questions, we seek not only to *record* our experience in looking at the painting but to *understand* it more fully.

Classification, then, begins by thinking about a body of material and trying to break it down into distinct parts, or categories.

Called *division* or *analysis,* this first task helps split an idea or object into usable components. Then, some of the parts can serve as categories into which the writer can fit individual pieces that share some common qualities.

For example, if the writer wanted to *analyze* the Van Gogh painting, she might begin with the large subject of painting. Then she could *divide,* or break the subject down, into two groups:

traditional painting

modern painting

Then, she could further *divide* the types of modern painting:

impressionist
postimpressionist
fauvist
art nouveau
cubist
art deco
abstract expressionist
op art
minimalist art

The purpose is to determine what the parts of the whole are. If we know what the components of *modern painting* are, then we can place or locate the Van Gogh painting in relation to other paintings. We would know whether it belonged in the soup aisle or the freezer section, so to speak. In this case, we would decide that it is *not* traditional painting, so that we would separate it from that group. We would place it in the modern group. Now we know which aisle it belongs in. But is it tomato or chicken soup? Now we relate it to the other modern types of painting, and place it in the postimpressionist group. Our decision is based on an analysis of the painter's use of color, his style, and the ways he differs from painters in the other groups.

Our analysis does not mean that the Van Gogh has nothing in common with traditional painting. Van Gogh, for instance, shares an interest in landscape and self-portraits with Rembrandt. But the bright, bold colors of his *Starry Night* are so dramatically different from the somber colors of the older Dutch painter's *Nightwatch* that we are inclined to emphasize their *division.* We could, for instance, set up a supermarket on the basis of what color the food labels were: all the red labels in one aisle, all the yellow labels together. But such a system would make it much harder to find what we wanted unless we were experts in package design. Similarly, our classification of painting is based on the most sensible method of division.

In this chapter, Judith Viorst classifies friends into eight groups, and even numbers them to make it is easy to follow her divisions. E. B. White analyzes three New Yorks, first separating its various strands for a close look at the city, but then weaving them back together to create the "whole" city he loved so much. James T. Baker brings together a variety of writing techniques to analyze the world of education with some humor. Amy Rashap chronicles the changing stereotypes American magazines have used to portray ethnicity. Each writer has a different purpose for classification, but each uses the same basic system of organization.

HOW DO WE READ CLASSIFICATION?

Reading classification involves the following steps:

- Identify what the author is classifying. Find the thesis to determine what the purpose or basis of the classification is.
- Make an outline of the essay. Find the divisions and the classifications into which the author has sorted the subject.
- Determine whether the categories are clearly defined. Do they overlap?
- Be alert for stereotypes. Has the author used them in order to build the groups? If so, see if the groups are oversimplified and thus unreliable.
- Identify the intended audience. How do we know who the audience is?

HOW DO WE WRITE CLASSIFICATION?

The four essayists in this chapter should provide you with enough examples of how to classify to make your writing task easy. Classification resembles outlining. Whether the subject is personal, technical, simple, complex, or abstract, the writer can organize material into categories, and can move carefully from one category to another in developing an essay.

Select your topic and begin to separate it into categories. Try drawing a tree with branches or use a model from a biology book that shows the division of life into genus, species, phyla, and so on. Or make lists. Think about how your library classifies books. Arranging books by the color of the covers might look attractive, but it would presume that all library users already knew what a book looked like before they came to the library. Instead, libraries divide books by type. They generally begin with two large groups: fiction and nonfiction. Within these categories, they create small ones: English fiction, Mexican fiction, Australian fiction. Within nonfiction, they divide books into history, religion, geography, mathematics, and so on. In this way, a reader can find a book based on need, and not prior knowledge. Keeping the library in mind, make a list of categories for your topic.

Make an outline and arrange the groups to avoid overlap from one group to the next.

Decide on a system of classification. Don't force objects into arbitrary slots, though. Don't ignore differences that violate your categories. Try to create a legitimate system that avoids stereotyping or oversimplification; don't classify invalidly. Be sure your categories are legitimate.

Write a thesis that identifies the purpose of your system of classification. Think of the ways in which your system can broaden a reader's understanding of the subject rather than narrow it.

Sample thesis statement:

> At least three groups of immigrants reach the United States today—political refugees seeking asylum, economic refugees looking for a better life, and religious dissidents looking for freedom to practice their chosen beliefs.

Writing the Draft

Write a rough draft. Be sure that you explain the categories and give examples for each one.

For each category, use definition, description, illustration, or narrative to help the reader see the distinct nature of the division you have created. Use transitions between each category or group.

Proofread for correctness. Make a final copy.

A STUDENT PARAGRAPH: CLASSIFICATION

The student who wrote the following paragraph considered the sample thesis statement on immigration appearing earlier, and then modified it to suit her approach to the topic. Observe her various strategies for paragraph development, especially the way she subdivides the last of her categories.

Thesis statement announces classification scheme

First category with brief examples

Second category with greater detail.

Transition "By contrast," introduces third category, further subdivided into two subcategories

Evidence supports position

Americans have mixed feelings about immigrants; they tend to judge different categories of immigrants—illegal aliens, poor immigrants, and political or religious refugees—very differently. Illegal aliens encounter the greatest degree of hostility, despite the fact that U.S. citizens often benefit from their work as maids, gardeners, and street vendors. The second category of immigrants, poor people who are here legally but who are looking to improve their standards of living, also tend to encounter some hostility from Americans. These immigrants, according to some Americans, compete for low-level jobs, go on welfare, and strain such social services as schools and hospitals. By contrast, Americans are usually more welcoming to political and religious refugees. For one thing, political refugees and religious dissidents are fewer in number, which automatically makes them less threatening. In addition, whether from Cuba, Iran, or the former Soviet Union, they are often better educated and wealthier than the illegal aliens and economic refugees, so they are perceived as less of a drain on resources. Undoubtedly, too, they receive a warmer welcome from many Americans because of the belief that their aims are "nobler" than those of illegal aliens or economic refugees, because they flee their homelands to maintain political and religious ideals, rather than simply to make more money.

Friends, Good Friends—and Such Good Friends

Judith Viorst

Judith Viorst, author of eight collections of poetry and five books of prose for adults, as well as twelve children's books, was born in Newark, New Jersey, on February 2, 1931. She graduated from Rutgers University with a degree in history, and went on to study at the Washington Psychoanalytical Institute. Her bestseller *Necessary Losses* (1986) explores the profound impact of loss on our lives. In *Imperfect Control* (1998), she writes about the struggle for control within human relationships. Viorst's children's books include the hugely popular "Alexander" stories, such as the classic *Alexander and the Terrible, Horrible, No Good Very Bad Day* (1972). Among her other works are her comic novel *Murdering Mr. Monti* (1994) and most recently *You're Officially a Grown-Up: The Graduate's Guide to Freedom, Responsibility, Happiness, Personal Hygiene, and the Conquest of Fear.* In this essay, Viorst examines types of friends in her life. Her pattern of development is easy to follow because she tends to stay on one level in the process of classification. As you read this essay, try to keep in mind the similarities and distinctions that Viorst makes among types of friends, as well as the principles of classification that she uses.

PREREADING: THINKING ABOUT THE ESSAY IN ADVANCE

Take a few moments to think about the types of friends that play various roles in your life. How many distinct varieties of friends can you identify? Do you act differently with each type or have different expectations? How does each type of friend make you feel?

Words to Watch

nonchalant (par. 3) showing an easy unconcern or disinterest

endodontist (par. 14) a dentist specializing in diseases of dental pulp and root canals

sibling (par. 16) brother or sister

dormant (par. 19) as if asleep; inactive

self-revelation (par. 22) self-discovery; self-disclosure

calibrated (par. 29) measured; fixed; checked carefully

Women are friends, I once would have said, when they totally love and support and trust each other, and bare to each other the secrets of their souls, and run—no questions asked—to help each other, and tell harsh truths to each other (no, you can't wear that dress unless you lose ten pounds first) when harsh truths must be told. 1

Women are friends, I once would have said, when they share the same affection for Ingmar Bergman, plus train rides, cats, warm rain, charades, Camus, and hate with equal ardor Newark and Brussels sprouts and Lawrence Welk and camping. 2

In other words, I once would have said that a friend is a friend all the way, but now I believe that's a narrow point of view. For the friendships I have and the friendships I see are conducted at many levels of intensity, serve many different functions, meet different needs and range from those as all-the-way as the friendship of the soul sisters mentioned above to that of the most nonchalant and casual playmates. 3

Consider these varieties of friendship: 4

1. Convenience friends. These are the women with whom, if our paths weren't crossing all the time, we'd have no particular reason to be friends: a next-door neighbor, a woman in our car pool, the mother of one of our children's closest friends or maybe some mommy with whom we serve juice and cookies each week at the Glenwood Co-op Nursery. 5

Convenience friends are convenient indeed. They'll lend us their cups and silverware for a party. They'll drive our kids to soccer when we're sick. They'll take us to pick up our car when we need a lift to the garage. They'll even take our cats when we go on vacation. As we will for them. 6

But we don't, with convenience friends, ever come too close or tell too much; we maintain our public face and emotional distance. "Which means," says Elaine, "that I'll talk about being overweight but not about being depressed. Which means I'll admit being mad but not blind with rage. Which means I might say that we're pinched this month but never that I'm worried sick over money." 7

But which doesn't mean that there isn't sufficient value to be found in these friendships of mutual aid, in convenience friends. 8

2. Special-interest friends. These friendships aren't intimate, and they needn't involve kids or silverware or cats. Their value lies in some interest jointly shared. And so we may have an office 9

friend or a yoga friend or a tennis friend or a friend from the Women's Democratic Club.

10 "I've got one woman friend," says Joyce, "who likes, as I do, to take psychology courses. Which makes it nice for me—and nice for her. It's fun to go with someone you know and it's fun to discuss what you've learned, driving back from the classes." And for the most part, she says, that's all they discuss.

11 "I'd say that what we're doing is *doing* together, not being together," Suzanne says of her Tuesday-doubles friends. "It's mainly a tennis relationship, but we play together well. And I guess we all need to have a couple of playmates."

12 I agree.

13 *My* playmate is a shopping friend, a woman of marvelous taste, a woman who knows exactly *where* to buy *what,* and furthermore is a woman who always knows beyond a doubt what one ought to be buying. I don't have the time to keep up with what's new in eyeshadow, hemlines and shoes and whether the smock look is in or finished already. But since (oh, shame!) I care a lot about eyeshadow, hemlines and shoes, and since I don't *want* to wear smocks if the smock look is finished, I'm very glad to have a shopping friend.

14 3. Historical friends. We all have a friend who knew us when . . . maybe way back in Miss Meltzer's second grade, when our family lived in that three-room flat in Brooklyn, when our dad was out of work for seven months, when our brother Allie got in that fight where they had to call the police, when our sister married the endodontist from Yonkers and when, the morning after we lost our virginity, she was the first, the only, friend we told.

15 The years have gone by and we've gone separate ways and we've little in common now, but we're still an intimate part of each other's past. And so whenever we go to Detroit we always go to visit this friend of our girlhood. Who knows how we looked before our teeth were straightened. Who knows how we talked before our voice got unBrooklyned. Who knows what we ate before we learned about artichokes. And who, by her presence, puts us in touch with an earlier part of ourself, a part of ourself it's important never to lose.

16 "What this friend means to me and what I mean to her," says Grace, "is having a sister without sibling rivalry. We know the texture of each other's lives. She remembers my grandmother's

cabbage soup. I remember the way her uncle played the piano. There's simply no other friend who remembers those things."

4. Crossroads friends. Like historical friends, our crossroads friends are important for *what was*—for the friendship we shared at a crucial, now past, time of life. A time, perhaps, when we roomed in college together; or worked as eager young singles in the Big City together; or went together, as my friend Elizabeth and I did through pregnancy, birth and that scary first year of new motherhood. 17

Crossroads friends forge powerful links, links strong enough to endure with not much more contact than once-a-year letters at Christmas. And out of respect for those crossroads years, for those dramas and dreams we once shared, we will always be friends. 18

5. Cross-generational friends. Historical friends and crossroads friends seem to maintain a special kind of intimacy—dormant but always ready to be revived—and though we may rarely meet, whenever we do connect, it's personal and intense. Another kind of intimacy exists in the friendships that form across generations in what one woman calls her daughter-mother and her mother-daughter relationships. 19

Evelyn's friend is her mother's age—"but I share so much more than I ever could with my mother"—a woman she talks to of music, of books and of life. "What I get from her is the benefit of her experience. What she gets—and enjoys—from me is a youthful perspective. It's a pleasure for both of us." 20

I have in my own life a precious friend, a woman of 65 who has lived very hard, who is wise, who listens well; who has been where I am and can help me understand it; and who represents not only an ultimate ideal mother to me but also the person I'd like to be when I grow up. 21

In our daughter role we tend to do more than our share of self-revelation; in our mother role we tend to receive what's revealed. It's another kind of pleasure—playing wise mother to a questing younger person. It's another very lovely kind of friendship. 22

6. Part-of-a-couple friends. Some of the women we call our friends we never see alone—we see them as part of a couple at couples' parties. And though we share interests in many things and respect each other's views, we aren't moved to deepen the relationship. Whatever the reason, a lack of time or—and this is more 23

likely—a lack of chemistry, our friendship remains in the context of a group. But the fact that our feeling on seeing each other is always, "I'm *so* glad she's here" and the fact that we spend half the evening talking together says that this too, in its own way, counts as a friendship.

24 (Other part-of-a-couple friends are the friends that came with the marriage, and some of these are friends we could live without. But sometimes, alas, she married our husband's best friend; and sometimes, alas, she *is* our husband's best friend. And so we find ourself dealing with her, somewhat against our will, in a spirit of what I'll call *reluctant* friendship.)

25 7. Men who are friends. I wanted to write just of women friends, but the women I've talked to won't let me—they say I must mention man-woman friendships too. For these friendships can be just as close and as dear as those that we form with women. Listen to Lucy's description of one such friendship:

26 "We've found we have things to talk about that are different from what he talks about with my husband and different from what I talk about with his wife. So sometimes we call on the phone or meet for lunch. There are similar intellectual interests—we always pass on to each other the books that we love—but there's also something tender and caring too."

27 In a couple of crises, Lucy says, "he offered himself, for talking and for helping. And when someone died in his family he wanted me there. The sexual, flirty part of our friendship is very small, but *some*—just enough to make it fun and different." She thinks—and I agree—that the sexual part, though small, is always *some,* is always there when a man and a woman are friends.

28 It's only in the past few years that I've made friends with men, in the sense of a friendship that's *mine,* not just part of two couples. And achieving with them the ease and the trust I've found with women friends has value indeed. Under the dryer at home last week, putting on mascara and rouge, I comfortably sat and talked with a fellow named Peter. Peter, I finally decided, could handle the shock of me minus mascara under the dryer. Because we care for each other. Because we're friends.

29 8. There are medium friends, and pretty good friends, and very good friends indeed, and these friendships are defined by their level of intimacy. And what we'll reveal at each of these levels of

intimacy is calibrated with care. We might tell a medium friend, for example, that yesterday we had a fight with our husband. And we might tell a pretty good friend that this fight with our husband made us so mad that we slept on the couch. And we might tell a very good friend that the reason we got so mad in that fight that we slept on the couch had something to do with that girl who works in his office. But it's only to our very best friends that we're willing to tell all, to tell what's going on with that girl in his office.

The best of friends, I still believe, totally love and support and trust each other, and bare to each other the secrets of their souls, and run—no questions asked—to help each other, and tell harsh truths to each other when they must be told. 30

But we needn't agree about everything (only 12-year-old girl friends agree about *everything*) to tolerate each other's point of view. To accept without judgment. To give and to take without ever keeping score. And to *be* there, as I am for them and as they are for me, to comfort our sorrows, to celebrate our joys. 31

BUILDING VOCABULARY

1. Find *antonyms* (words that mean the opposite of given words) for the following entries.
   a. harsh (par. 1)
   b. mutual (par. 8)
   c. crucial (par. 17)
   d. intimacy (par. 29)
   e. tolerate (par. 31)
2. The *derivation* of a word—how it originated and where it came from—can make you more aware of meanings. Your dictionary normally lists abbreviations (for instance, L. for Latin, Fr. for French) for word origins, and sometimes explains fully the way a word came into use. Look up the following words to determine their origins.
   a. psychology (par. 10)
   b. historical (par. 14)
   c. sibling (par. 16)
   d. Christmas (par. 18)
   e. sexual (par. 27)

THINKING CRITICALLY ABOUT THE ESSAY

Understanding the Writer's Ideas

1. What is Viorst's definition of friendship in the first two paragraphs? Does she accept this definition? Why or why not?
2. Name and describe in your own words the types of friends that Viorst mentions in her essay.
3. In what way are "convenience friends" and "special-interest friends" alike? How are "historical friends" and "crossroads friends" alike?
4. What does Viorst mean when she writes, "In our daughter role we tend to do more than our share of self-revelation; in our mother role we tend to receive what's revealed" (par. 22)?
5. How do part-of-a-couple friends who came with the marriage differ from primary part-of-a-couple friends?
6. Does Viorst think that men can be friends for women? Why or why not? What complicates such friendships?
7. For Viorst, who are the best friends?

Understanding the Writer's Techniques

1. Which paragraphs make up the introduction in this essay? How does Viorst organize these paragraphs? Where does she place her thesis sentence?
2. How does the thesis sentence reveal the principles of classification (the questions Viorst asks to produce the various categories) that the author employs in the essay?
3. Does Viorst seem to emphasize each of her categories equally? Is she effective in handling each category? Why or why not? Do you think that men belong in the article as a category? For what reasons?
4. Analyze the importance of illustration in this essay. From what sources does Viorst tend to draw her examples?
5. How do definition and comparison and contrast operate in the essay? Cite specific examples of these techniques.
6. The level of language in this essay tends to be informal at times, reflecting patterns that are as close to conversation as to formal writing. Identify some sentences that seem to resemble informal speech. Why does Viorst try to achieve a conversational style?

7. Which main group in the essay is further broken down into categories?
8. Analyze Viorst's conclusion. How many paragraphs are involved? What strategies does she use? How does she achieve balanced sentence structure (parallelism) in her last lines?

Exploring the Writer's Ideas

1. Do you accept all of Viorst's categories of friendship? Which categories seem the most meaningful to you?
2. Try to think of people you know who fit into the various categories established by Viorst. Can you think of people who might exist in more than one category? How do you explain this fact? What are the dangers in trying to stereotype people in terms of categories, roles, backgrounds, or functions?
3. Viorst maintains that you can define friends in terms of functions and needs (see paragraph 3 and paragraphs 29 to 31). Would you agree? Why or why not? What principle or principles do you use to classify friends? In fact, *do* you classify friends? For what reasons?

IDEAS FOR WRITING

Prewriting

Select a specific category of people—for example, teachers, friends, or family members—and freewrite for fifteen minutes about the characteristics of each type within the group.

Guided Writing

Using the classification method, write an essay on a specific group of individuals—for instance, types of friends, types of enemies, types of students, types of teachers, types of politicians, types of dates.

1. Establish your subject in the first paragraph. Also indicate to the reader the principle(s) of classification that you plan to use. (For guidelines look again at the second sentence in paragraph 3 of Viorst's essay.)
2. Start the body of the essay with a single short sentence that introduces categories, as Viorst does in paragraph 4. In the body,

use numbers and category headings ("Convenience friends" . . . "Special-interest friends") to separate groups.
3. Try to achieve a balance in the presentation of information on each category. Define each type and provide appropriate examples.
4. If helpful, use comparison and contrast to indicate from time to time the similarities and differences among groups. Try to avoid too much overlapping of groups, since this is harmful to the classification process.
5. Employ the personal "I" and other conversational techniques to achieve an informal style.
6. Return to your principle(s) of classification and amplify this feature in your conclusion. If you want, make a value judgment, as Viorst does, about which type of person in your classification scheme is the most significant.

Thinking and Writing Collaboratively

Form groups of three or four, and have each group member draw a diagram showing the types of teachers they have encountered in school and college. Then, discuss the various divisions and try to develop one combined diagram. Finally, present your findings to the class.

Writing About the Text

Are you persuaded by Viorst's opening sentence in paragraph 3? If so, explain. If not, write an essay showing that thinking in terms of the "types" of friends Viorst enumerates may in fact undermine friendship.

More Writing Projects

1. As journal practice, classify varieties of show business comedians, singers, talk-show hosts, star athletes, or the like.
2. In a paragraph, use division and (or) classification to explain the various roles that you must play as a friend.
3. Ask each student in your class to explain what he or she means by the term "friendship." List all responses and then divide the list into at least three categories. Using your notes, write a classification essay reporting your findings.

The Three New Yorks

E. B. White

E(lwyn). B(rooks). White (1899–1985) ranks among the great stylists in American letters. His famous essays, children's literature, and light verse are notable for their wit and perfection of form. Born in Mount Vernon, New York, White graduated from Cornell University. In 1926 he joined the staff of *The New Yorker* (the magazine had just been founded), and remained a regular contributor for most of his career. White also wrote a popular column for *Harper's* magazine, entitled "One Man's Meat," from 1938 to 1943. In his essays White looks on the problems of modern life with an unflinching but calm, amused, and deeply sympathetic eye. Generations of readers have been enchanted by his children's books which include *Stuart Little* (1945) and *Charlotte's Web* (1952). In 1959 White published a revised edition of *The Elements of Style,* first published by his professor William Strunk, Jr., in 1918. The book is one of the outstanding works on the use of American English. This selection, taken from White's tribute to New York City, *Here Is New York* (1949), remains remarkably fresh after more than fifty years. Look closely at the way White clearly defines his categories of classification, then skillfully blends them to create a vivid sense of the whole city.

PREREADING: THINKING ABOUT THE ESSAY IN ADVANCE

As you prepare to read White's essay, take a few minutes to think about the place where you live or, if you have lived in several locations, the place that you know best. What is the place like? Are there different classes of people in this place or different parts with specific features or functions? How would you divide the place in terms of people, sections, and functions?

Words to Watch

locusts (par. 1) migratory grasshoppers that travel in swarms, stripping vegetation as they pass over the land

disposition (par. 1) temperament; way of acting

deportment (par. 1) the way in which a person carries himself or herself

tidal (par. 1) coming in wavelike motions

continuity (par. 1) uninterrupted flow of events

slum (par. 1) a highly congested residential area marked by unsanitary buildings, poverty, and social disorder

indignity (par. 1) humiliating treatment

vitality (par. 2) lively and animated character

gloaming (par. 2) a poetic term for "twilight"

ramparts (par. 2) high, broad structures guarding a building

negligently (par. 2) nonchalantly; neglectfully

loiterer (par. 2) a person who hangs around aimlessly

spewing (par. 2) coming in a flood or gush

rover (par. 2) wanderer; roamer

1 There are roughly three New Yorks. There is, first, the New York of the man or woman who was born here, who takes the city for granted and accepts its size and its turbulence as natural and inevitable. Second, there is the New York of the commuter—the city that is devoured by locusts each day and spat out each night. Third, there is the New York of the person who was born somewhere else and came to New York in quest of something. Of these three trembling cities the greatest is the last—the city of final destination, the city that is a goal. It is this third city that accounts for New York's high-strung disposition, its poetical deportment, its dedication to the arts, and its incomparable achievements. Commuters give the city its tidal restlessness; natives give it solidity and continuity; but the settlers give it passion. And whether it is a farmer arriving from Italy to set up a small grocery store in a slum, or a young girl arriving from a small town in Mississippi to escape the indignity of being observed by her neighbors, or a boy arriving from the Corn Belt with a manuscript in his suitcase and a pain in his heart, it makes no difference; each embraces New York with the intense excitement of first love, each absorbs New York with the fresh eyes of an adventurer, each generates heat and light to dwarf the Consolidated Edison Company.

2 The commuter is the queerest bird of all. The suburb he inhabits has no essential vitality of its own and is a mere roost where he comes at day's end to go to sleep. Except in rare cases, the man who lives in Mamaroneck or Little Neck or Teaneck, and works in New York, discovers nothing much about the city except the time of arrival and departure of trains and buses, and the path to a quick lunch. He is deskbound, and has never, idly roaming in the gloaming, stumbled suddenly on Belvedere Tower in the Park, seen the ramparts rise sheer from the water of the pond, and the boys along

the shore fishing for minnows, girls stretched out negligently on the shelves of the rocks; he has never come suddenly on anything at all in New York as a loiterer, because he has had no time between trains. He has fished in Manhattan's wallet and dug out coins, but has never listened to Manhattan's breathing, never awakened to its morning, never dropped off to sleep in its night. About 400,000 men and women come charging onto the Island each week-day morning, out of the mouths of tubes and tunnels. Not many among them have ever spent a drowsy afternoon in the great rustling oaken silence of the reading room of the Public Library, with the book elevator (like an old water wheel) spewing out books onto the trays. They tend their furnaces in Westchester and in Jersey, but have never seen the furnaces of the Bowery, the fires that burn in oil drums on zero winter nights. They may work in the financial district downtown and never see the extravagant plantings of Rockefeller Center—the daffodils and grape hyacinths and birches of the flags trimmed to the wind on a fine morning in spring. Or they may work in a midtown office and may let a whole year swing round without sighting Governor's Island from the sea wall. The commuter dies with tremendous mileage to his credit, but he is no rover. His entrances and exits are more devious than those in a prairie-dog village; and he calmly plays bridge while his train is buried in the mud at the bottom of the East River. The Long Island Rail Road alone carried forty million commuters last year; but many of them were the same fellow retracing his steps.

The terrain of New York is such that a resident sometimes 3
travels farther, in the end, than a commuter. The journey of the composer Irving Berlin from Cherry Street in the lower East Side to an apartment uptown was through an alley and was only three or four miles in length; but it was like going three times around the world.

BUILDING VOCABULARY

1. Underline the numerous references in this essay to buildings, people, and areas in and around New York City and identify them. If necessary, consult a guidebook, map, or history of New York City for help.

2. Write *synonyms* (words that mean the same) for each of these words in the essay. Use a dictionary if necessary.
   a. turbulence (par. 1)
   b. inevitable (par. 1)
   c. quest (par. 1)
   d. high-strung (par. 1)
   e. incomparable (par. 1)
   f. essential (par. 2)
   g. deskbound (par. 2)
   h. drowsy (par. 2)
   i. extravagant (par. 2)
   j. devious (par. 2)

THINKING CRITICALLY ABOUT THE ESSAY

Understanding the Writer's Ideas

1. What are the three New Yorks?
2. What single-word designation does E. B. White assign to each of the three types of New Yorkers? Match up each of the three New Yorks you identified in the first question with each of the three types of New Yorkers.
3. For what reasons do people born elsewhere come to New York to live? What three illustrations of such people does White describe? What is the young girl's indignity? What is the occupation or hope of the boy from the Corn Belt? Why might he have "a pain in his heart"?
4. What does each type of New Yorker give to the city?
5. What is White's attitude toward the suburbs? What key phrases reveal this attitude?
6. What are some of the things commuters miss about New York by dashing in and out of the city? What does White ironically suggest will be the commuter's final fate?
7. Are we to take literally White's conclusion that "many of them were the same fellow retracing his steps"? Why or why not?
8. Explain the sentence "The terrain of New York is such that a resident sometimes travels farther, in the end, than a commuter." Be aware that White is using language figuratively.

9. The author tells of composer Irving Berlin's journey through an alley. He is referring to "Tin Pan Alley." Identify this place.

Understanding the Writer's Techniques

1. In this essay what is the thesis? Where is it? Is it developed fully?
2. What is the purpose of classification in this essay? What is the basis of the classification White uses? What key words at the beginning of paragraph 1 direct your attention to each category discussed? How do these key words contrast in tone with the descriptions in the first few sentences? What sort of rhythm is established?
3. White vividly *personifies* (see Glossary) New York City in paragraph 1. List and explain the effects of these personifications. Where else does he personify?
4. Refer to your answers to question 2 in the Building Vocabulary section. Are the literal meanings of those words appropriate to White's three types of New Yorkers? Defend your answer. Figuratively, what does each term make you think of? How do the figurative meanings enhance the essay?
5. How does White use *illustration* in this essay? Where does he use it most effectively?
6. What is the function of *negation* (see page 256) in the first part of paragraph 2? What is the *implied contrast* in this paragraph?
7. How is White's attitude toward New York reflected in the *tone* (see Glossary) of this essay?
8. White makes widespread use of *metaphor* (see Glossary) in this essay. How does his use of metaphor affect the tone of the essay? State in your own words the meaning of each of the following metaphors:
    a. the city that is devoured by locusts each day and spat out each night (par. 1)
    b. The commuter is the queerest bird of all. (par. 2)
    c. a mere roost (par. 2)
    d. idly roaming in the gloaming (par. 2)
    e. He has fished in Manhattan's wallet and dug out coins, but has never listened to Manhattan's breathing (par. 2)
    f. the great rustling oaken silence (par. 2)
9. Among all the metaphors, White uses just one *simile* (see Glossary). What is it? What is the effect of placing it where he did?

Exploring the Writer's Ideas

1. Is New York's turbulence "natural and inevitable" for any large city? What are some examples of turbulence in a city you know? How do you deal with disruptions in your environment?
2. White writes of "a young girl arriving from a small town in Mississippi to escape the indignity of being observed by her neighbors." What might cause her indignity? How can neighbors bring about such a condition?
3. Some people feel that the anonymity of a big city like New York makes it easier just to "be yourself" without having to worry about what others might say. Others feel such anonymity creates a terrible feeling of impersonality. What are the advantages and disadvantages of each attitude?
4. Do you agree that the suburbs have "no essential vitality"? Explain your response by referring to suburbs you have visited, have read about, or have inhabited.
5. White claims that those who choose to leave their homes and who come to live in New York give the place a special vitality. Do you know any people who chose to leave their places of birth to live in a large city like New York? Why did they move? How have things gone for them since they began living in the city? Have you noticed any changes? For what reasons do people leave one place to live in another? When have you moved from place to place? Why?
6. The World Trade Center disaster of 2002 threatened to cut down on the numbers of New York City's visitors. Yet tourists still visit in large numbers and commuters continue their daily rides in and out of the city. How do you account for the continued presence of "non-natives" in New York? What in White's essay helps you explain the way people over the country embrace New York City?

IDEAS FOR WRITING

Prewriting

Write "The Three __________" at the top of a sheet of paper, and fill in the blank with the name of your town or city. Below the title, draw a diagram or visual presentation in which you establish and label at least three types of people in your community.

Guided Writing

Organize a classification essay around the city or town in which you live.

1. Begin with a simple direct thesis statement that tells the reader how many categories of classification you will consider.
2. Briefly outline the different categories. Indicate each with a key organizational word or phrase.
3. Indicate which category is the most important. Tell why.
4. Develop this category with at least three vivid illustrations.
5. Define one of the categories through both negation and an implied contrast to another category.
6. Use figurative language (metaphors, similes, personification) throughout your essay.
7. Use specific name or place references.
8. End your essay with a brief factual narrative that gives the reader a feel for your town or city.

Thinking and Writing Collaboratively

Exchange your classification essay with a class member. Then assess the accuracy of your classmate's division of her or his subject into categories. Underline the subdivisions within the paper. Check to see that there is no overlap or omission of key categories. Recommend revisions, if any, and make any appropriate revisions suggested by your partner to your own paper.

Writing About the Text

Write an essay in which you examine the *tone* (see Glossary) of this essay. How is White's attitude reflected in the tone of the essay?

More Writing Projects

1. Use classification in a journal entry to capture at least three ways of viewing your college.
2. Write a classification paragraph on the suburbs or the country.
3. Select a cultural group and classify in an essay various characteristics common to that group. Be careful to avoid stereotyping.

How Do We Find the Student in a World of Academic Gymnasts and Worker Ants?

James T. Baker

James T. Baker is general editor for the "Creators of the American Mind" series, published by Harcourt Brace. Presently at work on a volume about Andrew Carnegie, Baker has contributed three books to the series—on Nat Turner, Eleanor Roosevelt, and Abraham Lincoln. Baker received his Ph.D. in 1968 from Florida State University and is currently Professor of History at Western Kentucky University. In this witty selection from the *Chronicle of Higher Education,* Baker classifies student types that you may well recognize as you look around your classrooms, school cafeteria, lecture halls, or gymnasium. The writer enhances his unique categories by using description, definition, and colloquial language, which help make his deliberate stereotypes come alive.

PREREADING: THINKING ABOUT THE ESSAY IN ADVANCE

Prior to reading this essay, think about the different types of students you have encountered and the forms of behavior distinguishing one from the other. Does each type behave in a predictable way? Which category would you place yourself in? Which types do you prefer or associate with, and why?

Words to Watch

musings (par. 3) dreamy, abstract thoughts

sabbatical (par. 3) a paid leave from a job earned after a certain period of time

malaise (par. 3) uneasiness; feelings of restlessness

impaired (par. 3) made less effective

clones (par. 4) exact biological replicas, asexually produced

recuperate (par. 5) to undergo recovery from an illness

esoteric (par. 7) understood by a limited group with special knowledge

primeval (par. 7) primitive; relating to the earliest ages

mundane (par. 8) ordinary

jaded (par. 20) exhausted; bored by something from overexposure to it

1 Anatole France once wrote that "the whole art of teaching is only the art of awakening the natural curiosity of young minds." I fully agree, except I have to wonder if, by using the word "only," he thought that the art of awakening such natural curiosity was an easy job. For me, it never has been—sometimes exciting, always challenging, but definitely not easy.

2 Robert M. Hutchins used to say that a good education prepares students to go on educating themselves throughout their lives. A fine definition, to be sure, but it has at times made me doubt that my own students, who seem only too eager to graduate so they can lay down their books forever, are receiving a good education.

3 But then maybe these are merely the pessimistic musings of someone suffering from battle fatigue. I have almost qualified for my second sabbatical leave, and I am scratching a severe case of the seven-year itch. About the only power my malaise has not impaired is my eye for spotting certain "types" of students. In fact, as the rest of me declines, my eye seems to grow more acute.

4 Has anyone else noticed that the very same students people college classrooms year after year? Has anyone else found the same bodies, faces, personalities returning semester after semester? Forgive me for violating my students' individual "personhoods," but reality makes it so tempting to see them as types. Doubtless you will recognize at least some of them. They have twins, or perhaps clones, on your campus, too.

5 There is the eternal Good Time Charlie (or Charlene), who makes every party on and off the campus, who by November of his freshman year has worked his face into a case of terminal acne, who misses every set of examinations because of "mono," who finally burns himself out physically and mentally by the age of 19 and drops out to go home and recuperate, and who returns at 20 after a long talk with Dad to major in accounting.

6 There is the Young General Patton, the one who comes to college on an R.O.T.C. scholarship and for a year twirls his rifle at basketball games while loudly sniffing out pinko professors, who at midpoint takes a sudden but predictable, radical swing from far right to far left, who grows a beard and moves in with a girl who refuses to shave her legs, who then makes the just as predictable, radical swing back to the right and ends up preaching fundamentalist sermons on the steps of the student union while the Good Time Charlies and Charlenes jeer.

7 There is the Egghead, the campus intellectual who shakes up his fellow students—and even a professor or two—with references to esoteric formulas and obscure Bulgarian poets, who is recognized by friend and foe alike as a promising young academic, someday to be a professional scholar, who disappears every summer for six weeks ostensibly to search for primeval human remains in Colorado caves, and who at 37 is shot dead by Arab terrorists while on a mission for the C.I.A.

8 There is the Performer—the music or theater major, the rock or folk singer—who spends all of his or her time working up an act, who gives barely a nod to mundane subjects like history, sociology, or physics, who dreams only of the day he or she will be on stage full time, praised by critics, cheered by audiences, who ends up either pregnant or responsible for a pregnancy and at 30 is either an insurance salesman or a housewife with a very lush garden.

9 There is the Jock, of course—the every-afternoon intramural champ, smelling of liniment and Brut, with bulging calves and a blue-eyed twinkle, the subject of untold numbers of female fantasies, the walking personification of he-manism—who upon graduation is granted managerial rank by a California bank because of his golden tan and low golf score, who is seen five years later buying the drinks at a San Francisco gay bar.

10 There is the Academic Gymnast—the guy or gal who sees college as an obstacle course, as so many stumbling blocks in the way of a great career or a perfect marriage—who strains every moment to finish and be done with "this place" forever, who toward the end of the junior year begins to slow down, to grow quieter and less eager to leave, who attends summer school, but never quite finishes those last six hours, who never leaves "this place," and who at 40 is still working at the campus laundry, still here, still a student.

11 There is the Medal Hound, the student who comes to college not to learn or expand any intellectual horizons but simply to win honors—medals, cups, plates, ribbons, scrolls—who is here because this is the best place to win the most the fastest, who plasticizes and mounts on his wall every certificate of excellence he wins, who at 39 will be a colonel in the U.S. Army and at 55 Secretary of something or other in a conservative Administration in Washington.

There is the Worker Ant, the student (loosely rendered) who takes 21 hours a semester and works 49 hours a week at the local car wash, who sleeps only on Sundays and during classes, who will somehow graduate on time and be the owner of his own vending-machine company at 30 and be dead of a heart attack at 40, and who will be remembered for the words chiseled on his tombstone: 12

All This Was Accomplished Without Ever Having So Much As Darkened The Door Of A Library 13

There is the Lost Soul, the sad kid who is in college only because teachers, parents, and society at large said so, who hasn't a career in mind or a dream to follow, who hasn't a clue, who heads home every Friday afternoon to spend the weekend cruising the local Dairee-Freeze, who at 50 will have done all his teachers, parents, and society said to do, still without a career in mind or a dream to follow or a clue. 14

There is also the Saved Soul—the young woman who has received, through the ministry of one Gospel freak or another, a Holy Calling to save the world, or at least some special part of it—who majors in Russian studies so that she can be caught smuggling Bibles into the Soviet Union and be sent to Siberia where she can preach to souls imprisoned by the Agents of Satan in the Gulag Archipelago. 15

Then, finally, there is the Happy Child, who comes to college to find a husband or wife—and finds one—and there is the Determined Child, who comes to get a degree—and gets one. 16

Enough said. 17

All of which, I suppose, should make me throw up my hands in despair and say that education, like youth and love, is wasted on the young. Not quite. 18

For there does come along, on occasion, that one of a hundred or so who is maybe at first a bit lost, certainly puzzled; who may well start out a Good Timer, an Egghead, a Performer, a Jock, a Medal Hound, a Gymnast, a Worker Ant; who may indeed have trouble settling on a major, who will be distressed by what sometimes passes for education, who might even be a temporary dropout; but who has a vital capacity for growth and is able to fall in love with learning, who acquires a taste for intellectual pleasure, who becomes in the finest sense of the word a Student. 19

20 This is the one who keeps the most jaded of us going back to class after class, and he or she must be oh-so-carefully cultivated. He or she must be artfully awakened, given the tools needed to continue learning for a lifetime, and let grow at whatever pace and in whatever direction nature dictates.

21 For I try always to remember that this student is me, my continuing self, my immortality. This person is my only hope that my own search for Truth will continue after me, on and on, forever.

BUILDING VOCABULARY

1. Explain these *colloquialisms* (see Glossary) in Baker's essay.
   - **a.** someone suffering from battle fatigue (par. 3)
   - **b.** I am scratching a severe case of the seven-year itch (par. 3)
   - **c.** worked his face into a case of terminal acne (par. 5)
   - **d.** burns himself out physically and mentally (par. 5)
   - **e.** loudly sniffing out pinko professors (par. 6)
   - **f.** working up an act (par. 8)
   - **g.** gives barely a nod (par. 8)
   - **h.** the walking personification of he-manism (par. 9)
   - **i.** to spend the weekend cruising the local Dairee-Freeze (par. 14)
   - **j.** he or she must be oh-so-carefully cultivated (par. 20)
2. Identify these references.
   - **a.** R.O.T.C. (par. 6)
   - **b.** C.I.A. (par. 7)
   - **c.** Brut (par. 9)
   - **d.** Dairee-Freeze (par. 14)
   - **e.** Gospel freak (par. 15)
   - **f.** Agents of Satan (par. 15)
   - **g.** Gulag Archipelago (par. 15)

THINKING CRITICALLY ABOUT THE ESSAY

Understanding the Writer's Ideas

1. In common language, describe the various categories of college students that Baker names.

2. Who is Anatole France? What process is described in the quotation from him? Why does Baker cite it at the beginning of the essay? What is his attitude toward France's idea?
3. For how long has Baker been teaching? What is his attitude toward his work?
4. About what age do you think Baker is? Why? Explain the meaning of the sentence: "In fact, as the rest of me declines, my eye seems to grow more acute" (par. 3).
5. Choose three of Baker's categories and paraphrase each description and meaning in a serious way.
6. What does Baker feel, overall, is the contemporary college student's attitude toward studying and receiving an education? How does it differ from Baker's own attitude toward these things?
7. Although Baker's classification may seem a bit pessimistic, he refuses to "throw up . . . [his] hands in despair" (par. 18). Why?
8. Describe the characteristics that are embodied in the category of *Student.* To whom does Baker compare the "true" Student? Why?

Understanding the Writer's Techniques

1. What is Baker's thesis in this essay? Does he state it directly or not? What, in your own words, is his purpose?
2. In this essay Baker deliberately creates, rather than avoids, stereotypes. He does so to establish exaggerated representatives of types. Why?

   For paragraphs 5 to 16, prepare a paragraph-by-paragraph outline of the main groups of students classified. For each, include the following information:

   a. type represented by the stereotype
   b. motivation of type for being a student
   c. main activity as a student
   d. condition in which the type ends up
3. This article was published in *The Chronicle of Higher Education,* a weekly newspaper for college and university educators and administrators. How do you think this audience influenced Baker's analysis of types of students? His tone and language?

4. What is Baker's tone in the essay? Give specific examples. In general, how would you characterize his attitude toward the contemporary college student? Why? Does his attitude or tone undergo any shifts in the essay? Explain.
5. Why does Baker use the term "personhoods" in paragraph 4? What attitude, about what subject, does he convey in his use of that word?
6. Why does the author capitalize the names he gives to the various categories of students? Why does he capitalize the word *Truth* in the last sentence?
7. What is the purpose of the one-sentence paragraph 13? Why does Baker set it aside from paragraph 12, since it is a logical conclusion to that paragraph? Why does he use a two-word sentence as the complete paragraph 17? In what ways do these words signal the beginning of the essay's conclusion?

MIXING PATTERNS

How does Baker use description to enhance his analysis in this essay? Which descriptive details do you find most convincing? What purpose does description serve?

What is the role of *process analysis?* (Process analysis, discussed in the next chapter, is telling how something is done or proceeds; see pages 338–341). Look especially at Baker's descriptions of each type of student. How does process analysis figure into the title of the essay?

Exploring the Writer's Ideas

1. Do you think Baker's classifications in this essay are fair? Are they representative of the whole spectrum of students? How closely do they mirror the student population at your school? The article was written in 1982: How well have Baker's classifications held up to the present conditions?
2. Into which category (or categories) would you place yourself? Why?
3. Based on your reaction to and understanding of this article, would you like to have Baker as your professor? Why or why not?

IDEAS FOR WRITING

Prewriting

Freewrite for fifteen minutes about the different types of students who are common to your campus. What are the traits or characteristics of each group? What do representatives of each group do? Where do they congregate? How many of these types can you recognize in this classroom?

Guided Writing

Write a classification of at least three "types" in a situation with which you are familiar, other than school—a certain job, social event, sport, or some such situation.

1. Begin your essay with a reference, direct or indirect, to what some well-known writer or expert said about this situation.
2. Identify your role in relation to the situation described.
3. Write about your attitude toward the particular situation and why you are less than thrilled about it at present.
4. Make sure you involve the reader as someone who would be familiar with the situation and activities described.
5. Divide your essay into exaggerated or stereotyped categories which you feel represent almost the complete range of types in these situations. In your categorization, be sure to include motivations, activities, and results for each type.
6. Use description to make your categories vivid.
7. Use satire and a bit of gentle cynicism as part of your description.
8. Select a lively title.
9. In the conclusion, identify another type that you consider the "purest" or "most truthful" representative of persons in this situation. Either by comparison with yourself or by some other means, explain why you like this type best.

Thinking and Writing Collaboratively

In groups of four to five class members, draft an article for your college newspaper in which you outline the types of students on the campus. Try to maintain a consistently lighthearted or humorous tone or point of view as you move from discussion to the drafting of the letter. Revise your paper, paying careful attention to the flow from one category to the next, before submitting the article for possible publication.

Writing About the Text

Much of the humor and energy of this essay comes from Baker's use of figurative language—from the title on. Write an essay in which you analyze the figurative language here. How does it contribute to the thesis? The tone?

More Writing Projects

1. In your journal, write your own classification of three college "types." Your entry can be serious or humorous.
2. In a 250-word paragraph, classify types of college dates.
3. Look in current magazines for advertisements directed at men or women, or both. Write an essay in which you classify current advertisements according to some logical scheme. Limit your essay to three to five categories.

The American Dream for Sale: Ethnic Images in Magazines

Amy Rashap

Amy Rashap (b. 1955) holds a Ph.D. from the University of Pennsylvania in the study of folklore and writes about American popular culture. Her current project is a book about food, dieting, and images of the body in American society. This selection appeared in the catalog published in conjunction with an exhibition mounted in 1984 at the Balch Institute for Ethnic Studies, a museum and research library in Philadelphia. Rashap classifies evolving ethnic images in U.S. popular magazines as these images have reflected the views and the assumed biases of readers and the society at large over the last century.

PREREADING: THINKING ABOUT THE ESSAY IN ADVANCE

One version of the American Dream conjures up the picture of boatfuls of immigrants floating by the Statue of Liberty onto the shores of the land of opportunity. How does the essay's title make use of this notion of America? What does the title imply about the role of advertising in relation to traditional notions of the American Dream?

Words to Watch

dictum (par. 1) an authoritative saying
plethora (par. 2) overabundance
subservience (par. 5) submissiveness
protagonists (par. 9) the main characters in a story
nominally (par. 9) in name only but not in fact
superficial (par. 10) shallow
impetus (par. 12) incentive, stimulus
indigenous (par. 13) from a particular region, ethnic

"Promise—large promise—is the soul of advertising," wrote Dr. Samuel Johnson in the eighteenth century. His dictum has remained remarkably accurate during the last two hundred and fifty years. Advertisements tell the viewer much more than the merits of a particular product. From the glossy and colorful pages of 1 magazines, catalogues, and newspaper supplements the reader can extract images of how to live the perfect American life. This exhibit shows how the depiction of ethnic groups has changed radically in the advertisements of nationally distributed magazines over the last century. The pictures tell a complex tale of economic power and mobility; of conflicting attitudes towards one's ethnic heritage and towards Anglo-American culture.

2 The development of modern advertising, with its sophisticated use of imagery and catchy phrases, grew hand-in-hand with the advent of the affordable monthly and weekly magazines. By the 1880's factories were churning out a plethora of ready-made goods, and the expanded system of railways and roads linked producer and consumer into a national network. During this period magazine production rose apace. Due to a variety of factors, ranging from improved typesetting techniques and low postal rates to the utilization of increasingly sophisticated photoengraving processes, publishers began to produce low-priced, profusely illustrated magazines fashioned to appeal to a national audience. The contents of the magazines, such as *Collier's, The Saturday Evening Post* and *The Ladies Home Journal,* covered a wide variety of topics: from homemaking to current events, new inventions to briskly paced fiction. By 1905 twenty general monthlies, each with a circulation of over 100,000, were in existence. Ranging in price from 10 to 15¢, easily within the budget of tens of thousands of Americans, they were an ideal vehicle for carrying the manufacturer's messages to a national audience.

3 What were the implications of advertising for the masses? As advertisers targeted their products towards a mass audience, the need arose to create an "average person," a type who embodied the qualities and attitudes of many others. Advertisers devised images that tapped into deeply held beliefs and myths of an "all-American" lifestyle—one that didn't just sell a product, but a way of life that people could buy.

4 The very nature of the advertising medium itself necessitates the use of symbols and character types that could be understood at a glance. If the advertisement was to be effective, its message had to be quickly absorbed and understood. Thus, in their depiction of ethnic groups, advertisers often used commonly held stereotypes. Within these stock images, however, one can observe various levels of complexity.

When the N.H.M. Hotels ad in figure 1 appeared in 1936, the nation was still in the midst of the Great Depression. The black railroad porter, with his knowledge of the rails and reputation for prompt and courteous service, was an effective spokesman for a hotel chain dependent for its livelihood upon Americans getting back on the move. The portrayal of the porter is interesting in this ad, for, beyond the obvious fact that the only blacks present are in service roles, the spokesman's subservience is visually reinforced by his deferential smile, slight stoop, and bent knees. As porters, blacks could assist in the resurgence of the American economy, but not fully participate in its benefits. 5

An advertisement for the Milwaukee Railroad from a 1945 *National Geographic* (figure 2) reveals another way in which ethnic groups are shown as outsiders—at the service of American culture while not actively participating in it. Here is the Noble Savage, not as the representative of any particular group of Native Americans, but as the symbol for the railroad itself, barely visible in the advertisement. In both the visuals and the copy the sale is made through stock images and associations. He is as familiar as a dime store Indian; a reassuring and time-honored part of the American landscape. However, while the Indian shown here still 6

FIGURE 1

Magazine advertisement, 1936

(Courtesy Balch Institute/ Historical Society of Pennsylvania)

brandishes his bow and arrow, he has been tamed. He gazes mutely over the changed landscape, another symbol of technological domination.

7 In a 1949 ad in *American Home,* Chiquita Banana entices us to buy her goods. Wearing a traditional ruffled skirt and fruit-laden hat, she embodies the stereotypical, fun-loving, gay Hispanic woman. While she occasionally doffs the more demure chef's hat, her smile and pert manner never waver. Her basic message is one of festivity, tempered with the American housewife's concern for nutrition: while bananas are good for you, they can be fun, too! They make mealtimes a party. In the later television ads of the 1960s, Chiquita Banana was transformed into a more overtly sexual figure doing the rumba. Singing her famous "I'm Chiquita Banana . . ." song in a Spanish accent, the advertisement's emphasis was more on festivity than wholesomeness.

8 The use of simple external attributes to symbolize ethnic identification has long been a favorite technique of advertisers. In a

FIGURE 2

National Geographic *advertisement, July 1945*

(Courtesy Balch Institute/ Historical Society of Pennsylvania)

Royal Crown Cola advertisement of 1938 (figure 3), the reader was urged to be like the thrifty "Scotchman" and buy the economical refreshment. Presenting its Scotsman with a broad grin and conspiratorial, chummy wink, the ad pokes gentle fun at the Scottish reputation for miserliness. Whether the character in Scottish garb is Scottish or not is incidental, for the white American can easily put on this ethnic persona without compromising or jeopardizing his identity. The Scottish stereotype can be invoked by using a few external character traits; the image does not extend beyond that initial statement. The black stereotype represented in the N.H.M. Hotel ad, however, reflects more deeply-held attitudes toward cultural differences. Compare the closeness of the two men in the RC Cola ad with the black porter and the white traveler in figure 1. Even the spacing between the characters in both ads is significant: while the men in the RC Cola ad display an easy intimacy, the black porter stands deferentially apart from the white traveler.

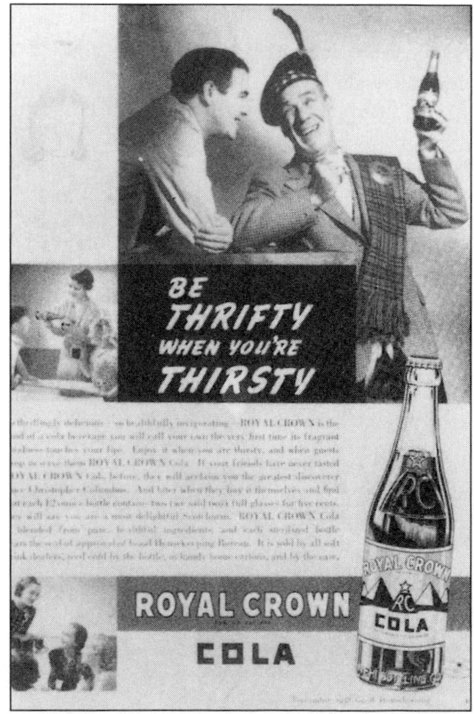

FIGURE 3

Good Housekeeping *advertisement, 1938*

(Courtesy Balch Institute/ Historical Society of Pennsylvania)

9 Advertisements were not the only medium that reflected the subservient role certain ethnic groups occupied within mainstream American culture. Magazine fiction too depicted a world in which white, Anglo-Americans were getting most of the world's material goods and occupying the more powerful roles in most human relationships. In story after story the heroes and heroines were of northern European stock, and in many cases when the protagonists were nominally foreign, their visual portrayal and characterization would belie the differences. This tendency is illustrated in a 1913 cover of the *Sunday Magazine of the Philadelphia Press,* which shows a pretty young Serbian dancer smiling languidly out at the viewer (figure 4). In her colorful native costume and dancc pose,

FIGURE 4

Magazine cover, November 9, 1913

(Courtesy Balch Institute/Historical Society of Pennsylvania)

she plays her role of "old country" ethnic. But while her dress presents an image of quaint and wholesome rusticity, her features bear a reassuringly western European stamp. She satisfied an American need for foreign experience and armchair travel without really challenging any assumptions about significant cultural variation.

Until the advent of the civil rights movement of the 1950's 10
and 60's, American businessmen and advertisers assumed, on the whole, that the best way to sell their products was to address their advertisements to the white Anglo-American. Hence magazine stories and ads were geared towards appealing to this constituency through the use of images and symbols that were familiar and appealing to them. In recent years, however, though advertisers have become increasingly concerned with the purchasing power of the different ethnic groups, the images they use continue to reassure the consumer that the group's "foreignness" is carefully controlled. Their cultural identity is often reduced to a few superficial symbols.

A Sprite ad (figure 5) reveals a group of smiling Americans of 11
all different lineages brandishing their favorite brand of soda. Yet

FIGURE 5

Newsweek *advertisement, 1983*

(Courtesy Balch Institute/ Historical Society of Pennsylvania)

while different ethnic groups are shown, they are all of the wholesome "all American" type. The advertisement's point is that the "you"—the American youth, who chose Sprite, now includes Asians, Hispanics and blacks.

12 Advertisements that have appeared in nationally distributed magazines targeted at specific ethnic groups also need mentioning. Until the Civil Rights movement gave many groups the impetus to speak out in their own voices, many of the advertisements in such magazines showed them displaying all the accoutrements and mannerisms of white, middle-class Americans. Thus the Ballantine Beer ad (figure 6) in a 1955 issue of *Ebony* portrays a group of thoroughly Anglicized and fair-complexioned black people. In black society light skin often gave a person enhanced prestige and eased acceptance into white American culture.

13 Today agencies have been formed to deal exclusively with advertisements targeted towards specific minority groups. Many of these more recent ads reveal the complex negotiations involved in attempting to reconcile indigenous cultural needs with societal acceptance: a crucial issue facing many ethnic Americans today.

FIGURE 6

Ebony *advertisement,* [illegible]

(Courtesy of Pabst Brewing Co., San Antonio, TX

BUILDING VOCABULARY

1. Advertisers necessarily work with commonly held views, powerful social myths, and broad social categories. Explain the meaning of and the common associations implied by these terms:
   - **a.** mobility (par. 1)
   - **b.** homemaking (par. 2)
   - **c.** stock images (par. 4)
   - **d.** dime store Indian (par. 6)
   - **e.** "all American" (par. 11)

THINKING CRITICALLY ABOUT THE ESSAY

Understanding the Writer's Ideas

1. According to the writer, what can we learn from advertisements in addition to information on particular products?
2. What main features of ethnic life in America do magazine ads of the last century display?
3. What factors accounted for the growth of modern advertising?
4. How did the availability of a mass audience affect the nature of magazine advertisements in general? Of advertisements that depicted members of ethnic groups?
5. How do the ads the writer has selected as illustrative examples distinguish between white Americans and others?
6. In addition to advertisements, what else "reflected the subservient role" of certain ethnic groups?
7. How did the civil rights movement affect the nature of magazine advertising?
8. How do contemporary magazine ads reflect changes in American culture?

Understanding the Writer's Techniques

1. What is the writer's thesis, and where does she state it?
2. Why does the writer provide a short history of advertising before showing the changing nature of images of ethnic groups in magazine ads?

3. The writer notes that ethnic images in advertisements are often stereotypes, but there are "various levels of complexity" within the stereotypes. What types, or categories, of stereotypes does the author present? Which examples in each category do you find most convincing?
4. How might this essay have been different if, instead of being written for an exhibition catalog, it had been written for a scholarly publication? As a guest editorial in a newspaper?
5. How does the writer organize her material to show "how the depiction of ethnic groups has changed"? How do her transitions help to move her essay forward in an orderly fashion?
6. The images of ethnic groups the writer discusses are visual images. Do you think the essay would have been as effective without the illustrations, the reproductions of actual ads? If yes, why do you think the illustrations are unnecessary? If no, what do you think the illustrations add to the essay?
7. What would the writer have had to do differently to write about images in literature? Provide some illustrative examples to support your point.
8. How does the conclusion draw the essay to an appropriate close?

Exploring the Writer's Ideas

1. Do you agree that advertising sells not just a product but a way of life (par. 3)? Support your answer with a few illustrative examples drawn from today's advertisments.
2. Could advertising, aimed naturally at large audiences, avoid stereotypes? Are the stereotypes used in advertising always "bad"—that is, somehow a distortion of the complex truth about the person or persons being depicted? Again, support your answer with illustrative examples.
3. Do you find the writer's interpretation of the ads she discusses to be fair? Look at the ads and the descriptions. On which points, if any, do you disagree? How, if at all, would your descriptions of the ads differ?
4. The essay's title can imply that advertising has turned something noble—the American dream—into something for sale. After having read the essay, are you persuaded that the advertising discussed does in fact turn something noble into a product? Why or why not?

IDEAS FOR WRITING

Prewriting

Look through a few magazines that you usually read—this time for the ads. Jot down a few of the most obvious ways in which these ads use stereotypes—ethnic or otherwise.

Guided Writing

Write an essay titled "The Image of . . . in Popular Magazine Advertising."

1. Begin with a clear statement about what you are going to classify—such as the image of women athletes, children, for example in magazine ads.
2. Classify the ads you have studied into at least three main categories, illustrating the way magazines draw on current social stereotypes to sell their products.
3. Choose one especially useful advertisement to illustrate each of the three categories. In each case, examine the stereotype in some detail.
4. Write a paragraph that reflects on the contemporary image you are presenting as it may differ from images ads portrayed in the past.
5. Consider whether these differences reflect a significant social shift (for example, greater equality for women) or simply a superficial change masking a persistence of an old stereotype.
6. Draw an appropriate conclusion, restating the main points of step 2.

Thinking and Writing Collaboratively

Work in small groups of four or five. Choose a well-known magazine (preferably one that none of the other groups is working on), and look through several issues, scrutinizing the advertising representations of ethnic groups. After discussing the ads as a group, report to the class on your findings, using sample ads to support your conclusions.

Writing About the Text

The writer presents several advertisements as illustrative of her theme. Do you find her analysis, ad by ad, to be impartial and persuasive? In an essay, say why. If you do not, offer a different reading of the ads. In a second part of the essay, look at the ads from a different perspective, the perspective of the advertiser. Which of these ads do you find to be especially effective? Which do you find to be least effective? What features of these ads make them effective or ineffective?

More Writing Projects

1. Choose one or two of your favorite ads—in print, on billboards, on television—and explain in your journal what you especially like about these ads.
2. Write two or three paragraphs examining one of your favorite advertisements that you feel effectively avoids stereotyping. Tell why you like the ad, and analyze what makes it work well—both text and visual elements—and how it avoids stereotyping.
3. Interview an executive at an advertising company in your community. Question the executive about the things she or he looks for in creating an ad to make it most effective. Write up your interview in an article of around 1000 words.

SUMMING UP: CHAPTER 8

1. Reread Judith Viorst's "Friends, Good Friends—and Such Good Friends" in this chapter. Then, write down the names of several of your closest friends. Keep a journal for one week in which you list what you did, how you felt, and what you talked about with each of these friends. Then write an essay that classifies these friends into three categories. Use entries from your journal to support your method of classification.
2. With the class divided into four groups, assemble a guide to the city, town, or neighborhood surrounding your campus. Each group should be responsible for one category of information: types of people; types of places; types of entertainment; types of services; and so on. Be sure that each category is covered in detail; you may refer to E. B. White's essay "The Three New Yorks" as a model. After each group has completed its work, choose someone to present findings to the class. Now write your own guide to the areas based on the classifications discussed.
3. Although Viorst's, Baker's, and Rashap's essays are classifications, they also present new ways of looking at a group of people. Viorst has an underlying message about how to choose friends, Baker has a warning about how not to be stereotyped, and Rashap shows how easily stereotype can dominate portrayals of people. Write a classification essay entitled "What to Avoid When __________." Fill in the blank with an activity that would involve a decision-making process on the part of the reader.
4. Many of the essays in this book deal with crucial experiences in the various authors' lives. Among others, Hughes and Wong tell us of coming-of-age experiences; Selzer writes of his special insights into human nature; and Dillard and Thomas describe their relationships to the world of nature. Try writing an essay that classifies the personal essays that you have read in this anthology.
5. Judith Viorst offers an account of friendships (especially among women) by classifying the many kinds of friendships she notices. Ellen Goodman, in contrast, aims to tease out some essential qualities of friendships, especially among women, by comparing and contrasting male and female friendships.

Rewrite their essays by switching the approaches—that is, take Viorst's material and turn her essay into one that mainly compares and contrasts; and take Goodman's material and write an essay that mainly classifies.

6. Write an essay classifying views of the American Dream using he essays in this book by Elizabeth Wong, David Brooks, Amy Rashap, Manning Marable (pp. 429–431), and Martin Luther King, Jr.

FROM SEEING TO WRITING

The person in this cartoon obviously has an unwieldy "family" of chairs that he needs to classify or sort into categories. Write your own humorous classification essay in which you put the chairs into categories and make clear the relations among members of each group. As an alternative, write a humorous classification essay about a "family" that might be real—for example, your own extended family—or more fanciful. Organize your essay around at least three categories that support your thesis.

"Attention, everyone! I'd like to introduce the newest member of our family."

Jeff Kaufman © *The New Yorker Magazine/The Cartoon Bank*

CHAPTER 9

Process Analysis

WHAT IS PROCESS ANALYSIS?

Process analysis explains to a reader how something is done, how something works, or how something occurs. Like classification, it is a form of analysis, or taking apart a process in order better to understand how it functions. This kind of writing is often called *expository* because it *exposes* or shows us information. If you use cookbooks, you are encountering process analysis each time you read a recipe. If you are setting up a new VCR, you may wish the writer of the manual were more adept at writing process analysis when you find the steps hard to follow. "How to" writing can therefore give the reader steps for carrying out a process. The writer might also analyze the steps someone took already in completing a process, such as explaining how Harriet Tubman organized the Underground Railroad or how women won the right to vote.

Planning a good process analysis requires the writer to include all the essential steps. Be sure you have all the tools or ingredients needed. Arrange the steps in the correct sequence. Like all good writing, a good process essay requires a thesis to tell the reader the *significance* of the process. The writer can tell the reader how to do something, but also should inform the reader about the usefulness or importance of the endeavor.

In this chapter, Henry Louis Gates, Jr., explains how to "de-kink" your hair. Jerrold G. Simon advises us how to write a resume. John Lantos explains the scary process of saving a baby's life. And, from Ernest Hemingway, we learn how to make our next experience of camping a success. As you read about these processes, watch how each writer uses the same technique to achieve a different result.

HOW DO WE READ PROCESS ANALYSIS?

Identify what process the writer is going to analyze. As you read, make a quick outline of the steps the writer introduces.

Watch the use of transitions as the writer moves from one step to the next.

Assess the audience that the writer has aimed at. Is the writer addressing innocents or experts? If the writer's purpose was to explain how to prepare beef stew, he would give different directions to a college freshman who has never cooked before than he would give to a cooking class at the Culinary Institute of America, where everyone was familiar with the fundamentals of cooking. Ask yourself, then: Is there enough information in the analysis? Too much?

How does the writer try to make the piece lively? Does it sound as dry as a technical manual, or is there an engaging tone?

HOW DO WE WRITE PROCESS ANALYSIS?

Decide to analyze a process with which you are very familiar. Unless you can do it well yourself, you won't be able to instruct or inform your readers.

Process begins with a good shopping list. Once you have your topic, make lists of ingredients or tools.

Arrange the essential steps in logical order. Don't assume your reader already knows how to do the process. As you know from those incomprehensible VCR instructions, the reader should be given *every* step.

List the steps to *avoid* when carrying out the procedure.

If possible, actually try out the process, using your list as a guide, if you are presenting a method for a tangible product, like making an omelet. Or imagine that you are explaining the procedure over the telephone.

If your topic is abstract, like telling someone how to become an American citizen, read it aloud to a willing listener to see if he or she can follow the steps clearly.

Use *definition* to explain terms the reader may not know, especially if you are presenting a technical process. At the same time, avoid jargon. Make the language as plain as possible.

Describe the appearance of the product or *compare* an unfamiliar item with a familiar one.

Be sure to think about your audience. Link the audience to the purpose of the process.

Formulate a thesis statement that tells what the process is, and why it is a good process to know.

Sample thesis statement:

> Buying and renovating an old car is a time-consuming process, but the results are worthwhile.

Writing the Draft

Write a rough draft. Turn your list into an essay by developing the steps into sentences, using your thesis to add significance and coherence to the process you are presenting. Don't just list; analyze the procedure as you go along. Keep in mind the techniques of writers like Ernest Hemingway, who doesn't just cook a trout but uses the process to represent the whole morality of "doing things right," raising his process analysis beyond the ordinary.

Add transitions when necessary to alert the reader that a new step is coming. The most common transition words help a reader to follow steps: *first, second, third; first, next, after, last.*

Proofread, revise, and create a final draft.

A STUDENT PARAGRAPH: PROCESS ANALYSIS

Process analysis lends itself to a variety of approaches, ranging from a methodical step-by-step explanation of a task such as how to prepare a pie, to assessment of a series of related historical events. As you read the following one-paragraph composition, consider the student's success in providing the reader with a flexible approach to a typical problem.

Topic sentence

Phrase "the first step" starts the process

"Next" signals the second step

Finding the right used car can be a real challenge. Unless you are totally open to possibilities, the first step in the process is to focus on one make and model that interests you. Next, you should consult the Blue Book, which lists car makes and models by year, and provides a rough guide to fair prices based on condition. It's a good idea to have the book handy before moving to the next stage in your search; you can probably disqualify a number of cars based on asking price alone. (If the asking price is significantly higher than the Blue Book suggests, the seller is not always trying to hoodwink you. There might be a good reason for the price—exceptionally good condition, or an unusual number of "add-ons," for example. Still, it makes sense to use caution in these cases.) At this point, you are ready to start the actual search, beginning with a scanning of these resources. Don't limit your search to these resources, however; continue your hunt by consulting more local venues, such as campus bulletin-board postings. There are several other promising routes to finding the wheels of your dreams: car rental companies usually sell off their rentals after they've reached a ripe old age—sometimes a venerable 3 to 5 years! Police auctions are another possibility, though the successful bidder is usually required to plunk down cash for the car right away, and the cars come with no warranty—you can find a real bargain here, but it's only really a safe bet if you can take along a mechanic. In fact, consulting a good mechanic should always be the last step in the process: after you have located the car of your dreams, get an inspection before you write that check, just to make sure that your dream machine doesn't explode.

Parenthetical remark qualifies earlier statement

"At this point" moves reader to third step

"Continue your hunt by consulting" advances the process

"Several other promising routes" adds to process

Concluding step cautions, adds humor

How to Write a Resume

Jerrold G. Simon

Few processes provoke more anxiety than presenting yourself as a candidate for a job. Here the psychologist and career development specialist Jerrold G. Simon provides a primer on how to get yourself started; it aims to be supportive, lucid, and useful. As you read this selection, look for the methods the writer uses to achieve these ends.

PREREADING: THINKING ABOUT THE ESSAY IN ADVANCE

What thoughts and emotions does searching for a job stir in you? What do you expect from a "How to" book or essay?

Words to Watch

formats (par. 6) general arrangements
chronological (par. 6) in order of occurrence
prospective (par. 8) potential
extracurricular (par. 13) outside of formal instruction
articulate (par. 28) able to speak well

If you are about to launch a search for a job, the suggestions I offer here can help you whether or not you have a high school or college diploma, whether you are just starting out or changing your job or career in midstream. 1

Before you try to find a job opening, you have to answer the hardest question of your working life: "What do I want to do?" Here's a good way. 2

Sit down with a piece of paper and don't get up till you've listed all the things you're proud to have accomplished. Your list might include being head of a fund-raising campaign, or acting a juicy role in the senior play. 3

Study the list. You'll see a pattern emerge of the things you do best and like to do best. You might discover that you're happiest working with people, or maybe with numbers, or words, or well, you'll see it. 4

Once you've decided what job area to go after, read more about it in the reference section of your library. "Talk shop" with any people you know in that field. Then start to get your resume together. 5

6 There are many good books that offer sample resumes and describe widely used formats. The one that is still most popular, the *reverse chronological,* emphasizes where you worked and when, and the jobs and titles you held.

7 Your name and address go at the top. Also phone number.

8 What job do you want? That's what a prospective employer looks at first. If you know exactly, list that next under *Job Objective.* Otherwise, save it for your cover letter (I describe that later), when you're writing for a specific job to a specific person. In any case, make sure your resume focuses on the kind of work you can do and want to do.

9 Now comes *Work Experience.* Here's where you list your qualifications. *Lead with your most important credentials.* If you've had a distinguished work history in an area related to the job you're seeking, lead off with that. If your education will impress the prospective employer more, start with that.

10 Begin with your most recent experience first and work backwards. Include your titles or positions held. And list the years.

11 The most qualified people always get the job. It goes to the person who presents himself most persuasively in person and on paper.

12 So don't just list where you were and what you did. This is your chance to tell *how well you did.* Were you the best salesman? Did you cut operating costs? Give numbers, statistics, percentages, increases in sales or profits.

13 No job experience? In that case, list your summer jobs, extracurricular school activities, honors, awards. Choose the activities that will enhance your qualifications for the job.

14 Next list your *Education*—unless you chose to start with that. This should also be in reverse chronological order. List your high school only if you didn't go on to college. Include college degree, postgraduate degrees, dates conferred, major and minor courses you took that help qualify you for the job you want.

15 Also, did you pay your own way? Earn scholarships or fellowships? Those are impressive accomplishments.

16 No diplomas or degrees? Then tell about your education: special training programs or courses that can qualify you. Describe outside activities that reveal your talents and abilities. Did you sell the most tickets to the annual charity musical? Did you take your motorcycle engine apart and put it back together so it works? These can help you.

Next, list any *Military Service.* This could lead off your resume if it is your only work experience. Stress skills learned, promotions earned, leadership shown. 17

Now comes *Personal Data.* This is your chance to let the reader get a glimpse of the personal you, and to further the image you've worked to project in the preceding sections. For example, if you're after a job in computer programming, and you enjoy playing chess, mention it. Chess playing requires the ability to think through a problem. 18

Include foreign languages spoken, extensive travel, particular interests or professional memberships, *if* they advance your cause. 19

Keep your writing style simple. Be brief. Start sentences with impressive action verbs: "Created," "Designed," "Achieved," "Caused." 20

Make sure your grammar and spelling are correct. And no typos! 21

Use 8½″ × 11″ bond paper—white or off-white for easy reading. Don't cram things together. 22

Make sure your original is clean and readable. Then have it professionally duplicated. No carbons. 23

Now that your resume is ready, start to track down job openings. How? Look up business friends, personal friends, neighbors, your minister, your college alumni association, professional services. Keep up with trade publications, and read help-wanted ads. 24

And start your own "direct mail" campaign. First, find out about the companies you are interested in—their size, location, what they make, their competition, their advertising, their prospects. Get their annual report—and read it. 25

Send your resume, along with a cover letter, to a specific person in the company, not to "Gentlemen" or "Dear Sir." The person should be the top in the area where you want to work. Spell his name properly! The cover letter should appeal to your reader's own needs. What's in it for him? Quickly explain why you are approaching *his* company (their product line, their superior training program) and what you can bring to the party. Back up your claims with facts. Then refer him to your enclosed resume and ask for an interview. 26

And now you've got an interview! Be sure to call the day before to confirm it. Meantime, *prepare yourself.* Research the company and the job by reading books and business journals in the library. 27

28 On the big day, arrive 15 minutes early. Act calm, even though, if you're normal, you're trembling inside at 6.5 on the Richter scale. At every chance, let your interviewer see that your personal skills and qualifications relate to the job at hand. If it's a sales position, for example, go all out to show how articulate and persuasive you are.

29 Afterwards, follow through with a brief thank-you note. This is a fine opportunity to restate your qualifications and add any important points you didn't get a chance to bring up during the interview.

30 Keep a list of prospects. List the dates you contacted them, when they replied, what was said.

31 And remember, someone out there is looking for someone *just like you.* It takes hard work and sometimes luck to find that person. Keep at it and you'll succeed.

BUILDING VOCABULARY

The writer advises that in composing a resume you should keep your writing style simple; be brief; and start sentences with action verbs.

Go through Simon's essay and pick out six to twelve examples of how he follows his own advice.

THINKING CRITICALLY ABOUT THE ESSAY

Understanding the Writer's Ideas

1. Where and how does the writer let you know what to expect from his essay?
2. Before writing a resume, what critical step must you take first?
3. The writer identifies headings that are important to guide your composing of a resume, as well as what kind of information should be emphasized under each heading. What is the consistent theme of the writer's advice about what to emphasize?
4. The writer advises a proactive approach to job hunting once the resume is finished. What are his recommendations for an active job search?

5. How does the writer's advice about how to behave in an interview mirror his advice about what to emphasize in your resume?
6. What follow-up does the writer recommend, even after the job interview?

Understanding the Writer's Techniques

1. This essay is a guide in the form of suggestions about how to do something. What determines the order of the writer's instructions?
2. What audience do you imagine the writer is addressing in this essay? How are the essay's *style* and *tone* appropriate to that audience?
3. Looking for work can be nerve-wracking. What techniques does the writer employ to quiet the reader's fears?
4. Taking a reader through a process requires definite *transitions* (see Glossary) from one step to the next. Make a list of several of the transitional words or phrases that the writer uses, and write a few words about why these transitional words or phrases are well suited to this purpose.

Exploring the Writer's Ideas

1. By advising the reader to follow the "most popular" formats for resumes, does the writer risk recommending something that will simply blend the result into the crowd of other resumes? If so, what steps could be taken to avoid this result? If not, why not?
2. What could you do to make your resume more individual and original? Does an original resume risk being dismissed as eccentric? How could you avoid such a reaction?
3. Does the you-can-do-it! approach of this essay perhaps set the reader up for disappointment? If so, what could the writer do to avoid such a result? If not, why not?

IDEAS FOR WRITING

Prewriting

Write an outline of the steps involved in writing a reference letter, or writing a lesson plan, or writing your will—or a similar process.

Guided Writing

Write an essay on how to write a job application letter.

1. Start by indicating to readers that whatever their age and whatever the job of their choice, what you are going to say will help them.
2. Identify two or three key questions that must be answered before you can start your application letter.
3. Take the reader through the main stages of an application letter, giving each stage a name.
4. Be careful to move from step to step by means of clear but active, even directive transitional words or phrases (e.g. "Next," or "Make sure . . .").
5. Be careful to assure the reader that the letter can be done well, that the reader has the gifts and record to win the job.
6. Indicate how an application letter should end so as to get helpfully to the next stage—the interview.
7. Give one or two tips about how to present yourself at the job interview.
8. Help the reader to adopt an easy method of tracking his or her applications.
9. End with a mild pep talk, encouraging the reader to take a positive attitude, because success will come in the end.

Thinking and Writing Collaboratively

In groups of four or five, share your experiences of applying to college. Compare and contrast the steps you took to decide where to apply and to decide how to apply.

Writing About the Text

Do you think meeting expectations can lead to mindless conformity? Write an essay that considers this question with reference to Simon's essay (look, too, at question 1 of Exploring the Writer's Ideas).

More Writing Projects

1. Discuss how students in the class have found full- or part-time or summer jobs. Then break up into smaller work groups and

develop job search guides for each category, remembering to offer full, detailed instructions to the reader.

2. Interview a group of alumni of your college about what they seek in a job applicant for their firm or profession. Write an article for the school paper based on the interviews.
3. Write a humorous essay about the comparisons and contrasts between you as a creation of your resume and you as a real person, in the context of a real or fictional interview for a job.

Life and Death in Neonatal Intensive Care

John Lantos

A graduate of Brown University and the University of Pittsburgh, John Lantos is section chief in general pediatrics at the University of Chicago's Pritzker School of Medicine. He is also associate director of the MacLean Center for Clinical Ethics. Moreover, he is the son of an internist and is married to a fellow University of Chicago pediatrician. Lantos has written two provocative books about the contemporary practice of medicine, with a sensitive awareness of the terrain where medical practice and profound ethical questions intersect. These books are *Do We Still Need Doctors?* (1997) and *The Lazarus Case: Life-and-Death Issues in Neonatal Intensive Care* (2001). He is also co-editor, with Carl Elliott, of *The Last Physician: Walker Percy and the Moral Life of Medicine* (1999). This selection, which originally appeared in *The Chronicle of Higher Education,* is excerpted from *The Lazarus Case.* Note how Lantos uses one of our society's most revered and rigorous processes—surgical practice—to raise subtle and complex questions about the relation between professionalism and ethics, and between unemotional, detached process and human responsibility.

PREREADING: THINKING ABOUT THE ESSAY IN ADVANCE

"Intensive care"—by themselves, the words sound happy, a promise of a great deal of something we all crave. But of course "neonatal intensive care" refers to a crisis center in a hospital—an "ICU." What kinds of associations does the essay's title arouse? Have you ever visited an ICU?

Words to Watch

neonatal (par. 1) newborn
euphoria (par. 5) great joy
resuscitative (par. 5) reviving
amorphous (par. 8) uncrystallized, vague
solicitous (par. 13) full of concern

It was while I was working in the neonatal intensive-care unit that I first achieved that dream of doctors everywhere: to actually save a patient's life. That happens a lot on TV but not so often in real life. Most of medicine is much more mundane—colds, rashes, vague aches and pains that can't be diagnosed, can't be cured, and don't go away. But every once in a while, it's not like that. For me, that first time, the patient was a 600-gram preemie, and I was on call as a second-year resident. 1

The obstetricians called to warn us that a woman was in labor at 25 weeks. I called the neonatology fellow, assuming that he would be there to take over. Alas, he was at home, 45 minutes away. Don't worry, he said, he'd get in as soon as he could. In the meantime, do my best. 2

Forty-five minutes? Do my best? Was he kidding? I was just a resident. I was just covering at night. I wasn't ready to solo. I panicked. I was angry. I felt abandoned. I froze. I didn't want to do this, didn't want to be there. It was a cold November night, nearly two years after I'd first visited a NICU and nearly passed out at the surreally minuscule patients and the machine-intensive otherworldliness of their treatment. Since then, I'd spent months caring for preemies, gotten to know the strange, almost papery feel of their underdeveloped skin, to recognize the hairline wisps of blue just beneath it as tiny veins, tiny but not so tiny that we couldn't cannulate them with even tinier plastic catheters. I was in the middle of a 36-hour shift, tired and alone, holding the bag for the neonatal fellow who was holding the bag for the neonatal attending physician. 3

As residents, we spent a lot of time in the NICU. Interestingly, that was not because anybody thought it was essential for our education as pediatricians to learn so much about neonatal intensive care. By this time, in the early 1980's, there was already a subspecialty board in neonatology. Any doctor who wanted to work in a NICU would have to do a three-year, post-residency fellowship in neonatology in order to become sub-board certified. Thus, most pediatric residents would never again work in a NICU, would never again take care of 600-gram preemies, and would probably never need the skills that we were so painstakingly learning and endlessly perfecting. But the NICU was the most labor-intensive unit in the hospital. Every tiny baby needed three or four professionals hovering over the bassinet. As a result of these personnel demands, such 4 units claimed a disproportionate amount of the residents' time. The NICU needed us, and the hospitals needed the NICU, so there we were, night after night, month after month.

5 My anxiety and fear were gradually replaced by a seeping sense of vindictive euphoria. Screw them, I thought, I can do this, or at least I'll try, and, in the end, nobody will really know or care how well I do, because the task itself is so meaningless. In a moment, they will hand me a baby who by all rights should just die, and I will run through the paces of the resuscitative routine that I've rehearsed and rehearsed and rehearsed until I could do it in my sleep. You could learn this stuff by watching TV. The ABC's: airway, breathing, circulation. Suction the trachea, intubate, check a pulse, start umbilical intravenous line, give some fluid. If the heart rate is low, give some adrenaline. This wasn't magic. It wasn't rocket science, either. I made sure my hair was combed, put on a clean scrub suit, and strolled over to the delivery room to see how the mom was doing.

6 It was a quiet scene. Doctors and nurses talking in whispers. I thought to myself, I should go to the woman on the table, who was the quietest of all, should introduce myself, should try to give the predelivery spiel: "Very high risk, may not be viable, we won't know for sure until the baby is born, we'll do what we can, I'll let you know as soon as we know." This conversation seems to offer important information but really offers almost none. It's just a chance to check each other out. How does she look? Caring and concerned, or strung out and indifferent? Is there a man in the picture? Another woman? The mom, perhaps? A friend? A lover? The words are placeholders, a vague recognition of shared humanity, a verbal handshake, valuable as gestures of caring rather than for what they mean.

7 Her eyes searched mine quickly, then turned away. What was she looking for in the gowned, gloved, masked figure who presented himself, out of the sky, at the precise moment of her life's most profound distress, at the moment when everything that was supposed to be good and beautiful and life-affirming had become horrific, terrifying, mournful? At the moment when fear and dependency defined her life as never before? She was certainly no health-care consumer negotiating a contract, purchasing some health-care services, dispassionately evaluating the risks and benefits of this or that intervention. She was sizing me up—not because

she had a decision to make, but just to see what hand she'd been dealt. Did I look experienced, trustworthy? Was I nervous? Did I know what I was doing? Would I be there for her? Could she talk to me?

What was she hoping for? That I would save her baby, right? 8
Maybe, or maybe that I would wisely allow her baby to die, saving for her a life unburdened by a NICU cripple? Or were her hopes more amorphous, a primitive fear and a longing for comfort and caring, the chance for some simple recognition as someone who is suffering? What sort of doctoring was called for here?

On the basis of that meeting, I might soon have had to make 9
some profound decisions about the baby about to be born. Should I have gone into more detail about the risks and benefits, the chances of intracranial bleeds or chronic lung disease or cerebral palsy, about the options for treatment or nontreatment? That sort of talk didn't seem appropriate to the powerful emotional tenor of the moment. There were big decisions to be made. In theory, we were supposed to make them together. In fact, we seemed to be all part of some larger script, and it wasn't clear that any of us had learned our lines well.

So, I introduced myself, made such explanations as I could. 10
She didn't ask questions, and it's just as well, because I didn't really want to answer them. My mind was already terrifyingly focused on the technical tasks ahead of me, the ones I might not be able to perform. And her questions, if they came, would probably have been about matters of judgment, about fears, about emotions. Questions that only a doctor who was ready to engage a patient at a deep level of shared humanity could answer. I hadn't really learned to be such a doctor yet. I was worrying about whether I'd be able to get the tube into the trachea. Mine was not to make decisions, to question why, mine was just to do, so that others did not die on my 36-hour shift.

She was silent and exhausted on the bed between contractions, 11
and then moaned with pain at every contraction, a low, mournful moan, not so much as of someone in acute pain, but someone in a sort of mourning. This was not where she wanted to be. The contractions seemed to be a sort of punishment.

She looked to be about my age—in her late 20's. An older 12
man sat beside the bed, holding her hand, saying little. I returned to the baby warmer and got to work.

13 The nurses, as always, were solicitous of a rookie. They helped me set out my equipment: A DeLee suction trap. A tiny laryngoscope to open the baby's airway and visualize the vocal cords. Endotracheal tubes in the smallest sizes made. An umbilical catheter. Syringe with some saline flush. We turned on the heat on the warming table, got the leads for the temperature monitor and the transcutaneous oxygen monitor ready. The tension was like the tension before a ballgame, or before a showdown. I kept thinking that the neonatology fellow would arrive any minute to rescue me, that I was really a bit player, a stuntman, maybe even a stagehand, certainly not the star. We watched the great big clock on the delivery-room wall. It was a little after 2 a.m.

14 Here it comes! The obstetricians are doing their final schtick. "One little push, thattagirl, here we go. OK, relax now. Ohhh. It's a girl! A pretty girl. Looking good. Just relax, now. Now we'll give her to the pediatricians. Lie back. There you go."

15 There you go! Check pulse—weak and thready, about 70. Respirations—an occasional gasp. Color—pale, blue. Give oxygen. Suction. Intubate. I get the laryngoscope, give me the 2.5 ET tube. There, I think that's in. Check breath sounds. With the puffs of the ambubag, her chest rises and falls. I'm amazed at my competence. Good. Heart rate? 100. Can we get a BP? It's not reading. Pulse is a little thready. Want to start a line, doctor? (This is the nurse's gentle way of telling me what to do, handing me the umbilical catheter.) I choose the larger umbilical vein, rather than struggling with the tiny arteries. No time for subtlety here. It goes in easily, good blood return. Give a bolus, 10 cc/kg would be what, 6 cc's. A teaspoon of saline. BP 40/20. OK, let's get her back to the NICU.

16 Again, I wanted to go talk to Mom, tell her what was happening, but I was needed at the bedside, I was the central technician, all eyes were on me. I beckoned to one of the lower-level nurses, "Go tell Mom that, so far, everything looks good." She looked at me with wonder and skepticism, but she went.

17 As we rolled into the NICU, the neonatology fellow strolled through the door, calmly shed his street coat, and slipped into the sterile yellow gown. He took over, effortlessly. The nurse read out the numbers to him, he listened, briefly, to heart rate and breath sounds, shook his head slowly, patted me on the back. "Nice job. The kid probably won't make it, but you did a nice job."

He was right. The baby died two days later, in spite of receiv- 18
ing all that neonatal intensive care could offer. There was no further discussion with the parents about whether or not to continue treatment. At the end, there was a short, symbolic attempt at cardiopulmonary resuscitation. And the fellow was right. I did a nice job. I got all the tubes in place, the lines started, the right doses of the right drugs calculated, calibrated, and delivered. I felt good about all that, but deeply bad about something that I couldn't quite name, about the conversations that hadn't happened but perhaps should have, or the things that had but didn't help. The doctors never talked about the case again. That was how, as residents, we learned about death and dying.

That routine is the essence of neonatal care: a calm and or- 19
derly response, a sequence of interventions designed to address, with some semblance of reason and order, the cascade of life-threatening events that follow premature birth.

Tiny preemies can't control their body temperature, can't 20
breathe, and can't maintain an appropriate blood pressure. They need to have their temperature and blood pressure and oxygen levels and glucose levels constantly monitored and kept neither too high nor too low. If that works, and they make it through the first crucial hours, then they begin to have other needs. They need intravenous nutrition for weeks or sometimes for months before they can eat on their own. They need monitoring of their livers and their kidneys, their lungs, brains, and bowels. Their immune systems are underdeveloped, so they need a sterile environment, but they are still at high risk for overwhelming infections. What they really need is an artificial womb, so we try to build one with our medical Tinkertoys. The result is something that works much better than nothing but much worse than the real thing. Most preemies live and do well. Some die. Worst of all, some end up somewhere in between.

Neonatal intensive care has gotten better over the years. There 21
are more good outcomes. Unfortunately, there are still many bad outcomes. They just occur today in smaller, more-premature babies.

Are the efforts worth it? The years when I was in the NICU 22
were the years when there were national controversies about decisions to withhold or withdraw life-sustaining treatment in both neonatal care and adult medicine. There were new journals devoted to bioethics in which writers struggled with the questions.

There were debates at national meetings, high-profile legal struggles, and policy statements by professional societies and other advocacy groups.

23 In some ways, the questions came down to one of perspective. To ask whether it was "worth it," one had to then ask, "Worth it to whom?"

BUILDING VOCABULARY

The specialist medical vocabulary in some ways is familiar—we all have been to the doctor, or visited a hospital, or watched *ER*—and yet it is altogether strange because it sounds so intensely technical. Lantos's essay cannot be thoroughly understood, without an understanding of its medical vocabulary. Here are some of the terms you will find useful to define. Look them up and write definitions in your own words.

- **a.** cannulate (par. 3)
- **b.** catheter (par. 3)
- **c.** trachea (par. 5)
- **d.** intubate (par. 5)
- **e.** intracranial (par. 9)
- **f.** endotrachael (par. 13)
- **g.** transcutaneous (par. 13)
- **h.** bolus (par. 15)
- **i.** cardiopulmonary (par. 18)

THINKING CRITICALLY ABOUT THE ESSAY

Understanding the Writer's Ideas

1. What unusual opportunity is the writer going to tell us about? Why is it unusual? How old is the writer at the time the events he writes about occur?
2. What was the writer's initial reaction to the task he was going to have to perform?
3. Why did residents spend a lot of time in the NICU?
4. What does the writer mean by "vindictive euphoria"?

5. The writer finds a "quiet scene" in the hospital room. At the center is a young woman his own age. How does the writer answer his own question about her, "What was she hoping for?"
6. Why does the writer say "we seemed to be all part of some larger script" (par. 9)?
7. Why was the writer relieved that the patient did not ask him any questions?
8. How did the nurses treat the writer, "a rookie"?
9. Why does the nurse look at the writer "with wonder and skepticism" when he tells her to inform the mother "that, so far, everything looks good" (par. 16)?
10. After the baby dies, the writer feels both good and bad. What is he proud of? What is he distressed about?
11. Why do "tiny preemies" often fail to survive?
12. In what ways do you think one might answer the writer's final question, "Worth it to whom?"

Understanding the Writer's Techniques

1. The writer undertakes in this essay to relate a narrative, or story, rooted in a process. Does this essay have a thesis statement? If so, where is the statement made? If not, how does the writer tell you what the essay is going to be about and what it will try to accomplish?
2. The writer introduces the process he is going to describe by setting the scene. In setting the scene, what information does he give us that we will need to follow his story of the process?
3. How does the writer's use of transitions move his essay forward? Identify at least three especially effective transitions, and say why they are effective.
4. The writer describes two processes—one, the process of informing the mother first about what he is going to do, then about what he is doing, and then about what to expect for her child. A second process is the process of "saving" the baby, the technical and medical process. How does he weave the two processes together? How do his techniques differ when he speaks of one process as opposed to the other?
5. How does the writer convey his feelings about the neonatology fellow?

6. How does the concluding section of the essay, from paragraph 18 to the end, differ from the rest of the essay? What does the writer aim to accomplish in paragraph 18? In paragraph 20? Why does the writer include these paragraphs in his essay?
7. What is your view of the writer's conclusion? Do you find it effective? Why or why not?

Exploring the Writer's Ideas

1. The essay's opening sentence says the writer had the opportunity "to actually save a patient's life." But the "preemie" dies. Why, then, does the writer begin as he does? Should he have fashioned a different opening, or is the opening a good one? Why?
2. To what extent are the writer's expectations of the process he is about to perform fulfilled? How was he well prepared for what he had to do? How was he ill prepared for what he had to do?
3. This essay appeared in *The Chronicle of Higher Education,* which is the professional newsmagazine of college teachers and administrators. Why did the writer choose to publish his essay there, rather than in, say, a professional medical journal? What audience do you think he had in mind, and how is his choice of audience reflected in his essay? What does the place of publication tell you about the intentions of the writer?

IDEAS FOR WRITING

Prewriting

The writer was given ample technical training to perform the process he describes, but its emotional dimensions and repercussions were left out of his education. Jot down some ideas for an essay on the technical versus emotional aspects of a job or other activity. If possible, base these ideas on your personal experience. Perhaps a doctor or some other professional was unprepared to meet your emotional needs. Or perhaps you yourself were the professional, who was unprepared for the emotional dimensions of a job, say, as coach to a child struggling to master a sport.

Guided Writing

Write an essay about the gap between technical and emotional skill involved in performing an important task. You can write as the person performing the task—taking care of a sick child or relative, providing help in some emergency, or having to assume some other role for which you do (or don't) feel that you are prepared. Or, write as a person being subjected to a process performed by, for example, someone who is trying to inform you of bad news—a physician giving you information about a sick relative, a teacher telling you about a poor grade, an employer telling you that you're not being hired or that you're being laid off. In either case, select an informative title for your essay, and be sure to include in your essay the details of the technical expertise required and of the process involved.

1. Open your essay by identifying the situation that called for your expertise, or the expertise of someone else (lawyer, teacher, coach, social worker, and so on).
2. In one or two paragraphs introduce the details of the expert process.
3. Now introduce the human dimension—the emotional stress of having to carry out the process skillfully and the dilemmas about what the situation requires in addition to technical know-how.
4. If you are the expert in the essay, discuss your mixed feelings about what the situation requires of you. If you are being subjected to an expert's process, indicate what, under the circumstances, you expected emotionally from the expert.
5. Reflect on the educational implications of the experience you have recounted.
6. In your conclusion, suggest the kinds of steps *you* would favor to rectify the lacks in professional education that you wrote about in your essay.

Thinking and Writing Collaboratively

In groups of four or five, share experiences—good and bad—that you have had with professionals under circumstances that required both expertise and emotional care. Make two lists, one of the kinds of things that can help ensure that caring will accompany expertise, and one of the consequences of the "careless" exercise of expertise.

Writing About the Text

Write an essay that explores how the writer might answer his own final question, "Worth it to whom?" by drawing on various clues in the selection. Consider, for example, the writer's attitude toward the neonatalogy fellow. The writer seems to have invested a great deal of emotional energy, and expertise, into the treatment of his preemie. He seems in a sense to resent the nonchalance of the neonatalogy fellow. And yet, the fellow is right: the baby does not survive. The writer, moreover, tells us just how unlikely, in medical terms, the baby's survival would be. So is the enormous effort and cost devoted to the baby "worth it"?

More Writing Projects

1. The writer is a "medical ethicist." From an ethical point of view, how is one to decide whether a treatment is "worth it"? What considerations *should* enter into such a decision? Who should bear the cost of extremely expensive care that has little—but some—chance of success? Respond to these questions in your journal.
2. By doing some research online, find out what a class in medical ethics consists of. Then write several paragraphs that reflect on whether such a class would have helped the writer know how to behave and what to do—emotionally, morally—in the situation he describes.
3. Rewrite Lantos's description of the medical process he undertook to include the human dimension, so that he could have been proud not only of his technical skills but of his "people" skills too.

Camping Out

Ernest Hemingway

Through his life and his work, Ernest Hemingway influenced world culture more than any other American writer of his time. Born in Oak Park, Illinois, in 1899, Hemingway began his writing career as a reporter, and throughout his life he worked for newspapers, often on the front lines of armed conflicts such as the Spanish Civil War (1936–1939) and the Second World War (1939–1945). His adventures brought him close to death several times—in the Spanish Civil War when shells landed in his hotel room, in the Second World War when he was struck by a taxi during a blackout, and in 1954 when his plane crashed in Africa.

Writing in an unadorned, unemotional but morally taut style, Hemingway placed the search for meaning in a world disenchanted with old ideals at the heart of his fiction. In his life as in his writing he was drawn to individuals committed to the art of doing things well regardless of the larger world's lack of direction or faith; he especially admired those who achieved grace or beauty in the face of death, such as bullfighters, hunters, and soldiers. His best-known books are *The Sun Also Rises* (1926), the novel that established his reputation; *A Farewell to Arms* (1929); *For Whom the Bell Tolls* (1940); and *The Old Man and the Sea* (1953). For the last he was awarded a Pulitzer Prize, and in the following year he received the Nobel Prize in Literature. Hemingway committed suicide in Ketchum, Idaho, in 1961.

In this essay, Hemingway uses the pattern of process analysis to order his materials on the art of camping. Hemingway wrote this piece for the *Toronto Star* in the early 1920s, before he gained worldwide recognition as a major American writer. In it, we see his lifelong interest in the outdoors and his desire to do things well.

PREREADING: THINKING ABOUT THE ESSAY IN ADVANCE

As you prepare to read Hemingway's essay, take a minute or two to think about your own experiences in nature or any unknown place you once visited. If you have ever camped out or attended summer camp, for example, how did you prepare for, enter into, and survive the experience? What problems did you encounter, and how did you overcome them?

Words to Watch

relief map (par. 2) a map that shows by lines and colors the various heights and forms of the land

Caucasus (par. 2) a mountain range in southeastern Europe

proprietary (par. 7) held under patent or trademark

rhapsodize (par. 9) to speak enthusiastically

browse bed (par. 9) a portable cot

tyro (par. 11) an amateur; a beginner in learning something

dyspepsia (par. 13) indigestion

mulligan (par. 18) a stew made from odds and ends of meats and vegetables

1 Thousands of people will go into the bush this summer to cut the high cost of living. A man who gets his two weeks' salary while he is on vacation should be able to put those two weeks in fishing and camping and be able to save one week's salary clear. He ought to be able to sleep comfortably every night, to eat well every day and to return to the city rested and in good condition.

2 But if he goes into the woods with a frying pan, an ignorance of black flies and mosquitoes, and a great and abiding lack of knowledge about cookery the chances are that his return will be very different. He will come back with enough mosquito bites to make the back of his neck look like a relief map of the Caucasus. His digestion will be wrecked after a valiant battle to assimilate half-cooked or charred grub. And he won't have had a decent night's sleep while he has been gone.

3 He will solemnly raise his right hand and inform you that he has joined the grand army of never-agains. The call of the wild may be all right, but it's a dog's life. He's heard the call of the tame with both ears. Waiter, bring him an order of milk toast.

4 In the first place he overlooked the insects. Black flies, no-see-ums, deer flies, gnats and mosquitoes were instituted by the devil to force people to live in cities where he could get at them better. If it weren't for them everybody would live in the bush and he would be out of work. It was a rather successful invention.

5 But there are lots of dopes that will counteract the pests. The simplest perhaps is oil of citronella. Two bits' worth of this purchased at any pharmacist's will be enough to last for two weeks in the worst fly and mosquito-ridden country.

Rub a little on the back of your neck, your forehead and your wrists before you start fishing, and the blacks and skeeters will shun you. The odor of citronella is not offensive to people. It smells like gun oil. But the bugs do hate it. 6

Oil of pennyroyal and eucalyptol are also much hated by mosquitoes, and with citronella they form the basis for many proprietary preparations. But it is cheaper and better to buy the straight citronella. Put a little on the mosquito netting that covers the front of your pup tent or canoe tent at night, and you won't be bothered. 7

To be really rested and get any benefit out of a vacation a man must get a good night's sleep every night. The first requisite for this is to have plenty of cover. It is twice as cold as you expect it will be in the bush four nights out of five, and a good plan is to take just double the bedding that you think you will need. An old quilt that you can wrap up in is as warm as two blankets. 8

Nearly all outdoor writers rhapsodize over the browse bed. It is all right for the man who knows how to make one and has plenty of time. But in a succession of one-night camps on a canoe trip all you need is level ground for your tent floor and you will sleep all right if you have plenty of covers under you. Take twice as much cover as you think that you will need, and then put two-thirds of it under you. You will sleep warm and get your rest. 9

When it is clear weather you don't need to pitch your tent if you are only stopping for the night. Drive four stakes at the head of your made-up bed and drape your mosquito bar over that, then you can sleep like a log and laugh at the mosquitoes. 10

Outside of insects and bum sleeping the rock that wrecks most camping trips is cooking. The average tyro's idea of cooking is to fry everything and fry it good and plenty. Now, a frying pan is a most necessary thing to any trip, but you also need the old stew kettle and the folding reflector baker. 11

A pan of fried trout can't be bettered and they don't cost any more than ever. But there is a good and bad way of frying them. 12

The beginner puts his trout and his bacon in and over a brightly burning fire; the bacon curls up and dries into a dry tasteless cinder and the trout is burned outside while it is still raw inside. He eats them and it is all right if he is only out for the day and going home to a good meal at night. But if he is going to face more trout and bacon the next morning and other equally well-cooked dishes for the remainder of two weeks he is on the pathway to nervous dyspepsia. 13

14 The proper way is to cook over coals. Have several cans of Crisco or Cotosuet or one of the vegetable shortenings along that are as good as lard and excellent for all kinds of shortening. Put the bacon in and when it is about half cooked lay the trout in the hot grease, dipping them in corn meal first. Then put the bacon on top of the trout and it will baste them as it slowly cooks.

15 The coffee can be boiling at the same time and in a smaller skillet pancakes being made that are satisfying the other campers while they are waiting for the trout.

16 With the prepared pancake flours you take a cupful of pancake flour and add a cup of water. Mix the water and flour and as soon as the lumps are out it is ready for cooking. Have the skillet hot and keep it well greased. Drop the batter in and as soon as it is done on one side loosen it in the skillet and flip it over. Apple butter, syrup or cinnamon and sugar go well with the cakes.

17 While the crowd have taken the edge from their appetites with flapjacks the trout have been cooked and they and the bacon are ready to serve. The trout are crisp outside and firm and pink inside and the bacon is well done—but not too done. If there is anything better than that combination the writer has yet to taste it in a lifetime devoted largely and studiously to eating.

18 The stew kettle will cook you dried apricots when they have resumed their predried plumpness after a night of soaking, it will serve to concoct a mulligan in, and it will cook macaroni. When you are not using it, it should be boiling water for the dishes.

19 In the baker, mere man comes into his own, for he can make a pie that to his bush appetite will have it all over the product that mother used to make, like a tent. Men have always believed that there was something mysterious and difficult about making a pie. Here is a great secret. There is nothing to it. We've been kidded for years. Any man of average office intelligence can make at least as good a pie as his wife.

20 All there is to a pie is a cup and a half of flour, one-half teaspoonful of salt, one-half cup of lard and cold water. That will make pie crust that will bring tears of joy into your camping partner's eyes.

21 Mix the salt with the flour, work the lard into the flour, make it up into a good workmanlike dough with cold water. Spread some flour on the back of a box or something flat, and pat the dough around a while. Then roll it out with whatever kind of round bottle you prefer. Put a little more lard on the surface of the sheet

of dough and then slosh a little flour on and roll it up and then roll it out again with the bottle.

Cut out a piece of the rolled out dough big enough to line a pie tin. I like the kind with holes in the bottom. Then put in your dried apples that have soaked all night and been sweetened, or your apricots, or your blueberries, and then take another sheet of the dough and drape it gracefully over the top, soldering it down at the edges with your fingers. Cut a couple of slits in the top dough sheet and prick it a few times with a fork in an artistic manner. 22

Put it in the baker with a good slow fire for forty-five minutes and then take it out and if your pals are Frenchmen they will kiss you. The penalty for knowing how to cook is that the others will make you do all the cooking. 23

It is all right to talk about roughing it in the woods. But the real woodsman is the man who can be really comfortable in the bush. 24

BUILDING VOCABULARY

For each word below write your own definition, based on how the word is used in the selection. Check back to the appropriate paragraph in the essay for more help, if necessary.

a. abiding (par. 2)
b. valiant (par. 2)
c. assimilate (par. 2)
d. charred (par. 2)
e. solemnly (par. 3)
f. requisite (par. 8)
g. succession (par. 9)
h. studiously (par. 17)
i. concoct (par. 18)
j. soldering (par. 22)

THINKING CRITICALLY ABOUT THE ESSAY

Understanding the Writer's Ideas

1. What is Hemingway's main purpose in this essay? Does he simply want to explain how to set up camp and how to cook outdoors?

2. What, according to the writer, are the two possible results of camping out on your vacation?
3. Why is oil of citronella the one insecticide that Hemingway recommends over all others?
4. Is it always necessary to pitch a tent when camping out? What are alternatives to it? How can you sleep warmly and comfortably?
5. Explain the author's process for cooking trout. Also explain his process for baking a pie.
6. Is it enough for Hemingway simply to enjoy "roughing it" while camping out?

Understanding the Writer's Techniques

1. Does the author have a stated thesis? Explain.
2. Identify those paragraphs in the essay that involve process analysis, and explain how Hemingway develops his subject in each.
3. What is the main writing pattern in paragraphs 1 and 2? How does this method serve as an organizing principle throughout the essay?
4. How would you characterize the author's style of writing? Is it appropriate to a newspaper audience? Is it more apt for professional fishermen?
5. In what way does Hemingway employ classification in this essay?
6. Analyze the tone of Hemingway's essay.
7. The concluding paragraph is short. Is it effective, nevertheless, and why? How does it reinforce the opening paragraph?

Exploring the Writer's Ideas

1. Camping out was popular in the 1920s, as it is today. What are some of the reasons that it remains so attractive today?
2. Hemingway's essay describes many basic strategies for successful camping. He does not rely on "gadgets" or modern inventions to make camping easier. Do such gadgets make camping more fun today than it might have been in the 1920s?
3. The author suggests that there is a right way and a wrong way to do things. Does it matter if you perform a recreational activity correctly as long as you enjoy doing it? Why?

IDEAS FOR WRITING

Prewriting

Freewrite for fifteen minutes about your favorite pastime, activity, or hobby. How do you approach this activity? What steps must be observed in order to be successful at it? How might other people fail at it whereas you are successful?

Guided Writing

Write an essay on how to do something wrong, and how to do it right—going on vacation, looking for a job, fishing, or whatever.

1. Reexamine the author's first three paragraphs and imitate his method of introducing the right and wrong ways about the subject, and the possible results.
2. Adopt a simple, informal, "chatty" style. Feel free to use a few well-placed clichés and other forms of spoken English. Use several similes.
3. Divide your subject into useful categories. Just as Hemingway treated insects, sleeping, and cooking, try to cover the main aspects of your subject.
4. Explain the process involved for each aspect of your subject. Make certain that you compare and contrast the right and wrong ways of your activity.
5. Write a short, crisp conclusion that reinforces your longer introduction.

Thinking and Writing Collaboratively

As a class, choose a process—for example, applying to college—which clearly involves a "right way" and "wrong way" of accomplishing the activity. Then divide the class into two groups, with one group outlining the correct steps and the other the incorrect or incomplete steps to completing the process. List both approaches on the chalkboard for comparative discussion.

Writing About the Text

Write an essay discussing Hemingway's view of doing things "the proper way" (par. 14), looking at how his personal views are translated into authoritative instructions. Is Hemingway being overly judgmental? Or does "the proper way" mean everything in life?

More Writing Projects

1. How do you explain the fascination that camping out holds for many people? Reflect on this question in your journal.
2. In a paragraph, describe how to get to your favorite vacation spot, and what to do when you get there.
3. If you have ever camped out, write a process paper explaining one important feature of setting up camp.

In the Kitchen

Henry Louis Gates, Jr.

One of the nation's leading literary scholars, Henry Louis Gates, Jr., was born in 1950 in Piedmont, West Virginia. Educated in the newly desegregated local public schools, Gates went on to receive his B.A. from Yale and his Ph.D. from Clare College at the University of Cambridge (England). Having begun his career writing for *Time* magazine in London, Gates established his reputation as a major literary critic with his book *The Signifying Monkey: Toward a Theory of Afro-American Literary Criticism* (1989), which received the National Book Award. He is editor of the authoritative *Norton Anthology of African American Literature* and co-editor of *Transition* magazine. His many awards include the prestigious MacArthur Foundation "genius award." Gates is W.E.B. Du Bois Professor of Humanities and Chair of Afro-American Studies at Harvard University. In this selection, which first appeared in *The New Yorker* in 1994, Gates examines the politics of the hairdo by recalling his experiences as a child in his mother's home beauty parlor.

PREREADING: THINKING ABOUT THE ESSAY IN ADVANCE

Michael Jackson, America's pop icon, was criticized by some in the African-American community for altering his appearance to conform to Anglo features (such as straight hair). Do you think you should have the right to change your looks even if it means trying to conform to the standards of beauty of an ethnic or cultural group other than your own?

Words to Watch

transform (par. 4) to change the appearance or form of

southpaw (par. 4) a left-handed person, especially a left-handed baseball pitcher

refrain (par. 7) repeated phrase or utterance

preposterous (par. 7) absurd

tiara (par. 24) a crown or fine headdress

1 We always had a gas stove in the kitchen, in our house in Piedmont, West Virginia, where I grew up. Never electric, though using electric became fashionable in Piedmont in the sixties, like

using Crest toothpaste rather than Colgate, or watching Huntley and Brinkley rather than Walter Cronkite. But not us: gas, Colgate, and good ole Walter Cronkite, come what may. We used gas partly out of loyalty to Big Mom, Mama's Mama, because she was mostly blind and still loved to cook, and could feel her way more easily with gas than with electric. But the most important thing about our gas-equipped kitchen was that Mama used to do hair there. The "hot comb" was a fine-toothed iron instrument with a long wooden handle and a pair of iron curlers that opened and closed like scissors. Mama would put it in the gas fire until it glowed. You could smell those prongs heating up.

2 I liked that smell. Not the smell so much, I guess, as what the smell meant for the shape of my day. There was an intimate warmth in the women's tones as they talked with my Mama, doing their hair. I knew what the women had been through to get their hair ready to be "done," because I would watch Mama do it to herself. How that kink could be transformed through grease and fire into that magnificent head of wavy hair was a miracle to me, and still is.

3 Mama would wash her hair over the sink, a towel wrapped around her shoulders, wearing just her slip and her white bra. (We had no shower—just a galvanized tub that we stored in the kitchen—until we moved down Rat Tail Road into Doc Wolverton's house, in 1954.) After she dried it, she would grease her scalp thoroughly with blue Bergamot hair grease, which came in a short, fat jar with a picture of a beautiful colored lady on it. It's important to grease your scalp real good, my Mama would explain, to keep from burning yourself. Of course, her hair would return to its natural kink almost as soon as the hot water and shampoo hit it. To me, it was another miracle how hair so "straight" would so quickly become kinky again the second it even approached some water.

4 My Mama had only a few "clients" whose heads she "did"—did, I think, because she enjoyed it, rather than for the few pennies it brought in. They would sit on one of our red plastic kitchen chairs, the kind with the shiny metal legs, and brace themselves for the process. Mama would stroke that red-hot iron—which by this time had been in the gas fire for half an hour or more—slowly but firmly through their hair, from scalp to strand's end. It made a scorching, crinkly sound, the hot iron did, as it burned its way through kink, leaving in its wake straight strands of hair, standing long and tall but drooping over at the ends, their shape like the top

of a heavy willow tree. Slowly, steadily, Mama's hands would transform a round mound of Odetta kink into a darkened swamp of everglades. The Bergamot made the hair shiny; the heat of the hot iron gave it a brownish-red cast. Once all the hair was as straight as God allows kink to get, Mama would take the well-heated curling iron and twirl the straightened strands into more or less loosely wrapped curls. She claimed that she owed her skill as a hairdresser to the strength in her wrists, and as she worked her little finger would poke out, the way it did when she sipped tea. Mama was a southpaw, and wrote upside down and backward to produce the cleanest, roundest letters you've ever seen.

The "kitchen" she would all but remove from sight with a 5 handheld pair of shears, bought just for this purpose. Now, the kitchen was the room in which we were sitting—the room where Mama did hair and washed clothes, and where we all took a bath in that galvanized tub. But the word has another meaning, and the kitchen that I'm speaking of is the very kinky bit of hair at the back of your head, where your neck meets your shirt collar. If there was ever a part of our African past that resisted assimilation, it was the kitchen. No matter how hot the iron, no matter how powerful the chemical, no matter how stringent the mashed-potatoes-and-lye formula of a man's "process," neither God nor woman nor Sammy Davis, Jr., could straighten the kitchen. The kitchen was permanent, irredeemable, irresistible kink. Unassimilably African. No matter what you did, no matter how hard you tried, you couldn't de-kink a person's kitchen. So you trimmed it off as best you could.

When hair had begun to "turn," as they'd say—to return to its 6 natural kinky glory—it was the kitchen that turned first (the kitchen around the back, and nappy edges at the temples). When the kitchen started creeping up the back of the neck, it was time to get your hair done again.

Sometimes, after dark, a man would come to have his hair done. It 7 was Mr. Charlie Carroll. He was very light-complected and had a ruddy nose—it made me think of Edmund Gwenn, who played Kris Kringle in "Miracle on 34th Street." At first, Mama did him after my brother, Rocky, and I had gone to sleep. It was only later that we found out that he had come to our house so Mama could iron his hair—not with a hot comb or a curling iron but with our very own Proctor-Silex steam iron. For some reason I never understood, Mr. Charlie would conceal his Frederick Douglass-like mane under a big white Stetson hat. I never saw him take it off except when he came to our house, at night, to have his hair pressed. (Later, Daddy would tell us about Mr. Charlie's most prized piece of knowledge, something that the man would only confide after his hair had been pressed, as a token of intimacy. "Not many people know this," he'd say, in a tone of circumspection, "but George Washington was Abraham Lincoln's daddy." Nodding solemnly, he'd add the clincher: "A white man told me." Though he was in dead earnest, this became a humorous refrain around our house—"a white man told me"—which we used to punctuate especially preposterous assertions.)

8 My mother examined my daughters' kitchens whenever we went home to visit, in the early eighties. It became a game between us. I had told her not to do it, because I didn't like the politics it suggested—the notion of "good" and "bad" hair. "Good" hair was "straight," "bad" hair kinky. Even in the late sixties, at the height of Black Power, almost nobody could bring themselves to say "bad" for good and "good" for bad. People still said that hair like white people's hair was "good," even if they encapsulated it in a disclaimer, like "what we used to call 'good.'"

9 Maggie would be seated in her high chair, throwing food this way and that, and Mama would be cooing about how cute it all was, how I used to do just like Maggie was doing, and wondering whether her flinging her food with her left hand meant that she was going to be left-handed like Mama. When my daughter was just about covered with Chef Boyardee Spaghetti-O's, Mama would seize the opportunity: wiping her clean, she would tilt Maggie's head to one side and reach down the back of her neck. Sometimes Mama would even rub a curl between her fingers, just to make sure that her bifocals had not deceived her. Then she'd sigh with satisfaction and relief: No kink . . . yet. Mama! I'd shout, pretending to be angry. Every once in a while, if no one was looking, I'd peek, too.

10 I say "yet" because most black babies are born with soft, silken hair. But after a few months it begins to turn, as inevitably as do the seasons or the leaves on a tree. People once thought baby oil would stop it. They were wrong.

11 Everybody I knew as a child wanted to have good hair. You could be as ugly as homemade sin dipped in misery and still be thought attractive if you had good hair. "Jesus moss," the girls at

Camp Lee, Virginia, had called Daddy's naturally "good" hair during the war. I know that he played that thick head of hair for all it was worth, too.

My own hair was "not a bad grade," as barbers would tell me when they cut it for the first time. It was like a doctor reporting the results of the first full physical he has given you. Like "You're in good shape" or "Blood pressure's kind of high—better cut down on salt." 12

I spent most of my childhood and adolescence messing with my hair. I definitely wanted straight hair. Like Pop's. When I was about three, I tried to stick a wad of Bazooka bubble gum to that straight hair of his. I suppose what fixed that memory for me is the spanking I got for doing so: he turned me upside down, holding me by my feet, the better to paddle my behind. Little *nigger,* he had shouted, walloping away. I started to laugh about it two days later, when my behind stopped hurting. 13

When black people say "straight," of course, they don't usually mean literally straight—they're not describing hair like, say, Peggy Lipton's (she was the white girl on "The Mod Squad"), or like Mary's of Peter, Paul & Mary fame; black people call that "stringy" hair. No, "straight" just means not kinky, no matter what contours the curl may take. I would have done *anything* to have straight hair—and I used to try everything, short of getting a process. 14

Of the wide variety of techniques and methods I came to master in the challenging prestidigitation of the follicle, almost all had two things in common: a heavy grease and the application of pressure. It's not an accident that some of the biggest black-owned companies in the fifties and sixties made hair products. And I tried them all, in search of that certain silken touch, the one that would leave neither the hand nor the pillow sullied by grease. 15

I always wondered what Frederick Douglass put on *his* hair, or what Phillis Wheatley put on hers. Or why Wheatley has that rag on her head in the little engraving in the frontispiece of her book. One thing is for sure: you can bet that when Phillis Wheatley went to England and saw the Countess of Huntingdon she did not stop by the Queen's coiffeur on her way there. So many black people still get their hair straightened that it's a wonder we don't have a national holiday for Madame C. J. Walker, the woman who invented the process of straightening kinky hair. Call it Jheri-Kurled or call it "relaxed," it's still fried hair. 16

17 I used all the greases, from sea-blue Bergamot and creamy vanilla Duke (in its clear jar with the orange-white-and-green label) to the godfather of grease, the formidable Murray's. Now, Murray's was some *serious* grease. Whereas Bergamot was like oily jello, and Duke was viscous and sickly sweet, Murray's was light brown and *hard.* Hard as lard and twice as greasy, Daddy used to say. Murray's came in an orange can with a press-on top. It was so hard that some people would put a match to the can, just to soften the stuff and make it more manageable. Then, in the late sixties, when Afros came into style, I used Afro Sheen. From Murray's to Duke to Afro Sheen: that was my progression in black consciousness.

18 We used to put hot towels or washrags over our Murray-coated heads, in order to melt the wax into the scalp and the follicles. Unfortunately, the wax also had the habit of running down your neck, ears, and forehead. Not to mention your pillowcase. Another problem was that if you put two palmfuls of Murray's on your head your hair turned white. (Duke did the same thing.) The challenge was to get rid of that white color. Because if you got rid of the white stuff you had a magnificent head of wavy hair. That was the beauty of it: Murray's was so hard that it froze your hair into the wavy style you brushed it into. It looked really good if you wore a part. A lot of guys had parts *cut* into their hair by a barber, either with the clippers or with a straightedge razor. Especially if you had kinky hair—then you'd generally wear a short razor cut, or what we called a Quo Vadis.

19 We tried to be as innovative as possible. Everyone knew about using a stocking cap, because your father or your uncle wore one whenever something really big was about to happen, whether sacred or secular: a funeral or a dance, a wedding or a trip in which you confronted official white people. Any time you were trying to look really sharp, you wore a stocking cap in preparation. And if the event was really a big one, you made a new cap. You asked your mother for a pair of her hose, and cut it with scissors about six inches or so from the open end—the end with the elastic that goes up to the top of the thigh. Then you knotted the cut end, and it became a beehive-shaped hat, with an elastic band that you pulled down low on your forehead and down around your neck in the back. To work well, the cap had to fit tightly and snugly, like a press. And it had to fit that tightly because it *was* a press: it pressed your hair with the force of the hose's elastic. If you greased your

hair down real good, and left the stocking cap on long enough, voilá: you got a head of pressed-against-the-scalp waves. (You also got a ring around your forehead when you woke up, but it went away.) And then you could enjoy your concrete do. Swore we were bad, too, with all that grease and those flat heads. My brother and I would brush it out a bit in the mornings, so that it looked—well, "natural." Grown men still wear stocking caps—especially older men, who generally keep their stocking caps in their top drawers, along with their cufflinks and their see-through silk socks, their "Maverick" ties, their silk handkerchiefs, and whatever else they prize the most.

A Murrayed-down stocking cap was the respectable version of the process, which, by contrast, was most definitely not a cool thing to have unless you were an entertainer by trade. Zeke and Keith and Poochie and a few other stars of the high-school basketball team all used to get a process once or twice a year. It was expensive, and you had to go somewhere like Pittsburgh or D.C. or Uniontown—somewhere where there were enough colored people to support a trade. The guys would disappear, then reappear a day or two later, strutting like peacocks, their hair burned slightly red from the lye base. They'd also wear "rags"—cloths or handkerchiefs—around their heads when they slept or played basketball. Do-rags, they were called. But the result was straight hair, with just a hint of wave. No curl. Do-it-yourselfers took their chances at home with a concoction of mashed potatoes and lye. 20

The most famous process of all, however, outside of the process Malcolm X describes in his "Autobiography," and maybe the process of Sammy Davis, Jr., was Nat King Cole's process. Nat King Cole had patent-leather hair. That man's got the finest process money can buy, or so Daddy said the night we saw Cole's TV show on NBC. It was November 5, 1956. I remember the date because everyone came to our house to watch it and to celebrate one of Daddy's buddies' birthdays. Yeah, Uncle Joe chimed in, they can do shit to his hair that the average Negro can't even *think* about—secret shit. 21

Nat King Cole was *clean.* I've had an ongoing argument with a Nigerian friend about Nat King Cole for twenty years now. Not about whether he could sing—any fool knows that he could—but about whether or not he was a handkerchief head for wearing that patent-leather process. 22

23 Sammy Davis, Jr.'s process was the one I detested. It didn't look good on him. Worse still, he liked to have a fried strand dangling down the middle of his forehead, so he could shake it out from the crown when he sang. But Nat King Cole's hair was a thing unto itself, a beautifully sculpted work of art that he and he alone had the right to wear. The only difference between a process and a stocking cap, really, was taste; but Nat King Cole, unlike, say, Michael Jackson, looked *good* in his. His head looked like Valentino's head in the twenties, and some say it was Valentino the process was imitating. But Nat King Cole wore a process because it suited his face, his demeanor, his name, his style. He was as clean as he wanted to be.

24 I had forgotten all about that patent-leather look until one day in 1971, when I was sitting in an Arab restaurant on the island of Zanzibar surrounded by men in fezzes and white caftans, trying to learn how to eat curried goat and rice with the fingers of my right hand and feeling two million miles from home. All of a sudden, an old transistor radio sitting on top of a china cupboard stopped blaring out its Swahili music and started playing "Fly Me to the Moon," by Nat King Cole. The restaurant's din was not affected at all, but in my mind's eye I saw it: the King's magnificent sleek black tiara. I managed, barely, to blink back the tears.

BUILDING VOCABULARY

For each word below write your own definition based on how the word is used in the selection. Check back to the appropriate paragraph in the essay for more help, if necessary.

a. galvanized (par. 5)
b. assertions (par. 7)
c. prestidigitation (par. 15)
d. follicle (par. 15)
e. din (par. 24)

THINKING CRITICALLY ABOUT THE ESSAY

Understanding the Writer's Ideas

1. The word *kitchen* in the title takes on two meanings in the essay. What are they?
2. Gas was used in this writer's kitchen even though people had turned to electricity in the 1960s. Why?
3. What does the writer mean when he states that his mother "did hair"?
4. What does the word *turn* (par. 6) describe?
5. What is the history behind "good" and "bad" hair?
6. As a child, how did the writer worry about his hair? Explain.
7. Describe the two things all hair-straightening techniques have in common.
8. What was it about Nat King Cole's hair that impressed this writer so much?
9. How were the hot irons used to straighten hair?
10. Hearing a Nat King Cole song while in Zanzibar, the writer says he had to "blink back the tears." What is going on?

Understanding the Writer's Techniques

1. Find the thesis and paraphrase it.
2. What process is described in paragraph 3? Give examples of the process described in paragraph 3.
3. Given the detailed descriptions of de-kinking hair, what audience does this writer have in mind in employing this strategy?
4. Where in the essay does the writer make a transition to describe two of the most common processes of hair straightening? How are these processes detailed?
5. Though the other de-kinking processes mentioned in the essay are detailed, the most famous one (Nat King Cole's) is not described at all. What might this suggest about the writer's attitude toward this subject?
6. What makes Gates's concluding paragraph different from others more common in essays?

MIXING PATTERNS

The essay's entire structure is not focused entirely on process. What other rhetorical pattern does the writer use? Identify the places where this pattern occurs.

Exploring the Writer's Ideas

1. Gates claims the "kitchen," those hairs on the back of the neck, are "unassimilably" African. Yet, his mother specialized in getting rid of the kitchen. Do you think this writer approves or disapproves of his mother's activity? Explain.
2. Gates tells of jokes about the "white man." Gates says he found the jokes funny even though he also admits he wanted good hair, like that of whites. How would you explain this writer's contradictory feelings about white people?
3. How do you feel about this writer's claims that most everyone he knew thought kinky hair was "bad"? Do you think this is an exaggeration? Why or why not?
4. Are there still examples today of people who remake themselves to look "white" or like those who are held up as role models, like Madonna or other rock stars? Is this impulse positive or negative? Why?
5. The author suggests that the de-kinking was physically painful. Does anything in the essay suggest all the pain was worth it? Explain.
6. By calling Nat King Cole's straightened hair a "black tiara" is this author concluding that straight hair (looking white) is indeed admirable? How do you feel?

IDEAS FOR WRITING

Prewriting

Use your journal to recall times when you felt good or bad about the way you look.

Guided Writing

Write an essay on how you once may have tried to make yourself look the "right" or "wrong" way. Remember the time you dressed for a date or to go to church or to get a job.

1. Examine Gates's first paragraph and imitate his method of introducing the thesis.
2. Divide your process into its important parts, like Gates who divides de-kinking into its steps: hot comb, the kitchen, the clients, the grease, and the pressure.
3. Make sure that your process is detailed in a way that keeps a general audience in mind (or people who don't know your process).
4. Try to use definition paragraphs to explain terms that describe your process which are unknown to your general audience.
5. Write a conclusion that tells a story, like Gates on Nat King Cole. Remember that this story should reflect an overall feeling you have about your topic.

Thinking and Writing Collaboratively

Your group has been assigned the task of creating a behavior code pamphlet for your school. Use process technique to make clear how students should act in different situations. Explain what happens (the process) if someone's behavior challenges the guidelines.

Writing About the Text

This essay is a reminiscence, an essay about a dear memory. Yet the writer seems ambivalent about his mother's hairdressing. Write an essay that explores the relation between Gates's *tone* and his attitude toward his subject.

More Writing Projects

1. In your journal, make notes on the ways that you have seen people change their looks to please others.
2. In a paragraph, describe the process by which people learn who looks the right way or the wrong way.
3. Write a process essay on something your parents or caregiver taught you as a child. Tell of learning to swim or to ride a bike.

SUMMING UP: CHAPTER 9

1. Divide into groups and choose one Guided Writing essay per group using the Gates, Lantos, or Hemingway selection. Collaboratively discuss, evaluate, correct, edit, and rewrite the Guided Writing process essay. By consensus, establish grades for the original and the revised essay. Present your findings to the class.
2. On the basis of your experience reading the four essays in the section, write about the types of processes the authors deal with (you may want to read the introduction to the previous chapter on classification) and how they manage these processes. Clarify the main steps that you consider to be important in the writing of any process analysis.
3. Jerrold G. Simon in his essay provides a kind of recipe for "brewing" a resume. To continue the metaphor, everyone has a favorite food. For this exercise, contribute a recipe for your favorite food to be included in a class cookbook. In addition to describing the step-by-step process for preparing the food, you should also tell something about the tradition behind the food, special occasions for eating it, the first time you ate it, and so forth. The goal should be to make the process clear and reassuring, to emphasize how following these simple steps can make anyone a great cook!
4. Three of the essays in this chapter tell us how to do things that can have direct and immediate effects on our lives—straightening hair, saving a baby, camping, getting a job. Try to write an essay that describes a process with much less immediate effect.
5. Interview a classmate about something that he or she does very well. Make sure the questions you ask don't omit any important steps or materials used in the process. Take careful notes during the interview, then try to replicate the process on your own. If there are any difficulties in accomplishing the process, reinterview your classmate. After you are satisfied that no steps or materials have been left out, write up the procedure in such a way that someone else could easily follow it.
6. John Lantos, Ernest Hemingway, and Henry Louis Gates, Jr.—each show how to perform a process with great rigor and devotion, not to say enthusiasm, and how to perform a process less carefully and even, according to Lantos and Hemingway,

indifferently. Choose a process that you care about—playing an instrument, cooking a dish, pitching a ball, and so on.—and discuss how to do it either well or poorly and what it means to you to see it done well and to see it done badly.

7. Many essays in this book look back to the writer's childhood—and frequently the writer remembers vividly the process of doing something, or of watching something being done, that epitomizes childhood. Write an essay about your childhood that focuses on a process—either something you did or something you watched being done that stands out as especially evocative of your childhood.
8. Choose an essay from Chapter 1, "On Writing," and analyze it as a process essay.

FROM SEEING TO WRITING

Consider the process the person in this photograph might have used to achieve her desired appearance. Imagine and describe the precise steps in the process she used, the order of those steps, and the relationship of the steps to the final impression that she makes. In your essay, help the reader understand the situation or circumstances under which the process was performed.

Michael Newman/PhotoEdit

CHAPTER 10

Cause-and-Effect Analysis

WHAT IS CAUSE-AND-EFFECT ANALYSIS?

Cause-and-effect analysis answers the basic human question: *Why?* Why do events occur, like hurricanes or the election of a new president? Why does one student do better in math than another? In addition, this form of analysis looks at the *expected* consequences of a chain of happenings. If we raise the minimum wage, what will the likely consequences be?

Basically, cause-and-effect analysis (also called causal analysis) looks for *causes* or conditions, and suggests or examines *results* or consequences (the effects).

Like most of the writing strategies you have been studying, causal analysis parallels a kind of thinking we do in everyday life. If you are a student who has returned to school after being away for several years, someone might ask you why you decided to come back. In answering, you would give causes: You needed a better job to support your children; you wanted to learn a new skill; your intellectual curiosity drove you back; and so on. These would be *causes.* Once you were attending school, a classmate might ask you what changes coming back to school have made in your life. You might consider the pride your children feel in your achievement, or the fact that you have less time to prepare meals, or that you sleep only four hours a night. Those are the *consequences* or results of your decision. In a few years' time, after graduation, the effects might be very different: a better job or a scholarship to graduate school might be one of the long-term results.

Thinking about causes can go beyond everyday life to help us understand social and political change: What were the causes of the American Civil War? What were the consequences for the nation? What caused the Great Depression? Why were women denied the vote until 1920? Why did so many Irish immigrants come to America around 1900, and what were the consequences for the growth of American industry?

In looking at such large questions, you will realize that there are different kinds of causes. First, there is the *immediate* cause that gives rise to a situation. This is the cause (or causes) most directly related, the one closest at hand. But as you can see from the historical questions in the previous paragraph, we also need to go beyond the immediate cause to the *ultimate* cause, the basic conditions that stimulated the more obvious or immediate ones.

For example, although we might identify the immediate cause of the 9/11 World Trade Center disaster of 2001 as the crashing of commercial airlines by suicide bombers, the ultimate causes for terrorism against the United States grew from long fomenting hatred and envy directed at out country by fanatics. To find the "real" causes, we have to think critically, to examine the situation deeply.

Often, a writer has to consider many causes and rank them in order of importance. Depending on the length of the essay, a writer may have to select from among many causes. If a small town begins to lose businesses to a large mall, the chamber of commerce may ask why businesses and customers prefer the mall to shopping in town. Convenience, parking, competitive pricing, and entertainment may be identified as causes: Since the town cannot solve all these problems at once, it may focus on one, and try to lure shoppers back downtown by building a larger municipal parking lot. The result, perhaps, will be that shoppers will return to Main Street.

One difficulty in working with causal analysis is that we cannot always prove that a cause or an effect is absolute. We can only do our best to offer as much evidence as possible to help the reader see the relation we wish to establish. Therefore, we have to support our causes and effects with specific details and evidence drawn from personal experience, from statistics, or from experts' statements in newspapers or books. A writer can interview people, for instance, and collect data about local shopping habits or visit the library to read articles on the Los Angeles riots.

In the essays in this chapter, you will find a variety of uses for causal analysis. Stephen King analyzes why we crave horror movies. Anne Roiphe looks at the causes for the failure of half the marriages in America. Harry Crews explains how he has come to settle in one particular place. Finally, Susan Jacoby combines both process analysis and narrative with causal analysis techniques to examine the reasons women opt out of courses in math and science. As you read each piece, keep in mind the kinds of causes the writers present and the ways in which they add support to their analysis.

HOW DO WE READ CAUSAL ANALYSIS?

Reading causal analysis requires us to ask ourselves these questions:

- What are the writer's topic and the main cause? Make an outline of the causes as you read.
- Are immediate causes or ultimate causes presented? How do you know?
- Does the author show the consequences of the event? Why or why not?
- How does the author develop the analysis? Identify the writing strategies used: narrative, description, illustration, process analysis, and so on. Which is most effective in supporting the causal analysis and why?
- What is the tone of the essay?

HOW DO WE WRITE CAUSAL ANALYSIS?

Select a topic you can manage. If you try to find the causes of psychological depression, you may need to study a great deal of Freud before you can write the essay. If, on the other hand, you decide to write about causes of suicide among college freshmen, you would narrow the scope of the essay and thus control it more easily.

Write a working thesis that tells the cause and effect you are analyzing. Why is it important?

Sample thesis statement:

> Many causes lie behind Americans' return to more healthful eating habits, but the most important are fear of disease, desire to lose weight, and curiosity about new types of food.

Make a list of the major causes and under each cause, add at least one specific example to support it.

Plan whether you want to concentrate on either causes or effects, or on a balance of the two.

Be sure that you have included all the necessary links in the chain of reasoning that you began in the thesis.

Avoid oversimplification.

Include both major and minor causes and effects.

Writing the Draft

Write an introduction that presents the thesis and your statement of the significance of the thesis.

Use transitions as you move from one cause to the next.

Use narrative, description, process analysis, and other techniques to support your causes.

Conclude by reminding your reader of the importance of understanding this chain of events.

Proofread your draft carefully. Ask a classmate to read it to see if your causes seem logical.

Make corrections and prepare a final copy.

A STUDENT PARAGRAPH: CAUSE-AND-EFFECT ANALYSIS

The student who wrote the following paragraph concentrated on one aspect of the thesis sentence provided earlier in this chapter introduction to focus her causal analysis. Examine the way she weaves examples as her support for an analysis of American's changing eating habits.

The arrival of ethnic restaurants and groceries in what used to be called "white-bread" neighborhoods has transformed the eating habits of mainstream American culture—in most cases, for the better. While chicharron de pollo (fried chicken cracklings) and jerk pork might not be much better for you nutritionally than what you can get at McDonald's, much of the newly arrived "exotic" food is far less fatty than typical fast-food fare. Phô (a Vietnamese noodle soup), rice and beans, hummus, chana saag (Indian chickpeas and spinach), and similar dishes provide leaner, more healthful fuel for the body than a Philly cheese steak and fries. Many people are beginning to think they taste better, too. The positive

Topic sentence

Contrasting examples

Supporting examples, with definitions

Transition "too" signals shift to related topic; examples follow

influence of these cuisines doesn't stop at the restaurant door, either. Many Americans are beginning to bring the culinary habits of other cultures into their own kitchens, imitating their techniques (stir frying, for example), adopting their principles (using meat as a flavoring, instead of the centerpiece of the meal), and borrowing their more healthful ingredients (yogurt instead of sour cream, olive oil instead of butter, a wider range of fresh vegetables and spices). In the process, the traditions of newly arrived immigrants receive appropriate recognition, and native habits evolve in a positive direction: the effect is not only better eating, but a broadening of the American cultural horizon.

Concluding sentence establishes main effect of altered eating habits

Why We Crave Horror Movies

Stephen King

Stephen King, America's best-known writer of horror fiction, was born in 1947 in Portland, Maine. He graduated from the University of Maine at Orono. King's masterly plots and prolific output reestablished horror as a hugely popular contemporary genre. Among his widely read novels are *The Shining* (1976), which was adapted into a classic of modern horror films, *It* (1986), and *The Girl Who Loved Tom Gordon* (1999). King also writes science fiction, and has published a series that features Roman Gilead, entitled *The Dark Tower.* His most recent volume in that series is *Wizard and Glass* (1997). In 2000 King became the first major author to publish his work, the story "Riding the Bullet," exclusively as an e-book. Because he is an acknowledged master of this genre, his thoughts on why people love horror movies offer an unusual insight into this question. King also gives us a unique glimpse into why he himself creates horror. This selection originally appeared in *Playboy* in January 1982.

PREREADING: THINKING ABOUT THE ESSAY IN ADVANCE

Do you think that we all have a dark side to our personalities that we rarely reveal? Explain.

Words to Watch

innately (par. 4) by essential characteristic; by birth

voyeur (par. 6) a person who derives sexual gratification from observing the acts of others

penchant (par. 7) a definite liking; a strong inclination

remonstrance (par. 10) an expression of protest

anarchistic (par. 11) active resistance and terrorism against the state

subterranean (par. 12) hidden; secret

1 I think that we're all mentally ill; those of us outside the asylums only hide it a little better—and maybe not all that much better, after all. We've all known people who talk to themselves, people who sometimes squinch their faces into horrible grimaces when they believe no one is watching, people who have some hysterical fear—of snakes, the dark, the tight place, the long drop . . . and, of

course, those final worms and grubs that are waiting so patiently underground.

When we pay our four or five bucks and seat ourselves at 2
tenth-row center in a theater showing a horror movie, we are daring the nightmare.

Why? Some of the reasons are simple and obvious. To show 3
that we can, that we are not afraid, that we can ride this roller coaster. Which is not to say that a really good horror movie may not surprise a scream out of us at some point, the way we may scream when the roller coaster twists through a complete 360 or plows through a lake at the bottom of the drop. And horror movies, like roller coasters, have always been the special province of the young; by the time one turns 40 or 50, one's appetite for double twists or 360-degree loops may be considerably depleted.

We also go to re-establish our feelings of essential normality; 4
the horror movie is innately conservative, even reactionary. Freda Jackson as the horrible melting woman in *Die, Monster, Die!* confirms for us that no matter how far we may be removed from the beauty of a Robert Redford or a Diana Ross, we are still light-years from true ugliness.

And we go to have fun. 5

Ah, but this is where the ground starts to slope away, isn't it? 6
Because this is a very peculiar sort of fun indeed. The fun comes from seeing others menaced—sometimes killed. One critic has suggested that if pro football has become the voyeur's version of combat, then the horror film has become the modern version of the public lynching.

It is true that the mythic, "fairytale" horror film intends to take 7
away the shades of gray. . . . It urges us to put away our more civilized and adult penchant for analysis and to become children again, seeing things in pure blacks and whites. It may be that horror movies provide psychic relief on this level because this invitation to lapse into simplicity, irrationality and even outright madness is extended so rarely. We are told we may allow our emotions a free rein . . . or no rein at all.

If we are all insane, then sanity becomes a matter of degree. If 8
your insanity leads you to carve up women like Jack the Ripper or the Cleveland Torso Murderer, we clap you away in the funny farm (but neither of those two amateur-night surgeons was ever caught, heh-heh-heh); if, on the other hand your insanity leads you only to talk to yourself when you're under stress or to pick your

nose on the morning bus, then you are left alone to go about your business . . . though it is doubtful that you will ever be invited to the best parties.

9 The potential lyncher is in almost all of us (excluding saints, past and present; but then, most saints have been crazy in their own ways), and every now and then, he has to be let loose to scream and roll around in the grass. Our emotions and our fears form their own body, and we recognize that it demands its own exercise to maintain proper muscle tone. Certain of these emotional muscles are accepted—even exalted—in civilized society; they are, of course, the emotions that tend to maintain the status quo of civilization itself. Love, friendship, loyalty, kindness—these are all the emotions that we applaud, emotions that have been immortalized in the couplets of Hallmark cards and in the verses (I don't dare call it poetry) of Leonard Nimoy.

10 When we exhibit these emotions, society showers us with positive reinforcement; we learn this even before we get out of diapers. When, as children, we hug our rotten little puke of a sister and give her a kiss, all the aunts and uncles smile and twit and cry, "Isn't he the sweetest little thing?" Such coveted treats as chocolate-covered graham crackers often follow. But if we deliberately slam the rotten little puke of a sister's fingers in the door, sanctions follow—angry remonstrance from parents, aunts and uncles; instead of a chocolate-covered graham cracker, a spanking.

11 But anticivilization emotions don't go away, and they demand periodic exercise. We have such "sick" jokes as, "What's the difference between a truckload of bowling balls and a truckload of dead babies?" (You can't unload a truckload of bowling balls with a pitchfork . . . a joke, by the way, that I heard originally from a ten-year-old.) Such a joke may surprise a laugh or a grin out of us even as we recoil, a possibility that confirms the thesis: If we share a brotherhood of man, then we also share an insanity of man. None of which is intended as a defense of either the sick joke or insanity but merely as an explanation of why the best horror films, like the best fairy tales, manage to be reactionary, anarchistic, and revolutionary all at the same time.

12 The mythic horror movie, like the sick joke, has a dirty job to do. It deliberately appeals to all that is worst in us. It is morbidity unchained, our most base instincts let free, our nastiest fantasies realized . . . and it all happens, fittingly enough, in the dark. For those reasons, good liberals often shy away from horror films. For

myself, I like to see the most aggressive of them—*Dawn of the Dead,* for instance—as lifting a trap door in the civilized forebrain and throwing a basket of raw meat to the hungry alligators swimming around in that subterranean river beneath.

Why bother? Because it keeps them from getting out, man. It 13
keeps them down there and me up here. It was Lennon and McCartney who said that all you need is love, and I would agree with that.

As long as you keep the gators fed. 14

BUILDING VOCABULARY

King uses descriptive language in this essay to re-create some of the scary images from horror stories, such as snakes and grubs (par. 1). Make a list of his scary words (at least five). Then find a synonym for each word and use each in a sentence.

THINKING CRITICALLY ABOUT THE ESSAY

Understanding the Writer's Ideas

1. King uses the cause-and-effect method to explore why people crave horror. He says we share an "insanity of man" (par. 11). What does he mean by *insanity?*
2. Due to what three reasons does the writer think we dare the nightmare?
3. What does King mean when he says the "'fairytale'" horror films "take away the shades of gray" (par. 7)?
4. How does King explain his view on anticivilization emotions?
5. King uses the image of alligators (the gator) to make a final point. How do you interpret this?

Understanding the Writer's Techniques

1. What is the thesis? Where is it? How does the essay's title reflect the writer's thesis?
2. King uses first person narration in this essay. What other rhetorical modes does he use to develop his essay?
3. In this cause-and-effect essay, what is the cause and what is the effect?

4. King says we are all insane. What tone does this create for the reader? Is he accusing? humorous? serious?
5. King uses both specific and broad generalizations to develop his thesis. Give an example of something specific and something generalized. Which better supports the thesis and why?
6. Notice how the last and concluding sentence of the essay suddenly addresses the reader ("you"). Why? What purpose does this shift to the second person serve in this essay's conclusion?

Exploring the Writer's Ideas

1. How do you feel about the writer's bold opening statement that we are all mentally ill? Does this statement make you want to stop reading? How do you feel about his assumption?
2. Do you go to horror movies or do you avoid them? Why do you or don't you go? Explain.
3. Why do you think King chose to write out his ideas rather than discuss them with a friend? In what way is the process of writing out our ideas different from the process of thinking out loud in conversation?
4. This writer claims he isn't defending anticivilization emotions (par. 11), but he tells us that we need to "scream and roll around in the grass" (par. 9). Which side is this writer on? Which side are you on? Why?
5. Is it true that in horror tales the villains are always destroyed and good always triumphs? Should this be the case? Why or why not?

IDEAS FOR WRITING

Prewriting

Make a scratch outline of your strongest feelings for or against horror stories.

Guided Writing

Write an essay in which you analyze your reactions to horror books or movies.

1. Begin the essay by stating your feelings on why you personally like or dislike horror. Use some examples to bring to life for the reader your experience with horror.
2. Describe two or more causes for the way you react to horror.
3. Analyze some of the effects you think horror movies may have on you or others who crave them.
4. Respond to the issue of horror allowing anticivilization emotions to be exercised so they don't "get out," as King says.
5. Conclude by addressing readers, telling them why they should embrace or avoid the horror genre.

Thinking and Writing Collaboratively

Working in a group of four to five students, research what experts say about the causes and effects of television violence on children. Then write an essay that makes these causes and effects clear to an audience of parents.

Writing About the Text

If King's opening statement contains little truth, his argument in effect falls apart. Write an essay that explores the validity of his opening and then analyzes the essay's argument based on your conclusions about its opening.

More Writing Projects

1. In your journal, write about something that scares you.
2. Write a paragraph that explains what causes you to fear something.
3. In an essay, examine the causes and effects of something in your life that frightens you (for example, stage fright, test anxiety, fear of flying, and so forth).

Why Marriages Fail

Anne Roiphe

The writer and journalist Anne Roiphe established her reputation with the widely read *Up the Sandbox!* (1970). She has since published four other books, including *Lovingkindness* (1997) and *1185 Park Avenue: A Memoir* (1999). Her most recent work, *For Rabbit with Love and Squalor* (2000), offers a highly personal reading of twentieth-century American fiction. Roiphe's column, "The New Yorker's Diary," appears biweekly in the *New York Observer.* In this essay from *Family Weekly,* notice how she presents a series of interconnected reasons for the currently high divorce rate.

PREREADING: THINKING ABOUT THE ESSAY IN ADVANCE

What experiences or assumptions do you bring to an essay about failed marriages? Do you know of marriages that have failed? If so, what were the causes?

Words to Watch

obsolete (par. 1) out-of-date; no longer in use
perils (par. 2) dangers
infertility (par. 2) the lack of ability to have children
turbulent (par. 2) very chaotic or uneasy
stupefying (par. 2) bewildering
obese (par. 3) very fat; overweight
entrapment (par. 4) the act of trapping, sometimes by devious methods
yearning (par. 4) a strong desire
euphoric (par. 7) characterized by a feeling of well-being
infidelity (par. 13) sexual unfaithfulness
proverbial (par. 13) relating to a proverb or accepted truth

1 These days so many marriages end in divorce that our most sacred vows no longer ring with truth. "Happily ever after" and "Till death do us part" are expressions that seem on the way to becoming obsolete. Why has it become so hard for couples to stay together? What goes wrong? What has happened to us that close to one-half of all marriages are destined for the divorce courts? How could we have created a society in which 42 percent of our children will

grow up in single-parent homes? If statistics could only measure loneliness, regret, pain, loss of self-confidence and fear of the future, the numbers would be beyond quantifying.

Even though each broken marriage is unique, we can still find 2
the common perils, the common causes for marital despair. Each marriage has crisis points and each marriage tests endurance, the capacity for both intimacy and change. Outside pressures such as job loss, illness, infertility, trouble with a child, care of aging parents and all the other plagues of life hit marriage the way hurricanes blast our shores. Some marriages survive these storms and others don't. Marriages fail, however, not simply because of the outside weather but because the inner climate becomes too hot or too cold, too turbulent or too stupefying.

When we look at how we choose our partners and what ex- 3
pectations exist at the tender beginnings of romance, some of the reasons for disaster become quite clear. We all select with unconscious accuracy a mate who will recreate with us the emotional patterns of our first homes. Dr. Carl A. Whitaker, a marital therapist and emeritus professor of psychiatry at the University of Wisconsin, explains, "From early childhood on, each of us carried models for marriage, femininity, masculinity, motherhood, fatherhood and all the other family roles." Each of us falls in love with a mate who has qualities of our parents, who will help us rediscover both the psychological happiness and miseries of our past lives. We may think we have found a man unlike Dad, but then he turns to drink or drugs, or loses his job over and over again or sits silently in front of the TV just the way Dad did. A man may choose a woman who doesn't like kids just like his mother or who gambles away the family savings just like his mother. Or he may choose a slender wife who seems unlike his obese mother but then turns out to have other addictions that destroy their mutual happiness.

A man and a woman bring to their marriage bed a blended 4
concoction of conscious and unconscious memories of their parents' lives together. The human way is to compulsively repeat and recreate the patterns of the past. Sigmund Freud so well described the unhappy design that many of us get trapped in: the unmet needs of childhood, the angry feelings left over from frustrations of long ago, the limits of trust and the recurrence of old fears. Once an individual senses this entrapment, there may follow a yearning to escape, and the result could be a broken, splintered marriage.

5 Of course people can overcome the habits and attitudes that developed in childhood. We all have hidden strengths and amazing capacities for growth and creative change. Change, however, requires work—observing your part in a rotten pattern, bringing difficulties out into the open—and work runs counter to the basic myth of marriage: "When I wed this person all my problems will be over. I will have achieved success and I will become the center of life for this other person and this person will be my center, and we will mean everything to each other forever." This myth, which every marriage relies on, is soon exposed. The coming of children, the pulls and tugs of their demands on affection and time, place a considerable strain on that basic myth of meaning everything to each other, of merging together and solving all of life's problems.

6 Concern and tension about money take each partner away from the other. Obligations to demanding parents or still-depended-upon parents create further strain. Couples today must also deal with all the cultural changes brought on in recent years by the women's movement and the sexual revolution. The altering of roles and the shifting of responsibilities have been extremely trying for many marriages.

7 These and other realities of life erode the visions of marital bliss the way sandstorms eat at rock and the ocean nibbles away at the dunes. Those euphoric, grand feelings that accompany romantic love are really self-delusions, self-hypnotic dreams that enable us to forge a relationship. Real life, failure at work, disappointments, exhaustion, bad smells, bad colds and hard times all puncture the dream and leave us stranded with our mate, with our childhood patterns pushing us this way and that, with our unfulfilled expectations.

8 The struggle to survive in marriage requires adaptability, flexibility, genuine love and kindness and an imagination strong enough to feel what the other is feeling. Many marriages fall apart because either partner cannot imagine what the other wants or cannot communicate what he or she needs or feels. Anger builds until it erupts into a volcanic burst that buries the marriage in ash.

9 It is not hard to see, therefore, how essential communication is for a good marriage. A man and a woman must be able to tell each other how they feel and why they feel the way they do; otherwise they will impose on each other roles and actions that lead to further unhappiness. In some cases, the communication patterns of childhood—of not talking, of talking too much, of not listening, of

distrust and anger, of withdrawal—spill into the marriage and prevent a healthy exchange of thoughts and feelings. The answer is to set up new patterns of communication and intimacy.

10 At the same time, however, we must see each other as individuals. "To achieve a balance between separateness and closeness is one of the major psychological tasks of all human beings at every stage of life," says Dr. Stuart Bartle, a psychiatrist at the New York University Medical Center.

11 If we sense from our mate a need for too much intimacy, we tend to push him or her away, fearing that we may lose our identities in the merging of marriage. One partner may suffocate the other partner in a childlike dependency.

12 A good marriage means growing as a couple but also growing as individuals. This isn't easy. Richard gives up his interest in carpentry because his wife, Helen, is jealous of the time he spends away from her. Karen quits her choir group because her husband dislikes the friends she makes there. Each pair clings to each other and are angry with each other as life closes in on them. This kind of marital balance is easily thrown as one or the other pulls away and divorce follows.

13 Sometimes people pretend that a new partner will solve the old problems. Most often extramarital sex destroys a marriage because it allows an artificial split between the good and the bad—the good is projected on the new partner and the bad is dumped on the head of the old. Dishonesty, hiding and cheating create walls between men and women. Infidelity is just a symptom of trouble. It is a symbolic complaint, a weapon of revenge, as well as an unraveler of closeness. Infidelity is often that proverbial last straw that sinks the camel to the ground.

14 All right—marriage has always been difficult. Why then are we seeing so many divorces at this time? Yes, our modern social fabric is thin, and yes the permissiveness of society has created unrealistic expectations and thrown the family into chaos. But divorce is so common because people today are unwilling to exercise the self-discipline that marriage requires. They expect easy joy, like the entertainment on TV, the thrill of a good party.

15 Marriage takes some kind of sacrifice, not dreadful self-sacrifice of the soul, but some level of compromise. Some of one's fantasies, some of one's legitimate desires have to be given up for the value of the marriage itself. "While all marital partners feel shackled at times, it is they who really choose to make the marital ties into confining chains or supporting bonds," says Dr. Whitaker.

Marriage requires sexual, financial and emotional discipline. A man and a woman cannot follow every impulse, cannot allow themselves to stop growing or changing.

16 Divorce is not an evil act. Sometimes it provides salvation for people who have grown hopelessly apart or were frozen in patterns of pain or mutual unhappiness. Divorce can be, despite its initial devastation, like the first cut of the surgeon's knife, a step toward new health and a good life. On the other hand, if the partners can stay past the breaking up of the romantic myths into the development of real love and intimacy, they have achieved a work as amazing as the greatest cathedrals of the world. Marriages that do not fail but improve, that persist despite imperfections, are not only rare these days but offer a wondrous shelter in which the face of our mutual humanity can safely show itself.

BUILDING VOCABULARY

1. Roiphe loads her essay with some very common expressions to make the discussion more easily understandable to the reader. Below is a list of ten such expressions. Use each in a sentence of your own.
   - **a.** ring with truth (par. 1)
   - **b.** crisis points (par. 2)
   - **c.** tender beginnings (par. 3)
   - **d.** mutual happiness (par. 3)
   - **e.** marriage bed (par. 4)
   - **f.** hidden strengths (par. 5)
   - **g.** marital bliss (par. 7)
   - **h.** healthy exchange (par. 9)
   - **i.** childlike dependency (par. 11)
   - **j.** social fabric (par. 14)
2. Locate and explain five terms that the author draws from psychology.

THINKING CRITICALLY ABOUT THE ESSAY

Understanding the Writer's Ideas

1. What are the "sacred vows" the author mentions in paragraph 1? Identify the source of the expressions "happily ever after" and

"till death do us part." What does she mean when she says that these expressions "seem on the way to becoming obsolete"?

2. What is a "single-parent home"?
3. How does Roiphe define "endurance" in a marriage? What does she mean by "outside pressures" in paragraph 2? What are some of these pressures? Does Roiphe feel they are the primary causes for marriages failing? Why?
4. According to the essay, how do we choose husbands and wives? What is the meaning of "our first homes" in paragraph 3? According to Roiphe, for what reason is the way we choose mates a possible cause for marriages failing?
5. What is the "basic myth" of marriage? How does it create a possibly bad marriage?
6. How have the women's movement and the sexual revolution created strains on modern marriages?
7. Explain what the writer means by "Real life, failure at work, disappointments, exhaustion, bad smells, bad colds, and hard times" in paragraph 7. How do they affect marriages?
8. What is the role of communication between husband and wife in a marriage? What are the results of poor communication? What solutions to this problem does Roiphe suggest?
9. What two types of "growth" does Roiphe suggest as necessary to a good marriage? Who are Richard, Helen, and Karen, named in paragraph 12?
10. According to Roiphe, what is the common cause of extramarital sexual affairs? What are her projected results of infidelity?
11. What does Roiphe identify as the primary cause of divorce? What does she propose as a solution to this problem?
12. According to the last paragraph, do you think Roiphe is in favor of divorce? Why? In this paragraph, she presents both the positive and negative effects of divorce. What are the positive effects? the negative effects?

Understanding the Writer's Techniques

1. Where does the writer place her thesis?
2. How does the title almost predict for the reader that the writer's main technique of development will be cause-and-effect analysis?
3. One strategy for developing an introductory paragraph is to ask a question. What is the purpose of the questions that the

author asks in the opening paragraph? What is the relationship among the questions? How do the questions themselves dictate a cause-and-effect pattern of development? How do they immediately involve the reader in the topic?

4. In which paragraph does Roiphe list the immediate or common causes of marital failure? Why is this placement effective?

5. The use of clear *topic sentences* for each paragraph can often be an important technique in writing a clear causal analysis because topic sentences usually identify main causes for the effect under discussion. Identify the topic sentences for paragraphs 3, 4, and 6. What causes for marriage failure does each identify?

6. What causal chain of behavior does Roiphe build in paragraphs 8 to 13?

7. Why does Roiphe begin paragraph 14 with the words "All right"? Whom is she addressing? How does this address compare with the technique used in her introduction?

8. What two authorities does Roiphe quote in this essay? How are their citations useful? How are they identified? In what ways do their identifications add to their credibility as sources of opinions or information on Roiphe's topic?

9. Where does Roiphe use statistics in this essay? Why is it especially important to the development of the article?
Locate other places where she uses definition.

10. In some essays, the introduction and conclusion are each simply the first and last paragraphs. In this essay, the writer uses more than one paragraph for each. Which paragraphs make up her introduction? Which make up the conclusion? Why might she have structured her introduction and conclusion in this way? How does the structure affect the essay?

11. You have learned that two of the most common types of comparisons used by writers to enliven their essays are *similes* and *metaphors.* Look up the definition of these terms in the Glossary to refresh your memory. In addition, writers may use *extended metaphors.* This technique relies upon a number of metaphoric comparisons that revolve around a main idea rather than a single comparison. Roiphe uses comparisons in a number of paragraphs in this essay. In each of the following cases identify and explain the comparisons indicated:

a. extended metaphor (par. 2)
b. metaphor (par. 7)

c. metaphor (par. 8)
d. metaphor (par. 9)
e. simile (par. 14)
f. metaphor (par. 15)
g. similes, metaphors (par. 16)

How does Roiphe's frequent use of metaphors and similes affect the tone of the essay?

12. Why does Roiphe end her essay with references to successful marriages? Would you consider that as being off the topic? Why or why not?

MIXING PATTERNS

Roiphe makes use of *definition* (see pages 254–258) in a number of places in this essay. What are her definitions of the following?

a. work [in a marriage] (par. 5)
b. A good marriage (par. 12)
c. Divorce (par. 16)
d. Marriages that do not fail but improve (par. 16)

Exploring the Writer's Ideas

1. Roiphe discusses quite a few causes for marriages failing. Discuss with the class some additional causes. Why are they also important?
2. Paragraph 6 states, "Couples today must also deal with all the cultural changes brought on in recent years by the women's movement and the sexual revolution." Identify these two social phenomena. Among the people you know, have these cultural changes affected their marriages? How? If you are not married, and plan to marry, do you feel that the changes will present any foreseeable problems? If you are not married, and do not plan to marry, have they influenced your decision in any ways? What other effects have these two movements had in American society? Do you think these influences have been positive or negative? Why?
3. If you are married or in a close relationship, how did you choose your mate? If you are not married or in a relationship, what qualities would you look for in a mate? Why?

4. In paragraphs 6 and 7, Roiphe mentions "realities of life" that destroy romantic notions of "marital bliss." What other realities can you add to her list?
5. Paragraph 15 discusses the idea of self-sacrifice in marriage. Roiphe writes, "Some of one's fantasies, some of one's legitimate desires have to be given up for the value of the marriage itself." However, some people insist that for a marriage to survive, each partner must maintain complete integrity, that is, must not be forced into major sacrifices of values or lifestyles. What is your opinion of these two opposing viewpoints?
6. Judy Brady in "I Want a Wife" (pages 456–458) provides some insights into marriage that complement Roiphe's. How does Brady's position compare with Roiphe's?

IDEAS FOR WRITING

Prewriting

Free-associate on a sheet of paper about the reasons or causes for *successful* marriages. In other words, which marriages survive despite the high rate of divorce in the United States?

Guided Writing

Using cause-and-effect analysis, write an essay in which you explain *why marriages succeed.*

1. Limit your topic sufficiently so that you can concentrate your discussion on closely interrelated cause-and-effect patterns.
2. In the introduction, involve your reader with a series of pertinent questions.
3. Identify what many people think are common or immediate causes of successful marriages; then show how other causes are perhaps even more important.
4. In the course of your essay, cite at least one relevant statistic that will add extra importance to your topic.
5. Try to use at least one quotation from a reputable authority. Consult your library for books and articles that deal with marriage. Be sure to include full identification of your source.

6. Use clear topic sentences in each paragraph as you present analyses of the various causes for successful marriages.
7. Make use of metaphors, similes, and extended metaphors.
8. In your essay, offer necessary definitions of terms that are especially important to your topic. Try for at least one definition by negation.
9. Write a conclusion in which you make some commentary upon divorce. Make your comment as an outgrowth of your discussion of a successful marriage.

Thinking and Writing Collaboratively

Divide the class into four equal groups. Have members of each group read their essays out loud. Next, select your group's strongest essay and list the reasons your group has selected it. Present your findings to the class, and if time permits, ask the writer of the best essay to read it to the class.

Writing About the Text

Write an essay that explores the impact of Roiphe's use of metaphors and similes on the *tone* and thus the *thesis* of her essay.

More Writing Projects

1. What is the "ideal marriage"? In your journal, speculate on those qualities that you think would make a perfect marriage. Share observations with others in the class.
2. In a paragraph, explain some of your reasons for ending a relationship (a marriage, a close friendship, a relationship with a girlfriend or boyfriend).
3. Write an essay in which you explain the effects of divorce on the lives of the couple involved. Here, do not concern yourself with causes; look only at the results of the failed marriage.

Why I Live Where I Live

Harry Crews

Harry Crews was born to a poor farming family in Alma, Georgia, in 1935. When he was 21 months old, his father died. At 17 Crews joined the Marines; he enrolled in the University of Florida at Gainesville upon his discharge and eventually received his B.A. Since 1968, when his novel *The Gospel Singer* was published, Crews has published thirteen novels, most recently *Celebration* (1998). A frequent contributor to *Playboy* and *Esquire,* where this selection first appeared, Crews has collected his nonfiction in *Blood and Grits* (1979) and *Florida Frenzy* (1982). He has also published a memoir, *A Childhood: The Biography of a Place* (1978). Crews writes in the gothic tradition of literature of the South, often, as in this selection, immersing his characters in a richly detailed and powerfully evocative Southern landscape.

PREREADING: THINKING ABOUT THE ESSAY IN ADVANCE

Why *do* people live where they live? Is it a matter of choice? Do certain climates, certain kinds of neighborhoods, certain styles of houses, certain views . . . agree with certain people and not with others? Or is it something that happens by accident—because of family or where the person was brought up or happens to have a job?

Words to Watch

pall (par. 1) to lose its attraction
indices (par. 2) plural of "index"
circuitous (par. 4) roundabout
skiff (par. 5) small boat, sometimes a rowboat but also a powerboat
slough (par. 5) creek in a marsh or swamp
precious (par. 7) affected
pretentious (par. 7) showy
symptomatic (par. 8) indicative
malaise (par. 8) moral illness

1 I can leave the place where I live a couple of hours before daylight and be on a deserted little strip of sand called Crescent Beach in time to throw a piece of meat on a fire and then, in a few minutes,

lie back sucking on a vodka bottle and chewing on a hunk of bloody beef while the sun lifts out of the Atlantic Ocean (somewhat unnerving but also mystically beautiful to a man who never saw a body of water bigger than a pond until he was grown) and while the sun rises lie on a blanket, brain singing from vodka and a bellyful of beef, while the beautiful bikinied children from the University of Florida drift down the beach, their smooth bodies sweating baby oil and the purest kind of innocent lust (which of course is the rankest sort) into the bright air. If all that starts to pall—and what *doesn't* start to pall?—I can leave the beach and be out on the end of a dock, sitting in the Captain's Table eating hearts-of-palm salad and hot boiled shrimp and sipping on a tall, icy glass of beer while the sun I saw lift out of the Atlantic that morning sinks into the warm, waveless Gulf of Mexico. It makes for a hell of a day. But that isn't really why I live in the north-central Florida town of Gainesville.

Nor do I live in Gainesville because seven blocks from my 2
house there are two enormous libraries filled with the most courteous, helpful people you can imagine, people who, after explaining some of the more intricate mysteries of how the place works, including the purposes of numerous indices, will go ahead and cheerfully find what I cannot: for example, the car capacity of drive-in theaters in Bakersfield, California, in 1950. A man never knows when he may need a bit of information like that, but it isn't enough to keep him living in a little town in Florida as opposed to, say, Ann Arbor, Michigan.

I love the size of Gainesville. I can walk anywhere I want to 3
go, and consequently I have very little to do with that abomination before the Lord, the car. It's a twenty-minute stroll to my two favorite bars, Lillian's Music Store and the Winnjammer; ten minutes to a lovely square of grass and trees called the Plaza of the Americas; less than ten minutes to the house of a young lady who has been hypnotizing me for six years. Some people get analyzed; I get hypnotized. It leaves me with the most astonishing and pleasurable memories. But there must be ten thousand towns like Gainesville in this country, and surely several hundred of them would have good places to drink and talk and at least one house where a young lady lived who would consent to hypnotize me into astonishing and pleasurable memories. So I cannot lean too heavily on walking and memories to justify being where I am.

The reason I live where I do is more complicated than the sorts 4
of things I've been talking about thus far—more complicated and,

I expect, ultimately inexplicable. Or, said another way: anyone other than I may find that the explanation does not satisfy. To start, I live right in the middle of town on three acres of land, land thick with pines a hundred feet tall, oak, wild plum trees, and all manner of tangled, unidentifiable underbrush. The only cleared space is the very narrow road leading down to the house. No lawn. (There are many things I absolutely refuse to do in this world, but the three things leading the list are: wash my car, shine my shoes, and mow a lawn.) The back wall of the room I work in at the rear of the house is glass, and when I raise my eyes from the typewriter I look past an enormous bull bay tree through a thin stand of reeds into a tiny creek, the banks of which are thick with the greenest fern God ever made. In my imagination I can follow that little creek upstream to the place where, after a long, circuitous passage, it joins the Suwannee River, and then follow the dark waters of the Suwannee upriver to the place where it rises in the nearly impenetrable fastness of the Okefenokee Swamp. Okefenokee: Creek Indian word for Land of the Trembling Earth, because most of the islands in the swamp—some of them holding hundreds of huge trees growing so thick that their roots are matted and woven as closely as a blanket—actually float on the water, and when a black bear crashes across one of them, the whole thing trembles.

5 I saw the Okefenokee Swamp long before I saw the Suwannee River, and the Suwannee River long before I saw the little creek I'm looking at as I write this. When I was a boy, I was in the swamp a lot, on the edges of it practically all the time that I was not in the fields working. I went deep into the Okefenokee with T. J., the husband of one of my first cousins. His left leg was cut off at the knee and he wore a peg, but he got along fine with it because we were usually in a flat skiff casting nets for crawfish, which he sold for fish bait at a penny apiece. I did not know enough then and do not know enough now to go into the deep middle swamp, but T. J. did; he knew the twisting maze of sloughs like his back yard, could read every sign of every living thing in the swamp, and made a good living with the crawfish nets and his string of traps and his gun. He sold alligator, wore alligator, and ate alligator. This was long before the federal government made the place a national wildlife refuge.

6 T. J. made his living out of the swamp, and I make mine now out of how the swamp shaped me, how the rhythms and patterns of speech in that time and place are still alive in my mouth today and, more important, alive in my ear. I feed off now and hope always to

feed off the stories I heard told in the early dark around fires where coffee boiled while our clothes, still wet from stringing traps all day, slowly dried to our bodies. Even when I write stories not set in Georgia and not at all about anything in the South, that writing is of necessity still informed by my notions of the world and of what it is to be caught in it. Those notions obviously come out of South Georgia and out of everything that happened to me there, or so I believe.

Living here in North Florida, I am a little more than a hundred miles from where I was born and raised to manhood. I am just far enough away from the only place that was ever mine to still see it, close enough to the only people to whom I was ever kin in ways deeper than blood to still hear them. I know that what I have just written will sound precious and pretentious to many people. So be it. Let them do their work as they will, and I'll do mine. 7

I've tried to work—that is, to write—in Georgia, but I could not. Even under the best of circumstances, at my mama's farm, for instance, it was all too much for me. I was too deep in it, too close to it to use it, to make anything out of it. My memory doesn't even seem to work when I'm writing in Georgia. I can't seem to hold a story in my head. I write a page, and five pages later what I wrote earlier has begun to slide out of focus. If this is all symptomatic of some more profound malaise, I don't want to know about it and I certainly don't want to understand it. 8

Living here in Gainesville seems to give me a kind of geographic and emotional distance I need to write. I can't write if I get too far away. I tried to work on a novel in Tennessee once and after a ruined two months gave it up in despair. I once spent four months near Lake Placid in a beautiful house lent to me by a friend—perfect place to write—and I didn't do a damn thing but eat my guts and look out the window at the mountains. 9

And that, all of it, precious, pretentious, or whatever, is why I live where I live. And unless something happens that I cannot control, I plan to die here. 10

BUILDING VOCABULARY

Central to the essay is the evocation of a certain place. One way that Crews achieves his evocative effects is through diction, that is, through his choice of words. Rewrite the sentences below, finding new words for those that are italicized.

a. ". . . and while the sun *rises lie* on a blanket, brain *singing* from vodka and a *bellyful* of beef, while the *beautiful* bikinied *children* from the University of Florida *drift* down the beach, their *smooth* bodies *sweating* baby oil and the *purest* kind of innocent *lust* (which of course is the *rankest* sort) into the *bright* air" (par. 1).

b. "The *back* wall of the room *where I work in* at the rear of the house is glass, and when I *raise my eyes* from the typewriter I *look past an enormous* bull bay tree *through a thin stand* of reeds into a *tiny* creek, the *banks* of which are *thick with the greenest* fern *God ever made*" (par. 4).

THINKING CRITICALLY ABOUT THE ESSAY

Understanding the Writer's Ideas

1. What do we learn about the writer from his opening paragraph?
2. Why does the writer bother to write his opening paragraph only to end it by saying "that isn't really why" he lives in Gainesville?
3. What do we learn about the writer from the second and third paragraphs? Why does he write these paragraphs if they, too, fail to explain why he lives in Gainesville?
4. In what ways is his reason for living in Gainesville "more complicated" (par. 4) than "the sorts of things" he writes about in paragraphs 1, 2, and 3?
5. Why is the Okefenokee Swamp important to the writer?
6. Why doesn't the writer live in South Georgia?

Understanding the Writer's Techniques

1. How does the writer introduce the *topic* of his essay?
2. In this cause-and-effect essay, what is the cause? Where in the essay is the cause identified?
3. The writer approaches his subject obliquely rather than head-on. Why do you think he takes this approach? What is gained and what is lost as a consequence of this approach?
4. The writer provides a great deal of detail to explain why he lives in Gainesville but little by way of generalizations or "abstract" reasons. His argument, in effect, is made by means of details. What do the details "say"?

5. Why does the writer describe what he sees outside his window (par. 4)?
6. Does this essay have a thesis statement? If so, where is it located in the essay? If not, how does the essay succeed without one?
7. In what ways could what the writer says be interpreted as being "precious and pretentious" (par. 7)?
8. What is the *tone* of this essay? Quote two examples to illustrate the tone.
9. Do you find the essay's conclusion effective? In accord with the tone of the rest of the essay?

Exploring the Writer's Ideas

1. The writer paints a fairly full portrait of himself. Do you like the man portrayed? Offer the details that lead you to like or dislike him, and explain why.
2. Does the writer want to be "liked" or does he want to be "understood"? Explain your answer.
3. Are Crews's reasons for living where he does "precious and pretentious"? Say why you think they are or are not.
4. The concluding sentences in paragraphs 7, 8, and 9 seem insistent or aggressive. Do you think that the writer is overdoing it, pushing away too hard at things he does not want to hear? Or is he just being in character, and explaining himself honestly? Support your answer.

IDEAS FOR WRITING

Prewriting

What sort of place would you *like* to live in? List some of the characteristics of such a place. Think about how that place compares and contrasts with the place where you live now.

Guided Writing

Write an essay titled "Why My Room Is the Way It Is."

1. Begin with an attractive or interesting detail about your room either at home or at college—but a detail that doesn't answer the question Why is my room the way it is?

2. Continue with another feature of your room that does go some way toward answering the question—but that doesn't get to the heart of the matter.
3. Finally, get at the main reason, which should try to mimic Crews in being fairly philosophical, or tending toward the existentially revealing ("I fear the disorder of life and therefore keep my room especially neat.").
4. Offer examples of your having tried to live in your room when it was quite different from the way it is today—and say why that didn't work.
5. End by reaffirming why your room is as it is and saying how you hope always to have a room like the one you have now.

Thinking and Writing Collaboratively

In small groups compare ideas about places people have lived in that they especially liked or disliked. Make a list of outstanding positive and negative qualities that advertisers for towns or cities could promote by claiming the town or city has—or doesn't have—them.

Writing About the Text

Write an essay with one of the following two titles: "Harry Crews: When Do I Get to Meet Him?" or "Harry Crews: A Man I Never Want to Meet." Support your perspective with evidence from the selection.

More Writing Projects

1. In your journal, write one or two real estate ads based on the collaborative project above, aimed at enticing residents to a particular town or city.
2. Choose an activity that you find especially satisfying—fishing, staying in bed till afternoon, collecting buttons—and write a paragraph or two about it as a way of drawing a portrait of yourself that highlights some of your essential qualities.
3. Read a work by Harry Crews—fiction or nonfiction—and write an essay comparing the "persona" that emerges from that work with the one found in this selection.

When Bright Girls Decide That Math Is "a Waste of Time"

Susan Jacoby

The journalist Susan Jacoby was born in 1945. She received a B.F.A. from the University of Iowa. She has published widely in newspapers and magazines, and is author of *Half-Jew: A Daughter's Search for Her Family's Buried Past* (2000). In this article, which appeared originally in the *New York Times* on June 2, 1983, Jacoby explains how cultural expectations and societal stereotyping are overshadowed by women's own decisions to keep themselves away from scientific and technological studies. Notice how she uses narrative and process analysis to reinforce the causes and effects she is exploring here.

PREREADING: THINKING ABOUT THE ESSAY IN ADVANCE

This article focuses on the reasons why women perform poorly in one academic subject, mathematics. How would you explain this phenomenon? What causes might you identify? Are there academic subjects or professional areas where women are less able or more able to succeed than men? Why or why not?

Words to Watch

sanguine (par. 3) cheerful, hopeful
vulnerable (par. 6) open to attack or suggestion
syndrome (par. 7) a group of symptoms that characterize a condition
akin to (par. 7) similar to
phobia (par. 7) an excessive fear of something
constitute (par. 7) to make up; compose
epitomize (par. 8) to be a prime example of
prone to (par. 15) disposed to; susceptible to
accede to (par. 16) give in to

Susannah, a 16-year-old who has always been an A student in every subject from algebra to English, recently informed her parents that she intended to drop physics and calculus in her senior year of high school and replace them with a drama seminar and a 1 work-study program. She expects to major in art or history in college, she explained, and "any more science or math will just be a waste of my time."

2 Her parents were neither concerned by nor opposed to her decision. "Fine, dear," they said. Their daughter is, after all, an outstanding student. What does it matter if, at age 16, she has taken a step that may limit her understanding of both machines and the natural world for the rest of her life?

3 This kind of decision, in which girls turn away from studies that would give them a sure footing in the world of science and technology, is a self-inflicted female disability that is, regrettably, almost as common today as it was when I was in high school. If Susannah had announced that she had decided to stop taking English in her senior year, her mother and father would have been horrified. I also think they would have been a good deal less sanguine about her decision if she were a boy.

4 In saying that scientific and mathematical ignorance is a self-inflicted female wound, I do not, obviously, mean that cultural expectations play no role in the process. But the world does not conspire to deprive modern women of access to science as it did in the 1930's, when Rosalyn S. Yalow, the Nobel Prize-winning physicist, graduated from Hunter College and was advised to go to work as a secretary because no graduate school would admit her to its physics department. The current generation of adolescent girls—and their parents, bred on old expectations about women's interests—are active conspirators in limiting their own intellectual development.

5 It is true that the proportion of young women in science-related graduate and professional schools, most notably medical schools, has increased significantly in the past decade. It is also true that so few women were studying advanced science and mathematics before the early 1970's that the percentage increase in female enrollment does not yet translate into large numbers of women actually working in science.

6 The real problem is that so many girls eliminate themselves from any serious possibility of studying science as a result of decisions made during the vulnerable period of midadolescence, when they are most likely to be influenced—on both conscious and subconscious levels—by the traditional belief that math and science are "masculine" subjects.

During the teen-age years the well-documented phenomenon of "math anxiety" strikes girls who never had any problem handling numbers during earlier schooling. Some men, too, experience this syndrome—a form of panic, akin to a phobia, at any task involving numbers—but women constitute the overwhelming majority of sufferers. The onset of acute math anxiety during the teen-age years is, as Stalin was fond of saying, "not by accident." 7

In adolescence girls begin to fear that they will be unattractive to boys if they are typed as "brains." Science and math epitomize unfeminine braininess in a way that, say, foreign languages do not. High-school girls who pursue an advanced interest in science and math (unless they are students at special institutions like the Bronx High School of Science where everyone is a brain) usually find that they are greatly outnumbered by boys in their classes. They are, therefore, intruding on male turf at a time when their sexual confidence, as well as that of the boys, is most fragile. 8

A 1981 assessment of female achievement in mathematics, based on research conducted under a National Institute for Education grant, found significant differences in the mathematical achievements of 9th and 12th graders. At age 13 girls were equal to or slightly better than boys in tests involving algebra, problem solving and spatial ability; four years later the boys had outstripped the girls. 9

It is not mysterious that some very bright high-school girls suddenly decide that math is "too hard" and "a waste of time." In my experience, self-sabotage of mathematical and scientific ability is often a conscious process. I remember deliberately pretending to be puzzled by geometry problems in my sophomore year in high school. A male teacher called me in after class and said, in a baffled tone, "I don't see how you can be having so much trouble when you got straight A's last year in my algebra class." 10

The decision to avoid advanced biology, chemistry, physics and calculus in high school automatically restricts academic and professional choices that ought to be wide open to anyone beginning college. At all coeducational universities women are overwhelmingly concentrated in the fine arts, social sciences and traditionally female departments like education. Courses leading to degrees in science- and technology-related fields are filled mainly by men. 11

12 In my generation, the practical consequences of mathematical and scientific illiteracy are visible in the large number of special programs to help professional women overcome the anxiety they feel when they are promoted into jobs that require them to handle statistics.

13 The consequences of this syndrome should not, however, be viewed in narrowly professional terms. Competence in science and math does not mean one is going to become a scientist or mathematician any more than competence in writing English means one is going to become a professional writer. Scientific and mathematical illiteracy—which has been cited in several recent critiques by panels studying American education from kindergarten through college—produces an incalculably impoverished vision of human experience.

14 Scientific illiteracy is not, of course, the exclusive province of women. In certain intellectual circles it has become fashionable to proclaim a willed, aggressive ignorance about science and technology. Some female writers specialize in ominous, uninformed diatribes against genetic research as a plot to remove control of childbearing from women, while some well-known men of letters proudly announce that they understand absolutely nothing about computers, or, for that matter, about electricity. This lack of understanding is nothing in which women or men ought to take pride.

15 Failure to comprehend either computers or chromosomes leads to a terrible sense of helplessness, because the profound impact of science on everyday life is evident even to those who insist they don't, won't, can't understand why the changes are taking place. At this stage of history women are more prone to such feelings of helplessness than men because the culture judges their ignorance less harshly and because women themselves acquiesce in that indulgence.

16 Since there is ample evidence of such feelings in adolescence, it is up to parents to see that their daughters do not accede to the old stereotypes about "masculine" and "feminine" knowledge. Unless we want our daughters to share our intellectual handicaps, we had better tell them no, they can't stop taking mathematics and science at the ripe old age of 16.

BUILDING VOCABULARY

1. Use a dictionary to look up any unfamiliar words in the phrases below from Jacoby's essay. Then, write a short explanation of each expression.
   - **a.** sure footing (par. 3)
   - **b.** cultural expectations (par. 4)
   - **c.** overwhelming majority (par. 7)
   - **d.** male turf (par. 8)
   - **e.** spatial ability (par. 9)
   - **f.** the exclusive province (par. 14)
   - **g.** ominous, uninformed diatribes (par. 14)
   - **h.** acquiesce in that indulgence (par. 15)
   - **i.** ample evidence (par. 16)
   - **j.** our intellectual handicaps (par. 16)
2. Explain the *connotations* (see Glossary) that the following words have for you. Use each word correctly in a sentence of your own.
   - **a.** disability (par. 3)
   - **b.** conspire (par. 4)
   - **c.** adolescent (par. 4)
   - **d.** vulnerable (par. 6)
   - **e.** acute (par. 7)

THINKING CRITICALLY ABOUT THE ESSAY

Understanding the Writer's Ideas

1. What condition is Jacoby trying to analyze? Is the main *effect* analyzed in this cause-and-effect analysis? On what primary cause does she blame women's "scientific and mathematical ignorance"? What exactly does she mean by that term? How is society to blame? What is the "process" mentioned in paragraph 4? What point does the example of Rosalyn S. Yalow illustrate?
2. Why does Jacoby think that the greater proportion of women students now in science and medical graduate and professional schools does not really mean that there are many women working in these areas?

3. According to Jacoby, when do most girls decide not to study the sciences? Why does this happen?
4. What is "math anxiety"? Who suffers more from it—boys or girls? Why? What does the author mean by "brains" (par. 8)?
5. Who was Joseph Stalin (par. 7)?
6. What subjects does Jacoby identify as "feminine"? Which are "unfeminine"?
7. According to the research evidence discussed in paragraph 9, how do the math abilities of girls and boys change between ninth and tenth grades? What does Jacoby say is the *cause* of this change? What are the *results?*
8. Explain what Jacoby means by the expression "self-inflicted female wound" (par. 4) and "self-sabotage" (par. 10). How are these expressions similar? How are they different?
9. What is the difference between what men and women study at coeducational universities?
10. What does Jacoby mean by "mathematical and scientific illiteracy" (par. 12)? Do only women suffer from this syndrome? According to Jacoby, why does it lead to "an incalculably impoverished vision of human experience"? What does she mean by this phrase? What examples of scientific illiteracy does Jacoby offer?
11. Why does the author think women feel more helpless than men do about scientific changes?
12. What suggestion does Jacoby offer in her conclusion?

Understanding the Writer's Techniques

1. What is the thesis statement of this essay? Why is it placed where it is? Find another statement before it that expresses a similar cause-and-effect relation. How are the two different?
2. Which paragraphs make up the introductory section of this essay? What cause-and-effect relation does Jacoby establish and how does she present it? How does Jacoby use narration in her introduction? How does she use illustration?
3. Both sentences of paragraph 5 begin with the phrase "It is true," yet the sentences contradict each other. How and why does the author set up this contradiction? What is the effect on Jacoby's analysis of beginning paragraph 6 with the words "The real problem is . . ."?

4. How does she use *process analysis* (see pages 411–412) from paragraph 6 to paragraph 8?
5. Where does the author use definition in this essay?
6. Trace the cause-and-effect developments in paragraphs 7 and 8.
7. In paragraph 9, Jacoby mentions a study conducted under "a National Institute for Education grant." How does the evidence she presents support her position in the essay?
8. What is the effect of the phrase "in my experience" in paragraph 10? What expository technique does she use there?
9. Trace the cause-and-effect patterns in paragraphs 11 through 13. Be sure to show the interrelation between the causes and the effects (that is, how the effect of something can also be the cause of something else).
10. How is the first sentence of paragraph 15 ("Failure to comprehend. . . .") a good example in itself of cause-and-effect development?
11. Why does Jacoby use quotation marks around the words "masculine" and "feminine" in the phrase "'masculine' and 'feminine' knowledge" (par. 16)?
12. What is the overall tone of this essay? At three points, Jacoby switches tone and uses *irony* (see Glossary). Explain the irony in the following sentences.
    - **a.** What does it matter if, at age 16, she has taken a step that may limit her understanding of both machines and the natural world for the rest of her life? (par. 2)
    - **b.** The onset of acute math anxiety during the teenage years is, as Stalin was fond of saying, "not by accident." (par. 7)
    - **c.** Unless we want our daughters to share our intellectual handicaps, we had better tell them no, they can't stop taking mathematics and science at the ripe old age of 16. (par. 16)

    Compare the irony in paragraph 16 with that in paragraph 2. How is the impact the same or different?
13. Who do you think is the intended audience for this essay? Cite evidence for your answer.
14. Jacoby uses a variety of transitional devices to connect smoothly the ideas expressed in the various paragraphs of this essay. Look especially at paragraphs 1 to 4. How does the writer achieve coherence between paragraphs? What transitional elements do you find in the opening sentences of each of those paragraphs? What other transitions do you find throughout the essay?

Exploring the Writer's Ideas

1. One of the underlying suggestions in this essay is that society has long considered there to be "masculine" and "feminine" subjects to study. What is your opinion on this issue? Do you feel that any subjects are particularly more suited to men or women? Which? Why? Are there any other school activities that you feel are exclusively masculine or feminine? Why? Are there any jobs that are more suited to men or women?
2. In paragraph 4, Jacoby mentions the "old expectations about women's interests." What do you think these expectations are? What do you consider *new* expectations for women?
3. A *stereotype* is an opinion of a category of people that is unoriginal and often based on strong prejudices. For example, some prejudicial stereotypes include "All immigrants are lazy"; "All Republicans are rich"; "All women are terrible drivers." What other stereotypes do you know? Where do you think they originate?
4. The general implication of paragraph 8 is that people minimize their skills in order to be socially acceptable. In your experience, where have you seen this principle operating? Do you agree that people sometimes pretend to be unable to achieve something? What motivates them, do you think?
5. A recent study shows that among major nations in the world America's students—boys and girls—are the worst mathematics students. How do you account for the poor showing of Americans as mathematicians? How would you remedy this situation?

IDEAS FOR WRITING

Prewriting

Think about an activity that seems either male-friendly or female-friendly. Take complete notes on the reasons or causes that explain the situations.

Guided Writing

Select a job or profession that is usually male-dominated. Write a cause-and-effect analysis explaining how and why women both have been excluded from this profession and (or) have self-selected themselves from the job. (Some examples may include fire fighters, physicians, marines, bank executives, and carpenters.)

1. Begin with an anecdote to illustrate the condition that you are analyzing.
2. Present and analyze the partial causes of this condition that arise from society's expectations and norms.
3. State your main point clearly in a thesis statement.
4. Clearly identify what you consider "the real problem."
5. If you believe that women have deliberately excluded themselves, explain when and how the process of self-selection begins for women.
6. Analyze the consequences of this process of self-selection and give examples of the results of it.
7. Provide evidence that supports your analysis.
8. Link paragraphs with appropriate transitions.
9. In your conclusion offer a suggestion to change or improve this situation.

Thinking and Writing Collaboratively

Exchange a draft version of your Guided Writing assignment with a classmate. Review your partner's essay for its success in following the recommended guidelines. Is the thesis stated clearly? Are both the main causes and minor causes presented, and with sufficient evidence to support the analysis? Write a brief evaluation of the essay, with recommendations for revision, before returning it.

Writing About the Text

Write an essay that explores Jacoby's assertion that lack of competence in science and math "produces an incalculably impoverished vision of human experience" (par. 13). Has she made a valid point?

More Writing Projects

1. In your journal, make a list of everything that comes into your mind about the word "mathematics." Do not edit your writing. When you are finished, share your list with other people in the class. How do your impressions compare? contrast?

2. In a paragraph, analyze why you think boys and men exclude themselves from a certain field or profession—nursing, cooking, grammar-school teaching, and so on.
3. Margaret Mead, the famous anthropologist, once wrote, "Women in our society complain of the lack of stimulation, of the loneliness, of the dullness of staying at home." In an essay write a causal analysis of this situation.

SUMMING UP: CHAPTER 10

1. Susan Jacoby analyzes a kind of "self-destructive behavior" on the part of young women. Write an essay about a friend, relative, or someone else close to you who is doing something that you feel will have a very negative effect on him or her. Analyze *why* he or she is doing this and what effects, both short- and long-term, these actions are likely to have.
2. In this chapter, we hear female voices analyzing some of the experiences of women in American life today. Using their approaches to causal analysis, examine these experiences and the impact that they have had on your own thinking and activities. Clarify the connections between what you have read and how your sense of self has deepened or been sharpened.
3. Working in small groups, develop a questionnaire focusing on male and female roles in our society. After the questionnaire has been prepared, each group member should interview at least three people. When all the interviews have been completed, each group should write a collective analysis of the results and present the analysis to the class.
4. For the next week, keep a journal about something that is currently causing you to have mixed emotions. (Note: This should not be the same issues you've written about in the Guided Writing exercise following the essay by Stephen King; it should be a *current* issue.) Try to write five reasons each day (or expand upon previous ones). At the end of the week, write an essay that analyzes how the issue is affecting your life or how you plan to deal with it in the future.
5. The essays in this chapter portray causes that are well captured by Anne Roiphe's distinction between "the outside weather" and "the inner climate" (par. 2). Do things happen because of an "inherent" cause or something external? Is Fate the maker of character or is character Fate? Write an essay to explore these alternative explanations of effects, using as resources the essays in this chapter.
6. The essays in this chapter identify inner drives that seem to function as compulsions—as things that just have to be, that have to come out of us no matter what. King writes about our anticivilizational emotions, Roiphe about seeking to rectify unconscious childhood longings through our choice of marriage partners, Crews about being driven to live where he does, and Jacoby about unconscious surrender to self-destructive forces.

Write an essay that analyzes these writers' responses to the compulsions they describe.

7. Compare and contrast Anne Roiphe's view of how cause and effect operates in failing marriages with Katha Pollitt's view of how it operates in child-rearing.
8. What do you think Anne Roiphe would say about Harry Crews's remark that if his needing to be not too close and not too far from home in order to write "is all symptomatic of some more profound malaise, [he doesn't] want to know about it and [he] certainly [doesn't] want to understand it"?
9. Do you think the causes Jacoby identifies for the general aversion many girls have to math are right? If so, what—if anything—do you believe schools or society could do to change things? If not, what other causes might you identify?

FROM SEEING TO WRITING

Why has the person in this photograph been stopped by a police officer? Analyze some of the possible causal relationships, moving from the obvious (she was speeding) to more subtle and complex causes. Offer a complete analysis in which you consider a range of possible main and secondary causes as well as possible effects.

Jim Whitmer/Stock Boston

CHAPTER 11

Argumentation and Persuasion

WHAT ARE ARGUMENTATION AND PERSUASION?

When we use *argumentation,* we aim to convince someone to join our side of an issue. Often, we want the readers or listeners to change their views and adopt ours. We also use *persuasion* when we want a person to take action in a way that will advance our cause. Both argumentation, which appeals to reason, and persuasion, which appeals to emotions, aim to convince an audience to agree with your opinion or position.

In everyday life we hear the word "argument" used as a synonym for "fight." In writing, however, an argument is not a brawl but a train of thought directed toward a well-focused goal. Usually an argument has a topic that can be debated, and an argument should reflect the ethical and critical standards that apply to debate. Although argument naturally includes emotion and even passion, a good argument avoids mere emotional appeals. A good argument appeals to reason. Consequently, argument relies on logic more than do other kinds of writing. At the same time, all writing—analysis, narrative, even description—can be said to be a form of argument. Whatever we write, we want the reader to get our point, and if possible to see it our way. This proposition can be reversed, as well. Just as all writing includes some form of argument, so, too, argumentation draws on all the writers' tools that you have learned so far. In preparing your argumentative essay, you will be able to rehearse and refine the skills you have learned to this point.

The first step in arguing successfully is to state your position clearly. This means that a good thesis is crucial to your essay. For argumentative or persuasive essays, the thesis is sometimes called a *major proposition,* or a *claim.* Through your major proposition, you take a definite position in a debate, and by taking a strong position, you give your essay its argumentative edge. Your readers must know what your position is and must see that you have supported your main idea with convincing minor points. The weakest arguments are those in which the writer tries to take both sides and as a result persuades no one. As you will see in the reading selections, writers often concede or yield a point to the opposition, but they do so only to strengthen the side that they favor.

Writing arguments should make you even more aware of the need to think about audience. In particular, in writing you need to think about the people who will make up their minds on the basis of your evidence. As you consider how to present your case, think about what kind of language, what kinds of examples, and what general tone will speak most persuasively to your audience. As well, keep in mind that readers are rarely persuaded simply by assertion; you can't just tell them something is true. You need to show them through well-organized support of the main and minor points that support your major proposition or claim. In this respect you might say that there are two audiences for an argumentative essay: the actual, living audience of readers; and something that you might see as the "court of standards"—the rules of logic and of evidence. The actual audience is in fact more likely to be convinced of your case if it follows these rules and meets the standards for debate. Moreover, an essential feature of argument is credibility. An excellent way to establish and sustain your credibility is to follow the rules of logic and of evidence faithfully.

Evidence or support can come from many sources. Among the most powerful forms of evidence are facts, whether these are drawn from the historical record, from reliable statistical sources, or from personal experience. Another common form of evidence is expert opinion. If, for example, you are writing an essay about cleaning up pollution in a river, you may want to rely on statements from scientists or environmental engineers to support your point. Indeed, you may have come to your own conclusions on the basis of authoritative information or opinion.

In addition to evidence, writers often depend on analysis of the opponent's points or the opponent's evidence to advance their own arguments. (See, for example, the essay by James Q. Wilson on pp. 449–452.) Finally, a writer can of course use narrative, description, comparison and contrast, illustration, and definition to persuade.

Because we use argument in everyday life, we may think it is easy to argue in writing—but just the opposite is true. If we are arguing with someone in person, we can *see* our opponent's response and quickly change our direction. In writing, we can only imagine the opponent and so must carefully prepare evidence for all possible responses. Moreover, although the evening news may expose us to arguments, about abortion clinics, increasing the minimum wage, or accusations of sexual harassment, we often see only what media experts call "sound bites," tiny fragments of information. We may see just a slogan as a picket sign passes a camera. We may hear only a few sentences out of hours of testimony. We seldom see or hear the entire argument. When we turn to writing arguments ourselves, we need to remember to develop a complete and detailed and *rational* argument.

This does not mean that written arguments lack emotion. Rather, written argument channels that emotion into a powerful eloquence that can endure much longer than a shouting match. The writer states the major proposition, or point he or she wants to make, and keeps it firmly in front of the reader. To do this, a writer must have a clear sense of his or her purpose and audience and play the argument accordingly.

A wide range of topics—and of purposes and intended audiences—are possible. For example, a writer may want to argue that the U.S. government should grant amnesty to illegal aliens who have been in the country for at least two years. He may be writing to his member of Congress to persuade her to take action on a proposed bill. Or the writer may want to convince a group of readers, such as readers of the local newspaper, that something is true—that single fathers make excellent parents, for example, or that wife abuse is an increasingly serious crime in our society.

Whatever the writer's topic, the keys to a good argument are

- a clear and effective major proposition or claim
- a reasonable tone
- an abundance of evidence
- an avoidance of personal attacks

ORGANIZATION OF THE CHAPTER

Because of the nature of argumentation, we have organized this chapter differently from the others so as to highlight more than usual the issues—the ideas, the techniques—raised in the selections. Since argument always implies an opposing view, we have, first, provided two sets of pro and con essays on topics of broad social interest: reparations for slavery and the death penalty. Second, to help readers get a view of the complexities of general themes, we have grouped essays under two thematic headings: issues of identity and issues of political rights. Here are the selections you will find in this chapter:

HOW DO WE READ ARGUMENTS?

Try to find out something about the background and credentials of the writer. In what way is he or she an expert on the topic?

Is the proposition presented in a rational and logical way? Is it credible and presented accurately and fairly? What reasons (or minor propositions) are used to support the writer's claim, and are they convincing?

Has the writer presented ample reliable evidence to back up the proposition? (If you look at the headlines on supermarket tabloid newspapers that try to persuade us that aliens have been keeping Elvis Presley alive on Mars, you will see why it is important to be able to evaluate a writer's evidence before accepting the proposition!)

Does the writer consider the counterarguments and deal effectively with the opposition?

HOW DO WE WRITE ARGUMENTS?

State a clear major proposition, and stick to it.

Convince readers of the validity of your thesis by making an essay plan that introduces *minor propositions.* These are assertions that help clarify the reasons you offer to support your main idea.

Use *refutation.* This is a technique in which you anticipate what an opponent will say and answer the objection ahead of time. Another technique is *concession.* You yield a small point to your opponent but at the same time claim a larger point on your own side. Using these techniques makes your argument seem fairer. You acknowledge that there *are* at least two sides to the issue. Moreover, these devices help you make your own point more effectively.

Be aware of these pitfalls:

- Avoid personal attacks on your opponent, and don't let excessive appeals to emotion damage the tone of your argument.
- Avoid hasty generalization—that is, using a general statement about a subject without properly supporting it.
- Avoid drawing a conclusion that does not follow from the evidence in your argument.
- Avoid faulty analogies—that is, comparing two things or situations that are not really comparable.

Writing the Draft

Begin the rough draft. State your thesis or main proposition boldly.
Back up all minor propositions with

statistics
facts
testimony from authorities
personal experience

Find a reliable listener and read your essay aloud. Encourage your listener to refute your points as strongly as possible.

Revise the essay, taking into account your listener's refutations. Find better support for your weakest points. Write a new draft.

Revise the essay carefully. Read it aloud again if possible. Prepare a final copy.

A STUDENT PARAGRAPH: ARGUMENTATION AND PERSUASION

In the following paragraph, the student begins quite forcibly by stating his position on custody battles during divorce cases—in other words, in an argumentative mode. Examine the simple but effective way he provides evidence for his position.

The outcomes of custody battles during divorce proceedings exemplify the outrageous prejudice against fathers in our culture. Recently, the Houston Chronicle reported on the outcome of a child custody case the paper had followed for nearly six months. In the case, both father and mother wanted sole custody of their only child. The mother, a defense attorney at a high-flying Houston firm, worked 60–70 hours a week; she had maintained this schedule from the time the child, now six, was two months old. She frequently spent at least one weekend day at the office; she traveled on business as many as 10 weeks out of the year. The father, a freelance writer who worked at home, was acknowledged by both spouses to be the child's primary caretaker, and to have filled this role from the time the child was two months old

Main proposition; "outrageous" a cue for sympathy

Cites authority to support main proposition

Case study provides evidence

and the wife returned to work. He typically woke the child, prepared breakfast, helped her choose clothing to wear, packed her a lunch, and walked her to school. He picked her up from school, accompanied her on playdates or took her to play in the park, made dinner for them both, helped the child with her homework, bathed her, read her a story, and put her to sleep. The mother ordinarily arrived home from work after the child was already asleep, and often left for work before the child was awake. Guess who got custody? The mother, of course. Sadly, judges persist in assuming that mothers are always the better—the more "natural"—caretaker. This assumption leads them all too often to award custody to the mother, despite evidence in many cases that the child has been raised primarily by the father, and would be better off continuing in his care.

Identification of opposition: conservative judges

Refutation and conclusion that reinforces main proposition

ARGUMENTS PRO AND CON: REPARATIONS FOR SLAVERY:

At the heart of the history of the United States is the grim legacy of slavery. The time when the United States was a slave-owning nation, moreover, is not that long ago: there are people alive today whose grandparents were slaves. What should be done about the legacy of slavery? The essays below, by two prominent African-American scholars, stake out sharply opposing views on this question. Manning Marable argues that "the fundamental problem of American democracy in the twenty-first century" is the "accumulated disadvantage" that black Americans continue to suffer because of "racist stereotypes and white indifference." He favors reparations for slavery. In contrast, Shelby Steele says that the "worst enemy black America faces today is not white racism but white guilt." White guilt, he says, distracts black Americans from attending to their own development, and so sustains injustice. He is opposed to reparations.

As you read these essays—both careful, eloquent, and reasoned—look attentively at the kinds of evidence these writers use to support their points. Do they agree on the evidence? What implicit and explicit values do these writers bring to their essays?

An Idea Whose Time Has Come . . .

Manning Marable

Manning Marable is Professor of History and Political Science as well as director of the Institute for Research in African-American Studies at Columbia University. A graduate of Earlham College with a Ph.D. from the University of Maryland (1976), Marable has published extensively on issues relating to African-Americans. His works include *How Capitalism Underdeveloped Black America* (1983), *Black Liberalism in Conservative America* (1997), and *Black Leadership* (1998). This selection appeared originally, along with the following selection by Shelby Steele, in *Newsweek* on August 27, 2001.

PREREADING: THINKING ABOUT THE ESSAY IN ADVANCE

How can past injustice be rectified? The victims of the Nazi Holocaust have received monetary reparations from the German government. Should the United States government, in a similar fashion, pay monetary reparations to the descendants of slaves? Is the United States now ready to accept this idea, which has been rejected in the past?

Words to Watch

Jim Crow (par. 1) name associated with a stereotypical black character in nineteenth century minstrel shows, later applied to laws and practices in the South that discriminated against African-Americans

paradoxically (par. 5) in apparent contradiction

net (par. 7) what is left (e.g., income or worth) after all deductions (taxes, costs, debts, etc.)

recession (par. 8) an economic downturn, when the economy is shrinking

1 In 1854 my great-grandfather, Morris Marable, was sold on an auction block in Georgia for $500. For his white slave master, the sale was just "business as usual." But to Morris Marable and his heirs, slavery was a crime against our humanity. This pattern of human-rights violations against enslaved African-Americans continued under Jim Crow segregation for nearly another century.

The fundamental problem of American democracy in the 21st century is the problem of "structural racism": the deep patterns of socioeconomic inequality and accumulated disadvantage that are coded by race, and constantly justified in public discourse by both racist stereotypes and white indifference. Do Americans have the capacity and vision to dismantle these structural barriers that deny democratic rights and opportunities to millions of their fellow citizens? 2

This country has previously witnessed two great struggles to achieve a truly multicultural democracy. 3

The First Reconstruction (1865–1877) ended slavery and briefly gave black men voting rights, but gave no meaningful compensation for two centuries of unpaid labor. The promise of "40 acres and a mule" was for most blacks a dream deferred. 4

The Second Reconstruction (1954–1968), or the modern civil-rights movement, outlawed legal segregation in public accommodations and gave blacks voting rights. But these successes paradoxically obscure the tremendous human costs of historically accumulated disadvantage that remain central to black Americans' lives. 5

The disproportionate wealth that most whites enjoy today was first constructed from centuries of unpaid black labor. Many white institutions, including Ivy League universities, insurance companies and banks, profited from slavery. This pattern of white privilege and black inequality continues today. 6

Demanding reparations is not just about compensation for slavery and segregation. It is, more important, an educational campaign to highlight the contemporary reality of "racial deficits" of all kinds, the unequal conditions that impact blacks regardless of class. Structural racism's barriers include "equity inequity," the absence of black capital formation that is a direct consequence of America's history. One third of all black households actually have negative net wealth. In 1998 the typical black family's net wealth was $16,400, less than one fifth that of white families. Black families are denied home loans at twice the rate of whites. 7

Blacks remain the last hired and first fired during recessions. During the 1990–91 recession, African-Americans suffered disproportionately. At Coca-Cola, 42 percent of employees who lost their jobs were black. At Sears, 54 percent were black. Blacks have significantly shorter life expectancies, in part due to racism 8 in the health establishment. Blacks are statistically less likely than whites to be referred for kidney transplants or early-stage cancer surgery.

9 In criminal justice, African-Americans constitute only one seventh of all drug users. Yet we account for 35 percent of all drug arrests, 55 percent of drug convictions and 75 percent of prison admissions for drug offenses.

10 White Americans today aren't guilty of carrying out slavery and segregation. But whites have a moral and political responsibility to acknowledge the continuing burden of history's structural racism.

11 A reparations trust fund could be established, with the goal of closing the socioeconomic gaps between blacks and whites. Funds would be targeted specifically toward poor, disadvantaged communities with the greatest need, not to individuals. Let's eliminate the racial unfairness in capital markets that perpetuates black poverty. A national commitment to expand black homeownership, full employment and quality health care would benefit all Americans, regardless of race.

12 Reparations could begin America's Third Reconstruction, the final chapter in the 400-year struggle to abolish slavery and its destructive consequences. As Malcolm X said in 1961, hundreds of years of racism and labor exploitation are "worth more than a cup of coffee at a white café. We are here to collect back wages."

BUILDING VOCABULARY

Issues involving ethnic identity are complex and emotional and touch on personal sensitivities as well as broad questions of social justice. The use of terms related to ethnicity and race is, therefore, a serious, even troubling matter. What is the proper and respectful word to use in referring to the descendants of American slaves? Martin Luther King, Jr., writing in 1963, uses the word *Negro* (see pp. 506–509). Shelby Steele uses the word *black.* And Manning Marable uses both *black* and the hyphenated expression *African-American.* Using etymological dictionaries and related sources, trace the evolution of these terms. What accounts for the use of these different terms? What other words in public discourse have also over time reflected the changing outlook and situation of groups within American society?

THINKING CRITICALLY ABOUT THE ESSAY

Understanding the Writer's Ideas

1. Why does Marable begin his essay by alluding to his great-grandfather?
2. What answer does Marable imply to the question he asks in paragraph 2?
3. According to Marable, what did "First Reconstruction" achieve? What did it not achieve?
4. What does Marable think the civil-rights movement left undone?
5. How, according to Marable, was the wealth of white Americans "constructed"?
6. In addition to being about compensation for past injustice, what purpose does the campaign for reparations serve?
7. What evidence does Marable provide to illustrate the continuing economic inequality suffered by African-Americans?
8. What would be the function of reparations, in economic and political terms?

Understanding the Writer's Techniques

1. What is Marable's "major proposition" (see p. 423)?
2. What minor propositions does Marable use to support his major one?
3. Paraphrase Marable's argument. Is it logical?
4. What kinds of evidence does Marable use to support his argument?
5. What do you think is Marable's strongest logical point? Discuss why you think this is so.
6. What do you think is Marable's strongest piece of evidence? Discuss why you think this is so. Why does Marable use examples to support some of his assertions while leaving other assertions unsupported?
7. How does Marable support his point that "whites have a moral and political responsibility to acknowledge the continuing burden of history's structural racism" (par. 10)?
8. Is Marable's conclusion an effective close for his argument? Why or why not?

MIXING PATTERNS

How does Marable use cause-and-effect analysis? Illustration?

Exploring the Writer's Ideas

1. Why is the "fundamental problem" we face in the coming century "structural racism"? What support does Marable provide for this statement? What kinds of supporting argument or evidence, if any, do you find lacking?
2. Marable says that the demand for reparations is mainly an educational campaign to highlight contemporary racial inequalities. Do you agree that this is an effective method for achieving that goal? Why or why not?
3. Steele makes the point that "there is no justice for past suffering" (p. 438). We can assume that Marable and Steele are familiar with each other's work and ideas. How, if at all, does Marable's essay reflect an awareness of Steele's point?
4. Does "acknowledgment" of "structural racism" (par. 10) necessarily translate into reparations? Does Marable persuasively argue for the connection? What other kinds of acknowledgments could you think of? Do you think that Marable would find these acceptable?

IDEAS FOR WRITING

Prewriting

Can you think of anything that happened to your grandparents or to other ancestors that might merit reparations? For example, were they forced to emigrate from their native land because of injustice? Did their work result in debilitating or fatal diseases, such as lung cancer? Think of what arguments you might make to justify a claim—against a government, a company—for reparations.

Guided Writing

Write an essay arguing for reparations by a local or national government for the descendants of people whose ancestors have been harmed by a former policy of that government. Before writing, research the topic to obtain some basic facts.

1. Begin by asserting that the people in question were victims of the policy.
2. Indicate the long-term consequences for these people of the policy—such as discrimination, economic loss, poor education, and so on.
3. Suggest that this great tragedy and its long-term effects have been downplayed, even though the effects persist to this day.
4. Suggest that a demand for reparations is as much an educational tool as a demand for compensation.
5. Indicate that compensation would reflect a final acknowledgment by the government of its responsibility for these problems.
6. Write a rebuttal to the objection that the people in question have overcome adversity and do not need reparations.
7. Conclude by saying that only reparations can close the book on this bitter chapter in history.

Thinking and Writing Collaboratively

Divide into two equal groups, one of which will argue in favor of Marable's point that "the fundamental problem of American democracy is the problem of 'structural racism'" and one of which will argue against this view. The group that supports Marable's view should think of arguments and facts to add to those he has already given to support this point. The group that opposes Marable's view should think of arguments and facts that refute his point. After debating the issue, reconvene as a class and discuss the arguments and evidence that each side has offered.

Writing About the Text

After a careful analysis of paragraphs 10 and 11 in Marable's essay, write an argument maintaining either that these paragraphs are the persuasive climax of his essay or that they expose serious weaknesses in his argument.

More Writing Ideas

1. Write notes in your journal for an essay that supports or takes issue with Marable's point that structural racism persists in today's America.
2. Write two or three paragraphs that take issue with Marable's argument, in paragraph 5, that the civil-rights movement has had a paradoxical effect.
3. Write an essay that explores the implications of Marable's view that contemporary society is responsible for tempering and offering recompense for injustices of the past.

. . . Or a Childish Illusion of Justice?

Shelby Steele

A research fellow at the Hoover Institution at Stanford University, Shelby Steele was born in Chicago in 1946 and educated at Coe College in Iowa, at Southern Illinois University, and at the University of Utah, from which he earned his Ph.D. Steele came to national attention with publication of the best-seller *The Content of Our Character: A New Vision of Race in America,* which won the National Book Critics Circle Award in 1991. A frequent commentator on *Nightline* and *60 Minutes,* Steele most recently has published *A Dream Deferred: The Second Betrayal of Black Freedom in America* (1999). This selection, along with the previous selection by Manning Marable, originally appeared in *Newsweek* on August 27, 2001.

PREREADING: THINKING ABOUT THE ESSAY IN ADVANCE

Is justice an illusion? Is there any way to repair the hurt of a victim of grave injustice? Even if injustice cannot be erased—what has happened, has happened—is there anything meaningful that can be done?

Words to Watch

plausibly (par. 1) reasonably
crucible (par. 2) a severe test
cuisine (par. 2) food culture
scion (par. 3) descendant
subsidized (par. 5) provided money for support
mark (par. 9) target

My father was born in the last year of the 19th century. His father was very likely born into slavery, though there are no official records to confirm this. Still, from family accounts, I can plausibly argue that my grandfather was born a slave. 1

When I tell people this, I worry that I may seem conceited, like someone claiming a connection to royalty. The extreme experience of slavery—its commitment to broken-willed servitude—was so intense a crucible that it must have taken a kind of genius to survive it. In the jaws of slavery and segregation, blacks created a life-sustaining form of worship, rituals for every human 2 initiation from childbirth to death, a rich folk mythology, a world-famous written literature, a complete cuisine, a truth-telling comic sensibility and, of course, some of the most glorious music the world has ever known.

3 Like the scion of an aristocratic family, I mention my grandfather to stand a little in the light of the black American genius. So my first objection to reparation for slavery is that it feels like selling our birthright for a pot of porridge. There is a profound esteem that comes to us from having overcome four centuries of oppression.

4 This esteem is an irreplaceable resource. In Richard Wright's "Black Boy," a black elevator operator makes pocket money by letting white men kick him in the behind for a quarter. Maybe reparations are not quite this degrading, but when you trade on the past victimization of your own people, you trade honor for dollars. And this trading is only uglier when you are a mere descendent of those who suffered but nevertheless prevailed.

5 I believe the greatest problem black America has had over the past 30 years has been precisely a faith in reparational uplift—the idea that all the injustice we endured would somehow translate into the means of uplift. We fought for welfare programs that only subsidized human inertia, for cultural approaches to education that stagnated skill development in our young and for affirmative-action programs that removed the incentive to excellence in our best and brightest.

6 Today 70 percent of all black children are born out of wedlock. Sixty-eight percent of all violent crime is committed by blacks, most often against other blacks. Sixty percent of black fourth graders cannot read at grade level. And so on. When you fight for reparational uplift, you have to fit yourself into a victim-focused, protest identity that is at once angry and needy. You have to locate real transformative power in white society, and then manipulate white guilt by seducing it with neediness and threatening it with anger. And you must nurture in yourself, and pass on to your own children, a sense of aggrieved entitlement that sees black success as an impossibility without the intervention of white compassion.

7 The above statistics come far more from this rippling sense of entitlement than from racism. And now the demand for reparations is yet another demand for white responsibility when today's problem is a failure of black responsibility.

8 When you don't know how to go forward, you find an excuse to go backward. You tell yourself that if you can just get a little

justice for past suffering, you will feel better about the challenges you face. So you make justice a condition of your going forward. But of course, there is no justice for past suffering, and to believe there is only guarantees more suffering.

The worst enemy black America faces today is not white racism but white guilt. This is what encourages us to invent new pleas rather than busy ourselves with the hard work of development. So willing are whites to treat us with deference that they are a hard mark to pass up. The entire civil-rights establishment strategizes to keep us the wards of white guilt. If these groups had to rely on black money rather than white corporate funding, they would all go under tomorrow. 9

An honest black leadership would portray our victimization as only a condition we faced, and nurture a black identity around the ingenuity by which we overcame it. It would see reparations as a childish illusion of perfect justice. I can't be repaid for my grandfather. The point is that I owe him a great effort. 10

BUILDING VOCABULARY

Argument is often cast in emotive terms. Rewrite the passage below by substituting other words for those in italics.

> We fought for welfare programs that only *subsidized human inertia,* for cultural approaches to education that *stagnated* skill development in our young and for affirmative-action programs that removed *the incentive to excellence in our best and brightest* (par. 5).

THINKING CRITICALLY ABOUT THE ESSAY

Understanding the Writer's Ideas

1. Why is Steele hesitant to claim a personal connection to slavery through his grandfather? Compare Steele's use of this information about his grandfather and Marable's allusion to his grandfather (p. 429).
2. What is Steele's first objection to reparations? How many other objections does he make, and what are they?

3. For what reason does Steele allude to Richard Wright's novel *Black Boy?*
4. What is Steele's objection to what he refers to as "reparational uplift"?
5. For what reason does Steele cite the statistics found in paragraph 6? How would Manning Marable interpret these same statistics? Why does Marable not cite these statistics? Why does Steele not cite the statistics Marable cites in paragraphs 7, 8, and 9 of his selection (p. 430-431)?
6. Why does Steele object to appeals on the part of blacks to "white responsibility" or "white guilt"?
7. What kind of position does Steele wish to see advocated by "black leadership"?

Understanding the Writer's Techniques

1. Why does Steele open his essay with an allusion to his grandfather?
2. Where does Steele's introduction end? Does his introduction include his thesis statement? If not, where in the essay is his thesis stated?
3. Compare and contrast the kinds of support that Steele and Marable use to make their arguments. Do they both rely equally on examples? Do they both rely equally on reason? Does one writer make a stronger appeal to emotion? Explain your answers.
4. What evidence does Steele cite to support his claim that the statistics mentioned in paragraph 6 "come far more from this crippling sense of entitlement than from racism" (par. 7)?
5. How does Steele support his point that the "worst enemy black America faces today is . . . white guilt" (par. 9)?
6. Explain how Steele's conclusion effectively ties the essay together, providing both coherence and closure.

Exploring the Writer's Ideas

1. What do you think Marable would say in response to Steele's point that "when you trade on the past victimization of your own people, you trade honor for dollars" (par. 4)?

2. Do you think Steele draws the most persuasive conclusion from the statistics he cites in paragraph 6? How else could this information be read?
3. It may be that "there is no justice for past suffering" (par. 8), but does that mean there can be no reparations? In either case, say why.
4. Are the positions that (a) reparations are a way to highlight the persistence of discrimination and that (b) "today's problem is a failure of black responsibility" mutually exclusive, that is, totally incompatible? Why or why not?

IDEAS FOR WRITING

Prewriting

Are there any examples in your life, or in the life of your family, that show how suffering or even oppression can lead to surprisingly positive achievements, such as creative acts or sustaining traditions? Write some notes about how you would explain this paradox to a stranger.

Guided Writing

Write an essay about how blaming others can be a way of avoiding personal initiative.

1. Open with an example of an injustice or grave hurt that clearly invites blaming the perpetrator and demanding redress.
2. Indicate that such a response perhaps should be examined more thoughtfully.
3. Allude to two examples—examples involving your family or others you know; or examples from history in general—that show the barrenness of ongoing rage and hate as well as the benefits that can be derived from overcoming great obstacles.
4. Return to the example of injustice you started with, and argue that, although it was an injustice, no good will be served by dwelling on blame.
5. Conclude by seeing adversity as not an obstacle to the future, but rather as a motive for improving it.

Thinking and Writing Collaboratively

Divide the class into two equal groups, one taking Marable's position and one taking Steele's. As a group, think of arguments and facts to add to those already given by the writer whose position you are taking and try to remedy weaknesses you may see in his essay. Take notes on this discussion, and use your notes to prepare an outline for a debate on the issue of reparations. After debating the issue, switch sides so that those who argued for Marable's position will now argue for Steele's side, and vice versa. Repeat the previous process. After this second debate, reconvene as a class and discuss the experience of taking both sides of an issue.

Writing About the Text

Write an essay that seeks to expand on this sentence of Steele's: "The above statistics [in par. 6] come far more from this crippling sense of entitlement than from racism" (par. 7).

More Writing Projects

1. Respond in your journal to question 3 in Exploring the Writer's Ideas, above.
2. Write an imaginary interview conducted by Manning Marable of Steele, or vice versa.
3. Read Richard Wright's *Black Boy,* and write an essay which assesses Marable's and Steele's essays in light of that novel.

ARGUMENTS PRO AND CON: THE DEATH PENALTY

Are some crimes so heinous that the only appropriate punishment is death? How can such a question be answered? The essays that follow assume that, putting all else aside, the legal process that establishes innocence or guilt in capital cases must be utterly fair and impartial in order for the death penalty to be imposed. But Bob Herbert suggests that the death penalty can never be imposed fairly, whereas James Q. Wilson says there is no evidence that the death penalty is being imposed unfairly or that innocent people are being executed.

How can the same evidence yield two such opposing views?

Death-Penalty Dissenters

Bob Herbert

Bob Herbert, whose column "In America" appears in the *New York Times* twice weekly, was born in Brooklyn, New York, on March 7, 1945. He has written on politics, urban affairs, and current social trends for the *Times* since 1993. Herbert began his career as a reporter with the *Star-Ledger* of Newark, New Jersey, and he worked as a reporter and editor at the *Daily News* in New York from 1976 to 1985, when he became a member of its editorial board. In 1990 Herbert was a founding panelist on *Sunday Edition* for CBS and the host of *Hotline* on WNYC-TV. He is recipient of the American Society of Newspaper Editors award for distinguished newspaper writing. In this selection, a column published on July 9, 2001, Herbert says almost nothing in his own voice about capital punishment, relying instead on exceptionally powerful illustrations to make his point. As you read the selection, consider how it would be different with other illustrations, or without any illustrations at all. What makes these illustrations so effective?

PREREADING: THINKING ABOUT THE ESSAY IN ADVANCE

Think about the main points that people for and against the death penalty usually make. Which of these main points do you find most persuasive, or disturbing? What image comes to your mind at the mention of "death penalty dissenters"? Do Herbert's illustrations conform to your preconceptions of such dissenters?

Words to Watch

tenure (par. 1) the length of time a position is held
staunch (par. 2) steadfast
to stay (par. 4) to halt
fraught (par. 6) filled or loaded with
viability (par. 9) capable of surviving or thriving
moratorium (par. 9) a suspension of activity

Harry A. Blackmun was 85 years old and near the end of his tenure on the Supreme Court when he declared in 1994 that he could no longer support the imposition of the death penalty. 1

2 This was especially noteworthy because Justice Blackmun was seen as a staunch "law and order" judge when he was appointed to the court by Richard Nixon in 1970, and he played a significant role in the restoration of capital punishment in the U.S. in 1976.

3 But he was a thoughtful man. And what turned him around on the death penalty, after decades of trying to ensure that it was imposed fairly, was his realization that it could never be imposed fairly.

4 In a solitary dissent from the court's refusal to stay an execution in Texas, Justice Blackmun wrote in February 1994, "The problem is that the inevitability of factual, legal and moral error gives us a system that we know must wrongly kill some defendants, a system that fails to deliver the fair, consistent and reliable sentences of death required by the Constitution."

5 He said that he and a majority of his colleagues on the court had struggled unsuccessfully for more than 20 years to bring an acceptable level of fairness to the system of capital punishment. But despite all good-faith efforts, he said, "I feel morally and intellectually obligated simply to concede that the death penalty experiment has failed."

6 Justice Blackmun could no longer bring himself to roll the dice with a person's life at stake. He would no longer participate in a system that he described as "fraught with arbitrariness, discrimination, caprice and mistake."

7 "From this day forward," he said, "I no longer shall tinker with the machinery of death."

8 Justice Blackmun died in 1999.

9 In January 2000, another unlikely individual stepped forward with concerns about the viability of capital punishment. Gov. George H. Ryan of Illinois, a pro-death-penalty Republican, imposed a moratorium on executions in Illinois because of his state's "shameful record of convicting innocent people and putting them on death row."

10 More than a dozen men who had been sentenced to death in Illinois since 1977 eventually were found to have been innocent and were freed.

11 Anthony Porter was one, and he came frighteningly close to dying for a crime he hadn't committed. Mr. Porter was convicted of murdering a young couple in a park in Chicago. He spent 16 years on death row and came within 48 hours of actually being executed. He was released from prison in February 1999, after a group of

Northwestern University students, working with their journalism professor, uncovered evidence that showed he was innocent.

Echoing Justice Blackmun, Governor Ryan said, "I cannot support a system which, in its administration, has proven so fraught with error, and has come so close to the ultimate nightmare, the state's taking of innocent life." 12

The latest voice to be heard on this critical issue was that of Supreme Court Justice Sandra Day O'Connor, who is also a supporter of the death penalty. "If statistics are any indication," said Justice O'Connor, in an address last week to a gathering of lawyers in Minnesota, "the system may well be allowing some innocent defendants to be executed." 13

With that stunningly understated observation, Justice O'Connor became the second pro-death-penalty Supreme Court justice to raise the horrifying specter of innocents being delivered to the death chambers. "Perhaps," she said, "it's time to look at minimum standards for appointed counsel in death cases and adequate compensation for appointed counsel when they are used." 14

Justice Blackmun would have called that tinkering. He did not believe the courts could develop procedures that would provide "consistency, fairness and reliability" in the administration of the death penalty. 15

He was more optimistic, he said, that the Supreme Court would eventually have no choice but to declare the death penalty a failure and abandon it altogether. "I may not live to see that day," he said, "but I have faith that eventually it will arrive." 16

He concluded his opinion on the 1994 case as follows: "The path the court has chosen lessens us all. I dissent." 17

BUILDING VOCABULARY

Explain the meaning of the following examples of figurative language (see Glossary). Rewrite the sentences by putting the figure of speech in your own words.

- **a.** . . . Justice Blackmun was seen as a staunch *"law and order"* judge. . . . (par. 2)
- **b.** Justice Blackmun could no longer bring himself to *roll the dice* with a person's life at stake (par. 6).
- **c.** "I no longer shall *tinker with the machinery* of death" (par. 7).

THINKING CRITICALLY ABOUT THE ESSAY

Understanding the Writer's Ideas

1. What details about Harry A. Blackmun does the writer offer in his two opening paragraphs that make Blackmun's views on the death penalty especially noteworthy?
2. What is the effect of the first sentence of paragraph 3?
3. How does the phrase "solitary dissent" (par. 4) support the first sentence of paragraph 3?
4. What grounds does Blackmun provide for his view that "the death penalty experiment has failed" (par. 5)?
5. What is the writer's purpose in telling us that Justice Blackmun died in 1999?
6. What makes Gov. Ryan an "unlikely individual" to raise concerns about capital punishment?
7. Why does Gov. Ryan say Illinois' record on capital punishment is "shameful"?
8. What do Justices Blackmun and O'Connor have in common?
9. Why does the writer say Justice Blackmun was "optimistic" about how future Supreme Courts would regard the death penalty?

Understanding the Writer's Techniques

1. What is the thesis statement of this essay? Where does it appear?
2. This essay is divided into three sections, each an illustration intended to support the essay's thesis. What transitions does the writer use to move from one section to the next?
3. Outline the essay to highlight the way in which each section contributes facts or arguments to the essay's thesis.
4. Discuss how each illustration echoes the points made by the others; discuss how each illustration has a special point to contribute to the essay.
5. The illustrations chosen by the writer are set out in chronological order. Is there any other reason for the order in which the illustrations appear? Explain.
6. The writer punctuates his essay with evocative words or phrases intended to support the intellectual argument with emotional force, such as "to roll the dice" in the opening sentence of

paragraph 6. List three more examples of such words or phrases, and explain how these words or phrases contribute to (or detract from) the writer's argument.

7. What are the main characteristics of these "death-penalty dissenters"? Why do you think the writer has chosen dissenters with these characteristics to illustrate his point of view?
8. How does the initial portrait—of Justice Blackmun—serve to help unify the essay?
9. Do you think the final paragraph is a good conclusion to the essay? Why or why not?

Exploring the Writer's Ideas

1. In illustrating a "type"—death-penalty dissenters—the writer has, paradoxically, chosen three public figures who favor the death penalty. How would the essay have been different if he had chosen public figures with a record of long opposition to the death penalty? Which group of illustrations do you think would be more representative of U.S. public opinion on this issue? Which group of illustrations do you think would be most effective in persuading readers to adopt his view? Explain.
2. Is "dissent" a good or a bad quality? Do you automatically associate good qualities with dissenters, or bad ones? Or does your response depend on what they dissent from? Is it influenced by how dissenters are portrayed? What qualities would you attach to a "dissenter" to encourage positive associations in the audience? To encourage negative associations?
3. The three dissenters whom the writer quotes seem to bring different considerations to bear on the question of the viability of the death penalty. Justice Blackmun is concerned with the fairness of the judicial process, objecting to "arbitrariness, discrimination, caprice and mistake." Governor Ryan is concerned with avoiding "the ultimate nightmare, the state's taking of innocent life." And Justice O'Connor is concerned to ensure fair defense for those accused, suggesting "it's time to look at minimum standards for appointed counsel." Which of these considerations do you find the most serious? Why? Do you think each of these concerns ought to be styled "dissent" from the death penalty? Explain.

IDEAS FOR WRITING

Prewriting

List the pros and cons of the death penalty. Then list the kinds of prominent individuals who might serve as exceptionally convincing advocates for these pros and cons.

Guided Writing

Search the on-line archives of the *New York Times* or of some other newspaper or magazine or search valid websites for articles on the death penalty. Look for writers who support the death penalty and articles about prominent death-penalty supporters. Write an essay illustrating the viability of the death penalty through three examples of individuals who, despite their otherwise liberal views, favor the death penalty. Title the essay "Supporters of the Death Penalty."

1. Open your essay by introducing your most persuasive example, an individual who is well-known for his or her liberal views and who in the past has opposed the death penalty.
2. Use a paragraph to illustrate this person's record.
3. Offer an example that shows why the person has finally come down on the side of the death penalty.
4. Introduce your second example, another individual who has concluded that the death penalty is necessary.
5. Introduce your final example.
6. Draw the essay to a close by alluding again to your opening illustration.

Thinking and Writing Collaboratively

Divide into three groups. Each group should prepare for a debate on the death penalty, conducting research on this issue in the library or on the Web. The aim of the preparation should be to win the debate through persuasive illustration. Stage the debate, with one group arguing in favor of the death penalty and the second group arguing against it. The third group will act as jury. The jury should vote on a winner and articulate the reasons for its verdict in a written "judgment."

Writing About the Text

Building on question 3 of Exploring the Writer's Ideas, write an essay that challenges or affirms the writer's choice of illustrations. Your essay should maintain *either* that the writer has fairly and persuasively used a range of examples *or* that the writer has unfairly lumped together three incompatible examples, making a weak case for his point of view.

More Writing Projects

1. In the form of one-paragraph journal entries, write impressionistically about the electric chair; hanging by the neck until dead; lethal injections.
2. The death penalty is fraught with paradoxes: the Ten Commandments say: "Thou shalt not kill"; those sentenced to be killed have usually been condemned because they have killed; the deterrent to killing is killing. Are these paradoxes—a paradox is an *apparent* contradiction—actually outright contradictions, or can further explanation reconcile what seem on their face to be fundamentally conflicting elements? Take one position or the other, and write an extended paragraph explaining your position.
3. Critics of the death penalty, like Herbert's dissenters, usually stress the unfairness or unworkableness of the death penalty. Advocates often concede some of the criticisms of the system but maintain that the death penalty is the only possible deterrent to violent crime and acts such as murder. Write an essay that argues for alternative deterrents to the death penalty, using illustrations to carry the weight of your argument.

What Death-Penalty Errors?

James Q. Wilson

Professor Emeritus of Government at Harvard, James Q. Wilson has long enjoyed a reputation as a distinguished political analyst. His main works include *Political Organizations* (1973), *Crime and Human Nature* (1985), *American Government* (1995), and his widely read *The Moral Sense* (1993). Wilson, who earned his Ph.D. at the University of Chicago in 1959, served as chairman of the White House Task Force on Crime in 1966 and is chairman of the Council of Academic Advisors of the American Enterprise Institute. This selection appeared on July 10, 2000, a year earlier than the Herbert piece.

PREREADING: THINKING ABOUT THE ESSAY IN ADVANCE

Would your views on the death penalty be affected in any way if it were discovered that some people are being sentenced to death for crimes they did not in fact commit?

Words to Watch

DNA (par. 14) deoxyribonucleic acid, found in cell nuclei, and hence a "building block" of life, bearing the precise chemical identification of an individual

indigent (par. 14) poor

certify (par. 14) to attest authoritatively

plausible (par. 15) credible

foreclose (par. 17) to shut out

1 For those who support capital punishment, as I do, the possibility that innocent people could be executed is profoundly disturbing. No human arrangement can guarantee perfection, but if perfection is not possible, then the number of errors ought to kept as low as possible. For that reason, it is worth studying "Broken System: Error Rates in Capital Cases," the recent report by Professor James Liebman and others at the Columbia University Law School, especially since that document has stimulated an outpouring of media coverage.

Its essential finding is that, for the last two decades or so, 2
courts have found "serious, reversible error" in a large fraction of the cases they reviewed. These errors, the report claimed, often involved weak or incompetent defense attorneys and the withholding of important evidence from the juries.

But notice what the report did not say. Its authors did not at- 3
tempt to discover whether any innocent person had been executed, and they made no claim that this has happened. Instead, they said that the large number of appeals leaves "grave doubt whether we do catch" all of the errors. The clear implication is that, were the truth known, we might well be killing many innocent people.

But that truth is not known. The Death Penalty Information 4
Center, a rallying point for opponents of execution, reports that since 1973, when the Supreme Court reinstated the death penalty, 69 people have been released from death row after they were found to be innocent. But the center does not say that any innocent person has been put to death, though if it had found such a case it surely would have proclaimed it.

The Columbia University report shows that death sentences 5
are intensively reviewed by appeals courts. Some critics of these reviews think they take too long and involve too many unnecessary bites at the apple, and that may be true. But if we are to err, it is best that we err on the side of safety.

Nine or 10 years usually pass between the imposition of the 6
death penalty and its being carried out. It took 19 years and appeals heard by more than 30 judges before Gary Graham was executed last month in Texas. It is hard to imagine that this much time is necessary for an adequate appeal, but offsetting the cost and delay is the assurance of only a small chance that an innocent person will be killed. The 5,760 death sentences handed out since 1973 had, by 1995, led to only 313 executions.

Mr. Liebman suggests that the high rate of appeals means that 7
serious errors are often made by the trial courts. But before we can accept that conclusion, we must first know whether the errors were serious enough to affect the outcomes of the cases when they were sent back for new trials. Did an "error" cause a new trial that set aside the death penalty? Unfortunately, Mr. Liebman was able to learn this for only a small number of the reversals.

Because of Supreme Court decisions, every death-penalty 8
conviction leads to an appeal to the state's highest court. About two-fifths of these cases were reversed. As I read the report, we have no information about what happened in the new trials.

9 Then there are state appeals after convictions. These also led to many reversals, but we don't know what happened to the great majority of these cases when they were retried because trial courts ordinarily do not publish their findings. Mr. Liebman and his colleagues managed to find 301 cases that had been retried, but we have no idea whether these were representative of all of those appealed or were only a few dramatic ones that somehow came to the attention of outsiders.

10 Of these 301 new actions by trial courts, 22 found that the defendant was not guilty of a capital crime, 54 reimposed the death sentence and 247 imposed prison sentences.

11 Then there were appeals to the federal courts that also led to reversals in about two-fifths of the cases, but again we are not certain what happened in all the new trials.

12 The report also lumps together cases going back to 1973 with those decided more recently, even though the Supreme Court in 1976 created new procedural guarantees that automatically overturned many of the death-penalty decisions made between 1973 and 1976. It is not clear from the Columbia report what fraction of its reversals date back to these big changes in the rules.

13 In short, in the vast majority of death-penalty cases we have no idea whether the finding of error that led to a reversal was based on a legal technicality, a changing high-court standard about how a capital crime ought to be tried or a judgment that the defendants might be innocent. All we know for certain is that a lot of death-penalty cases are reviewed over a long period of time—a fact that dramatically reduces the chances of innocent people having been executed.

14 More procedural reforms may be coming. Congress is now considering a bill that would require federal courts to order DNA testing, at government expense if the defendant is indigent, whenever DNA evidence from the crime is available. It also would require states seeking federal crime-control funds to certify that they have effective systems for providing competent legal services to indigent defendants in death-penalty cases.

15 But more might be done at the state level. States ought to have laws that create imprisonment without possibility of parole for first-degree murder convictions, and the judge in every such case should instruct the jurors in the sentencing phase that they can choose that or the death penalty. This allows jurors who may have some doubts about the strength of the evidence or some other plausible worry to hedge their bets if they are so inclined.

Not every state now has such laws. In Texas, the alternative to the death sentence is life in prison, but without an absolute guarantee that the offender will actually spend his life there. Jurors rightly suspect that the perpetrator will find some way to get back on the street, and so they often vote for death. 16

The American Law Institute, a group of legal scholars that designs uniform state legal codes, has recommended that even when a jury decides that capital punishment is appropriate, the judge should be allowed to bar the death penalty if the evidence "does not foreclose all doubt respecting the defendant's guilt." The states have not adopted this rule, but perhaps they should, especially if this change could be coupled with procedures designed to reduce the seemingly endless number of post-trial appeals. 17

In the meantime, we ought to calm down. No one has shown that innocent people are being executed. The argument against the death penalty cannot, on the evidence we now have, rest on the likelihood of serious error. It can only rest, I think, on moral grounds. Is death an excessive penalty for any offense? I think not, but those who disagree should make their views on the morality of execution clear and not rely on arguments about appeals, costs and the tiny chance that someday somebody innocent will be killed. 18

BUILDING VOCABULARY

This selection requires knowledge of some of the basic vocabulary of our legal system. Define, and where relevant describe the function of, the following:

- **a.** appeals courts (par. 5)
- **b.** trial courts (par. 7)
- **c.** Supreme Court (par. 8)
- **d.** state appeals (par. 9)
- **e.** federal courts (par. 11)
- **f.** first-degree murder (par. 15)
- **g.** the sentencing phase (par. 15)

THINKING CRITICALLY ABOUT THE ESSAY

Understanding the Writer's Ideas

1. What prompted Wilson's essay?

2. According to Wilson, what are the main findings of Professor Liebman's report?
3. What does the report "not say"? Why is what the report does not say important to the writer?
4. What evidence in Professor Liebman's report supports the views of those who favor the death penalty?
5. Why does the writer question Professor Liebman's view that the "high rate of appeals means that serious errors are often made by the trial courts" (par. 7)?
6. According to the writer, what is the only thing "we know for certain" about legal procedures in death penalty cases (par. 13)?
7. What new federal procedural reforms does Wilson foresee?
8. According to the writer, what steps might the states take to reform legal procedures in death penalty cases?
9. Why does the writer urge us "to calm down" with respect to the findings of the Liebman report?

Understanding the Writer's Techniques

1. What is the thesis of this essay? Where does it appear?
2. What argumentative function does Wilson's opening serve?
3. What kinds of authoritative sources does Wilson use to support his argument? How does Wilson's use of these sources help or hinder his case?
4. Wilson relies heavily on *analysis* to support his case. Which do you see as his most persuasive analytical argument? Why do you find it persuasive? What is his least persuasive analytical argument? Why do you not find it persuasive?
5. How do paragraphs 15–17 support Wilson's position?
6. List two or three of Wilson's most effective transitions, and say why they are effective.
7. What does the title contribute to the essay?
8. What is your view of the conclusion? Is it effective? Why or why not?

Exploring the Writer's Ideas

1. Wilson concentrates his rebuttal of the Liebman report on the fact that "no one has shown that innocent people are being executed" (par. 18). Is Wilson's focus on this criterion reasonable? Might there be good reason to doubt the fairness or

justness of death sentences even if there is no positive proof that innocent people are being executed? Why or why not?

2. Is the "morality" of executions as easily separated from the soundness, reliability, and fairness of the system as Wilson contends? Why or why not? In general the courts, for example, place great emphasis on the integrity of procedure. Can procedural flaws therefore affect the "morality" of a death sentence, or of the system of trial and sentencing?
3. What aspects of Wilson's method cause you to have confidence in his conclusions (if any)? What aspects of Wilson's method cause you to distrust him (if any)?

Prewriting

List the *moral* arguments for and against the death penalty.

Guided Writing

Write an essay that argues for or against the death penalty *strictly on moral grounds.*

1. Begin the essay with Wilson's conclusion that the death penalty cannot be argued against on the grounds that errors are made. If you are arguing against the death penalty, say that you will, however, argue against it on moral grounds. If you are arguing for it, say that furthermore there are moral grounds for the death penalty.
2. State your moral position and the main ground for your position.
3. In separate paragraphs, offer at least two supporting points for the main ground of your argument.
4. In separate paragraphs, rebut the main objections to your position (offer at least two objections).
5. Conclude by restating your main position in light of your supporting points and your rebuttal of opposing views.

Thinking and Writing Collaboratively

Divide the class into three groups to mount a debate on the death penalty: one group will argue for, one against, and the third will offer a verbal and written judgment of the debate. Base the debate on a range of considerations—moral and other. Each group should research the topic sufficiently to be able to sustain a formal, forty-minute debate.

Writing About the Text

Write an essay that explores whether arguments based on numbers and statistics and moral arguments interact with respect to the death penalty. In other words, if one could show, for example, that innocent people were being executed, would this affect moral arguments in favor of the death penalty? What about if one could should show that sentences are biased against certain groups? Or could an argument for the death penalty on moral grounds be made independent of such considerations? Explain your responses to these questions in your essay.

More Writing Projects

1. Look up the Liebman report. In your journal argue either that Wilson fairly summarized and analyzed the report or that he distorted it in order to refute its conclusions.
2. Write a letter to the editor that takes issue with Wilson's conclusions.
3. Look into the matter of DNA testing, and write an essay on its potential impact on the death penalty.

ISSUES OF IDENTITY

Who am I? Am I a unique individual, with certain physical and emotional traits and with the habits and tastes that I myself have chosen to develop? Or am I the product of a certain group, community, nation, race, religion? Am I who I feel myself to be on the inside? Or am I the person others perceive me to be? These are among the most charged issues about which we, as Americans, tend to argue. But how can we discuss issues of identity fairly and reasonably? How can we persuade others of the rightness of our own views and the limits of theirs? As you read the following selections, pause to reflect not only about what the writer has to say but also about *how* the writer says it. What approaches do you find most persuasive? Which rhetorical devices appeal to you most? What can you take from these essays for your own use in your own essays?

I Want a Wife

Judy Brady

Judy Brady, born in San Francisco in 1937 and educated at the University of Iowa, is active in the women's movement and other social and political causes. In this essay Brady, a wife and mother of two children, argues for a wife of her own. Although her argument might seem strange, her position will become apparent once you move into the essay. She presents many points to support her position, so you want to keep in mind those that you think are the strongest. This essay appeared originally in the first issue of *Ms.* in 1971—two years before Brady and her husband separated.

PREREADING: THINKING ABOUT THE ESSAY IN ADVANCE

As you prepare to read this satirical essay, consider the traditional roles that men and women play in their mutual relationships. What is expected conventionally of a husband? of a wife? Do you accept these roles? Why or why not?

Words to Watch

nurturant (par. 3) giving affectionate care and attention

hors d'oeuvres (par. 6) food served before the regular courses of the meal

monogamy (par. 8) the habit of having only one mate; the practice of marrying only once during life

I belong to that classification of people known as wives. I am A Wife. And, not altogether incidentally, I am a mother. 1

Not too long ago a male friend of mine appeared on the scene fresh from a recent divorce. He had one child, who is, of course, with his ex-wife. He is obviously looking for another wife. As I thought about him while I was ironing one evening, it suddenly occurred to me that I, too, would like to have a wife. Why do I want a wife? 2

I would like to go back to school so that I can become economically independent, support myself, and, if need be, support those dependent upon me. I want a wife who will work and send me to school. And while I am going to school I want a wife to keep 3 track of the children's doctor and dentist appointments. And to keep track of mine, too. I want a wife to make sure my children eat properly and are kept clean. I want a wife who will wash the children's clothes and keep them mended. I want a wife who is a good nurturant attendant to my children, who arranges for their schooling, makes sure that they have an adequate social life with their peers, takes them to the park, the zoo, etc. I want a wife who takes care of the children when they are sick, a wife who arranges to be around when the children need special care, because, of course, I cannot miss classes at school. My wife must arrange to lose time at work and not lose the job. It may mean a small cut in my wife's income from time to time, but I guess I can tolerate that. Needless to say, my wife will arrange and pay for the care of the children while my wife is working.

4 I want a wife who will take care of *my* physical needs. I want a wife who will keep my house clean. A wife who will pick up after me. I want a wife who will keep my clothes clean, ironed, mended, replaced when need be, and who will see to it that my personal things are kept in their proper place so that I can find what I need the minute I need it. I want a wife who cooks the meals, a wife who is a *good* cook. I want a wife who will plan the menus, do the necessary grocery shopping, prepare the meals, serve them pleasantly, and then do the cleaning up while I do my studying. I want a wife who will care for me when I am sick and sympathize with my pain and loss of time from school. I want a wife to go along when our family takes a vacation so that someone can continue to care for me and my children when I need a rest and change of scene.

5 I want a wife who will not bother me with rambling complaints about a wife's duties. But I want a wife who will listen to me when I feel the need to explain a rather difficult point I have come across in my course of studies. And I want a wife who will type my papers for me when I have written them.

6 I want a wife who will take care of the details of my social life. When my wife and I are invited out by my friends, I want a wife who will take care of the babysitting arrangements. When I meet people at school that I like and want to entertain, I want a wife who will have the house clean, will prepare a special meal, serve it to me and my friends, and not interrupt when I talk about the things that interest me and my friends. I want a wife who will have arranged that the children are fed and ready for bed before my guests arrive so that the children do not bother us. I want a

wife who takes care of the needs of my guests so that they feel comfortable, who makes sure that they have an ashtray, that they are passed the hors d'oeuvres, that they are offered a second helping of the food, that their wine glasses are replenished when necessary, that their coffee is served to them as they like it.

And I want a wife who knows that sometimes I need a night 7
out by myself.

I want a wife who is sensitive to my sexual needs, a wife who 8
makes love passionately and eagerly when I feel like it, a wife who makes sure that I am satisfied. And, of course, I want a wife who will not demand sexual attention when I am not in the mood for it. I want a wife who assumes the complete responsibility for birth control, because I do not want more children. I want a wife who will remain sexually faithful to me so that I do not have to clutter up my intellectual life with jealousies. And I want a wife who understands that *my* sexual needs may entail more than strict adherence to monogamy. I must, after all, be able to relate to people as fully as possible.

If, by chance, I find another person more suitable as a wife 9
than the wife I already have, I want the liberty to replace my present wife with another one. Naturally, I will expect a fresh, new life; my wife will take the children and be solely responsible for them so that I am left free.

When I am through with school and have a job, I want my 10
wife to quit working and remain at home so that my wife can more fully and completely take care of a wife's duties.

My God, who *wouldn't* want a wife? 11

BUILDING VOCABULARY

1. After checking a dictionary, write definitions of each of these words.
   a. attendant (par. 3)
   b. adequate (par. 3)
   c. peers (par. 3)
   d. tolerate (par. 3)
   e. rambling (par. 5)
   f. replenished (par. 6)
   g. adherence (par. 8)
2. Write an original sentence for each word above.

THINKING CRITICALLY ABOUT THE ESSAY

Understanding the Writer's Ideas

1. What incident made Brady think about wanting a wife?
2. How would a wife help the writer achieve economic independence?
3. In what ways would a wife take care of the writer's children? Why would the writer like someone to assume those responsibilities?
4. What physical needs would Brady's "wife" take care of?
5. How would a wife deal with the writer's social life? Her sex life?

Understanding the Writer's Techniques

1. What is Brady's *major proposition?* Is it simply what she says in paragraph 2, or is the proposition more complex than that? State it in your own words.
2. What is the value of the question Brady asks in paragraph 2? Where else does she ask a question? What value does this other question have in its place in the essay? What impact does it have on the reader?
3. What *minor propositions* does Brady present to show why she wants a wife? In which instances do they serve as topic sentences within paragraphs? What details does she offer to illustrate those minor propositions?
4. In what order has the writer chosen to arrange the minor propositions? Why has she chosen such an order? Do you think she builds from the least to the most important reasons for having a wife? What changes, if any, would you urge in the order of the minor propositions?
5. Brady's style is obviously straightforward, her sentences for the most part simple and often brief. Why has she chosen such a style? What is the effect of the repetition of "I want" at the start of so many sentences? Why has Brady used several short paragraphs (1, 7, 10, 11) in addition to longer ones?
6. What is the author's *tone* (see Glossary)? Point out the uses of *irony* (see Glossary) in the essay. How does irony contribute to Brady's main intent in this essay? How does the fact that Brady is a woman contribute to this sense of irony?

MIXING PATTERNS

Most of the paragraphs here develop through illustration. Where has Brady used a simple listing of details? Why has she chosen that format? How does the illustration strategy help advance the argument?

Exploring the Writer's Ideas

1. By claiming that she wants a wife, Brady is showing us all the duties and responsibilities of the woman in a household at the time this essay was written. Has Brady represented these duties fairly? Do husbands still generally expect their wives to do all these things?
2. To what degree do wives today fit Brady's description? How could a wife avoid many of the responsibilities spelled out in the essay? How does the "modern husband" figure in the way many couples meet household responsibilities now?
3. Brady has characterized all the traditional and stereotyped roles usually assigned to wives. What "wifely responsibilities" has she left out?
4. Answer the question in the last line of the essay.
5. Read the essays "Night Walker" by Brent Staples (pages 183–186) and "How Do We Find the Student in a World of Academic Gymnasts and Worker Ants?" by James T. Baker (pages 315–319). Compare the use of stereotyping in these essays. How is it different from Brady's stereotypes?

IDEAS FOR WRITING

Prewriting

Freewrite for fifteen minutes about why you want a husband or wife, trying to poke fun at or ridicule (as Brady does) the traditional expectations that we bring to this issue.

Guided Writing

Write an essay of 750 to 1,000 words titled, "I Want a Husband."

1. Write the essay from the point of view of a *man*. As Brady wrote as a woman who wanted a wife, you write this essay as a man who wants a husband.
2. Start your essay with a brief personal story as in paragraph 2 of "I Want a Wife."
3. Support your main point with a number of minor points. Expand each minor point with details that explain your premises.
4. Arrange your minor premises carefully so that you build to the most convincing point at the end.
5. Use a simple and straightforward style. Connect your points with transitions; use repetition as one transitional device.
6. Balance your longer paragraphs with occasional shorter ones.
7. End your essay with a crisp, one-sentence question of your own.

Thinking and Writing Collaboratively

Divide the class into one group consisting entirely of males and the other of females. Working in these groups, have the men list the advantages of having a husband, and the women list the advantages of having a wife. Each group should list its key advantages on the chalkboard for class discussion.

Writing About the Text

Has Brady presented a balanced picture of the issues or is her argument one-sided? Support your opinion with specific references to the essay. Could the author have dealt effectively with opposing arguments? Why or why not? What might these opposing arguments be?

More Writing Projects

1. In your journal, copy any three sentences from Brady's essay that you find particularly provocative, challenging, strange, or unbelievable. Explain why you chose them.
2. Write a paragraph in which you argue *for* or *against* this issue: "A married woman belongs at home."
3. Write an essay in which you argue about whose role you think is harder to play effectively in today's society: the role of the mother or the role of the father.

Are the Homeless Crazy?

Jonathan Kozol

Jonathan Kozol was educated at Harvard University and Magdalen College, Oxford. He rose to national prominence with his startling account of his experience as a teacher in an urban school, *Death at an Early Age* (1967). Writing frequently about inequities in education and in American society, Kozol has reached wide audiences with best-selling books such as *Rachel and Her Children: Homeless Families in America* (1989) and *Savage Inequalities: Children in America's Schools* (1992). This selection, derived from "Distancing the Homeless," appeared originally in the *Yale Review* in 1988. Kozol examines the idea that much of the homelessness of the late 1980s resulted from the release of patients from mental hospitals in the 1970s. The essay discusses how we tend to impose a disturbing identity on those outside the circle of social respectability.

PREREADING: THINKING ABOUT THE ESSAY IN ADVANCE

What are your views of the homeless in American society? Should we classify the homeless as crazy, lazy, unfortunate, or abject failures? Why or why not?

Words to Watch

deinstitutionalized (par. 1) let inmates out of hospitals, prisons, and so forth

conceding (par. 2) acknowledging; admitting to

arson (par. 4) the crime of deliberately setting a fire

subsidized (par. 5) aided with public money

destitute (par. 6) very poor

afflictions (par. 7) ills; problems

stigma (par. 7) a mark of shame or discredit

complacence (par. 7) self-satisfaction

bulk (par. 10) the main part

de facto (par. 11) actually; in reality

resilience (par. 12) ability to recover easily from misfortune

paranoids (par. 13) psychotic people who believe everyone is persecuting them

vengeance (par. 14) retribution; retaliation

1 It is commonly believed by many journalists and politicians that the homeless of America are, in large part, former patients of large mental hospitals who were deinstitutionalized in the 1970s—the consequence, it is sometimes said, of misguided liberal opinion that favored the treatment of such persons in community-based centers. It is argued that this policy, and the subsequent failure of society to build such centers or to provide them in sufficient number, is the primary cause of homelessness in the United States.

2 Those who work among the homeless do not find that explanation satisfactory. While conceding that a certain number of the homeless are or have been mentally unwell, they believe that, in the case of most unsheltered people, the primary reason is economic rather than clinical. The cause of homelessness, they say with disarming logic, is the lack of homes and of income with which to rent or acquire them.

3 They point to the loss of traditional jobs in industry (2 million every year since 1980) and to the fact that half of those who are laid off end up in work that pays a poverty-level wage. They point out that since 1968 the number of children living in poverty has grown by 3 million, while welfare benefits to families with children have declined by 35 percent.

4 And they note, too, that these developments have occurred during a time in which the shortage of low-income housing has intensified as the gentrification of our major cities has accelerated. Half a million units of low-income housing are lost each year to condominium conversion as well as to arson, demolition, or abandonment. Between 1978 and 1980, median rents climbed 30 percent for people in the lowest income sector, driving many of these families into the streets. Since 1980, rents have risen at even faster rates.

5 Hard numbers, in this instance, would appear to be of greater help than psychiatric labels in telling us why so many people become homeless. Eight million American families now use half or more of their income to pay their rent or mortgage. At the same time, federal support for low-income housing dropped from $30 billion (1980) to $7.5 billion (1988). Under Presidents Ford and Carter, 500,000 subsidized private housing units were constructed. By President Reagan's second term, the number had dropped to 25,000.

6 In our rush to explain the homeless as a psychiatric problem even the words of medical practitioners who care for homeless people have been curiously ignored. A study published by the Massachusetts Medical Society, for instance, has noted that, with

the exceptions of alcohol and drug use, the most frequent illnesses among a sample of the homeless population were trauma (31 percent), upper-respiratory disorders (28 percent), limb disorders (19 percent), mental illness (16 percent), skin diseases (15 percent), hypertension (14 percent), and neurological illnesses (12 percent). Why, we may ask, of all these calamities, does mental illness command so much political and press attention? The answer may be that the label of mental illness places the destitute outside the sphere of ordinary life. It personalizes an anguish that is public in its genesis; it individualizes a misery that is both general in cause and general in application.

There is another reason to assign labels to the destitute and single out mental illness from among their many afflictions. All these other problems—tuberculosis, asthma, scabies, diarrhea, bleeding gums, impacted teeth, etc.—bear no stigma, and mental illness does. It conveys a stigma in the United States. It conveys a stigma in the Soviet Union as well. In both nations the label is used, whether as a matter of deliberate policy or not, to isolate and treat as special cases those who, by deed or word or by sheer presence, represent a threat to national complacence. The two situations are obviously not identical, but they are enough alike to give Americans reason for concern. 7

The notion that the homeless are largely psychotics who belong in institutions, rather than victims of displacement at the hands of enterprising realtors, spares us from the need to offer realistic solutions to the deep and widening extremes of wealth and poverty in the United States. It also enables us to tell ourselves that the despair of homeless people bears no intimate connection to the privileged existence we enjoy—when, for example, we rent or purchase one of those restored town houses that once provided shelter for people now huddled in the street. 8

What is to be made, then, of the supposition that the homeless are primarily the former residents of mental hospitals, persons who were carelessly released during the 1970s? Many of them are, to be sure. Among the older men and women in the streets and shelters, as many as one-third (some believe as many as one-half) may be chronically disturbed, and a number of these people were deinstitutionalized during the 1970s. But to operate on that assumption in a city such as New York—where nearly half the homeless are small children whose average age is six—makes no sense. Their parents, with an average age of twenty-seven, are not likely to have been hospitalized in the 1970s, either. 9

10 A frequently cited set of figures tells us that in 1955 the average daily census of non-federal psychiatric institutions was 677,000, and that by 1984 the number had dropped to 151,000. But these people didn't go directly from a hospital room to the street. The bulk of those who had been psychiatric patients and were released from hospitals during the 1960s and early 1970s had been living in low-income housing, many in skid-row hotels or boardinghouses. Such housing—commonly known as SRO (single-room occupancy) units—was drastically diminished by the gentrification of our cities that began in the early '70s. Almost 50 percent of SRO housing was replaced by luxury apartments or office buildings between 1970 and 1980, and the remaining units have been disappearing even more rapidly.

11 Even for those persons who are ill and were deinstitutionalized during the decades before 1980, the precipitating cause of homelessness in 1987 is not illness but loss of housing. SRO housing offered low-cost sanctuaries for the homeless, providing a degree of safety and mutual support for those who lived within them. They were a demeaning version of the community health centers that society had promised; they were the de facto "halfway houses" of the 1970s. For these people too—at most half of the homeless single persons in America—the cause of homelessness is lack of housing.

12 Even in those cases where mental instability is apparent, homelessness itself is often the precipitating factor. For example, many pregnant women without homes are denied prenatal care because they constantly travel from one shelter to another. Many are anemic. Many are denied essential dietary supplements by recent federal cuts. As a consequence, some of their children do not live to see their second year of life. Do these mothers sometimes show signs of stress? Do they appear disorganized, depressed, disordered? Frequently. They are immobilized by pain, traumatized by fear. So it is no surprise that when researchers enter the scene to ask them how they "feel," the resulting reports tell us that the homeless are emotionally unwell. The reports do not tell us that we have *made* these people ill. They do not tell us that illness is a natural response to intolerable conditions. Nor do they tell us of the strength and the resilience that so many of these people retain despite the miseries they must endure.

13 A writer in the *New York Times* describes a homeless woman standing on a traffic island in Manhattan. "She was evicted from her small room in the hotel just across the street," and she is determined

to get revenge. Until she does, "nothing will move her from that spot. . . . Her argumentativeness and her angry fixation on revenge, along with the apparent absence of hallucinations, mark her as a paranoid." Most physicians, I imagine, would be more reserved in passing judgment with so little evidence, but this reporter makes his diagnosis without hesitation. "The paranoids of the street," he says, "are among the most difficult to help."

Perhaps so. But does it depend on who is offering the help? Is anyone offering to help this woman get back her home? Is it crazy to seek vengeance for being thrown into the street? The absence of anger, some psychiatrists believe, might indicate much greater illness. 14

"No one will be turned away," says the mayor of New York City, as hundreds of young mothers with their infants are turned from the doors of shelters season after season. That may sound to some like a denial of reality. "Now you're hearing all kinds of horror stories," says the President of the United States as he denies that anyone is cold or hungry or unhoused. On another occasion he says that the unsheltered "are homeless, you might say, by choice." That sounds every bit as self-deceiving. 15

The woman standing on the traffic island screaming for revenge until her room has been restored to her sounds relatively healthy by comparison. If 3 million homeless people did the same, and all at the same time, we might finally be forced to listen. 16

BUILDING VOCABULARY

1. Throughout this essay, Kozol uses medical and psychiatric *jargon* (see Glossary). List the medical or psychiatric terms or references that you find here. Then look up any five in the dictionary and write definitions for them.
2. Explain in your own words the meanings of the following phrases. Use clues from the surrounding text to help you understand.
   - **a.** sufficient number (par. 1)
   - **b.** primary cause (par. 1)
   - **c.** poverty-level wage (par. 3)
   - **d.** median rents (par. 4)
   - **e.** low-income housing (par. 5)
   - **f.** sheer presence (par. 7)
   - **g.** intimate connection (par. 8)
   - **h.** chronically disturbed (par. 9)

i. skid-row hotels (par. 10)
j. precipitating cause (par. 11)
k. low-cost sanctuaries (par. 11)
l. mutual support (par. 11)
m. demeaning version (par. 11)
n. natural response (par. 12)
o. intolerable conditions (par. 12)
p. angry fixation (par. 13)

THINKING CRITICALLY ABOUT THE ESSAY

Understanding the Writer's Ideas

1. According to Kozol, who has suggested that the deinstitutionalizing of mental-hospital patients is the major cause of homelessness? Does he agree? If not, what does he identify as the major causes?
2. In the opening paragraph, what two groups does Kozol link together? Why? What relation between them does he suggest?
3. In New York City today, what percentage of the homeless are children? What is the average age of their parents? In the past twenty years, has the number of children living in poverty increased or decreased? What about welfare payments to families with children? How has this affected the homelessness situation?
4. What are "gentrification" and "condominium conversion" (par. 4)? How have they affected homelessness?
5. Explain the meaning of the statement: "Hard numbers, in this instance, would appear to be of greater help than psychiatric labels in telling us why so many people become homeless" (par. 5).
6. List in descending order the most common illnesses among the homeless. From what does Kozol draw these statistics? What is his conclusion about them?
7. In your own words, summarize why Kozol feels that journalists and politicians concentrate so heavily on the problems of mental illness among the homeless.
8. What are SROs? Explain how they figure in the homeless situation.
9. What is meant by the "press" (par. 6)? What are "halfway houses" (par. 11)?

10. What is Kozol's attitude toward former President Reagan? toward former New York City Mayor Ed Koch? Explain your answers with specific references to the beginning and ending of the essay.
11. Summarize in your own words the *New York Times* story to which Kozol refers. According to the *Times* reporter, why did the homeless woman mentioned refuse to move from the traffic island? Does Kozol agree with the reporter's interpretation? Explain.
12. In one sentence, state in your own words the opinion Kozol expresses in the last paragraph.

Understanding the Writer's Techniques

1. Which sentence states the *major proposition* of the essay?
2. Describe Kozol's argumentative purpose in this essay. Is it primarily to *convince* or to *persuade?* Explain.
3. In paragraph 1, the author uses a particular verbal construction that he doesn't repeat elsewhere in the essay. He writes: "It is commonly believed . . ."; "it is sometimes said . . ."; and "It is argued. . . ." Why does he use the "it is" construction? What effect does it have? How does he change that pattern in paragraph 2? Why?
4. In paragraph 2, Kozol uses the phrase "mentally unwell" instead of the more common "mentally ill," and he uses "unsheltered people" instead of "homeless people." Why does he use these less-expected phrases? Does he use them again in the essay? Why?
5. *Cynicism* adds an edge of pessimism or anger to a statement that might otherwise be perceived as *irony* (see Glossary). In the sentence, "The cause of homelessness, they say with disarming logic, is the lack of homes and of income with which to rent or acquire them" (par. 2), the clause set off by commas might be considered cynical. Why? Find and explain several other examples of cynicism in this essay. Are they effective? Are they justified?
6. Identify the *minor proposition* statements in this essay. How do they add *coherence* (see Glossary) to the essay?
7. How important is Kozol's use of *statistics* in this essay? Why does he use them?

8. What is the difference between *refutation* (see Glossary) and *negation*? Kozol uses refutation as a major technique in this essay. Analyze his use of refutation in paragraphs 1 and 2. List and discuss at least three other instances where he uses refutation. Where in the essay does he specifically use negation?
9. Characterize the overall *tone* of the essay. How and why does Kozol develop this tone? Who is the intended *audience* for this essay? What is the *level of diction?* How are the two connected? What assumption about the audience is implied in the last sentence of paragraph 8?
10. Writers often use *rhetorical questions* in order to prompt the reader to pay special attention to an issue, but rhetorical questions are usually not meant to be answered. Evaluate Kozol's use of rhetorical questions in paragraph 12. What is the effect of the one-word answer, "Frequently"? Where else does he use rhetorical questions? What message does he attempt to convey with them?
11. Returning to the thesis in the course of an essay is often an effective technique to refocus the reader's attention before beginning a new analysis or a conclusion. Explain how Kozol uses this technique in paragraph 11 to make it a key turning point in the essay.
12. Although Kozol cites various studies and authorities, he makes little use of *direct quotations.* Why? Identify and analyze the three instances where he *does* use direct quotations. How does it help to convey his attitude toward the material he's quoting?
13. Evaluate Kozol's conclusion. How does he establish an aura of unreality in paragraphs 15 and 16? Why does he do so? Does he effectively answer the title question? Explain.

MIXING PATTERNS

Kozol draws on a number of rhetorical strategies to advance his argument. How effective is his use of *cause-and-effect analysis* in paragraphs 1 through 6. In paragraph 12, how does Kozol revise the more commonly cited causal relation between homelessness and mental illness? How effective is Kozol's use of *comparison* in paragraph 7. In what ways does he use *illustration?* How is his use of illustration in the last paragraph different from his other uses of it?

Exploring the Writer's Ideas

1. In small groups, discuss your own experiences, both positive and negative, with homeless people.

2. If possible, conduct an interview with one or more homeless people. Try to find out:
   a. how they became homeless
   b. how long they've been homeless
   c. what they do to survive
   d. whether they feel there may be an end to their homelessness

   Write a report based on your interviews and share it with your classmates.

3. This essay is an excerpt from a much longer essay entitled "Distancing the Homeless," published in the *Yale Review.* How is the theme of that title expressed in this essay?

4. Kozol presents an impressive array of statistics. Working in small groups, compile as many other statistics about homelessness as possible. Each group should then draw a subjective conclusion from the data and be prepared to present and defend it to the class as a whole.

5. Read the following description of New York City's Bowery district:

> Walk under the El at night and all you feel is a sort of cold guilt. Touched for a dime, you try to drop the coin and not touch the hand, because the hand is dirty; you try to avoid the glance, because the glance accuses. This is not so much personal menace as universal—the cold menace of unresolved human suffering and poverty and the advanced stages of the disease alcoholism. On a summer night the drunks sleep in the open. The sidewalk is a free bed, and there are no lice. Pedestrians step along and over and around the still forms as though walking on a battlefield among the dead. In doorways, on the steps of the savings bank, the bums lie sleeping it off. Standing sentinel at each sleeper's head is the empty bottle from which he drained his release. Wedged in the crook of his arm is the paper bag containing his things.

This description is from E. B. White's 1949 essay "Here Is New York," the same essay from which the selection "The Three New Yorks" (pages 308–310) is drawn. It is but one small indication that the current problem of homelessness is nothing new. Try to find other examples, either written or visual, that indicate that homelessness is a long-standing social issue. (You may want to contact such organizations as the Coalition for the Homeless and the Salvation Army.)

In your own experience, how have the conditions of homelessness changed in your own environment over the past five years? The past one year?

IDEAS FOR WRITING

Prewriting

Draft a brief outline arguing for or against a specific issue of campus concern—for example, date rape, political correctness, drugs, or AIDS counseling. In your outline, list at least three main reasons that support the position you are advocating.

Guided Writing

Choose a controversial local issue about which you hold a strong opinion that is not the generally accepted one. (For example, you might write about a decision by the town council to build a new shopping mall on an old vacant lot; the limiting of public library hours in order to save money; a decision to open a halfway house in your neighborhood; and so forth.) Write an essay that will convince the reader of the validity of your stance on the issue.

1. Begin your essay with a discussion of the commonly held opinion on this issue. Use the verbal construction "it is" to help distance you from that opinion.
2. In the next section, strongly refute the commonly held opinion by stating your major proposition clearly and directly.
3. Develop your opinion by the use of comparative statistics.
4. While trying to remain as objective as possible, establish a slightly cynical edge to your tone.
5. If appropriate, include some jargon related to the issue.
6. Explain and refute the causal logic (cause-and-effect analysis) of the common opinion.
7. About midway through the essay, return to the thesis in a paragraph that serves as a "pivot" for your essay.
8. Link ideas, statistics, and opinions by means of well-placed minor proposition statements.

9. Continue to refute the common opinion by
   a. using rhetorical questions
   b. citing and showing the invalidity of a recent media item on the issue
   c. lightly ridiculing some of the "big names" associated with the common opinion on the issue
10. Conclude your essay with a somewhat unrealistic, exaggerated image that both reinforces your opinion and invokes the reader to reexamine the issue more closely.

Thinking and Writing Collaboratively

In groups of four to five, discuss the alternatives or the opposition viewpoint to the arguments presented in your Guided Writing essay. Jot down notes, and then incorporate the opposition viewpoint—and your refutation or answer to it—in your final draft.

Writing About the Text

Write an essay in which you evaluate Kozol's use of statistics in this essay. Which do you find most impressive? Which do you find less than convincing? How do statistics advance the essay's thesis? What other kinds of statistics might Kozol have used?

More Writing Projects

1. In your journal, freewrite about this topic: the homeless. Do not edit your writing. Write nonstop for at least fifteen minutes. When you finish, exchange journal entries with another student in the class. How do your responses compare? contrast?
2. Do you think it is correct to give money to panhandlers? Write a paragraph in which you state and defend your opinion.
3. Write an essay in the form of a letter to your local chief executive (mayor, town supervisor, and so forth) in which you express your opinion about the local homeless situation. Include some specific measures that you feel need to be enacted. Draw freely on your journal entry in question 1 of this exercise.

Psychiatry and Homosexuality

Robert L. Spitzer

Robert L. Spitzer, professor of psychiatry at Columbia University and a leading psychiatric researcher, argues in this essay that, within bounds, individuals can control their sexual identity rationally. A heterosexual male, for example, may seek therapy on how to minimize his homosexual fantasies on the basis of a rational desire to remain married. This selection, published originally in the *Wall Street Journal* on May 23, 2001, advances the view that science achieves its discoveries by asking questions that may go against established social views or political preferences. As you read Spitzer's essay, look carefully at the way he presents his position, and at the tension in his essay between scientific objectivity and personal opinion.

PREREADING: THINKING ABOUT THE ESSAY IN ADVANCE

Do you think of sexual identity as fixed or fluid (changeable)? Is it prejudice or discrimination in a veiled form to entertain the idea that homosexuals may wish to become heterosexuals?

Words to Watch

orthodoxy (par. 1) established doctrine

psychiatric disorders (par. 1) illnesses related to mental or emotional states

caveat (par. 6) warning, for example, of limitations

autonomy (par. 12) independence, self-direction

1 In 1973, I opposed the prevailing orthodoxy in my profession by leading the effort to remove homosexuality from the official list of psychiatric disorders. For this, liberals and the gay community respected me, even as it angered many psychiatric colleagues. I said then—as I say now—that homosexuals can live happy, fulfilled lives. If they claim to be comfortable as they are, they should not be accused of lying or of being in denial.

2 Now, in 2001, I find myself challenging a new orthodoxy. This challenge has caused me to be perceived as an enemy of the gay community, and of many in the psychiatric and academic communities.

3 The assumption I am now challenging is this: that every desire for change in sexual orientation is always the result of societal

pressure and never the product of a rational, self-directed goal. This new orthodoxy claims that it is impossible for an individual who was predominantly homosexual for many years to change his sexual orientation—not only in his sexual behavior, but also in his attraction and fantasies—and to enjoy heterosexuality. Many professionals go so far as to hold that it is unethical for a mental-health professional, if requested, to attempt such psychotherapy.

This controversy erupted recently, when I reported the results 4
of a study that asked an important scientific question: Is it really true that no one who was predominantly homosexual for many years could strongly diminish his homosexual feelings and substantially develop heterosexual potential?

What I found was that, in the unique sample I studied, many 5
made substantial changes in sexual arousal and fantasy—and not merely behavior. Even subjects who made a less substantial change believed it to be extremely beneficial. Complete change was uncommon.

My study concluded with an important caveat: that it should 6
not be used to justify a denial of civil rights to homosexuals, or as support for coercive treatment. I did not conclude that all gays should try to change, or even that they would be better off if they did. However, to my horror, some of the media reported the study as an attempt to show that homosexuality is a choice, and that substantial change is possible for any homosexual who decides to make the effort.

In reality, change should be seen as complex and on a contin- 7
uum. Some homosexuals appear able to change self-identity and behavior, but not arousal and fantasies; others can change only self-identity; and only a very few, I suspect, can substantially change all four. Change in all four is probably less frequent than claimed by therapists who do this kind of work; in fact, I suspect the vast majority of gay people would be unable to alter by much a firmly established homosexual orientation.

I certainly believe that parents with homosexually oriented 8
sons and daughters should love their children—no matter how their children decide to live their lives—and should not use my study to coerce them into unwanted therapy.

However, I continue to hold that desire for change cannot al- 9
ways be reduced to succumbing to society's pressure. Sometimes, such a choice can be a rational, self-directed goal. Imagine the following conversation between a new client and a mental-health professional.

10 *Client:* "I love my wife and children, but I usually am only able to have sex with my wife when I fantasize about having sex with a man. I have considered finding a gay partner, but I prefer to keep my commitment to my family. The homosexual feelings never felt like who I really am. Can you help me diminish those feelings and increase my sexual feelings for my wife?"

11 *Professional:* "You are asking me to change your sexual orientation, which is considered by my profession as impossible and unethical. All I am permitted to do is help you become more comfortable with your homosexual feelings."

12 The mental health professions should stop moving in the direction of banning such therapy. Many patients, informed of the possibility that they may be disappointed if the therapy does not succeed, can make a rational choice to work toward developing their heterosexual potential and minimizing their unwanted homosexual attractions. In fact, such a choice should be considered fundamental to client autonomy and self-determination.

13 Science progresses by asking interesting questions, not by avoiding questions whose answers might not be helpful in achieving a political agenda. Gay rights are a completely separate issue, and defensible for ethical reasons. At the end of the day, the full inclusion of gays in society does not, I submit, require a commitment to the false notion that sexual orientation is invariably fixed for all people.

BUILDING VOCABULARY

Define the following terms from the professional vocabulary of psychology:

- **a.** sexual orientation (par. 3)
- **b.** societal pressure (par. 3)
- **c.** self-directed goal (par. 3)
- **d.** self-identity (par. 7)
- **e.** self-determination (par. 12)

THINKING CRITICALLY ABOUT THE ESSAY

Understanding the Writer's Ideas

1. What prevailing orthodoxy did the writer oppose in 1973? How was his opposition received?

2. What prevailing orthodoxy does the writer oppose today? What has been the reaction to his opposition?
3. Why has controversy erupted over the writer's position?
4. Why does the writer call his sample "unique" (par. 5)?
5. What did the writer discover in his study?
6. What does the writer mean when he says change should be seen "on a continuum" (par. 7)?
7. In addition to changes in behavior, what other kinds of changes did the writer notice in some people he studied?
8. Why does the writer believe that "change cannot always be reduced to succumbing to society's pressure" (par. 9)?
9. What kind of choice does the writer believe "should be considered fundamental to client autonomy" (par. 12)?

Understanding the Writer's Techniques

1. Why does the writer open an essay written in 2001 with something he did in 1973?
2. Where does the writer's introduction end? Does his introduction include his thesis statement? If not, where is his thesis statement to be found?
3. Summarize the two sides of the issue Spitzer is discussing.
4. What kind of evidence does Spitzer use to support his position?
5. What is the effect of the transitional phrase with which Spitzer opens paragraph 7 ("In reality")?
6. What is the argumentative effect of the writer's transitions in the first sentences of paragraphs 7, 8, and 9?
7. How would you characterize the *tone* of this essay? How does the tone reflect the subject of the essay?
8. Do you think the points made in the writer's extended conclusion (pars. 12 and 13) are warranted? Why or why not?

EXPLORING THE WRITER'S IDEAS

1. What is your view of the writer's personal involvement in this issue—as evidenced, for example, in his reference to a position he took thirty years ago, his reference to a study he conducted and the press reaction, and his extensive use of the first person? Is there too much of the personal here? Would the essay be stronger if it were more impersonal? Or does the

personal connection add interest and weight to the essay? Explain your response.

2. Many of the desirable ends the writer advocates involve emphasis on the self—"self-directed," "self-identity," "self-determination." Does this suggest a misplaced emphasis, tending towards selfishness? Or is Spitzer properly concerned with the individual's right to make his or her own choices? Why do you feel as you do?
3. Clearly, Spitzer, as a scientist, is entitled to research whatever interests him. But why did he not think that the question he chose to study (par. 4) would not raise suspicions, that is, suspicions that he was looking for ammunition to use against the "orthodoxy" that homosexuality is just another normal and unchangeable form of sexuality? What would you expect would be the media reaction to a study asking the question that Spitzer did?
4. Some psychiatrists have criticized the methods Spitzer used in the research on which he based this argument: he used a very small sample of subjects and he conducted his interviews largely by phone. Why might such methods be a problem?

IDEAS FOR WRITING

Prewriting

Are homosexuality and heterosexuality something people are born into or just develop? Jot down some of your thoughts on this question.

Guided Writing

Imagine that you are the parent of a son or daughter who has revealed an important fact about himself or herself that surprises you. Perhaps he or she has religious views that differ from yours or has decided to live with a partner outside of marriage. Your child has just written you a letter about this fact. Write a letter in response.

1. Begin by acknowledging the seriousness of the revelation.
2. Note your views on the subject, and explain why you hold them.

3. Indicate that you love your child and will support your child's decision, whatever it may be.
4. Ask if your child is ready for the consequences of a decision about this fact no matter how things turn out.
5. Say that you are committed to your child's autonomy and self-determination, and ask how else you can be helpful.

Thinking and Writing Collaboratively

In small groups, share your papers that grew out of the Guided Writing assignment. Discuss the dilemma of the parent in this case—how much to intervene; how to weigh the parent's own preferences against those of the child, and so on. Is there a class consensus on the best advice the parent can give the child?

Writing About the Text

Spitzer presents himself as a scientist asking interesting questions (par. 13). Write an essay that closely analyzes his research question (par. 4). What elements of the text seem scientific to you? Where is Spitzer's writing unscientific?

More Writing Projects

1. Spitzer refers to a "new orthodoxy" about sexual orientation without naming any names. Do some research to discover who the proponents of the view Spitzer is challenging are, and what they think, and record the information in your journal.
2. Write a paragraph that explores the writer's reasoning and its implications in paragraph 12. Do you agree with his concluding sentence in that paragraph? Why or why not?
3. Spitzer identifies four elements of sexual orientation: self-identity, behavior, arousal, and fantasy (par. 7). Write an essay to address the question of whether one can look at these elements independently of the others. Can one change one's behavior and not one's identity? If your fantasies change, can your behavior remain the same? Are these elements of sexual orientation usually stable or fluid?

The Harmful Myth of Asian Superiority

Ronald Takaki

Ronald Takaki, whose grandparents were Japanese plantation workers in Hawaii, is Professor of Ethnic Studies at the University of California, Berkeley. He received his Ph.D. from Berkeley in 1967 and has since published widely in the area of ethnic studies. His works include *Pau Hana: Plantation Life and Labor in Hawaii* (1983) and *Strangers from a Different Shore: A History of Asian Americans* (1989). His most recent publication is *Hiroshima* (2001). In this selection, written in 1990, Takaki argues that stereotyping Asian-Americans as uniformly successful not only belies the facts but also is a veiled form of racist attack on other American ethnic groups, in particular African-Americans.

PREREADING: THINKING ABOUT THE ESSAY IN ADVANCE

How are we to gauge whether the American dream is truly available to all Americans? Is race a factor? How do you account for the success of some recent immigrants in the face of the poverty of many who have lived in the United States for generations? Is the success of some immigrants used unfairly to bolster racial stereotyping, for example, by appealing to the argument: If they can do it, why can't you?

Words to Watch

ubiquity (par. 2) presence everywhere

pundits (par. 3) authoritative opinion-shapers

superfluous (par. 3) unnecessary

acquiring (par. 5) obtaining

median (par. 12) a number or value in a set (say, the set of all incomes) such that there are an equal number of greater and lesser numbers or values

paragons (par. 12) models of excellence

exacerbates (par. 15) worsens

1 Asian Americans have increasingly come to be viewed as a "model minority." But are they as successful as claimed? And for whom are they supposed to be a model?

Asian Americans have been described in the media as "excessively, even provocatively" successful in gaining admission to universities. Asian American shopkeepers have been congratulated, as well as criticized, for their ubiquity and entrepreneurial effectiveness. 2

If Asian Americans can make it, many politicians and pundits ask, why can't African Americans? Such comparisons pit minorities against each other and generate African American resentment toward Asian Americans. The victims are blamed for their plight, rather than racism and an economy that has made many young African American workers superfluous. 3

The celebration of Asian Americans has obscured reality. For example, figures on the high earnings of Asian Americans relative to Caucasians are misleading. Most Asian Americans live in California, Hawaii, and New York—states with higher incomes and higher costs of living than the national average. 4

Even Japanese Americans, often touted for their upward mobility, have not reached equality. While Japanese American men in California earned an average income comparable to Caucasian men in 1980, they did so only by acquiring more education and working more hours. 5

Comparing family incomes is even more deceptive. Some Asian American groups do have higher family incomes than Caucasians. But they have more workers per family. 6

The "model minority" image homogenizes Asian Americans and hides their differences. For example, while thousands of Vietnamese American young people attend universities, others are on the streets. They live in motels and hang out in pool halls in places like East Los Angeles; some join gangs. 7

Twenty-five percent of the people in New York City's Chinatown lived below the poverty level in 1980, compared with 17 percent of the city's population. Some 60 percent of the workers in the Chinatowns of Los Angeles and San Francisco are crowded into low-paying jobs in garment factories and restaurants. 8

"Most immigrants coming into Chinatown with a language barrier cannot go outside this confined area into the mainstream of American industry," a Chinese immigrant said. "Before, I was a painter in Hong Kong, but I can't do it here. I got no license, no education. I want a living; so it's dishwasher, janitor, or cook." 9

10 Hmong and Mien refugees from Laos have unemployment rates that reach as high as 80 percent. A 1987 California study showed that three out of ten Southeast Asian refugee families had been on welfare for four to ten years.

11 Although college-educated Asian Americans are entering the professions and earning good salaries, many hit the "glass ceiling"—the barrier through which high management positions can be seen but not reached. In 1988, only 8 percent of Asian Americans were "officials" and "managers," compared with 12 percent for all groups.

12 Finally, the triumph of Korean immigrants has been exaggerated. In 1988, Koreans in the New York metropolitan area earned only 68 percent of the median income of non-Asians. More than three-quarters of Korean greengrocers, those so-called paragons of bootstrap entrepreneurialism, came to America with a college education. Engineers, teachers, or administrators while in Korea, they became shopkeepers after their arrival. For many of them, the greengrocery represents dashed dreams, a step downward in status.

13 For all their hard work and long hours, most Korean shopkeepers do not actually earn very much: $17,000 to $35,000 a year, usually representing the income from the labor of an entire family.

14 But most Korean immigrants do not become shopkeepers. Instead, many find themselves trapped as clerks in grocery stores, service workers in restaurants, seamstresses in garment factories, and janitors in hotels.

15 Most Asian Americans know their "success" is largely a myth. They also see how the celebration of Asian Americans as a "model minority" perpetuates their inequality and exacerbates relations between them and African Americans.

BUILDING VOCABULARY

This selection draws on concepts from economics and sociology. Define the terms below:

a. cost(s) of living (par. 4)
b. the national average (par. 4)
c. the poverty level (par. 8)
d. unemployment rates (par. 10)
e. welfare (par. 10)

THINKING CRITICALLY ABOUT THE ESSAY

Understanding the Writer's Ideas

1. Why have Asian-Americans been viewed as a "model minority"?
2. What's wrong with such a categorization, according to Takaki?
3. How has the "celebration of Asian Americans . . . obscured reality" (par. 4)?
4. How does the "model minority" image homogenize Asian-Americans?
5. What is the consequence of the language barrier faced by Chinese immigrants?
6. How has the "triumph" of Korean immigrants been "exaggerated" (par. 12)?

Understanding the Writer's Techniques

1. What is the writer's thesis statement?
2. The writer begins by stating the view he is going to oppose, and asks two questions to probe the opposing view. How does he answer these two questions? What evidence does he use in each case?
3. Categorize the examples the writer uses to show that the "celebration of Asian Americans has obscured reality" (par. 4).
4. Much of the writer's supporting evidence is in the form of examples. How does he develop his essay and maintain coherence?
5. What do you think is the writer's strongest piece of evidence for his point of view? What is the weakest? What is his strongest argument? His weakest?
6. The writer saves the word *myth* for last. Does that decision strengthen his use of the word to sum up his essay? Is the conclusion effective?

MIXING PATTERNS

How does the writer solve the problem of definition that his essay involves, that is, the definition of "Asian American"? How do comparison and contrast and classification operate as strategies in Takaki's essay?

Exploring the Writer's Ideas

1. Is the writer's reliance on example excessive? Are some of his examples more persuasive than others? Are some of his examples liable to other interpretations? Is it a problem for his argument that he does *not* give certain examples, such as the statistics on Asian-American admissions to universities? What other strategies might the writer have considered as alternatives to the one he chose? Explain your answers.
2. African-Americans often identify themselves as a coherent group. Despite their different standpoints, Manning Marable and Shelby Steele both, for example, use statistics about African-Americans to support their views. Why is it inappropriate to do the same with Asian-Americans?
3. Takaki cites examples and statistics about Asian-Americans that seem, unintentionally, to be very positive. He says, for example, that Asian-Americans work long hours, cooperate as families, have entered the professions, and have higher family incomes than whites. Are these examples a contradiction of his thesis? Why or why not?

IDEAS FOR WRITING

Prewriting

Is it fair to make any generalizations about "groups," or do groups simply consist of individuals who should be judged on their own merits? Write down ideas about the two sides of this question.

Guided Writing

Write an essay titled "The Harmful Myth of . . ." Make your myth a positive perception that nonetheless can have repercussions for those inside or outside the group. For example, the myth that all Ivy League students are brainy might be a positive perception that leads people to undervalue the academic achievements of other students or, say, the athletic achievements of Ivy League students.

1. Begin by stating the myth. Raise two questions that expose the myth as distorting the reality.
2. Indicate kinds of negative repercussions the myth can have.
3. Use four examples to demonstrate that the reality is more complex than the myth allows. In discussing these examples

and elsewhere in your essay, draw on strategies of definition, comparison and contrast, and classification—as needed—to advance your thesis.

4. End by restating how the myth obscures the reality and can be used negatively.

Thinking and Writing Collaboratively

Debate the question of whether a focus on ethnic or racial identification is a positive or negative phenomenon in the context of our multiethnic society. One half of the class should prepare the case that such a focus is harmful because, for example, it obscures differences within the group and discourages the appreciation of individuals as individuals. The other half should make the case that such a focus is beneficial because, for example, solidarity within a group can promote the economic and political progress of the individuals within the group.

Writing About the Text

Write an essay that explores the question of success as Takaki sees it. What is "success"? What are the main factors that make a person successful in America today? How important is the individual's race or ethnicity in success? How does race or ethnicity play a role?

More Writing Ideas

1. Many essays in *The Short Prose Reader* are by members of minority ethnic or racial groups. How do these essays influence your reading of Takaki? How does your reading of Takaki affect your appreciation for these other essays? Write journal entries that answer these questions.
2. Write a portrait of a city street, either your own street or one you have visited recently. Choose one with a clear ethnic identity. What ethnic groups are represented? What effect has each group had on the life of this street?
3. Interview Asian-American immigrants in your community, town, or city about their notion of the American Dream. Did they have an idea of the American Dream before they arrived in the United States? What do they think of the American Dream now? Has being part of the American Dream changed their identity? Write an essay based on the interviews.

Women Are Just Better

Anna Quindlen

The journalist and novelist Anna Quindlen, born in 1953, became widely known when she was a columnist for the *New York Times* from 1981 to 1984. Some of these columns were collected in *Living Out Loud* (1987), from which the current selection is taken, and *Thinking Out Loud* (1993). Winner of the Pulitzer Prize for Commentary, Quindlen has published three best-selling novels, *Object Lessons* (1991), *One True Thing* (1994), and *Black and Blue* (1998). She now writes the prestigious "Last Word" column for *Newsweek.*

PREREADING: THINKING ABOUT THE ESSAY IN ADVANCE

In human affairs one person is always slightly different from another, one group different from another. Does difference necessarily imply inequality? These days many people say men and women are equal. But is that what, deep down, they truly believe?

Words to Watch

specious (par. 1) only apparently correct

inherent (par. 4) based in the essential character of something

hormonally (par. 6) hormones are secretions of body cells that produce specific effects with male or female characteristics

stereotypes (par. 10) group characteristics

1 My favorite news story so far this year was the one saying that in England scientists are working on a way to allow men to have babies. I'd buy tickets to that. I'd be happy to stand next to any man I know in one of those labor rooms the size of a Volkswagen trunk and whisper "No, dear, you don't really need the Demerol; just relax and do your second-stage breathing." It puts me in mind of an old angry feminist slogan: "If men got pregnant, abortion would be a sacrament." I think this is specious. If men got pregnant, there would be safe, reliable methods of birth control. They'd be inexpensive, too.

2 I can almost hear some of you out there thinking that I do not like men. This isn't true. I have been married for some years to a man and I hope that someday our two sons will grow up to be men. All three of my brothers are men, as is my father. Some of my best friends are men. It is simply that I think women are superior to

men. There, I've said it. It is my dirty little secret. We're not supposed to say it because in the old days men used to say that women were superior. What they meant was that we were too wonderful to enter courtrooms, enjoy sex, or worry our minds about money. Obviously, this is not what I mean at all.

The other day a very wise friend of mine asked: "Have you 3
ever noticed that what passes as a terrific man would only be an adequate woman?" A Roman candle went off in my head; she was absolutely right. What I expect from my male friends is that they are polite and clean. What I expect from my female friends is unconditional love, the ability to finish my sentences when I am sobbing, a complete and total willingness to pour their hearts out to me, and the ability to tell me why the meat thermometer isn't supposed to touch the bone.

The inherent superiority of women came to mind just the 4
other day when I was reading about sanitation workers. New York City has finally hired women to pick up the garbage, which makes sense to me, since, as I discovered, a good bit of being a woman consists of picking up garbage. There was a story about the hiring of these female sanitation workers, and I was struck by the fact that I could have written that story without ever leaving my living room—a reflection not upon the quality of the reporting but the predictability of the male sanitation workers' responses.

The story started by describing the event, and then the two 5
women, who were just your average working women trying to make a buck and get by. There was something about all the maneuvering that had to take place before they could be hired, and then there were the obligatory quotes from male sanitation workers about how women were incapable of doing this job. They were similar to quotes I have read over the years suggesting that women are not fit to be rabbis, combat soldiers, astronauts, fire-fighters, judges, ironworkers, and President of the United States. Chief among them was a comment from one sanitation worker, who said it just wasn't our kind of job, that women were cut out to do dishes and men were cut out to do yard work.

As a woman who has done dishes, yard work, and tossed a fair 6
number of Hefty bags, I was peeved—more so because I would fight for the right of any laid-off sanitation man to work, for example, at the gift-wrap counter at Macy's, even though any woman knows that men are hormonally incapable of wrapping packages and tying bows.

7 I simply can't think of any jobs any more that women can't do. Come to think of it, I can't think of any job women don't do. I know lots of men who are full-time lawyers, doctors, editors and the like. And I know lots of women who are full-time lawyers and part-time interior decorators, pastry chefs, algebra teachers, and garbage slingers. Women are the glue that holds our day-to-day world together.

8 Maybe the sanitation workers who talk about the sex division of duties are talking about girls just like the girls that married dear old dad. Their day is done. Now lots of women know that if they don't carry the garbage bag to the curb, it's not going to get carried—either because they're single, or their husband is working a second job, or he's staying at the office until midnight, or he just left them.

9 I keep hearing that there's a new breed of men out there who don't talk about helping a woman as though they're doing you a favor and who do seriously consider leaving the office if a child comes down with a fever at school, rather than assuming that you will leave yours. But from what I've seen, there aren't enough of these men to qualify as a breed, only as a subgroup.

10 This all sounds angry; it is. After a lifetime spent with winds of sexual change buffeting me this way and that, it still makes me angry to read the same dumb quotes with the same dumb stereotypes that I was reading when I was eighteen. It makes me angry to realize that after so much change, very little is different. It makes me angry to think that these two female sanitation workers will spend their days doing a job most of their co-workers think they can't handle, and then they will go home and do another job most of their co-workers don't want.

BUILDING VOCABULARY

This selection depends significantly on topical allusions. Identify the following:

- **a.** Volkswagen (par. 1)
- **b.** Demerol (par. 1)
- **c.** second-stage breathing (par. 1)
- **d.** Roman candle (par. 3)
- **e.** Hefty bags (par. 6)
- **f.** girls just like the girls that married dear old dad (par. 8)

THINKING CRITICALLY ABOUT THE ESSAY

Understanding the Writer's Ideas

1. Quindlen is often direct, but she also makes many of her points implicitly or through irony. What is the point of her opening paragraph?
2. Why does the writer call thinking that women are superior to men her "dirty little secret" (par. 2)?
3. Restate in your own words the distinction the writer makes between men and women in paragraph 3.
4. Why was the writer "peeved" (par. 6) by the reaction of the male sanitation workers to the hiring of women?
5. Why does the writer think that women "are the glue that holds our day-to-day world together" (par. 7)?
6. What does the writer say she is angry about?
7. What does Quindlen mean when she says there is a "sub-group" rather than "breed" of new men (par. 9)?

Understanding the Writer's Techniques

1. What is the *tone* of this essay? Compare and contrast her tone with those of Molly Ivins (pp. 493–494) and Judy Brady (pp. 456–458)?
2. Why does the writer open her essay with a discussion of men having babies?
3. How does the writer set about showing that women are *better* than men? What kinds of evidence does she use?
4. How did reading about sanitation workers remind the writer of the "inherent" (par. 4) superiority of women? What evidence does she provide for their *inherent* superiority? Do you find the evidence persuasive?
5. What audience do you think the writer has in mind? What makes you think so?
6. Is the writer trying to persuade? If so, what is her main persuasive strategy? If not, what is her purpose in writing?
7. In addition to showing that women are "superior," what is the writer mainly aiming to show?
8. Outline the steps in the writer's argument. Do you find that the argument rambles, or is there a logical development to the argument? Support your answer.
9. What point is being made in the final sentence of the essay? How does that sentence create an effective conclusion?

MIXING PATTERNS

From the title on, Quindlen draws on comparison and contrast techniques to advance her argument. She also uses illustration to support her main proposition. How effective is the use of these rhetorical strategies? In what ways are they essential to the argument?

Exploring the Writer's Ideas

1. Why does Quindlen argue that women are better than, rather than equal to, men?
2. The writer ends paragraph 7 with the sentence "Women are the glue that holds our day-to-day world together." How does this conclusion follow from the evidence presented in the paragraph? Why does she refer to the "day-to-day world"? What other world is there? Is the implication that while men are off doing the "big things," women are keeping the wheels turning? Or is something else implied?
3. Is it really the case that there are no more "girls like the girls that married dear old dad"? Why or why not? What would a girl like the girl who married dear old dad say to Quindlen? What would a stay-at-home, or a "soccer" mom say?
4. How does the tone of Quindlen's essay suggest that not only are men unconvinced that women are better but also that many women may not be convinced either? Why might you agree or disagree with this notion?

IDEAS FOR WRITING

Prewriting

Make two lists. Head one, "Men Do It Better" and the other "Women Do It Better."

Guided Writing

Write an essay entitled "Some Men Are Better—and Women Think So, Too."

1. Begin by reference to a provocative news article or event that can set the tone for your essay as well as establish your main proposition—an article about a beauty pageant queen, for example, or an article about a heroic action.

2. Admit your secret prejudice.
3. If possible, tell an incident in which a wise male friend helped you realize the truth of your prejudice.
4. Offer a supporting illustration that shows that some men are better and also shows that women think so, too.
5. Say that after all these years of women's liberation you're tired of all the same lame clichés.
6. End by reaffirming your main proposition.

Thinking and Writing Collaboratively

In small groups compare the lists you made for the Prewriting exercise. Discuss the reasons people selected certain activities as done better by men or women.

Writing About the Text

Write an essay on Quindlen's style. Examine her word choice and sentence structure. How does humor come into play here? What does the fact that Quindlen wrote this as a newspaper column suggest about the writing style?

More Writing Ideas

1. For a journal entry, summarize the discussion that took place for Thinking and Writing Collaboratively. Stress some aspect of the experience that especially struck you.
2. Write a paragraph about an experience you have had in which, to your surprise, your gender seemed to become an important issue.
3. Write an essay titled "Women Are Better—but Men Are Stronger."

ISSUES OF POLITICAL RIGHTS

Issues of political rights arise from conflicting conceptions of freedom, government, progress, and human welfare. Men and women over the centuries have argued passionately about politics. Is freedom the freedom to be left to my own devices—and thus, freedom from government interference in my life (individual rights)? Or is freedom being treated fairly and equally—and thus, freedom sustained by government so I can run my life as I please (civil rights)? What is the appropriate balance between the individual and the State? In the United States these issues tend to be argued about in the context of the law, specifically the Bill of Rights and the Constitution in general. In the selections that follow, look carefully at the arguments and how they draw on American law and American tradition even as they attempt to change that tradition or to apply it to unprecedented situations. Broadly speaking, these essays use irony, reason, and rhetoric to advance their views. Which do you find most persuasive, and why? What can you take from these essays for use in your own essays?

Get a Knife, Get a Dog, but Get Rid of Guns

Molly Ivins

Born in Monterey, California, in 1944, political columnist Molly Ivins grew up in Houston, Texas. She graduated from Smith College and from the prestigious Columbia University School of Journalism. Ivins's column for the Fort Worth *Star-Telegram* is syndicated in 113 newspapers. Author of the best-selling *Molly Ivins Can't Say That Can She?* (1990), Ivins is known for her brash, amusing writing. In addition to appearing regularly in major American publications, she writes about press issues for the American Civil Liberties Union. This selection from her *Nothin' but Good Times Ahead* (1993) attacks "gun nuts" in a spirited, wry, and sometimes angry tone. As a professional writer for popular audiences, Ivins is alert to the need to be both persuasive and entertaining. Keep an eye out for how she manages to achieve these goals.

PREREADING: THINKING ABOUT THE ESSAY IN ADVANCE

Stop a moment to explore your attitudes about guns. Can you say *why* you think what you do? Are your opinions based on reliable evidence? Are your opinions well-reasoned?

Words to Watch

ricochet (par. 3) bounce off a surface

civil libertarian (par. 4) a person who believes strongly in freedom of speech and action

infringed (par. 5) violated

perforating (par. 6) making holes in

lethal (par. 8) deadly

wreak . . . carnage (par. 8) cause great bloodshed

martial (par. 12) warlike

literally (par. 13) actually

psychosexual (par. 13) having to do with the emotional aspects of sexuality

psyches (par. 14) emotional make-up

1 Guns. Everywhere guns.

2 Let me start this discussion by pointing out that I am not anti-gun. I'm pro-knife. Consider the merits of the knife.

3 In the first place, you have to catch up with someone in order to stab him. A general substitution of knives for guns would promote physical fitness. We'd turn into a whole nation of great runners. Plus, knives don't ricochet. And people are seldom killed while cleaning their knives.

4 As a civil libertarian, I, of course, support the Second Amendment. And I believe it means exactly what it says:

5 *A well-regulated militia being necessary to the security of a free state, the right of the people to keep and bear arms shall not be infringed.* Fourteen-year-old boys are not part of a well-regulated militia. Members of wacky religious cults are not part of a well-regulated militia. Permitting unregulated citizens to have guns is destroying the security of this free state.

6 I am intrigued by the arguments of those who claim to follow the judicial doctrine of original intent. How do they know it was the dearest wish of Thomas Jefferson's heart that teenage drug dealers should cruise the cities of this nation perforating their fellow citizens with assault rifles? Channeling?

7 There is more hooey spread about the Second Amendment. It says quite clearly that guns are for those who form part of a well-regulated militia, that is, the armed forces, including the National Guard. Their reasons for keeping them away from everyone else get clearer by the day.

8 The comparison most often used is that of the automobile, another lethal object that is regularly used to wreak great carnage. Obviously, this society is full of people who haven't enough common sense to use an automobile properly. But we haven't outlawed cars yet.

9 We do, however, license them and their owners, restrict their use to presumably sane and sober adults, and keep track of who sells them to whom. At a minimum, we should do the same with guns.

10 In truth, there is no rational argument for guns in this society. This is no longer a frontier nation in which people hunt their own food. It is a crowded, overwhelmingly urban country in which letting people have access to guns is a continuing disaster. Those who want guns—whether for target shooting, hunting, or potting rattlesnakes (get a hoe)—should be subject to the same restrictions

placed on gun owners in England, a nation in which liberty has survived nicely without an armed populace.

The argument that "guns don't kill people" is patent nonsense. Anyone who has ever worked in a cop shop knows how many family arguments end in murder because there was a gun in the house. Did the gun kill someone? No. But if there had been no gun, no one would have died. At least not without a good foot race first. Guns do kill. Unlike cars, that is all they do. 11

Michael Crichton makes an interesting argument about technology in his thriller *Jurassic Park.* He points out that power without discipline is making this society into a wreckage. By the time someone who studies the martial arts becomes a master—literally able to kill with bare hands—that person has also undergone years of training and discipline. But any fool can pick up a gun and kill with it. 12

"A well-regulated militia" surely implies both long training and long discipline. That is the least, the very least, that should be required of those who are permitted to have guns, because a gun is literally the power to kill. For years I used to enjoy taunting my gun-nut friends about their psychosexual hang-ups—always in a spirit of good cheer, you understand. But letting the noisy minority in the NRA force us to allow this carnage to continue is just plain insane. 13

I do think gun nuts have a power hang-up. I don't know what is missing in their psyches that they need to feel they have the power to kill. But no sane society would allow this to continue. 14

Ban the damn things. Ban them all. 15

You want protection? Get a dog. 16

BUILDING VOCABULARY

1. Identify the following:
   - **a.** the Second Amendment (par. 4)
   - **b.** the judicial doctrine of original intent (par. 6)
   - **c.** Michael Crichton's *Jurassic Park* (par. 12)
   - **d.** NRA (par. 13)
2. This is an essay that argues a certain point of view. It therefore wishes to undermine opposing ideas. List five words or phrases in this essay that aim to strengthen the writer's position by making fun of or otherwise undermining the opposition.

THINKING CRITICALLY ABOUT THE ESSAY

Understanding the Writer's Ideas

1. Why does the writer devote her first three paragraphs to the knife?
2. In your own words, state the writer's interpretation of the Second Amendment.
3. What is the point of comparing guns and cars?
4. In the view of the writer, was there ever an argument for the unlimited access to firearms?
5. What is the writer's response to the argument that "guns don't kill people," it is people using guns who do?
6. Why does the writer allude to *Jurassic Park?*

Understanding the Writer's Techniques

1. What is the *tone* (see Glossary) of this essay? How does the tone support the writer's argument?
2. What is the rhetorical effect of beginning the essay by a discussion of knives? How does the first sentence frame this discussion?
3. This essay lists and responds to the main arguments in *favor* of unlimited sale and possession of guns. Identify these positive arguments in the order they are presented.
4. Why does the writer present the arguments for guns in the order that she does?
5. In addition to responding to arguments by the opposition, the writer puts forward her own arguments against guns. Identify these in the order that they are presented.
6. How does the concluding paragraph reinforce the writer's argument?

Exploring the Writer's Ideas

1. Is the writer too "argumentative"? That is, does she overstep credibility by mocking those who oppose her views? Explain your view.
2. Meddling with amendments to the Constitution is a serious matter, for these provisions have governed the nation well for hundreds of years. Does the writer do justice to the gravity of

the documents whose meaning she is interpreting? Could she advance her argument in a less provocative way? Explain.

3. Are you persuaded by the writer's arguments regarding militias? If so, explain why. If not, explain why not.
4. Write a response to the writer's taunt that progun advocates must have something "missing in their psyches."

IDEAS FOR WRITING

Prewriting

Using the same tone as the writer, write a few sentences in support of guns.

Guided Writing

Write an essay which allows you to mock a well-established but controversial position, such as the advocacy of unlimited access to pornography on the grounds of free speech.

1. Begin the essay with a bold mocking statement that puts those opposed to your view on the defensive. Make sure you can usefully return to the example or tactic of your opening at other points in your essay.
2. State the main argument for the opposition point of view, preferably one referring to its basis in law.
3. Refute this argument by short, dismissive sentences and examples.
4. State two or three other arguments for the opposing point of view, again using short, pointed, and mocking retorts.
5. End your essay by a return, in the form of a pithy summary, to the ploy of your opening paragraph.

Thinking and Writing Collaboratively

Divide the class arbitrarily in two. Assign one group the progun position, and the other the antigun position. Have each group take the writer's main points and amplify or refute them.

Writing About the Essay

Ivins states in paragraph 10, "In truth there is no rational argument for guns in this society." How well has she supported this argument? What examples or details best support it? Has the essay convinced you to accept her argument? Why or why not? Address these questions in an essay that analyzes "Get a Knife, Get a Dog, but Get Rid of Guns."

More Writing Projects

1. Visit a firing range and interview some people there about their views on guns. Write an outline for an essay about your visit.
2. Read the debates that led to the original adoption of the Second Amendment. Write an essay that reflects on the relevance or irrelevance of the arguments of that time to our own.
3. Write an essay that argues for a favored solution of your own to the problem of violence in our society.

The (No) Free Speech Movement

Julie Bosman

In March 2001, when Julie Bosman was an undergraduate at the University of Wisconsin–Madison and editor-in-chief of the student newspaper, the *Badger Herald,* she wrote this essay, which was published in national news media. In her essay, Bosman addresses a classic conflict between those who advocate free speech and those who, persuaded by the rightness of their cause, believe that certain issues should not be allowed space in a public medium, like a newspaper. Look carefully at Bosman's presentation of the case, noting her use of reasoning and thinking about the validity of her evidence.

PREREADING: THINKING ABOUT THE ESSAY IN ADVANCE

You will better understand this selection if you have some familiarity with the Free Speech Movement, a 60s student protest movement that saw itself as fighting for free speech on U.S. college campuses. A good source of information is *www.lib.berkeley.edu/BANC/FSM/.* More generally, do you think there are any circumstances that warrant the restriction of speech?

Words to Watch

mea culpa (par. 4) the Latin phrase from the prayer of confession, meaning "through my own fault" but used generally as an acknowledgement of fault

cohorts (par. 6) like-minded group

discourse (par. 7) discussion, verbal or written

One hundred screaming protesters outside the doors of a small newspaper office can be intimidating, especially for the editor who is the main target of their abuse. 1

The protesters swarmed outside the office of my paper, the Badger Herald, at the University of Wisconsin–Madison, after first marching across campus brandishing placards that read "Badger Herald Racist." They demonstrated for more than an hour, demanding my resignation as editor, because the Herald had run a paid advertisement entitled "Ten Reasons Why Reparations for Slavery Is a Bad Idea—and Racist Too." The ad was written and 2 placed by David Horowitz, a conservative author, and had appeared on the last day of Black History Month, a full six days before the demonstration, which took place March 6.

3 The 10 anti-reparations reasons listed ranged from the commonplace ("There is no single group clearly responsible for the crime of slavery," or "Only a tiny minority of white Americans ever owned slaves") to the very controversial ("What about the debt blacks owe to America?"). But our decision to publish was based on the straight forward view that our paper believes in free speech.

4 The Horowitz ad was published elsewhere too, and the hostile response to it was as disturbing as the mobbing of our offices. Angry protesters confronted staffers of the Daily Californian at the University of California, Berkeley, after the ad had run. The Daily Cal's editor, Daniel Hernandez, printed a front-page apology for running the ad, calling his paper "an inadvertent vehicle for bigotry" and acknowledging, in a mea culpa wrung from him by the protesters, that the ad had not passed through the proper channels.

5 We were also under pressure to abase ourselves. But the Herald editorial board refused to run an apology. Instead, we published an editorial saying that "at the Badger Herald, we only regret that the editors of the Daily Californian allowed themselves to give in to pressure in the manner that unfortunately violated their professional integrity and journalistic duty to protect speech with which they disagree."

6 The issues raised here go to the heart of a critical question: Are American university campuses free and open to a spirit of inquiry, or closed places where activist cohorts can determine what is, or isn't, acceptable? Signs of rot can be detected in the fact that at least 15 college newspapers—including those at Harvard, Columbia, Notre Dame, the University of Washington, Georgia Tech and the University of Virginia—have rejected the Horowitz ad on grounds that it was politically unacceptable.

7 This is not to say that newspapers must print all advertisements submitted. The Herald does not prints ads that are completely false. The ad submitted (and rejected) last weekend by the Multicultural Student Coalition calling the Herald a "racist propaganda machine" would fall into this category. But the Horowitz ad is well within the bounds of political discourse.

8 One student (and student-government representative) at the Badger Herald rally shouted, "This isn't free speech, it's hate speech." Really? Most people outside of college campuses no

doubt would be amazed to find that reparations for slavery has become, for some, a nondebatable subject.

On a traditionally liberal campus like ours, any opinions originating from the right tend to be stomped out with a vengeance. Rather than rebut Mr. Horowitz's arguments, the protesters simply tried to drown out his message with name-calling directed at the Herald. It's woefully apparent that the same campuses that once stood for idealistic causes in the '60s and '70s now tolerate only political hyper-correctness and unchallenged "progressive" thought. Though the students who protested at the doors of the Herald say they demand "diversity"—UW–Madison's latest buzzword—they appear not to accept that principle when it comes to expression or beliefs. 9

The most consistent criticism of the Herald's action in printing the Horowitz ad has been our alleged lack of sensitivity to students of color on campus. While I do not deny the passionate reaction by many students to the advertisement, this is one of the painful and inescapable by-products of the free-speech principle by which ethical journalists must abide. 10

Shamefully for the culprits, the most recent maneuver in the speech wars at UW–Madison is an illegal and cowardly one. Several students have witnessed others throwing away stacks of Heralds from their racks in university buildings, while several Herald staff members have retrieved heaps of bundled papers from garbage cans in the same buildings. How ironic it is that the diversity of viewpoints the activists are demanding is trashed along with the open forum in which it can be represented. 11

BUILDING VOCABULARY

Argument involves persuasion; persuasion involves trying to sway the reader, often by careful selection of emotionally charged words. Rewrite the sentences below to make the presentation more "neutral" by choosing different words for those in italics.

- **a.** One hundred *screaming* protesters outside the doors of a *small* newspaper office can be *intimidating,* especially for the editor who is the main target of their *abuse* (par. 1).
- **b.** The Horowitz ad was published elsewhere too, and the *hostile response* to it was *as disturbing as the mobbing of our offices.* (par. 4)

THINKING CRITICALLY ABOUT THE ESSAY

Understanding the Writer's Ideas

1. When was the Horowitz ad printed in the writer's newspaper? How was the timing important? Why does the writer stress that the ad appeared "a full six days" before the demonstration?
2. What "anti-reparation reasons" did the ad propose?
3. What happened on other campuses with respect to the Horowitz ad?
4. Why did the *Herald* editorial board refuse to run an apology for having taken the ad?
5. What, according to the writer, are the issues raised by the response to the ad?
6. What does the writer mean by "signs of rot" (par. 6)?
7. In the view of the writer, under what circumstances does a newspaper *not* have to print an ad?
8. Why does the writer disagree with the view that the Horowitz ad is "hate speech"?
9. What evidence does the writer offer to support her point that once-idealistic campuses "now tolerate only political hyper-correctness"?
10. What rationale does the writer offer for permitting speech that some individuals may find personally wounding?
11. What, in the writer's view, is ironic about the demands for diversity made by some students on her campus?

Understanding the Writer's Techniques

1. What is the thesis of this essay? Where is it located?
2. How does the writer frame the issues she wishes to address?
3. The writer's essay divides into three sections: identify where each section begins and ends. What are the functions of each of the sections of the essay?
4. How does the writer link the three sections of the essay?
5. Which arguments justify a refusal to run the Horowitz ad? Where and how does the writer present these arguments?
6. How does the writer present her own argument? What is her argument? What are some of the main kinds of support or evidence that she uses to advance it? Give examples of each.

(See pp. 423–424 for a discussion of the kinds of support used in argumentative essays.)

7. How does Bosman's title affect the essay? Why does she place the word *No* in parentheses?
8. How does the writer's concluding paragraph support the main argument here? What is your reaction to the metaphor "the diversity of viewpoints . . . is trashed along with the open forum in which it can be represented"? What elements earlier in the paragraph help set up this metaphor?

Exploring the Writer's Ideas

1. Is the writer's presentation of the facts impartial? Cite passages that provide evidence of or call into question her impartiality.
2. The writer concedes that the exercise of free speech may cause pain to some individuals. She argues, however, that this pain is one of the "inescapable by-products of the free speech principle" (par. 10). Is the writer's argument "insensitive" or simply realistic? Explain your point.
3. Should an advertisement fall under the category "free speech"? Should a newspaper print all the ads submitted to it, or only those that are not "completely false" (par. 7)? Explain your answers.
4. Is a college newspaper indistinguishable from a commercial newspaper, or is a college paper different and subject to different rules and expectations?

Prewriting

Draw a line down the middle of a page, and list on one side reasons or circumstances that might justify restrictions on free speech and on the other arguments against those reasons.

Guided Writing

Write an essay to argue that newspapers are under no obligation to print any advertisements that are submitted to them and that newspapers should be free not to publish advertisements of which, for whatever reasons, they do not approve.

1. Begin by making reference to the controversy over the Horowitz ad, and say that people have miscast the issue inherent in the controversy as a free speech issue.
2. Assert that it is not a free speech issue but a different one: What are the obligations of newspapers to print advertisements submitted to them? Offer two or three possibilities and analyze the elements of each in separate paragraphs. These elements, of course, will *oppose* your argument. Nevertheless, present them fairly and logically. You might say that advertising is just marketing, and as a business decision, ads should appear if the newspaper wants to build its revenue no matter how provocative or unpleasant the ad. Or, to take another example, you might point out that ads are like any kind of free speech and should be completely unrestricted.
3. Restate your rejection of one or more of these views.
4. Conclude with a reaffirmation of your thesis and support it.

Thinking and Writing Collaboratively

In small groups of four or five, study the ads in a daily newspaper or a popular magazine. Pick a few ads that people might find offensive (for any reason), and list arguments for and against refusing to publish these potentially offensive ads.

Writing About the Text

The Horowitz ad argues against the idea of paying reparations for slavery. The writer does not say what her opinion on this subject might be. Write an essay that nevertheless seeks, on the basis of the evidence in the writer's essay, to tease out the writer's general political views. Try to be clear and definitive. Say, for example, that the evidence clearly shows the writer is a conservative like Horowitz and therefore she was comfortable with his ad. Or, to choose another possibility, say that the evidence shows that the writer is a libertarian, and, although she does not sympathize with Horowitz's views, she is committed to his right to have his say. Support your argument with references to the text.

More Writing Projects

1. Interview the editors of your college newspaper to discover their policy on publishing ads. In your journal, write a report of your interview, carefully restating the position of your school paper's editorial board.
2. Write a paragraph or two that explores the rights of advertisers in the context of free speech.
3. Read the Horowitz ad (you may be able to find a print copy in your library, or a copy on the Internet) and write an essay stating why, if you were the editor of your school paper, you would or would not print the ad.

I Have a Dream

Martin Luther King, Jr.

Martin Luther King, Jr. (1929–1968), American clergyman and Nobel Prize winner, was one of the main leaders of the civil-rights movement of the 1960s and a passionate advocate of nonviolent protest. His assassination in 1968 became an international rallying cry in the struggle for racial justice. A native of Atlanta, Georgia, King was educated at Morehouse College and Boston University. In 1957 King helped to found the Southern Christian Leadership Conference, and he soon led a series of protests throughout the South to desegregate the society. In 1963 King organized the now-legendary March on Washington, at the conclusion of which, standing before the Lincoln Memorial, he delivered the "I Have a Dream" speech, printed below, to an audience of more than 200,000 people. Immediately adopted into the canon of great American oratory, King's speech, with its distinctive use of religious language and emotional allusion to American images of freedom, merits careful attention as an example of powerful and historic argument.

PREREADING: THINKING ABOUT THE ESSAY IN ADVANCE

The essay's title is cast in the present tense: the speaker *has* a dream. How would the essay be different if the title were cast in the past tense? It's unlikely that you have not heard of Martin Luther King, Jr., or of this essay. But it was originally not an essay: it was a speech on a highly public occasion. What expectations does King raise by speaking of a dream rather than, say, a goal, or an ambition, or a purpose?

Words to Watch

symbolic (par. 1) representative
emancipation (par. 1) liberation
proclamation (par. 1) official publication
unalienable (par. 3) incapable of being surrendered or taken away
interposition (par. 16) interference
nullification (par. 16) the impeding by a state of federal law
prodigious (par. 21) vast

Five score years ago, a great American, in whose symbolic shadow we stand, signed the Emancipation Proclamation. This momentous decree came as a great beacon light of hope to millions of Negro slaves who had been seared in the flames of withering injustice. It came as a joyous daybreak to end the long night of captivity. 1

But one hundred years later, we must face the tragic fact that the Negro is still not free. One hundred years later, the life of the Negro is still sadly crippled by the manacles of segregation and the chains of discrimination. One hundred years later, the Negro lives on a lonely island of poverty in the midst of a vast ocean of material prosperity. One hundred years later, the Negro is still languishing in the corners of American society and finds himself an exile in his own land. So we have come here today to dramatize an appalling condition. 2

In a sense we have come to our nation's capital to cash a check. When the architects of our republic wrote the magnificent words of the Constitution and the Declaration of Independence, they were signing a promissory note to which every American was to fall heir. This note was a promise that all men would be guaranteed the unalienable rights of life, liberty, and the pursuit of happiness. 3

It is obvious today that America has defaulted on this promissory note insofar as her citizens of color are concerned. Instead of honoring this sacred obligation, America has given the Negro people a bad check; a check which has come back marked "insufficient funds." But we refuse to believe that the bank of justice is bankrupt. We refuse to believe that there are insufficient funds in the great vaults of opportunity of this nation. So we have come to cash this check—a check that will give us upon demand the riches of freedom and the security of justice. We have also come to this hallowed spot to remind America of the fierce urgency of *now.* This is no time to engage in the luxury of cooling off or to take the tranquilizing drugs of gradualism. *Now* is the time to make real the promises of Democracy. *Now* is the time to rise from the dark and desolate valley of segregation to the sunlit path of racial justice. *Now* is the time to open the doors of opportunity to all of God's children. *Now* is the time to lift our nation from the quicksands of racial injustice to the solid rock of brotherhood. 4

It would be fatal for the nation to overlook the urgency of the moment and to underestimate the determination of the Negro. This 5 sweltering summer of the Negro's legitimate discontent will not pass until there is an invigorating autumn of freedom and equality. 1963 is not an end, but a beginning. Those who hope that the Negro needed to blow off steam and will now be content will have a rude awakening if the nation returns to business as usual. There will be neither rest nor tranquility in America until the Negro is granted his citizenship rights. The whirlwinds of revolt will continue to shake the foundations of our nation until the bright day of justice emerges.

6 But there is something that I must say to my people who stand on the warm threshold which leads into the palace of justice. In the process of gaining our rightful place we must not be guilty of wrongful deeds. Let us not seek to satisfy our thirst for freedom by drinking from the cup of bitterness and hatred. We must forever conduct our struggle on the high plane of dignity and discipline. We must not allow our creative protest to degenerate into physical violence. Again and again we must rise to the majestic heights of meeting physical force with soul force. The marvelous new militancy which has engulfed the Negro community must not lead us to a distrust of all white people, for many of our white brothers, as evidenced by their presence here today, have come to realize that their destiny is tied up with our destiny and their freedom is inextricably bound to our freedom. We cannot walk alone.

7 And as we walk, we must make the pledge that we shall march ahead. We cannot turn back. There are those who are asking the devotees of civil rights, "When will you be satisfied?" We can never be satisfied as long as the Negro is the victim of the unspeakable horrors of police brutality. We can never be satisfied as long as our bodies, heavy with the fatigue of travel, cannot gain lodging in the motels of the highways and the hotels of the cities. We cannot be satisfied as long as the Negro's basic mobility is from a smaller ghetto to a larger one. We can never be satisfied as long as a Negro in Mississippi cannot vote and a Negro in New York believes he has nothing for which to vote. No, no, we are not satisfied, and will not be satisfied until justice rolls down like waters and righteousness like a mighty stream.

8 I am not unmindful that some of you have come here out of great trials and tribulations. Some of you have come fresh from narrow jail cells. Some of you have come from areas where your quest for freedom left you battered by the storms of persecution and staggered by the winds of police brutality. You have been the

veterans of creative suffering. Continue to work with the faith that unearned suffering is redemptive.

Go back to Mississippi, go back to Alabama, go back to South 9
Carolina, go back to Georgia, go back to Louisiana, go back to the slums and ghettos of our northern cities, knowing that somehow this situation can and will be changed. Let us not wallow in the valley of despair.

I say to you today, my friends, that in spite of the difficulties 10
and frustrations of the moment I still have a dream. It is a dream deeply rooted in the American dream.

I have a dream that one day this nation will rise up and live 11
out the true meaning of its creed: "We hold these truths to be self-evident; that all men are created equal."

I have a dream that one day on the red hills of Georgia the 12
sons of former slaves and the sons of former slaveowners will be able to sit down together at the table of brotherhood.

I have a dream that one day even the state of Mississippi, a 13
desert state sweltering with the heat of injustice and oppression, will be transformed into an oasis of freedom and justice.

I have a dream that my four little children will one day live in 14
a nation where they will not be judged by the color of their skin but by the content of their character.

I have a dream today. 15

I have a dream that one day the state of Alabama, whose gover- 16
nor's lips are presently dripping with the words of interposition and nullification, will be transformed into a situation where little black boys and black girls will be able to join hands with little white boys and white girls and walk together as sisters and brothers.

I have a dream today. 17

I have a dream that one day every valley shall be exalted, 18
every hill and mountain shall be made low, the rough places will be made plain, and the crooked places will be made straight, and the glory of the Lord shall be revealed, and all flesh shall see it together.

This is our hope. This is the faith with which I return to the 19
South. With this faith we will be able to hew out of the mountain of despair a stone of hope. With this faith we will be able to transform the jangling discords of our nation into a beautiful symphony of brotherhood. With this faith we will be able to work together, to pray together, to struggle together, to go to jail together, to stand up for freedom together, knowing that we will be free one day.

20 This will be the day when all of God's children will be able to sing with new meaning

> My country, 'tis of thee,
> Sweet land of liberty,
> Of thee I sing:
> Land where my fathers died,
> Land of the pilgrims' pride,
> From every mountain-side
> Let freedom ring.

21 And if America is to be a great nation this must become true. So let freedom ring from the prodigious hilltops of New Hampshire. Let freedom ring from the mighty mountains of New York. Let freedom ring from the heightening Alleghenies of Pennsylvania!

22 Let freedom ring from the snowcapped Rockies of Colorado!

23 Let freedom ring from the curvaceous peaks of California!

24 But not only that; let freedom ring from Stone Mountain of Georgia!

25 Let freedom ring from Lookout Mountain of Tennessee!

26 Let freedom ring from every hill and molehill of Mississippi. From every mountainside, let freedom ring.

27 When we let freedom ring, when we let it ring from every village and every hamlet, from every state and every city, we will be able to speed up that day when all of God's children, black men and white men, Jews and Gentiles, Protestants and Catholics, will be able to join hands and sing in the words of the old Negro spiritual, "Free at last! free at last! thank God almighty, we are free at last!"

BUILDING VOCABULARY

King's speech is highly metaphorical. Rewrite the words in italics below in simple declarative language:

- **a.** "slaves who had been *seared in the flames of withering* injustice" (par. 1).
- **b.** "the Negro *lives on a lonely island of poverty in the midst of a vast ocean of material prosperity*" (par. 2).
- **c.** "We refuse to believe that *there are insufficient funds in the great vaults of opportunity* of this nation" (par. 4).
- **d.** *"from the quicksands of racial injustice to the solid rock of brotherhood"* (par. 4).

THINKING CRITICALLY ABOUT THE ESSAY

Understanding the Writer's Ideas

1. Who is the "great American" King speaks about in the first sentence of his essay?
2. What is the "appalling condition" that King says he and his followers have come to Washington to dramatize?
3. What does King mean when he says "we have come to our nation's capital to cash a check" (par. 3)?
4. Why does King emphasize the word *now* in par. 4?
5. What does King advise as proper for his followers as they stand "on the warm threshold" of justice?
6. How does King respond to the charge that his demands are insatiable?
7. Summarize in one sentence the point King makes in paragraphs 10–18.
8. How does King connect his faith and hope with the tradition of American patriotism?
9. Why does King end his speech with a passage from a Negro spiritual?

Understanding the Writer's Techniques

1. What aspects of King's address illustrate that it is a speech and not an essay? What is the purpose of King's speech?
2. King casts the purpose of the March on Washington in surprisingly monetary terms. The Constitution and Declaration of Independence were, he says, a "promissory note" on which America has "defaulted." But King has come to Washington "to cash this check." In what ways is this extended metaphor appropriate to advance King's cause? Or do you think it is too much to do with money and demeans his cause?
3. King, a preacher, makes abundant use of biblical allusion and biblical language to make his points. In paragraph 2, for example, King speaks of the Negro as being in "exile in his own land." How does this analogy appeal to Judeo-Christian tradition? What other examples of biblical allusion or biblical language do you find especially effective?
4. What is King's thesis? Where does he state it?
5. To whom do you think King addressed this speech? Support your answer by quoting pertinent passages.

6. How does King, as an orator, seek to move his audience?
7. Why does King include the opening of "My Country, 'Tis of Thee"? Why does he refer to so many different places in his final paragraphs? What is especially significant in his choice of Mississippi for his final geographical reference?
8. What argumentative strategies does King use? Which do you find most effective?
9. How does repetition affect the essay? Cite some examples and explain why you think King used repetition as he did.
10. How do the final words of the speech form an especially effective conclusion?

Exploring the Writer's Ideas

1. In the opening paragraphs of his speech, King uses metaphors related to money and payment in explaining the reason for his speech. Later in the speech, however, he calls upon a whole new set of references as he talks about his dream, a dream that doesn't seem to have much to do with money at all. Explain why you think that these two parts of his speech do or do not fit well together.
2. Do you think that King would today advocate the kind of nonviolent protest, known as "passive resistance," that he advocated in 1963 (par. 6)? Do you think that passive resistance would succeed in obtaining justice for people struggling for their rights today, within the United States or outside of it? Explain your answers.
3. Few ideas in American life are more powerful than the idea that "all men are created equal" (par. 11). But how does King intend us to understand that phrase? Does he mean that all people are entitled to the same things? Why does he not mention women? And can we achieve this entitlement? Does King mean that we are all equal in the eyes of God? If so, what does that imply for political equality? Economic equality? Should the government of the United States ensure that all people in the nation enjoy economic equality? Explain your thinking.
4. Do you find King's intensely religious way of speaking, with its echoes of biblical language and its heavy use of biblical metaphors, a strength or a weakness of his speech? Explain your answer.

IDEAS FOR WRITING

Prewriting

How should social or political grievances be settled within our democracy? Jot down some ideas about how you would go about changing some common practice or law that many people find oppressive—say, the laws that establish the age at which young people can drink; or the laws about marriage between people of the same sex; or . . .

Guided Writing

Write a speech intended to stir your classmates to conduct a sit-in or other protest at the college administration building, the mayor's or governor's offices, or a similar location to call attention to an injustice that you think affects many people.

1. Begin by making an allusion to a famous American or famous alumnus or alumna, etc., with the purpose of showing that this person acted to correct an injustice.
2. Then note that many years have passed and yet today injustices remain.
3. In metaphorical language, indicate the injustice that you want to rouse your audience to oppose.
4. Say that the moral high ground demands action—but action that avoids violence.
5. Emphasize King's notion that "unearned suffering is redemptive" (par. 8).
6. In your concluding paragraph or paragraphs, paint a picture of what you dream will come to pass.
7. Conclude the essay with an emotional sentence or phrase from a hymn or spiritual or popular patriotic or protest song.

Thinking and Writing Collaboratively

Almost half a century has passed since King delivered this famous speech. In small groups discuss whether his dream has been realized. Jot down the evidence for and against the view that his dream has been realized. Compare the conclusion arrived at by your group with the conclusions of the other groups in the class.

Writing About the Text

Argument depends mainly on reason. But clearly King does not mainly rely on reason. He often appeals directly to emotion. Is there then an inherent conflict between the fairly cool and objective standards of argument and the inevitably emotional methods of persuasion? Write an essay that considers whether in King's speech, his rational arguments support or undermine his more emotional writing, his methods of persuasion; and whether, on the other hand, the emotional passages of the essay tend to support or undermine the passages that rely more on reason.

More Writing Projects

1. Will social inequality always exist or can we eliminate it? In your journal record your responses to this question.
2. Write a paragraph about King's conception of justice based on what you can reasonably conclude from the references and metaphors of his speech.
3. On the basis of some research, write an essay in which you describe the picture of America in 1963 that emerges from King's speech, and do research to determine whether that picture was or was not accurate.

SUMMING UP: CHAPTER 11

1. Keep a journal in which you record your thoughts on, and observations of, homelessness in your part of the country. Try to gather specific data from reading, television viewing, or observation. Ask such questions as:

   How many are male? female?
   How many are children?
   How many are elderly?
   How many appear to be mentally ill?
   What symptoms or signs do they exhibit?

   Use the data, along with your observations, to present your position on homelessness in a letter to the editor of your campus or local newspaper.
2. Invite a local expert to class to speak on a current controversial issue. Write an essay of support for, or opposition to, the speaker's opinions.
3. Justify the inclusion of the essays by Kozol, Ivins, Brady, and Quindlen under the category "Argumentation and Persuasion." Treat the major issues that they raise, their positions on these issues, their minor propositions and use of evidence, and the tone of their language. Finally, establish the degree to which you are persuaded by these arguments.
4. Exchange with a classmate an essay that you've each written for a Guided Writing exercise in this chapter. Even if you agree with your partner's opinion, write a strongly worded response opposing it. Be sure you touch on the same, or similar, major and minor propositions.
5. Fill in the blanks in the following essay topic as you please, and use it as the major proposition for a well-developed argumentation-persuasion paper. Draw on the expository writing skills you have studied throughout the book. "I am very concerned about ____________, and I believe it's necessary to ____________."
6. Compare and contrast the viewpoints on men offered by Brady and Quindlen. Do you agree with their positions? Why or why not?

7. How do you think Marable and Steele would respond to the situation described by Julie Bosman in "The (No) Free Speech Movement"?
8. Write an essay that seeks to reconcile the views of Marable and Steele or of Herbert and Wilson.
9. The United States was once known as a "melting pot," meaning that the beauty of American life was its ability to meld different people, regardless of origin, into one nation. Today we speak instead of diversity as characterizing America. Write an essay that explores the implications of these two characterizations, using the selections relating to identity in this chapter as resources.
10. Shelby Steele and James Q. Wilson are considered to be "conservative" writers. Argue for or against the proposition that their conservative biases prevent them from presenting their arguments fairly and accurately.
11. Manning Marable and Bob Herbert are known as "liberal" or progressive writers. Argue for or against the proposition that their liberal biases prevent them from presenting their arguments fairly or accurately.
12. Reread the essays by Brady, Spitzer, and Quindlen and then select your favorite one, arguing why it is the best essay on the subject of identity.
13. Brady, Quindlen, and Ivins use various comic strategies to advance their arguments. Analyze these comic elements in a comparative essay.

FROM SEEING TO WRITING

What is this protestor's argument and how does he advocate it? Do you support or oppose his decision to engage in civil disobedience? Take your own stand on a specific environmental issue, and state your main proposition. Offer three reasons to support your position, and supply evidence for each. Deal with the opposing viewpoints. In your conclusion, either support or reject the use of civil disobedience as a way of advancing your viewpoint.

Bob Daemmrich/Stock Boston

APPENDIX:
A Guide to Research and Documentation

WHAT ARE RESEARCH AND DOCUMENTATION?

A *research* paper grows out of careful investigation of books, periodicals, on-line resources, and other documents and texts to support a thesis. Research writing can be a form of problem-solving or a careful investigation of a subject. You may identify a problem, form a hypothesis (an unproven thesis, theory, or argument), gather and organize information from various sources, assess and interpret data, evaluate alternatives, reach conclusions, and provide documentation. Other research writing projects may involve the discovery or revision of facts, theories, or applications. In either kind of research paper, your purpose is to demonstrate how other researchers approach a problem and how you treat that problem. A good research paper subtly blends your ideas and the ideas or discoveries of others. In research writing, you become part of a larger academic, social, or cultural conversation. You synthesize ideas that have already been made public—carefully documenting the sources of those ideas—and you contribute your own unique insights and conclusions.

Documentation refers to the rules and conventions by which academic researchers acknowledge the sources on which their work is based. As you research your subject, you will use documentation to note carefully where you find your information so that readers of your work can retrace your sources. Documentation also allows you to give proper credit to the work of other writers. Not providing full and accurate documentation can leave you open to charges of plagiarism.

THE RESEARCH PROCESS

The research process involves thinking, searching, reading, writing, and rewriting. The final product—the research paper—is the result of your discoveries about your topic as well as your contribution to the ongoing academic conversation about your topic. More than any other form of college writing, the research paper evolves gradually through a series of stages. As you develop as a writer and researcher, you will probably adapt this process according to your own strengths and style. As a beginning researcher and writer, however, you may find that a more methodical approach to this process will help you structure your library work as well as your writing.

PHASE I: CHOOSING AND LIMITING A TOPIC

- Browsing
- Limiting the topic

↓

PHASE II: GATHERING AND ORGANIZING DATA

- Developing a working bibliography
- Assessing and evaluating sources
- Taking notes
- Developing a thesis
- Organizing your notes and writing an outline

↓

PHASE III: WRITING THE PAPER

- Drafting
- Incorporating sources
- Revising your draft
- Preparing the final manuscript

↓

PHASE IV: DOCUMENTING SOURCES

Phase I: Choosing and Limiting a Topic

Although you may receive a very specific research topic from your professor, you are far more likely to meet your first research challenge before you even set foot in the library: What will you write about? One of the great challenges of academic research is learning how to ask the kind of question that will lead to a terrific research topic. You can save time, effort, and anxiety if you approach your research project as a problem to be investigated and solved, a controversy to take a position on, or a specific question to be answered. As a basis for your research, you need at least a hunch or a calculated guess—an idea that will lead to a strong hypothesis or working thesis.

- Before you can formulate a hypothesis, you need to start with a general idea of what subject you want to explore, what your purpose is going to be, and how you plan to select and limit a topic from your larger subject area.

To find and limit that topic, you'll want to begin with some preliminary browsing in the library.

Browsing

When you *browse,* you inspect, informally, books and articles in your general area of interest. These points will help you browse in the library as you explore a topic idea:

- The *library reference section* provides encyclopedias, almanacs, and other reference books for an overview of your area of interest. These resources may be print, on-line, or on CD-ROM. General reference resources can be useful for background reading and an introduction to your topic. However, these general resources should only be the beginning of your research—do not rely exclusively on these sources, which may not be the most up-to-date or in-depth.
- The *library catalog* lists information by author, title, subject, and keyword. It will suggest possible subtopics under the general topic heading and also give you an idea of how many books have been written about your topic. Your library may have both a card catalog and an on-line catalog; if so, your browsing will be more fruitful if you use both. Ask your reference librarian for guidance on using both the on-line and card catalogs.

- In your catalog browsing, you will notice that books on your topic most likely share a *call number,* or have call numbers within the same range. Go to that area of your library where books with these call numbers are shelved. Because library classification systems group all books on similar topics near one another, you have many approaches to your topic at your fingertips. Select books that have the most recent copyright dates, which you'll find on the first few pages of the book (ten years is a good boundary). Examine the table of contents, the index, the glossary, and the appendices. Look at the illustrations, if there are any. Read a paragraph or two from the preface or introduction.
- A *periodical index* is an alphabetical listing (usually annual) of authors, titles, and subjects of articles in magazines, journals, or newspapers. Some *databases,* which your library may have on CD-ROM or on-line, may also provide summaries or complete texts of articles. Indexes are both general (covering major newspapers, journals, and magazines, and a wide range of topics) and very subject-specific. Ask your reference librarian for indexes specific to your subject. Like a library catalog, an index or database shows you at a glance the kinds of subtopics current writers have addressed as parts of larger topics. Reading over the titles of current articles, you can see a variety of approaches to your topic.
- *Search engines* on-line can help you find a broad range of information about your general topic—but that very broadness of information can be overwhelming. Your instructor may be able to recommend useful sites, as can your reference librarian. Search engines such as Google, Dogpile, and HotBot hunt through vast numbers of pages at websites, seeking those that mention key words that you specify. Browsing through the "hits" you get through such a search engine can give you a spectrum of ideas about your topic. However, you will probably want to check with your instructor about any websites you may wish to use as a basis for your research. Print out the first page of the website, which will give you the URL (the site's address); you can then ask your instructor to visit the website and evaluate its reliability as a source.

Limiting the Topic

The first step in research writing is to *limit* your research to a *researchable topic.* Such a topic is appropriate in scope for your assignment, promises an adventure for you in the realm of ideas, and interests your audience. Developing a hypothesis, or a question that requires more than a simplistic answer, will lead to a researchable topic. The following chart shows examples of general topics narrowed to researchable topics.

NARROWING THE TOPIC

Too General	*Still Broad*	*Less Broad*	*Narrow Enough*
Teaching	teaching number concepts	teaching number concepts to children	teaching number concepts at home to children under five
Religion	religious customs	ancient religious customs in North America	Anazazi religious customs in America's Midwest
Pollution	fighting air pollution	fighting air pollution in California	the government's role in fighting air pollution in Los Angeles
World War II	effects of WWII	effects of WWII in the United States	economic effects of WWII in Detroit

After your first effort to limit your topic as a result of browsing and of some preliminary thinking, you should expect to limit your topic even further. Two further strategies for narrowing your topic are *freewriting* and *feedback.* Try the following freewriting exercise:

1. Why does this topic interest me so strongly?
2. What do I already know about this topic?
3. What three or four questions do I have about this topic, based on my preliminary browsing?
4. What are my opinions about problems related to this topic?

Sharing your freewriting with other students in a discussion group, with your instructor, or with some other friendly reader will give you additional insight into your topic.

Phase II: Gathering and Organizing Material

Developing a Working Bibliography

The purpose of compiling a working bibliography is to keep an accurate record of all the sources you consulted with all the critical information about them. If you are required to do so, you can prepare a list of works cited (see pages A-18 – A-26) from the data in your working bibliography. Although you may wish to keep your working bibliography as a computer document, you may find it more useful and efficient to use 4 × 6-inch index cards. Index cards allow you to do the following:

- Arrange the cards easily in alphabetical order as sources are added or deleted (your final bibliography will be alphabetically organized)
- Make quick notes to yourself about your first impressions of the materials to help you decide later whether to return to the source for closer study
- Carry them easily to the library for quick notes, where a computer is not always convenient

Use a standard form for your working bibliography, whether you use cards or computer entries, to simplify the task of preparing your final Works Cited or References section.

INFORMATION FOR A WORKING BIBLIOGRAPHY

Record the following information for a book:

1. Name(s) of author(s)
2. Title of book, underlined
3. Place of publication
4. Publisher's name
5. Date of publication
6. Call number or location in library

continued

Record the following information for an article in a periodical:

1. Name(s) of author(s)
2. Title of article, in quotation marks
3. Title of periodical, underlined
4. Volume number or issue number
5. Date of publication
6. Page numbers on which article appears
7. Call number or location in library

For on-line sources, record all of the above information as well as the complete URL (site address) and date of access on-line.

Sample working bibliography card: Article

Gladwell, Malcolm. "Examined Life." The New Yorker 17 Dec. 2001: 86–92.

Assessing and Evaluating Sources

At this phase in the research process, you will have amassed a variety of sources and perspectives. Your task now is to revisit those articles, books, websites, and other sources—using your working bibliography as a constant guide. Begin by *skimming* your sources. Skimming is not random or casual reading, but a careful examination of the material to sort out the useful sources from those that aren't helpful. For a book, check the table of contents and index for information on your topic; then determine whether the information is relevant to your topic (your hypothesis, question, or problem). For an article, see if the abstract or topic sentences in the body of the essay apply to your topic.

On-line sources require careful and critical evaluation on your part. In general, librarians have recommended or chosen the books that you find in your school library. In addition, editors and experts in the field have for the most part reviewed books and articles in print. To the contrary, unbiased or authoritative experts may or may not have examined materials located on the Web. When in doubt, ask your instructor or a reference librarian.

EVALUATING PRINT AND ON-LINE SOURCES

1. Is the source directly relevant to your topic? Does it confirm your hypothesis, answer your question, or propose a solution to your problem?
2. Does the source present relatively current information, especially for research in the social and natural sciences?
3. Does the source indicate the author's expertise (background, education, other publications)? Do other writers refer to this author as a reliable expert?
4. Does the source provide information comparable to that in other reputable sources?
5. Does the source supply notes, a bibliography, or other information to document its own sources?
6. Does an on-line source identify its author? Is the site sponsored by a particular business, agency, or organization? Is contact information provided for the author or sponsor?
7. Does an on-line source supply useful, appropriate links? Are the links current and relevant? Are many of the links broken? (Many broken links indicate that the site has not been recently updated.)

Taking Notes

Once you have assembled relevant, useful sources, you can begin to read these sources more closely and take detailed notes. Accurate, well-chosen notes will help you build your research essay. You want to select and summarize the general ideas that will form the outline of your paper, to record specific evidence to support your ideas, and to copy exact statements you plan to quote for evidence or interest.

Many researchers find it useful to take notes on 4 × 6-inch cards. By keeping your notes on cards, you can easily rearrange information from different sources; compare ideas from different sources; and build a visual outline when it's time to draft your research essay.

There are three kinds of notes that you can take as you do your research:

- *Summaries* of material keep track of specific facts, overall perspectives, reminders of what particular sources provide.
- *Paraphrases* of material compel you to think carefully about what you read so that you can express it in your own words. Paraphrase helps you to summarize specific ideas and arguments without having to copy out, word for word, a particular source.
- *Direct quotations* are exact copies of an author's own words. Use direct quotations for ideas and concepts that are concise, specific, and that state the author's opinion or conclusion.

GUIDELINES FOR TAKING NOTES ON YOUR TOPIC

1. Write the author's last name, the title of the book or article, and the page number on each index card. Be sure that you also have an entry for this source in your working bibliography. This will help you accurately document your sources and save you time later.
2. Copy only one idea, group of closely related facts, or quote on each card. This will make it easier for you to organize the information when you begin to draft your research essay.
3. List a subtopic at the top of the card. This will permit you to arrange your cards into groups, which can then serve as the basis of your outline. Keep a separate list of these subtopics and be sure that you don't use a new term for each card!
4. If applicable, add your own ideas to each card—perhaps using a different color ink, or on the reverse side of the card.

The sample cards below illustrate each of these note-taking strategies.

1: Sample note card: Summary

Subtopic	*N.A.T./college admissions*
Author/title	*Gladwell, "Examined Life"*
Page number(s)	*86–88*
Summary	*The University of California in 2001 proposed using measures other than the N.A.T. when considering students for admission, because a study of UC students found that the N.A.T was the least reliable measure of potential student success.*

2: Sample note card: Paraphrase

Subtopic	*N.A.T./college admission*
Author/title	*Gladwell, "Examined Life"*
Page number(s)	*86–88*
Paraphrase	*A University of California study showed that achievement tests like the N.A.T.* II *were far more likely than the N.A.T. in predicting student success. High school grade point averages were also found by the study to be a more reliable way to determine student success. The study was based on the records of UC students from 1996–1999. Achievement tests were found, overall, to be more fair to students because they measure what students have already learned.*

3: Sample note card: Direct Quotation

Subtopic	*N.A.T./college admissions*
Author/title	*Gladwell, "Examined Life"*
Page number(s)	*86–88*
Direct quotation	*Gladwell quotes Richard Atkinson, the president of the University of California: "Achievement tests are fairer to students because they measure accomplishment rather than promise . . . they tell students that a college education is within the reach of anyone with the talent and determination to succeed."*

Developing a Thesis

As you read your material and take notes, you should start developing ideas for your proposal or thesis. You began your research with a *hypothesis*—an unproven idea, hunch, or question that guided your reading and helped you to narrow your topic. Your *thesis* is the main idea of your research essay. Although your thesis may change a bit as you draft your research paper and continue to think about different ideas and perspectives, writing your thesis down before you begin your outline will give you a solid foundation for your outline and draft.

HYPOTHESIS	THESIS
Fashion magazines promote an unrealistic body image.	The self-esteem of adolescent girls determines how they respond to unreal images of women in fashion magazines.

Organizing Your Notes and Writing an Outline

Because you must organize all of this material you have gathered in a clear, logical way, an outline is especially valuable for a research essay. Plan to spend as much time as you can in drafting your outline and organizing your evidence, as this will make the actual writing of your research essay much more efficient. Your instructor may require you to submit an outline at some stage of writing the research essay; be sure that you understand the required format. You may also find it useful to ask your instructor, or fellow students, to review your outline and make suggestions. A good outline should allow a reader to follow easily the lines of your argument and see how each piece of evidence will fit in to the final essay.

THE ORGANIZING PROCESS

1. Gather all your note cards. Be sure they include source information (p. A-10).
2. Group your note cards by subtopic. Can any subtopics be combined? Are any subtopics so large that you can divide them further?

continued

3. Do any note cards duplicate each other? Set aside any cards which, within a subtopic grouping, duplicate information.
4. Are there any subtopics that include just one or two cards, or that don't seem to "fit" anywhere? Set those aside.
5. Number your note cards within each subtopic. Use capital letters for each subtopic, followed by a dash and a numeral for the card number (the first subtopic's cards would be numbered A-1, A-2; the next subtopic's cards would be B-1, B-2; and so on). This will help you save time as you write your rough draft.
6. Do not throw away any note cards. Even if you don't see an obvious place for a card in your outline, you never know what might prove useful as you write. Set those cards aside for now.
7. Do not feel obliged to use every note card when you write your paper. You may be overwhelmed by the number of note cards you have—but you probably won't use every single quotation, paraphrase, and piece of information in your final paper.

This grouping of cards by subtopic should provide you with the basic structure of an outline. If your instructor requires a formal outline, follow the guidelines provided. If not, follow these basic principles as you arrange your note cards within each subgrouping:

I. (Most important points)
    A.
    B. (Next most important point)
        1.
        2.
        3. (Supporting points)
            a.
            b. (Relevant details, minor points)

Phase III: Writing the Paper

As you begin the third phase of the research process, keep in mind that your research paper will be a formal essay, not a collection of notes. You should be prepared to take your research effort through multiple drafts, each time reconsidering the relevance and "fit" of your evidence.

Drafting

For your rough draft, concentrate on filling in the shape of your outline. Take the time to organize your note cards in the topic order of your outline. In this way you will be able to integrate notes and writing more efficiently.

Remember that your outline is a *guide* for your writing—you are not obliged to adhere to it. As you write, you may find subtle points taking on new importance, or additional evidence that needs to be included. Your purpose in writing a rough draft is to work out the shape and content of your research essay, and you should expect to make many changes and adjustments as you write.

You may choose to incorporate direct quotations from your notes into the rough draft. Some writers prefer to save time by indicating in the draft which note card to return to later in order to copy out the entire paraphrase or quote. If you have numbered your note cards as suggested above, you might find this a valuable time-saving strategy.

As you work through your outline, organizing your sources, you must contribute your own commentary. You will arrange details in an effective order, sort out conflicting claims and interpretations, and solve problems. Writing the rough draft of a research paper is much more complex than a mere transcription of facts and quotations. The process of writing is an effort to work in a logical way from the introduction and the statement of your thesis, through the evidence, to the outcome or conclusion that supports everything that has come before.

You may not use every note card in your rough draft. Again, set aside those that you do not use, or that do not seem to "fit." *Do not throw away any note cards!* At the same time, you may find as you write that you need further information on a particular point. Try to phrase that "missing" information in the form of questions, and write those questions on a separate piece of paper. Consult your working bibliography and all of your note cards (those you are using as well as those you have set aside). Can you answer your questions from sources you already have? If not, what sources will you consult (or return to) in order to get the information you need?

Incorporating Sources

As you draft, you will refer to your note cards for ideas as well as information. Introducing that information—hard facts, paraphrases, or direct quotations—into the flow of your own writing requires that you make it clear to your reader that the following information or words come from a different source. At the same time, you do not want to interrupt the flow of your own argument by randomly dropping in chunks of outside information. Gracefully incorporating research sources into your essay supports your own ideas without confusing the reader. Think of this as a kind of conversational skill; by including other voices in your research essay and clearly identifying each of those voices, you are allowing your "listener"—your reader—to take part in the ongoing academic "conversation" about your research topic. For example:

> Recently, some colleges and universities have reconsidered the importance of S.A.T. scores in admissions decisions. "Seventy-five years ago, the S.A.T. was instituted because we were more interested, as a society, in what a student was capable of learning than in what he had already learned. Now, apparently, we have changed our minds . . ." (Gladwell 88).

In revision, this writer used paraphrase to help make the transition from her argument to Gladwell's observation:

> Discussing the recent decision by the University of California to use measures other than the S.A.T. in admissions decisions, Malcolm Gladwell points out that "seventy-five years ago, the S.A.T. was instituted because we were more interested, as a society, in what a student was capable of learning than in what he had already learned" (Gladwell 88), whereas today's educators realize that it is more fair to assess what students have already accomplished.

Using conversation verbs rather than simply "says" or "writes" can enliven your introduction of sources without confusing your reader. The writer above uses the verb phrase "points out." Other possibilities include:

> Malcolm X forcefully argues that . . .
> Annie Dillard vividly describes . . .
> Lewis Thomas suggests that . . .
> Susan Jacoby compares the results of . . .
> Katha Pollitt admits that . . .

You will notice that this system does not rely on footnotes or end notes to give credit to the source of information. When you write your research essay and incorporate outside sources, be sure to include the author's last name and the page number on which you found the ideas to which you are referring. You must provide this information for paraphrases and factual information as well as direct quotations. For more information on in-text citation, see p. A-17 of this appendix.

Revising Your Draft

In your rough draft you thought and wrote your way through your problem or hypothesis, considering different kinds of evidence and various points of view. In revision, you rethink and rewrite in order to give better form and expression to your ideas. Your instructor may ask you to share your rough draft with other students, which allows you to test the structure of your argument and the strength of your evidence. Even if you are not required to share your paper in class, you might find it very helpful to exchange drafts with another student for comment and feedback at this stage.

GUIDELINES FOR REVISING YOUR RESEARCH WRITING

1. Does my title clearly indicate the topic of my essay? Does it capture my reader's interest?
2. Does my opening paragraph clearly establish and limit my topic?
3. Is my thesis statement clear, limited, and interesting?
4. Do all my body paragraphs support the thesis? Is there a single topic and main idea for each paragraph? Is there sufficient evidence in each paragraph to support the main idea?
5. Are there clear and effective transitions linking my ideas within and between paragraphs?
6. Do I incorporate evidence gracefully and logically? Do I acknowledge other people's ideas properly? Do I clearly indicate the sources of facts and evidence?
7. Is my conclusion strong and effective? Does it clearly and obviously echo my thesis statement?
8. If I share my paper with a student reader, does that reader have any questions about my argument or my evidence? What further information would my reader suggest I add?

continued

9. Are my sentences grammatically correct and complete? Have I varied my sentences effectively?
10. Is my use of punctuation correct?
11. Are all words spelled correctly? Have I printed out and read through my paper to catch any spelling errors that a computerized "spellcheck" function might miss?

Preparing the Final Manuscript

Leave time in your research writing to prepare a neat, clean manuscript. Consult your instructor for the required format, and carefully follow those guidelines for your final manuscript. Store your word processor file on a backup disk, and print or duplicate an extra copy for your own records.

Phase IV: Documenting Sources

Documenting your sources throughout your paper and in a section called Works Cited tells your audience just how well you have conducted your research. It offers readers the opportunity to check and review the same sources you used in writing your paper. Failure to provide proper documentation for your paper can have very serious consequences, including charges of *plagiarism.* Plagiarism, or the use of material without giving proper credit to the source, is considered a kind of intellectual theft. The disciplinary consequences of plagiarism in academic writing can range from a failing grade for that assignment to dismissal from the college. The consequences for plagiarism in the workplace are even more severe, ranging from dismissal from a job to criminal charges.

MATERIALS THAT REQUIRE DOCUMENTATION

1. Direct quotations
2. Paraphrased material
3. Summarized material
4. Any key idea or opinion adapted and incorporated into your paper
5. Specific data (whether quoted, paraphrased, or tabulated)
6. Disputed facts
7. Illustrations (maps, charts, graphs, photographs, etc.)

In–Text Citations, in the Style of the Modern Language Association (MLA)

Briefly identifying sources in the text of your paper, either as part of your sentence or within parentheses, is the most common method of indicating sources. In MLA style, include the author's name and the page number of the source. Then list complete information alphabetically by author or title (if the source has no specific author), in the Works Cited section.

GUIDELINES FOR PARENTHETICAL (IN-TEXT) DOCUMENTATION

1. Give enough information so that the reader can readily identify the source in the Works Cited section of your paper.
2. Give the citation information in parentheses placed where the material occurs in your text.
3. Make certain that the complete sentence containing the parenthetical documentation is readable and grammatically correct.

The following examples illustrate how to cite a source in the text. The MLA guidelines require you to include the author's last name and the page number where the quotation or information is located. If you state the author's name in the text, do not repeat it in the citation. Other professional organizations, such as the American Psychological Association (APA), require alternate citation styles.

Page Number(s) for a Book

> The play offers what many audiences have found a satisfying conclusion (Hansberry 265–76).

> Garcia Marquez uses another particularly appealing passage as the opening of the story (105).

Page Number(s) for an Article in a Journal or Magazine

> Barlow's description of the family members includes "their most notable strengths and weaknesses" (18).

Section and Page Number(s) for a Newspaper Article

> A report on achievement standards for high school courses found "significant variation among schools" (Mallory B1).

Page Number(s)for a Work Without an Author

> Computerworld has developed a thoughtful editorial on the issue of government and technology ("Uneasy Silence" 54).

Works Cited list

To prepare your Works Cited list of sources, simply transcribe those bibliography cards or entries that you actually used to write the paper. The Works Cited page is a separate page at the end of your research paper (see p. A-37 for an example).

GUIDELINES FOR THE WORKS CITED LIST

1. Use the title *Works Cited.* Center this title at the top of the page. Do not underline this title or place it in quotation marks.
2. Arrange the list of sources alphabetically according to the author's last name or according to the title of the work if there is no author. Ignore *A, An,* or *The.*
3. List alphabetically according to title other works by the same author, directly under the first entry for the author's name.
4. For works by more than one author, list the entry under the last name of the first author, giving other writers' names in regular order (first name, middle, last).
5. Begin each entry at the left margin. Indent everything in an entry that comes after the first line by one-half inch or five spaces.
6. Double-space every line.
7. Punctuate with periods after the three main divisions in most entries: author, title, and publishing information.

Book by One Author

Notice the punctuation and underlining in the basic entry for a book.

Aldrich, Marcia. Girl Rearing. New York: Norton, 1998.

Muller, Eddie. Dark City: The Lost World of Film Noir. New York: St. Martin's-Griffin, 1998.

Several Books by One Author

If you use several books by one author, list the author's name in the initial entry. In the next entry or entries, replace the name with three hyphens.

Aldrich, John Herbert. Why Parties? The Origin and Transformation of Political Parties in America. Chicago: U of Chicago P, 1995.

- - - . Before the Convention: Strategies and Choices in Presidential Nomination Campaigns. Chicago: U of Chicago P,1980.

Book with Two or Three Authors or Editors

List the names of several authors in the sequence in which they appear in the book. Begin with the last name of the author listed first because it is used to determine the alphabetical order for entries. Then identify the other authors by first and last names.

Trueba, Henry T., Grace Pung Guthrie, and Kathryn Hu-Pei Au, eds. Culture and the Bilingual Classroom: Studies in Classroom Ethnography. Rowley: Newbury, 1981.

Work with More than Three Authors or Editors

Name all those involved, or list only the first author or editor with *et al.,* for "and others."

Nordhus, Inger, Gary R. VandenBos, Stig Berg, and Pia Fromholt, eds. Clinical Geropsychology. Washington: APA, 1998.

Nordhus, Inger, et al., eds. Clinical Geropsychology. Washington: APA, 1998.

Work with Group or an Organization as Author

National PTA. National Standards for Parent/Family Involvement Programs. Chicago: National PTA, 1997.

Work without an Author

A Visual Dictionary of Art. Greenwich, CT: New York Graphic Society, 1974.

Work in a Collection of Pieces All by the Same Author

Malamud, Bernard. "The Assistant." A Malamud Reader. New York: Farrar, 1967. 750–95.

Work in an Anthology

McCorkle, Jill. "Final Vinyl Days." It's Only Rock and Roll: An Anthology of Rock and Roll Short Stories. Ed. Janice Eidus and John Kastan. Boston: Godine, 1998. 19–33.

Work Translated from Another Language

Rostand, Edmund. <u>Cyrano de Bergerac</u>. Trans. Anthony Burgess. New York: Applause, 1998.

New Edition of an Older Book

Wharton, Edith. <u>The Custom of the Country</u>. 1913. NY Public Library Collector's Edition. New York: Doubleday, 1998.

Entry from a Reference Volume

Treat less common reference books like other books, including place of publication, publisher, and date. For encyclopedias, dictionaries, and other familiar references, simply note the edition and its date. No page numbers are needed if the entries appear in alphabetical order in the reference volume.

"Fox, Luke." <u>Encyclopedia Americana: International Edition.</u> 1996 ed.

Minton, John. "Worksong." <u>American Folklore: An Encyclopedia</u>. Ed. Jan Harold Brunvand. New York: Garland, 1996.

Article in a Journal with Pagination Continuing through Each Volume

Pistol, Todd A. "Unfinished Business: Letters from a Father to His Son, 1922–1928." <u>Journal of Men's Studies</u> 7 (1999): 215–31.

Article in a Journal with Pagination Continuing Only through Each Issue

Add the issue number after the volume number.

Guyer, Jane I. "Traditions of Invention in Equatorial Africa." African Studies Review 39.3 (1996):1–28.

Article in a Weekly or Biweekly Periodical

Cowley, Geoffrey. "Cancer and Diet." Newsweek 30 Nov. 1998: 60–66.

Lemonick, Michael D. "The Biological Mother Lode." Time 16 Nov. 1998: 96–97.

Article in a Monthly or Bimonthly Periodical

If an article in a magazine or a newspaper does not continue on consecutive pages, follow the page number on which it begins with a plus sign.

Blow, Richard. "The Great American Whale Hunt." Mother Jones Sept.–Oct. 1998:49+.

Article in a Daily Newspaper

Morson, Berny. "Tuft-eared Cats Make Tracks in Colorado." Denver Rocky Mountain News 4 Feb. 1999: 5A+.

Article with No Author

"Iguanas Cruise the Caribbean." New Scientist 10 Oct. 1998: 25.

"People in the News." US News and World Report 11 Jan. 1999:16.

Editorial in a Periodical

Fogarty, Robert W. "Fictional Families." Editorial. Antioch Review 56 (1998): 388.

Letter Written to the Editor of a Periodical

Paley, James A. Letter. "New Haven Renaissance." New York Times 30 Jan. 1999: A26.

Film, Videotape

Start with any actor, producer, director, or other person whose work you wish to emphasize. Otherwise, simply begin with the title of the recording. Note the form cited—videocassette, film, and so forth.

Olivier, Laurence, prod. and dir. Richard III. By William Shakespeare. Videocassette. London Film Productions, 1955.

Visions of the Spirit: A Portrait of Alice Walker. By Elena Featherston. Videocassette. Women Make Films, 1989.

Programs on Radio or Television

"Alone on the Ice." The American Experience. PBS. KRMA, Denver. 8 Feb. 1999.

CD or Other Recording

Identify the format if the recording is not on a compact disk.

Basie, Count. "Sunday at the Savoy." 88 Basie Street. Rec. 11–12 May 1983. LP. Pablo Records, 1984.

Cherry, Don. "When Will the Blues Leave?" Art Deco. A&M Records, 1989.

Published or Personal Interview

Gerard, William. Personal interview. 16 May 1999.

Previn, Andre. Interview. "A Knight at the Keyboard." By Jed Distler. Piano and Keyboard. Jan.–Feb. 1999: 241–29.

Book, Article, or Other Source Available On-line

Besides author and title, add any translator or editor and the date of electronic publication or last update. Conclude with the date on which you visited the electronic site where the source is located and the site's address.

Land-Webber, Ellen. To Save a Life: Stories of Jewish Rescue. 1999. 5 Feb. 1999 <http://sorrel.humboldt/edu/~rescuers/>.

Latham, Ernest. "Conducting Research at the National Archives into Art Looting, Recovery, and Restitution." National Archives Library. 4 Dec. 1998. National Archives and Records

Administration. 5 Feb. 1999 <http://www.nara.gov/research/assets/sympaper/latham.html>.

Marvell, Andrew. Last Instructions to a Painter. Poet's Corner. 11 Nov. 1997. 5 Feb. 1999 <http://www.geocities.com/~spanoudi/poems/marvel04.html>.

Wollstonecraft, Mary. "A Vindication of the Rights of Women: With Strictures on Political and Moral Subjects." Project Bartleby Archive. Ed. Steven van Leeuwen. Jan. 1996. Columbia U. 5 Feb. 1999 <http://www.cc.columbia.edu/acis/bartleby/wollstonecraft>.

Magazine Article Available On-line

Chatsky, Jean Sherman. "Grow Your Own Employee Benefits." Money.com 30–31 Jan. 1999. 7 Feb. 1999 <http://www.pathfinder.com/money/moneytalk>.

Database Available On-line

Bartleby Library. Ed. Steven van Leeuwen. 1999. 5 May 1999 <http://www.bartleby.com>.

Newspaper Article Available On-line

Wolf, Mark. "Finding Art in Albums." @ The Post: World Wide Web Edition of the Cincinnati Post 5 Feb. 1999. 5 Feb. 1999 <http://www.cincypost.com/living/album020599.html>.

Article from an Electronic Journal

Warren, W. L. "Church and State in Angevin Ireland." Chronicon: An Electronic History Journal 1 (1997): 6 pars. 6 Feb. 1999 <http://www.ucc.ie/chronicon/warren.htm>.

Electronic Posting to a Group

Faris, Tommy L. "Tiger Woods." Online posting. 3 Sept. 1996. H-Net: Humanities & Social Sciences Online Posting. 7 Feb. 1999 <http://www.h-net.msu.edu/~arete/archives/threads/tiger.html>.

SAMPLE STUDENT RESEARCH PAPER

Yeager 1

Frances Yeager

Professor Richard Kelaher

Expository Writing

June 3, 2001

Who Wants to Be a Cover Girl?: Media and Adolescent Body Image

Title clearly defines topic

In our consumer-focused society, the average American encounters between 400 and 600 advertisements per day. One in every 11 of those advertisements contains a message directly related to beauty (Wolf 35). And yet many Americans—especially adolescents—are not critical about the power that the advertising media holds. For so many young people, advertisements are the ultimate determining judgment of what is *chic* and what is *passé.* This holds especially true for women. Research has shown that girls are more inclined to become vulnerable to the ideal body images projected by the media than boys are. Many studies conducted on this issue have

All lines double-spaced

Opening establishes common audience experience and interests concluded that our culture places more importance on physical beauty in the assessment of women and girls than it does on boys or men. According to Naomi Wolf, females of all ages have been "consistently taught from an early age that their self-worth is largely dependent on how they look. The fact that women earn more money than men in only two job categories, those of modeling and prostitution, serves to illustrate this point" (50). Unrealistic images of the female body in advertising and the media can lead to distorted body image and eating disorders in young women immersed in our media culture.

Last sentence of paragraph is the thesis statement.

Certainly, the print media geared towards young women seems to confirm this argument. A study of five popular fashion and beauty magazines geared variously towards women between the ages of 13 and 40 (Paper, Seventeen, Cosmopolitan, Glamour, and Teen Vogue), found that approximately 65 percent of

Specific evidence to support thesis is introduced.

Yeager 3

their advertising consisted of products and services directly related to beauty (Stice and Shaw 289). Most of these advertisements used one or more of the following in their ads: models, sexual images, celebrities or other icon figures, and images of happiness, popularity, success, and love. In a study where the four most popular women's magazines were compared to the four most popular men's magazines, it was found that out of forty-eight issues of each, there was a total of sixty three diet food ads for women and one diet food ad for men (Mollin, Scully, and Irwin). What is even more disconcerting is that in the magazines geared more towards teens and young adults (Seventeen, Teen Vogue), this same study found that the average of sexual images and ads related to sex was much higher than in magazines geared for older women (Cosmopolitan, Paper, Glamour). The magazines targeted to adolescent girls and young women also used icons and

Summarized information is correctly cited.

On-line source does not need a page number for in-text citation.

Yeager 4

celebrities more often to sell products, as well as popularity gimmicks, implying that "popular" people buy <u>this</u> product and people who have fun use <u>that</u> product.

A typical advertisement from the May 2001 issue of the teen magazine <u>Seventeen</u> is for the shampoo "Herbal Essence" (15). The ad features a picture of the popular singer Britney Spears, with a caption reading: "Does this look like a girl who stays home on Friday nights to wash her hair? YES!" The clear implication is that even famous—and famously sexy—young girls clear their calendar to shampoo with "Herbal Essence," and therefore young girls who idolize Britney Spears should do so as well. (Of course, the older sisters of <u>Seventeen</u> readers are targeted by a much more explicit television campaign for "Herbal Essence," implying that washing with the shampoo is an "organic" experience—but with a blatant implication that it's really "orgasmic." One commercial even featured "sex expert" Dr. Ruth

Advertisements—print and other media—also require citation.

Westheimer praising the "organic" pleasures of the shampoo.)

Television, magazines, and other popular media seem at once to create and perpetuate our culture's values for beauty, and what is currently found acceptable for body shape and size, style, and attitude. Magazines, television ads, billboards, music videos, and movies all reveal images of tall, thin, tanned, and beautiful young people, linking them smoothly to other images of love, success, happiness, prestige, popularity, and wealth for women. It has been found that "repeated exposure to the thin ideal via the various media can lead to the internalization of this ideal" (Richins 75), and Stice and Shaw find that, to women who have internalized these ideals, the fantasy begins to seem an attainable goal. Studies also suggest that exposure to the idealized images lowered women's satisfaction with their own attractiveness; and that immediately after viewing these images women began to

The direct quote, from a print source, is immediately cited with a page number. The paraphrased on-line study is identified by the authors' names in the text.

experience shame, guilt, body dissatisfaction, depression, and stress (Richins 83). These results leave women even more vulnerable to ever-enticing advertisements selling them happiness, beauty and confidence in a bottle of shampoo or tube of lipstick.

For many young women, the effort to remake themselves in the idealized images perpetuated by the media becomes life-threatening. A 1991 study that tracked the incidents of anorexia nervosa over a fifty-year period found that the incidents of the disease among American females aged 10 to 19 reflected directly changes in fashion and its ideal body image. Many of the subjects also stated that they felt the greatest pressure of body weight ideals primarily from the media, with additional but lesser influence from peers and family. Even more devastating is that these results of the media's influence do not only affect adolescents and adults, but also children (Lucas et al). A study conducted by the

This paragraph summarizes the conclusions of two studies, demonstrating the *cause* and *effect* of the author's thesis (unreal media images—the "cause"—can lead to eating disorders—the "effect.").

American Association of University Women (1990) found that girls who had a negative body image were three times as likely as boys to believe that others perceived them negatively. The study also established that a negative body image has been directly linked to a higher risk of suicide for girls, and not boys.

A 1997 study by the Kaiser Family Foundation finds that that young women are receiving conflicting views and reflections of their bodies and social roles. In some circumstances, "women are shown being self-reliant and using intelligence, honesty and efficiency to achieve their goals," and magazines "reinforce these messages by encouraging their readers to rely on themselves and resolve situations in honest and direct ways." However, many other television shows targeted to adolescent females broadcast "stereotypical messages about appearance, relationships and careers, as well as more subtle signals about girls' value and importance"

Yeager 8

(Signorelli). Commenting on these findings, a study for the Vanier Institute of the Family notes that it has been discovered that the more television girls and young women watch, the more likely they would be to create a hypothetical female television character "who is rich and thin, concerned about popularity, clothes, money, and looking attractive, and who wants to be a model or a famous actress" (Moscovitch). These conflicting messages can have a powerful and confusing influence on young women at a vulnerable stage of their development.

The study, published electronically, does not require a page number for in-text citation

Moscovitch's article is also published electronically.

Young women—and young men, too—want to be popular. But an increasing body of evidence suggests that young women in particular believe that the route to popularity and success depends on their physical beauty, and their ability to meet rigid definitions of "beauty" perpetuated by the media. Cynical advertising campaigns exploit this anxiety among young women, encouraging them to buy beauty-related

Paragraph reminds readers of author's thesis and key points.

products to make them as popular, beautiful, and successful as Britney Spears or the latest supermodel. Everyone wants to look in the mirror and be happy with what they see, but the fact is few young women are happy when they are comparing themselves to the covers of Teen Vogue or In Style. The fashion world knows this, the advertising companies know this, and they also know that most women will pay a large price for a temporary fix of their shame and self-dissatisfaction. Women are sold on a quick pick-me-up with the latest lipstick, or the new and trendy jeans.

The research cited above suggests that the media's strong influence on women and girls wreaks havoc on the mental, physical, and emotional condition of America's female population. As the media and advertising companies continue to sell to the insecurities that the media itself created, the cycle of distorted body image and associated eating disorders will continue.

Conclusion makes a prediction based on assembled evidence. The author's language is strong, but she has amassed enough evidence to support her opinion.

Yeager 10

Pagination continues from body of paper

Works Cited

Title centered

All entries double-spaced

All entries in alphabetical order by author

First line at left margin; subsequent lines indented 5 spaces or one-half inch (one hit on "tab" key)

American Association of University Women. Shortchanging Girls, Shortchanging America: Full Data Report. Washington, D.C.: American Association of University Women, 1990.

Herbal Essences by Clairol. Advertisement. Seventeen May 2001: 15.

Lucas, A. R., C. M. Beard, W. M. O'Fallon, and L. T. Kurland. "50-Year Trends in the Incidence of Anorexia Nervosa in Rochester, Minn.: A Population-Based Study." American Journal of Psychiatry 148:7 (1991): 917–922.

Mellin, L. M., S. Scully, and C. E. Irwin. "Disordered Eating Characteristics in Preadolescent Girls: Meeting of the American Dietetic Association." Las Vegas: 1986. Abstract. About-Face.org. 1996–2001. 15 May 2001 <*http://www.about-face.org*>.

Moscovitch, Arlene. "Electronic Media and the Family." 1998. The Vanier Institute of the Family. 20 May 2001 <http://www.vifamily.ca/cft/ media/media.htm>.

Richins, M. L. "Social Comparison and the Idealized Images of Advertising." Journal of Consumer Research 18 (1991): 71–83.

Signorelli, Nancy. "A Content Analysis: Reflections of Girls in the Media." April 1997. The Kaiser Family Foundation. 20 May 2001 <http://www.kff.org/oontont/ archive/1260/gendr. html#top>.

Stice, E., and H. E. Shaw. "Adverse Effects of the Media-Portrayed Thin Ideal on Women and Linkages to Bulimic Symptomatology." Journal of Social and Clinical Psychology 13 (1994): 288–308.

Wolf, Naomi. The Beauty Myth. New York: Doubleday, 1992

Glossary

Abstract and concrete are ways of describing important qualities of language. Abstract words are not associated with real, material objects that are related directly to the five senses. Such words as "love," "wisdom," "patriotism," and "power" are abstract because they refer to ideas rather than to things. Concrete language, on the other hand, names things that can be perceived by the five senses. Words like "table," "smoke," "lemon," and "halfback" are concrete. Generally you should not be too abstract in writing. It is best to employ concrete words naming things that can be seen, touched, smelled, heard, or tasted in order to support your more abstract ideas.

Allusion is a reference to some literary, biographical, or historical event. It is a "figure of speech" (a fresh, useful comparison) used to illuminate an idea. For instance, if you want to state that a certain national ruler is insane, you might refer to him as a "Nero"—an allusion to the emperor who burned Rome.

Alternating method in comparison and contrast involves a point by point treatment of the two subjects that you have selected to discuss. Assume that you have chosen five points to examine in a comparison of the Volkswagen Jetta (subject A) and the Honda Accord (subject B): cost, comfort, gas mileage, road handling, and frequency of repair. In applying the alternating method, you would begin by discussing cost in relation to A + B; then comfort in relation to A + B; and so on. The alternating method permits you to isolate points for a balanced discussion.

Ambiguity means uncertainty. A writer is ambiguous when using a word, phrase, or sentence that is not clear. Ambiguity usually results in misunderstanding, and should be avoided in essay writing. Always strive for clarity in your compositions.

Analogy is a form of figurative comparison that uses a clear illustration to explain a difficult idea or function. It is unlike a formal comparison in that its subjects of comparison are from different categories or areas. For example, an analogy likening "division of labor" to the activity of bees in a hive makes the first concept more concrete by showing it to the reader through the figurative comparison with the bees.

Antonym is a word that is opposite in meaning to that of another word: "hot" is an antonym of "cold"; "fat" is an antonym of "thin"; "large" is an antonym of "small."

Argumentation is a type of writing in which you offer reasons in favor of or against something. (See Chapter 11)

Audience refers to the writer's intended readership. Many essays (including most in this book) are designed for a general audience, but a writer may also try to reach a special group. For example, William Zinsser in his essay "Simplicity" (pp. 39–44) might expect to appeal more to potential writers than to the general reading public. Similarly, Elizabeth Wong's "The Struggle to Be an All-American Girl" (pp. 142–144) could mean something particularly special to young Chinese Americans. The intended audience affects many of the writer's choices, including level of diction, range of allusions, types of figurative language, and so on.

Block method in comparison and contrast involves the presentation of all information about the first subject (A), followed by all information about the second subject (B). Thus, using the objects of comparison explained in the discussion of the "alternating method," you would for the block method first present all five points about the Volkswagen. Then you would present all five points about the Honda. When using the block method, remember to present the same points for each subject, and to provide an effective transition in moving from subject A to subject B.

Causal analysis is a form of writing that examines causes and effects of events or conditions as they relate to a specific subject (see Chapter 10).

Characterization is the description of people. As a particular type of description in an essay, characterization attempts to capture as vividly as possible the features, qualities, traits, speech, actions, and personality of individuals.

Chronological order is the arrangement of events in the order that they happened. You might use chronological order to trace the history of the Vietnam War, to explain a scientific process, or to present the biography of a close relative or friend. When you order an essay by chronology, you are moving from one step to the next in time.

Classification is a pattern of writing in which the author divides a subject into categories and then groups elements in each of those categories according to their relation to each other (see Chapter 8).

Clichés are expressions that were once fresh and vivid, but have become tired and worn from overuse. "I'm so hungry that I could eat a horse" is a typical clichè. People use clichès in conversation, but writers generally should avoid them.

Closings or "conclusions" are endings for your essay. Without a closing, your essay is incomplete, leaving the reader with the feeling that something important has been left out. There are numerous closing possibilities available to writers: summarizing main points in the essay; restating the main idea; using an effective quotation to bring the essay to an end; offering the reader the climax to a series of events; returning to the introduction and echoing it; offering a solution to a problem; emphasizing the topic's significance; or setting a new frame of reference by generalizing from the main thesis. Whatever type of closing you use, make certain that it ends the essay in a firm and emphatic way.

Coherence is a quality in effective writing that results from the careful ordering of each sentence in a paragraph, and each paragraph in the essay. If an essay is coherent, each part will grow naturally and logically from those parts that come before it. Coherence depends on the writer's ability to organize materials in a logical way, and to order segments so that the reader is carried along easily from start to finish. The main devices used in achieving coherence are transitions, which help to connect one thought with another.

Colloquial language is language used in conversation and in certain types of informal writing, but rarely in essays, business writing, or research papers. There is nothing wrong with colloquialisms like "gross," "scam," or "rap" when used in conversational settings. However, they are often unacceptable in essay writing—except when used sparingly for special effects.

Comparison/contrast is a pattern of essay writing treating similarities and differences between two subjects (See Chapter 6).

Composition is a term used for an essay or for any piece of writing that reveals a careful plan.

Conclusion (See *Closings*)

Concrete (See *Abstract and concrete*)

Connotation/denotation are terms specifying the way a word has meaning. Connotation refers to the "shades of meaning" that a word might have because of various emotional associations it calls up for writers and readers alike. Words like "American," "physician," "mother," "pig," and "San Francisco" have strong connotative overtones to them. With denotation, however, we are concerned not with the suggestive meaning of a word but with its exact, literal meaning. Denotation refers to the "dictionary definition" of a word—its exact meaning. Writers must understand the connotative and denotative value of words, and must control the shades of meaning that many words possess.

Context clues are hints provided about the meaning of a word by another word or words, or by the sentence or sentences coming before or after it. Thus in the sentence, "Mr. Rome, a true *raconteur,* told a story that thrilled the guests," we should be able to guess at the meaning of the italicized word by the context clues coming both before and after it. (A "raconteur" is a person who tells good stories.)

Definition is a method of explaining a word so that the reader knows what you mean by it. (See Chapter 7.)

Denotation (See *Connotation/denotation*)

Derivation is how a word originated and where it came from. Knowing the origin of a word can make you more aware of its meaning, and more able to use it effectively in writing. Your dictionary normally lists abbreviations (for example, O.E. for Old English, G. for Greek) for word origins and sometimes explains fully how they came about.

Description is a type of writing that uses details of sight, color, sound, smell, and touch to create a word picture and to explain or illustrate an idea. (See Chapter 3.)

Dialogue is the exact duplication in writing of something people say to each other. Dialogue is the reproduction of speech or conversation; it can add concreteness and vividness to an essay, and can also help to reveal character. When using dialogue, writers must be careful to use correct punctuation. Moreover, to use dialogue effectively in essay writing, you must develop an ear for the way other people talk, and an ability to create it accurately.

Diction refers to the writer's choice or use of words. Good diction reflects the topic of the writing. Malcolm X's diction, for example, is varied, including subtle descriptions in standard diction and conversational sarcasms. Levels of diction refer both to the purpose of the essay and to the writer's audience. Skillful choice of the level of diction keeps the reader intimately involved with the topic.

Division is that aspect of classification (see Chapter 8) in which the writer divides some large subject into categories. For example, you might divide "fish" into saltwater and freshwater fish; or "sports" into team and individual sports. Division helps writers to split large and potentially complicated subjects into parts for orderly presentation and discussion.

Effect is a term used in causal analysis (see Chapter 10) to indicate the outcome or expected result of a chain of happenings. When dealing with the analysis of effects, writers should determine whether they want to work with immediate or final effects, or both. Thus, a writer analyzing the effects of an accidental nuclear explosion might choose to analyze effects immediately after the blast, as well as effects that still linger.

Emphasis suggests the placement of the most important ideas in key positions in the essay. Writers can emphasize ideas simply by placing important ones at the beginning or at the end of the paragraph or essay. But several other techniques help writers to emphasize important ideas: (1) key words and ideas can be stressed by repetition; (2) ideas can be presented in climactic order, by building from lesser ideas at the beginning to the main idea at the end; (3)figurative language (for instance, a vivid simile) can call attention to a main idea; (4) the relative proportion of detail offered to support an idea can emphasize its importance; (5) comparison and contrast of an idea with other ideas can emphasize its importance; and (6) mechanical devices like underlining, capitalizing, and using exclamation points (all of which should be used sparingly) can stress significance.

Essay is the name given to a short prose work on a limited topic. Essays take many forms, ranging from a familiar narrative account of an event in your life to explanatory, argumentative, or critical investigations of a subject. Normally, in one way or the other, an essay will convey the writer's personal ideas about the subject.

Euphemism is the use of a word or phrase simply because it seems less distasteful or less offensive than another word. For instance, "mortician" is a euphemism for "undertaker"; "sanitation worker" for "garbage collector."

Fable is a story with a moral. The story from which the writer draws the moral can be either true or imaginary. When writing a fable, a writer must clearly present the moral to be derived from the narrative, as Rachel Carson does in "A Fable for Tomorrow" (see pp. 223–225.)

Figurative language, as opposed to *literal,* is a special approach to writing that departs from what is typically a concrete, straightforward style. It involves a vivid, imaginative comparison that goes beyond plain or ordinary statements. For instance, instead of saying that "Joan is wonderful," you could write that "Joan is like a summer's rose" (a *simile*); "Joan's hair is wheat, pale and soft and yellow" (a *metaphor*); "Joan is my Helen of Troy" (an *allusion*); or use a number of other comparative approaches. Note that Joan is not a rose, her hair is not wheat, nor is she some other person named Helen. Figurative language is not logical; instead, it requires an ability on the part of the writer to create an imaginative comparison in order to make an idea more striking.

Flashback is a narrative technique in which the writer begins at some point in the action and then moves into the past in order to provide necessary background information. Flashback adds variety to the narrative method, enabling writers to approach a story not only in terms of straight chronology, but in terms of a back-and-forth movement. However, it is at best a very difficult technique and should be used with great care.

General/specific words are necessary in writing, although it is wise to keep your vocabulary as specific as possible. General words refer to broad categories and groups, while specific words capture with more force and clarity the nature of a term. The distinction between general and specific language is always a matter of degree. "A woman walked down the street" is more general than "Mrs. Walker walked down Fifth Avenue," while "Mrs. Webster, elegantly dressed in a muslin suit, strolled down Fifth Avenue" is more specific than the first two examples. Our ability to use specific language depends on the extent of our vocabulary. The more words we know, the more specific we can be in choosing words.

Hyperbole is obvious and intentional exaggeration.

Illustration is the use of several examples to support an idea (see Chapter 5).

Imagery is clear, vivid description that appeals to our sense of sight, smell, touch, sound, or taste. Much imagery exists for its own sake, adding descriptive flavor to an essay, as when Richard Selzer in "The Discus Thrower" writes, "I unwrap the bandages from the stumps, and begin to cut away the black scabs and the dead, glazed fat with scissors and forceps. A shard of white bone comes loose." However, imagery can also add meaning to an essay. For example, when Orwell writes at the start of "A Hanging," "It was in Burma, a sodden morning of the rains. A sickly light, like yellow tinfoil, was slanting over the high walls into the jail yard," we see that the author uses imagery to prepare us for the somber and terrifying event to follow. Writers can use imagery to contribute to any type of wording, or they can rely on it to structure an entire essay. It is always difficult to invent fresh, vivid description, but it is an effort that writers must make if they wish to improve the quality of their prose.

Introductions are the beginning or openings of essays. Introductions should perform a number of functions. They should alert the reader to the subject, set the limits of the essay, and indicate what the *thesis* (or main idea) will be. Moreover, they should arouse the reader's interest in the subject, so that the reader will want to continue reading into the essay. There are several devices available to writers that will aid in the development of sound introductions.

1. Simply state the subject and establish the thesis. See the essay by Amartya Sen (p. 200).
2. Open with a clear, vivid description that will become important as your essay advances. Save your thesis for a later stage, but indicate what your subject is. See the essay by George Orwell (p. 158).
3. Ask a question or a series of questions, which you might answer in the introduction or in another part of the essay. See the Takaki essay (p. 478–480).

4. Tell an anecdote (a short, self-contained story of an entertaining nature) that serves to illuminate your subject. See the Staples essay (pp. 183–184).
5. Use comparison or contrast to frame your subject and to present the thesis. See the Goodman essay (p. 238).
6. Establish a definitional context for your subject. See the Ingrassia essay (p. 245).
7. Begin by stating your personal attitude toward a controversial issue. See the Ivins essay (p. 493).

These are only some of the devices that appear in the introductions to essays in this text. Writers can also ask questions, give definitions, or provide personal accounts—there are many techniques that can be used to develop introductions. The important thing to remember is that you *need* an introduction to an essay. It can be a single sentence or a much longer paragraph, but it must accomplish its purpose—to introduce readers to the subject, and to engage them so that they want to explore the essay further.

Irony is the use of language to suggest the opposite of what is stated. Writers use irony to reveal unpleasant or troublesome realities that exist in life, or to poke fun at human weaknesses and foolish attitudes. For instance, in Orwell's "A Hanging," the men who are in charge of the execution engage in laughter and lighthearted conversation after the event. There is irony in the situation and in their speech because we sense that they are actually very tense—almost unnerved—by the hanging; their laughter is the opposite of what their true emotional state actually is. Many situations and conditions lend themselves to ironic treatment.

Jargon is the use of special words associated with a specific area of knowledge or a specific profession. It is similar to "shop talk" that members of a certain trade might know, but not necessarily people outside it. For example, the medical jargon in Kozol's essay helps him defend his opinion on a nonmedical subject. Use jargon sparingly in your writing, and be certain to define all specialized terms that you think your readers might not know.

Journalese is a level of writing associated with prose types normally found in newspapers and popular magazines. A typical newspaper article tends to present information factually or objectively; to use simple language and simple sentence structure; and to rely on relatively short paragraphs. It also stays close to the level of conversational English without becoming chatty or colloquial.

Metaphor is a type of figurative language in which an item from one category is compared briefly and imaginatively with an item from another area. Writers create metaphors to assign meaning to a word in an original way.

Narration is telling a story in order to illustrate an important idea (see Chapter 4).

Objective/subjective writing refers to the attitude that writers take toward their subject. When writers are objective, they try not to report their own personal feelings about their subject. They attempt to control, if not eliminate, their own attitude toward the topic. Thus in the essay by Roiphe (pp. 293–297), we learn about the underlying causes of divorce, but the writer doesn't try to convince us of the rightness or wrongness of it. Many essays, on the other hand, reveal the authors' personal attitudes and emotions. In Frisina's essay, the author's personal approach to the process of reading seems clear. She takes a highly subjective approach to the topic. Other essays, such as Kozol's (see pp. 462–466), blend the two approaches to help balance the author's expression of a strong opinion. For some kinds of college writing, such as business or laboratory reports, research papers, or literary analyses, it is best to be as objective as possible. But for many of the essays in composition courses, the subjective touch is fine.

Order is the manner in which you arrange information or materials in an essay. The most common ordering techniques are *chronological order* (involving time sequence); *spatial order* (involving the arrangement of descriptive details); *process order* (involving a step-by-step approach to an activity); *deductive order* (in which you offer a thesis and then the evidence to support it); and *inductive order* (in which you present evidence first and build toward the thesis). Some rhetorical patterns such as comparison and contrast, classification, and argumentation require other ordering techniques. Writers should select those ordering principles that permit them to present materials clearly.

Paradox is a statement that *seems* to be contradictory but actually contains an element of truth. Writers use it in order to call attention to their subject.

Parallelism is a variety of sentence structure in which there is "balance" or coordination in the presentation of elements. "I came, I saw, I conquered" is a good example of parallelism, presenting both pronouns and verbs in a coordinated manner. Parallelism can also be applied to several sentences and to entire paragraphs (see the Brady essay, pp. 456–458). It can be an effective way to emphasize ideas.

Personification is giving an object, thing, or idea lifelike or human qualities. Like all forms of figurative writing, personification adds freshness to description, and makes ideas vivid by setting up striking comparisons.

Point of view is the angle from which a writer tells a story. Many personal or informal essays take the *first-person* (or "I") point of view, as the essays by Malcolm X, Hughes, Orwell, and others reveal. The first-person "I" point of view is natural and fitting for essays when the writer wants to speak in a familiar and intimate way to the reader. On the other hand, the *third-person* point of view ("he," "she," "it," "they") distances the reader somewhat from the writer. The third-person point of view is useful in essays where writers are not talking exclusively about themselves, but about other people, things, and events, as in the essays by Kozol and Carson. Occasionally, the *second-person* ("you") point of view will appear in essays, notably in essays involving process analysis where the writer directs the reader to do something; part of Ernest Hemingway's essay (which also uses a third-person point of view) uses this strategy. Other point-of-view combinations are possible when a writer wants to achieve a special effect—for example, combining *first-* and *second-person* points of view. The position that you take as a writer depends largely on the type of essay you write.

Prefix is one or more syllables attached to the front of another word in order to influence its meaning or to create a new word. A knowledge of prefixes and their meanings aids in establishing the meanings of words and in increasing the vocabulary that we use in writing. Common prefixes and their meanings include *bi-* (two), *ex-* (out, out of), *per-* (through), *pre-* (before), *re-* (again), *tele-* (distant), and *trans-* (across, beyond).

Process analysis is a pattern of writing that explains in a step-by-step way the methods for doing something or reaching a desired end (see Chapter 9).

Proposition is the main point in an argumentative essay. It is like a *thesis,* except that it usually presents an idea that is debatable or can be disputed.

Purpose refers to what a writer hopes to accomplish in a piece of writing. For example, the purpose may be *to convince* the reader to adopt a certain viewpoint (as in Quindlen's "Women Are Just Better," pp. 485–487), *to explain* a process (as in Hemingway's "Camping Out," pp. 360–364), or to allow the reader *to feel a dominant impression* (as in Woolf's "The Death of the Moth," pp. 127–130). Purpose helps a writer to determine which expository technique will dominate the essay's form, as well as what kinds of supporting examples will be used. Purpose and *audience* are often closely related.

Refutation is a technique in argumentative writing where you recognize and deal effectively with the arguments of your opponents. Your own argument will be stronger if you can refute—prove false or wrong—all opposing arguments.

Root is the basic part of a word. It sometimes aids us in knowing what the larger word means. Thus if we know that the root doc- means "teach" we might be able to figure out a word like "doctrine." *Prefixes* and *suffixes* are attached to roots to create words.

Sarcasm is a sneering or taunting attitude in writing. It is designed to hurt by ridiculing or criticizing. Basically, sarcasm is a heavy-handed form of irony, as when an individual says, "Well, you're exactly on time, aren't you" to someone who is an hour late, and says it with a sharpness in the voice, designed to hurt. Writers should try to avoid sarcastic writing and to use more acceptable varieties of irony and satire to criticize their subject.

Satire is the humorous or critical treatment of a subject in order to expose the subject's vices, follies, stupidities, and so forth. Brady, for instance, satirizes stereotyped notions of wives, hoping to change these attitudes by revealing them as foolish. Satire is a better weapon than sarcasm in the hands of the writer because satire is used to correct, whereas sarcasm merely hurts.

Sentimentality is the excessive display of emotion in writing, whether it is intended or unintended. Because sentimentality can distort the true nature of a situation, writers should use it cautiously, or not at all. They should be especially careful when dealing with certain subjects, for example the death of a loved one, the remembrance of a mother or father, a ruined romance, the loss of something valued, that lend themselves to sentimental treatment. Only the best writers—like Thomas, Woolf, Hughes, and others in this text—can avoid the sentimental traps rooted in their subjects.

Simile is an imaginative comparison using "like" or "as." When Orwell writes, "A sickly light, like yellow tinfoil, was slanting over the high walls into the jail yard," he uses a vivid simile in order to reinforce the dull description of the scene.

Slang is a level of language that uses racy and colorful expressions associated more often with speech than with writing. Slang expressions like "Mike's such a dude" or "She's a real fox" should not be used in essay writing, except when the writer is reproducing dialogue or striving for a special effect. Hughes is one writer in this collection who uses slang effectively to convey his message to the reader.

Subjective (See *Objective/subjective*)

Suffix is a syllable or syllables appearing at the end of a word and influencing its meaning. As with prefixes and roots, you can build vocabulary and establish meanings by knowing about suffixes. Some typical suffixes are *-able* (capable of), *-al* (relating to), *-ic* (characteristic of), *-ion* (state of), *-er* (one who), which appear often in standard writing.

Symbol is something that exists in itself but also stands for something else. Thus the "stumps" in paragraph 19 of Selzer's essay "The Discus Thrower" are not just the patient's amputated legs, but they serve as symbols of the man's helplessness and immobility. As a type of figurative language, the symbol can be a strong feature in an essay, operating to add depth of meaning, and even to unify entire essays.

Synonym is a word that means roughly the same as another word. In practice, few words are exactly alike in meaning. Careful writers use synonyms to vary word choice, without ever moving too far from the shade of meaning intended.

Theme is the central idea in an essay; it is also often termed the *thesis.* Everything in an essay should support the theme in one way or another.

Thesis is the main idea in an essay. The *thesis sentence,* appearing early in the essay, and normally somewhere in the first paragraph, serves to convey the main idea to the reader in a clear way. It is always useful to state your central idea as soon as possible, and before you introduce other supporting ideas.

Title for an essay should be a short, simple indication of the contents of your essay. Titles like "Spanglish" (pp. 259–261) and "I Want a Wife" (pp. 456–458) convey the central subjects of these essays in brief, effective ways. Others, such as "I Have a Dream" (pp. 505–509) and "Night Walker" (pp.183–186), also convey the central idea, but more abstractly. Always provide titles for your essays.

Tone is the writer's attitude toward his or her subject or material. An essay writer's tone may be objective ("Death in the Open"), ironic ("I Want a Wife"), comic ("Catfish in the Bathtub"), nostalgic ("One Writer's Beginnings"), or a reflection of numerous other attitudes. Tone is the "voice" that you give to an essay; every writer should strive to create a "personal voice" or tone that will be distinctive throughout any type of essay under development.

Transition is the linking of one idea to the next in order to achieve essay coherence (see *Coherence*). Transitions are words that connect these ideas. Among the most common techniques to achieve smooth transition are: (1) repeating a key word or phrase; (2) using a pronoun to refer back to a key word or phrase; (3) relying on traditional connectives like "thus," "for example," "moreover," "therefore," "however," "finally," "likewise," "afterward," and "in conclusion"; (4) using parallel structure (see *Parallelism*); and (5) creating a sentence or an entire paragraph that serves as a bridge from one part of your essay to the next. Transition is best achieved when the writer presents ideas and details carefully and in logical order. Try not to lose the reader by failing to provide for adequate transition from idea to idea.

Unity is that feature in an essay where all material relates to a central concept and contributes to the meaning of the whole. To achieve a unified effect in an essay, the writer must design an introduction and conclusion, maintain a consistent tone and point of view, develop middle paragraphs in a coherent manner, and always stick to the subject, never permitting unimportant elements to enter. Thus, unity involves a successful blending of all elements that go into the creation of a sound essay.

Vulgarisms are words that exist below conventional vocabulary, and are not accepted in polite conversation. Always avoid vulgarisms in your own writing, unless they serve an illustrative purpose.

Credits

Baker, James T. "How Do We Find the Student in a World of Academic Gynmasts and Worker Ants?" by James T. Baker in *Chronicle of Higher Education,* 1982. Reprinted by permission of the author.

Baker, Russell. "On Becoming a Writer" from *Growing Up* by Russell Baker, pp. 186–189. Copyright © 1983. Reprinted with permission from Don Congdon Associates.

Bosman, Julie. "The (No) Free Speech Movement" by Julie Bosman as appeared in *The Wall Street Journal,* 3/14/01. Reprinted with permission by Julie Bosman.

Brady, Judy. "Why I Want a Wife" by Judy Brady. Copyright © 1970 by Judy Brady. Reprinted by permission.

Brooks, David. "The Organization" by David Brooks from *The Atlantic Monthly,* April 2001. Reprinted by permission of the author.

Carson, Rachel. "A Fable for Tomorrow" from *Silent Spring* by Rachel Carson. Copyright © 1962 by Rachel L. Carson. Copyright renewed 1990 by Roger Christie. Reprinted by permission of Houghton Mifflin Company. All rights reserved.

Castro, Janice with Dan Cook and Cristina Garcia. "Spanglish Spoken Here" from *Time,* July 11, 1988. Copyright © 1988 Time Inc. Reprinted by permission.

Cofer, Judith Ortiz. "Volar" by Judith Ortiz Cofer. Reprinted with permission from the author.

Crews, Harry. "Why I Live Where I Live" by Harry Crews. Copyright © 1980 by Harry Crews. Reprinted with permission from John Hawkins & Associates.

Dillard, Annie. "In The Jungle" from *Teaching a Stone to Talk: Expeditions and Encounters* by Annie Dillard. Copyright © 1982 by Annie Dillard. Reprinted by permission of HarperCollins Publishers Inc.

Ehrenreich, Barbara. "What I've Learned from Men" by Barbara Ehrenreich from *Ms.* Magazine, 1985. Reprinted with permission from the publisher.

Frisina, Ellen Tashie. "'See Spot Run': Teaching My Grandmother to Read" by Ellen Tashie Frisina. Copyright © 1998. Reprinted by permission of the author.

Gates, Henry Louis, Jr. "In the Kitchen" by Henry Louis Gates, Jr., originally published in *The New Yorker,* 1994. Copyright © 1994 by Henry Louis Gates, Jr. Reprinted with permission of the author.

Goodman, Ellen. "The Tapestry of Friendships." Reprinted with the permission of Simon & Schuster from *Close to Home* by Ellen Goodman. Copyright © 1979 by The Washington Post Company.

Hemingway, Ernest. "Camping Out" reprinted with permission of Scribner, a Division of Simon & Schuster, Inc., from *Ernest Hemingway: Dateline: Toronto,* edited by William White. Copyright © 1985 by Mary Hemingway, John Hemingway, Patrick Hemingway and Gregory Hemingway.

Herbert, Bob. "Death Penalty Dissenters" by Bob Herbert from *The New York Times,* July 9, 2001. Copyright © 2001 The New York Times Co. Reprinted by permission.

Hughes, Langston. "Salvation" from *The Big Sea* by Langston Hughes. Copyright © 1940 by Langston Hughes. Copyright renewed 1968 by Arna Bontemps and George Houston Bass. Reprinted with permission from Hill and Wang, a division of Farrar, Straus & Giroux, Inc.

Ingrassia, Michele. "The Body of the Beholder" by Michele Ingrassia from *Newsweek,* June 24, 1995. Copyright © 1995 Newsweek, Inc. All rights reserved. Reprinted by permission.

Ivins, Molly. Excerpt from *Nothin' But Good Times* by Molly Ivins. Copyright © 1993 by Molly Ivins. Used by permission of Random House, Inc.

Jacoby, Susan. "When Bright Girls Decide that Math is a 'Waste of Time'" by Susan Jacoby. Copyright © 1983 by Susan Jacoby. Originally published in *The New York Times.* Reprinted by permission of Georges Borchardt, Inc.

Jordan, Suzanne Britt. "Fun. Oh, Boy. Fun. You Could Die from It." by Suzanne Britt Jordan in *The New York Times,* December 23, 1979. Copyright © 1979 The New York Times Co. Reprinted by permission.

King, Martin Luther, Jr. "I Have a Dream" speech by Martin Luther King, Jr. Copyright © 1963 by Martin Luther King, Jr., copyright renewed 1991 by Coretta Scott King. Reprinted by arrangement with The Heirs to the Estate of Martin Luther King, Jr. c/o Writers House, Inc. as agent for the proprietor.

King, Stephen. "Why We Crave Horror Movies" by Stephen King. Copyright © 1982 by Stephen King. All rights reserved. Reprinted with permission.

Kingston, Maxine Hong. "Catfish in the Bathtub" from *The Woman Warrior* by Maxine Hong Kingston. Copyright © 1975, 1976 by Maxine Hong Kingston. Used by permission of Alfred A. Knopf, a division of Random House, Inc.

Kozol, Jonathan. "Are the Homeless Crazy?" by Jonathan Kozol from *Rachel and Her Children,* Crown Publishers, 1988. Reprinted by permission of the author.

Lantos, John. From *The Lazarus Case: Life and Death Issues in the Neonatal Intensive Care* by John Lantos. Reprinted with permission from The Johns Hopkins University Press.

Malcolm X. Excerpt from *The Autobiography of Malcolm X* by Malcolm X and Alex Haley. Copyright © 1964 by Alex Haley and Macolm X. Copyright © 1965 by Alex Haley and Betty Shabazz. Used by permission of Random House, Inc.

Marable, Manning. "An Idea Whose Time Has Come . . ." by Manning Marable from *Newsweek,* August 27, 2001. Copyright © 2001 Newsweek, Inc. All rights reserved. Reprinted by permission.

Naylor, Gloria. "A Word's Meaning Can Often Depend on Who Says It" by Gloria Naylor as appeared in *The New York Times Magazine.* Copyright © 1986 by Gloria Naylor. Reprinted by permission of Sterling Lord Literistic, Inc.

Orwell, George. "A Hanging" from *Shooting an Elephant and Other Essays* by George Orwell. Copyright © 1950 by Sonia Brownell Orwell and renewed 1978 by Sonia Pitt-Rivers. Reprinted by permission of Harcourt, Inc.

Paley, Grace. "Traveling" by Grace Paley, originally published in *The New Yorker,* September 8, 1997, pp. 42–43. Reprinted by permission of the Elaine Markson Literary Agency.

Pollitt, Katha. "Why Boys Don't Play with Dolls" by Katha Pollitt from *The New York Times,* October 8, 1995. Copyright © 1995 The New York Times Co. Reprinted by permission.

Quindlen, Anna. Excerpt from *Living Out Loud* by Anna Quindlen. Copyright © 1987 by Anna Quindlen. Used by permission of Random House, Inc.

Rashap, Amy. "The American Dream for Sale: Ethnic Images in Magazines" as written for a catalog published in conjunction with an exhibition at the Balch Institute for Ethnic Studies. Reprinted with permission.

Roiphe, Anne. "Why Marriages Fail" by Anne Roiphe. Copyright © 1983 by Anne Roiphe. Reprinted by permission of International Creative Management, Inc.

Selzer, Richard. "The Discus Thrower" from *Confessions of a Knife* by Richard Selzer. Copyright © 1987, 2001 by Richard Selzer. Reprinted by permission of Georges Borchardt, Inc.

Sen, Amartya. "A World Not Neatly Divided" by Amartya Sen from *The New York Times,* November 23, 2001. Copyright © 2001 The New York Times Co. Reprinted by permission.

Simon, Jerrold G. "How to Write a Resume" by Jerrold G. Simon. Originally published in *Power of the Written Word,* International Paper Company, 1987. Copyright © 1987 by Jerrold G. Simon, Ed. D.

Spitzer, Dr. Robert L. "Psychiatry and Homosexuality" by Dr. Robert L. Spitzer as appeared in *The Wall Street Journal,* May 23, 2001. Reprinted by permission.

Staples, Brent. "Just Walk on By: A Black Man Ponders His Power to Alter Public Space" by Brent Staples as appeared in *Ms.* Magazine. Reprinted by permission of the author.

Steele, Shelby. ". . . or a Childish Illusion of Justice" by Shelby Steele from Newsweek, August 27, 2001. Copyright © 2001 *Newsweek,* Inc. All rights reserved. Reprinted by permission.

Takaki, Ronald. "The Harmful Myth of Asian Superiority" by Ronald Takaki from *The New York Times,* June 16, 1990. Copyright © 1990 The New York Times Co. Reprinted by permission.

Tan, Amy. "Mother Tongue" by Amy Tan. Copyright © 1990 by Amy Tan. First appeared in *The Threepenny Review.* Reprinted by permission of the author and the Sandra Dijkstra Literary Agency.

Thomas, Lewis. "Death in the Open" from *The Lives of a Cell* by Lewis Thomas. Copyright © 1973 by The Massachusetts Medical Society. Used by permission of Viking Penguin, a division of Penguin Putnam, Inc.

Viorst, Judith. "Friends, Good Friends—and Such Good Friends," Copyright © 1977 by Judith Viorst. Originally appeared in *Redbook.* Reprinted by permission of Lescher & Lescher, Ltd.

Vonnegut, Kurt, Jr. "How to Write with Style" by Kurt Vonnegut, Jr. Copyright © 1996 International Paper Company. Reprinted with permission.

Welty, Eudora. Reprinted by permission of the publisher from *One Writer's Beginnings* by Eudora Welty, Cambridge, Mass.: Harvard University Press. Copyright © 1983, 1984 by Eudora Welty.

White, E. B. "The Three New Yorks" from *Here is New York* by E. B. White. Copyright © 1949. Reprinted with permission from International Creative Management.

Wilson, James Q. "What Death Penalty Errors?" by James Q. Wilson from *The New York Times,* July 10, 2000. Copyright © 2000 The New York Times Co. Reprinted by permission.

Wong, Elizabeth. "The Struggle to Be an All-American Girl" by Elizabeth Wong. Reprinted by permission of the author.

Woolf, Virginia. "The Death of a Moth" from *The Death of the Moth and Other Essays* by Virginia Woolf. Copyright © 1942 by Harcourt, Inc., and renewed 1970 by Marjorie T. Parsons, Executrix. Reprinted by permission of the publisher.

Zinsser, William. "Simplicity" from *On Writing Well,* 6th Edition by William Zinsser. Copyright © 1976, 1980, 1985, 1988, 1990, 1994, 1998 by William K. Zinsser. Reprinted by permission of the author.

Index of Authors and Titles